PALGRAVE MACMILLAN
GREAT DEBATES IN LAW

PALGRAVE MACMILLAN
GREAT DEBATES IN LAW

Series editor
Jonathan Herring
Professor of Law,
University of Oxford

Contract Law
Jonathan Morgan

Criminal Law
Jonathan Herring

Employment Law
Simon Honeyball

Family Law
Jonathan Herring, Rebecca Probert and Stephen Gilmore

Property Law
David Cowan, Lorna Fox O'Mahony and Neil Cobb

Other titles are in course of preparation.

If you would like to comment on this book, or on any other law text published by Palgrave Macmillan, please write to lawfeedback@palgrave.com.

PALGRAVE MACMILLAN
GREAT DEBATES IN LAW

GREAT DEBATES IN
CONTRACT LAW

JONATHAN MORGAN

Fellow and Tutor in Law
St Catherine's College, Oxford

palgrave
macmillan

First published 2012 by PALGRAVE MACMILLAN

Palgrave Macmillan in the UK is an imprint of Macmillan Publishers Limited,
registered in England, company number 785998, of Houndmills, Basingstoke,
Hampshire RG21 6XS.

Palgrave Macmillan in the US is a division of St Martin's Press LLC,
175 Fifth Avenue, New York, NY 10010.

Palgrave Macmillan is the global academic imprint of the above companies
and has companies and representatives throughout the world.

Palgrave® and Macmillan® are registered trademarks in the United States,
the United Kingdom, Europe and other countries.

ISBN: 978–0–230–29290–1 paperback

This book is printed on paper suitable for recycling and made from fully
managed and sustained forest sources. Logging, pulping and manufacturing
processes are expected to conform to the environmental regulations of the
country of origin.

A catalogue record for this book is available from the British Library.

10 9 8 7 6 5 4 3 2 1
21 20 19 18 17 16 15 14 13 12

Printed and bound in Great Britain by
The Lavenham Press Ltd, Suffolk.

For Edward and Janette Morgan

CONTENTS

1. FORMATION OF CONTRACT   1

2. ENFORCEABILITY: CONSIDERATION,
INTENTION AND ESTOPPEL   29

3. STANDARD FORMS AND WRITTEN CONTRACTS   68

4. CONTRACTUAL CONTENT: TERMS AND THEIR MEANING   89

5. FRUSTRATION   120

6. MISREPRESENTATION AND MISTAKE   153

7. INEQUALITY OF BARGAINING POWER   185

8. PARTY-AGREED REMEDIES   211

9. JUDICIAL REMEDIES: PERFORMANCE OR COMPENSATION?   230

10. THIRD PARTIES   265

ACKNOWLEDGEMENTS

I am most grateful to St Catherine's College, Oxford for granting me sabbatical leave in Michaelmas Term 2011 during which this book was largely written. I will soon be leaving the college and I would like to thank the Master, Fellows and all of my Catz students for making my time there so very rewarding. This book is also a tribute to the University of Oxford: *Dominus illuminatio mea*.

I cannot imagine editors more supportive and encouraging than Rob Gibson at Palgrave Macmillan and Jonathan Herring of Exeter College. I am obliged to David Ibbetson and John Cartwright for *The Owl and the Pussycat* and Herodotus (respectively). David Winterton kindly shared with me his unpublished paper 'Money awards substituting for performance' upon which I have drawn in Chapter 9. David Campbell has assisted throughout the writing process.

Moving house is never a good time to write a book – nor vice versa. That I somehow managed both simultaneously is entirely due to Sophie. She has had to put up with a garden like Onegin's during the authorial process – an overgrown home for pensive Dryads.[1] For this forbearance and for so much else I owe her my deepest gratitude.

The book is dedicated to my parents.

---

[1] Pushkin, Евгéний Онéгин (1833) II.1.

INTRODUCTION

This book sets out to introduce exciting debates that are taking place across the law of contract. It is not a beginner's guide but has been written for students who already have some knowledge of the legal rules. The coverage has had to be selective. The choice was made to analyse a smaller number of areas in greater depth. I hope you will find food for thought in the chapters that follow.

There are numerous schools of contract scholarship. The primary division is between those who conceive of private law as a closed system of self-sufficient doctrine based on moral rights and duties,[1] and those who view law as an instrument for various goals of social policy. The latter group is inevitably more disparate. A divide between the 'market individualist' and 'social welfarist' approaches has been identified.[2] But this is hardly an exhaustive classification. Other currents running through the instrumental scholarship are sociological analysis,[3] regulatory approaches[4] and, above all, Law and Economics. The present book aims to introduce all of these perspectives and subject them to critical examination. Can we really deduce all the rules of commercial contract law by reflecting on the morality of promise keeping? How are judges to apply the complex recommendations of economic analysis?

The key texts in each Debate are collected at the end of each chapter. In addition, the following works are universally recommended for further reading. For the historical foundations without which the common law cannot properly be understood, see D.J. Ibbetson, *A Historical Introduction to the Law of Obligations*.[5] The classic reference work on Law and Economics remains R.A. Posner, *Economic Analysis of Law*.[6] A systematic examination of theoretical perspectives (ultimately rejecting instrumental analysis) is S.A. Smith's *Contract Theory*.[7] An unsystematic collection which is highly stimulating and rewarding to read is P.S. Atiyah's

---

[1] E.g. C. Fried, *Contract as Promise* (Harvard University Press, 1981); E.J. Weinrib, *The Idea of Private Law* (Harvard University Press, 1995); M. Hogg, *Promises and Contract Law: Comparative Perspectives* (Cambridge University Press, 2011).

[2] J. Adams & R. Brownsword, *Understanding Contract Law* (Sweet & Maxwell, 5th edn, 2007).

[3] Seminally S. Macaulay, 'Non-Contractual Relations in Business: A Preliminary Study' (1963) 28 *American Sociological Rev* 1.

[4] H. Collins, *Regulating Contracts* (Oxford University Press, 1999).

[5] Oxford University Press, 1999.

[6] Aspen, 8th edn, 2010.

[7] Clarendon Press, 2004.

Essays on Contract.[8] A critical examination is J. Wightman's, *Contract: A Critical Commentary*.[9] There are many fine textbooks and casebooks on contract; it would be tedious to list them all but invidious to choose. Nevertheless, I would single out H. Collins, *The Law of Contract* as a highly original and distinctive approach to a subject which usually follows a well-worn pattern.[10] Finally, for those wishing to research the law beyond these recommendations – which I would warmly encourage! – an excellent starting point is A. Kramer, *Contract Law: An Index and Digest of Published Writings*.[11]

---

[8] Oxford University Press, 1990.
[9] Pluto, 1996.
[10] Cambridge University Press, 4th edn, 2003.
[11] Hart, 2009.

CASES

Aberdeen CC v Stewart Milne
   Group [2011] UKSC 56   95–96
The Achilleas [2008] UKHL 48   116
Actionstrength Ltd v International
   Glass Engineering [2003]
   2 AC 541   55
Addis v Gramophone Co [1909]
   AC 488   252
Aerial Advertising Co v Bachelor's
   Peas [1938] 2 All ER 788   214
Ailsa Craig Fishing Co Ltd v
   Malvern Fishing Co Ltd
   [1983] 1 WLR 964   103, 223
The Albazero [1977] AC 774   266, 227,
   278–79, 285
ALCOA v Essex Group 499
   F Supp 43 (W.D. Pa. 1980)   150
Alec Lobb (Garages) v Total Oil
   [1983] 1 WLR 87   201
The Alecos M [1991]
   1 Lloyd's Rep 120   249
The Alev [1989] 1 Lloyd's Rep 138   190
Ali v BCCI [2002] 1 AC 251   94, 103–5,
   221
Allcard v Skinner (1887)
   36 Ch D 145   196–98, 199–200
Allen v Flood [1898] AC 1   190, 191
Alman and Benson v Associated
   Newspapers Group Ltd (1980,
   unreported)   81
Amalgamated Investment & Property v
   John Walker [1976] 3 All ER 509   123
The Angelia [1973] 1 WLR 210   214
The Antaios [1985] AC 191   92

Antons Trawling v Smith [2003]
   2 NZLR 23   34
Appleby v Myers (1867)
   LR 2 CP 651   144–45
Arcos Ltd v Ronaasen & Son
   [1933] AC 470   94, 216–17
Ashby v White (1703)
   2 Ld Raym 938   246
Ashington Piggeries v
   Christopher Hill [1972] AC 441   75
Associated Japanese Bank
   (International) Ltd v Credit du
   Nord SA [1989]
   1 WLR 255   175, 178, 183
Astley v Weldon (1801) 2 B & P 346   222
The Atlantic Baron [1979]
   QB 705   185, 194
Atlas Express v Kafco [1989] QB 833   49
AG v Blake [1998] Ch. 439
   and [2001] 1 AC 268   224–25, 251,
   254–63, 289
AG v R [2003] UKPC 22   187, 192
AG of Belize v Belize Telecom
   [2009] 1 WLR 1988   107, 111
Axa Sun Life Services plc v
   Campbell Martin Ltd [2011]
   EWCA Civ 133   81, 83

Balfour v Balfour [1919]
   2 KB 571   41–42
Bank Line v Arthur Capel
   [1919] AC 435   133
Bank of Boston v European Grain
   and Shipping [1989] AC 1056   142

Banque Brussels Lambert v Australian
    National Industries (1989) 21
    NSWLR 502   92
Barclays Bank plc v O'Brien [1994]
    AC 180   157
Barton v Armstrong [1976] AC 104   187,
    188
Bashir v Ali [2011] EWCA Civ 707   101
Beale v Thompson (1803)
    3 B & P 405   137
Bell v Lever Bros [1932] AC 161   156,
    163, 165, 167, 175, 176–79, 182
Bellgrove v Eldridge (1954)
    90 CLR 613   248
Bence Graphics v Fasson
    [1998] QB 87   262
Benedetti v Sawiris
    [2010] EWCA Civ 1427   22, 24
Beswick v Beswick
    [1968] AC 58   266, 270, 276, 280
Bettini v Gye (1876) LR 1 QBD 183   213
BJ Aviation Limited v Pool
    Aviation Ltd [2002] P&CR 25   107
Blackburn Bobbin v TW Allen & Sons
    [1918] 1 KB 540;
    [1918] 2 KB 467   122–23
Blomley v Ryan (1956) 99 CLR 362   201
BOC Group plc v Centeon LLC
    [1999] 1 All ER (Comm) 970   102
Boulton v Jones (1857)
    6 Weekly Reporter 108   169
BP Exploration Co (Libya) Ltd v Hunt
    (No 2) [1979] 1 WLR 783
    and [1981] 1 WLR 232   142–45
Bridge v Campbell Discount Co
    [1962] AC 600   57, 223
Brikom Investments v Carr
    [1979] QB 467   56
The Brimnes [1975] QB 929   11
Brinkibon v Stahag Stahl
    [1982] 1 All ER 293   11
British Movietonews v London and
    District Cinemas [1951] 1 KB 190
    and [1952] AC 166   125, 132

British Steel v Cleveland Bridge &
    Engineering Co
    [1984] 1 All ER 504   22–23, 27
British Westinghouse v London
    Underground [1912] AC 673   189
Brogden v Metropolitan Railway
    (1877) 2 App Cas 666   13
Bromage v Genning
    (1617) 1 Rolle 368   235
Broome v Cassell & Co
    [1972] AC 1027   254
Bunge v Tradax
    [1981] 1 WLR 711   215–16
Butler Machine Tool Co v Ex-Cell-O
    Corp [1979] 1 WLR 401   14–18
Bwllfa and Merthyr Dare Steam
    Collieries (1891) Ltd. v Pontypridd
    Waterworks Co [1903] AC 426   97

Canada Steamship Lines v
    The King [1952] AC 192   102–3, 138
Candler v Crane, Christmas & Co
    [1951] 2 KB 164   183
Cantiare San Rocco SA v Clyde
    Shipbuilding & Engineering Co Ltd
    [1924] AC 226   142, 146
Carlill v Carbolic Smoke Ball Co
    [1893] 1 Q.B. 256   14
Carlisle & Cumberland Banking Co v
    Bragg [1911] 1 KB 489   173
Central London Property Trust v High
    Trees House [1947] KB 130   44, 62
Centrovincial Estates v Merchant
    Investors Assurance
    [1983] Com LR 158   4, 159
Chandler v Webster
    [1904] 1 KB 493   142
Chappell & Co Ltd v Nestle Co Ltd
    [1960] AC 87   39
Chartbrook Ltd v Persimmon Homes
    Ltd [2007] 1 All ER (Comm)
    1083, [2008] EWCA Civ 183
    and [2009] 1 AC 1101   90, 95,
    98–101

Charter Reinsurance v Fagan
[1997] AC 313   92
Chatfield v Jones
[1990] 3 NZLR 285   180
Cheese v Thomas
[1994] 1 All ER 35   200
Chwee Kin Keong v Digilandmall.com
[2004] 2 SLR 594   159
CIBC Mortgages v Pitt
[1994] AC 200   199
Cie Noga d'Importation v Abacha
[2003] EWCA Civ 1100   47
City of New Orleans v Firemen's
Charitable Association
(1891) 9 So 486   251
Clark Contracts v Burrell Co (No 2)
2003 SLT 73   280
Clarke v Earl of Dunraven,
The Satanita [1897] AC 59   12
Cleaver v Schyde Investment Ltd
[2011] EWCA Civ 929   83
Cobbe v Yeoman's Row [2006]
EWCA Civ 1139   60
Cohen & Sons v M. Lurie Woolen Co
(1921) 232 NY 112   25
Collier v Wright [2008] 1 WLR 643   53,
57, 62
Combe v Combe [1951]
2 KB 215   31, 55, 62–63, 65, 270
Commission for the New Towns v
Cooper [1995] Ch 259   99, 182
Commonwealth v Verwayen
(1990) 170 CLR 394   55, 57, 59
Companhia de Navegaceo Lloyd
Brasilerio v Blake
(1929) 34 F 2d 616   126
Co-operative Insurance Society v
Argyll Stores [1998] AC 1   238, 240,
245
Co-operative Wholesale Society Ltd v
National Westminster Bank plc
[1995] 1 EGLR 97   92
Couldery v Bartrum (1880)
LR 19 Ch D 394   48

Coulls v Bagot's Executor
(1967) 119 CLR 460   268
The Countess of Rutland's Case
(1604) 5 Co Rep 25b   94
Countrywide Communications Ltd v
ICL Pathway Ltd (Unreported,
QBD, 1999)   21, 22, 24
Credit Lyonnais v Burch
[1997] 1 All ER 144   203
Creswell v Potter [1978]
1 WLR 255 (note)   201
Crossley v Faithful & Gould Holdings
[2004] EWCA Civ 293   111, 113
CTN Cash & Carry v Gallagher
[1994] 4 All ER 714   191–93
Cundy v Lindsay (1876)
LR 1 QBD 348 and (1878)
LR 3 App Cas 459   168, 172–73

Darlington BC v Wiltshier Northern
[1995] 1 WLR 68   266–67, 268,
272, 279
Davis Contractors Ltd v Fareham UDC
[1956] AC 696   120–21, 124
D&C Builders v Rees
[1965] 2 QB 617   50, 189
De Beers v Atos Origin IT Services
[2010] EWHC 3276 (TCC)   248
Decro-Wall v Practitioners in
Marketing [1971] 1 WLR 361   214
De Mattos v Gibson
(1858) 4 De G & J 276   292–93
Dennis v MoD
[2003] EWHC 793 (QB)   234
Denny, Mott & Dickson v Fraser
[1944] AC 265   125
Donoghue v Stevenson
[1932] AC 562   217
Drennan v Star Paving Co
(1958) 51 Cal 2d 409   5
DSND Subsea Ltd v Petroleum Geo-services
ASA (unreported, 2000)   191
Dunlop v Lambert (1839)
6 Cl & F 600   278–81, 285, 286

Dunlop Pneumatic Tyre Co Ltd v New Garage and Motor Co Ltd
[1915] AC 79   222, 224, 227
Dunlop Pneumatic Tyre Co v Selfridge & Co [1915] AC 847   31, 268

Earl Beauchamp v Winn
(1873) LR 6 HL 223   183
Eastwood v Kenyon (1840)
11 Ad & El 438   31, 35, 268
Edwards v Skyways [1964]
1 WLR 349   42
Elder, Dempster & Co Ltd v Paterson Zochonis & Co Ltd
[1924] AC 522   273
Entores Ltd v Miles Far East Corporation [1955] 2 QB 327   10
Equitable Life v Hyman
[2002] 1 AC 408   106
Equiticorp Finance Ltd (in Liq) v Bank of New Zealand (1993)
32 NSWLR 50   192
ERDC Group v Brunel University
[2006] EWHC 687 (TCC)   24
Erlanger v New Sombrero Phosphate Co
(1878) 3 App Cas 1218   181
Ertel Bieber v Rio Tinto
[1918] AC 260   122
Esso Petroleum Co Ltd v Harper's Garage (Stourport) Ltd
[1968] AC 269   85
Esso Petroleum Co Ltd v Kingswood Motors [1974] QB 142   294
Esso Petroleum Co Ltd v Mardon
[1976] QB 801   79
Esso Petroleum Co Ltd v Niad Ltd
[2001] EWHC (Ch) 458   224, 255
The Eugenia [1964] 2 QB 226   124, 125, 134
The Eurymedon, New Zealand Shipping v A M Satterthwaite & Co
[1975] AC 154   14, 18, 34, 273, 275
Evans & Son v Merzario Ltd
[1976] 2 All ER 930   79

The Evia Luck [1992] 2 AC 152   186, 187, 188
EVRA Corp v Swiss Bank Corp
673 F.2d 951 (1982)   116
Experience Hendrix v PPX Enterprises
[2003] EWCA Civ 323   259
Export Credits Guarantee Dept v Universal Oil Products [1983]
2 All ER 205   224

Falck v Williams [1900] AC 176   164
Felthouse v Bindley (1862)
11 CBNS 869   9
Fibrosa Spolka Akcyjna v Fairbairn Lawson Combe Barbour Ltd
[1943] AC 32   142
Fisher v Bell [1961] 1 QB 394   12
Foakes v Beer (1884)
L.R. 9 App Cas 605   44, 47, 50
Foley v Classique Coaches
[1934] 2 KB 1   25
Ford Motor Co v Amalgamated Union of Engineering and Foundry Workers
[1969] 2 QB 303   42, 43, 290
Foster v Mackinnon
(1869) LR 4 CP 704   173
Fry v Lane (1888) 40 Ch 312   201

G Percy Trentham Ltd v Archital Luxfer Ltd [1993] 1 Lloyd's Rep. 25   25
Gallie v Lee [1969] 2 Ch 17 and
[1970] AC 1004 (*sub nom.
Saunders v Anglia BS*)   78, 173–74
Gamerco SA v ICM/Fair Warning (Agency) Ltd
[1995] 1 WLR 1226   143
George Mitchell v Finney Lock Seeds
[1983] QB 284 and [1983]
2 AC 803   77, 83, 102, 236
Gibson v Manchester City Council
[1978] 1 WLR 520 and
[1979] 1 WLR 294   12–14
Gillespie Bros & Co v Cheney, Eggar & Co
[1896] 2 QB 59   79

Giumelli v Giumelli (1999)
73 ALJR 547   60
Glynwed Distribution v Koronka
1977 SLT 65   19
Goebel v Linn (1882)
47 Mich 489   50–52
Gold Group Properties v BDW Trading
[2010] EWHC 323 (TCC)   140
The Golden Victory [2007] UKHL 12   262
Gollins v Gollins [1964] AC 644   57
Goodson v Richardson
(1874) LR 9 Ch App 221   258
Goss v Lord Nugent (1833)
5 B & Ad 58   78
The Great Peace [2003] QB 679   164,
165, 167, 175, 177, 178, 182–83
The Gregos [1994] 1 WLR 1465   215
Grist v Bailey [1967] Ch 532   183
GUS Property Management Ltd. v
Littlewoods Mail Order Stores Ltd
1982 SLT 533   276

Habib Bank v Habib Bank Zurich
[1981] 1 WLR 1265   54
Hadley v Baxendale
(1854) 9 Ex 341   116–18
Hammond v Osborne [2002]
EWCA Civ 885   200
The Hannah Blumenthal [1983]
1 AC 854   3, 140
The Hansa Nord [1976] QB 44   215
Hart v O'Connor [1985]
1 AC 1004   197, 201, 203
Hartog v Colin & Shields [1939]
3 All ER 566   3, 75, 159, 163
Hawkes v Saunders (1782)
1 Cowper 289   31
Hedley Byrne v Heller [1964] AC 465   79
Heilbut, Symonds & Co v
Buckleton [1913] AC 30   79
Henderson v Merrett Syndicates
[1995] 2 AC 145   55
Henthorn v Fraser (1880)
LR 5 CPD 344   10

The Heron II [1969] 1 AC 350   116
HIH Casualty Insurance v Chase
Manhattan Bank
[2003] UKHL 6   102–3, 138
Hillas v Arcos (1932)
43 LlL Rep 359   25
Hills v Colonial Government
(1904) 21 SCC 59   227
Hirji Mulji v Cheong Yue Steamship Co
Ltd [1926] AC 497   124, 140
Holt v Markham [1923] 1 KB 504   23
Holwell Securities v Hughes
[1974] 1 WLR 155   11
Hong Kong Fir Shipping v Kawasaki
Kisen Kaisha (The Hong Kong Fir)
[1962] 2 QB 261   213–15, 217, 220
Howe v Smith (1884) 27 Ch D 89   224
Hutton v Warren (1836)
1 M&W 460   108
Hutton v West Cork Railway
(1883) LR 23 Ch D 654   33
Huyton v Cremer [1999]
1 Lloyd's Rep 620   188, 192–93
Huyton v DIPASA [2003]
2 Lloyd's Rep 780   183
Hyde v Wrench (1840)
3 Beav 334   11, 15

ING Bank NV v Ros Roca SA
[2011] EWCA Civ 353   101
Ingram v Little [1961]
1 QB 31   168, 169, 171
Inntrepreneur v East Crown Ltd
[2000] 2 Lloyd's Rep. 611   79–80
Interfoto v Stiletto [1989]
1 QB 433   75–78, 154
Inverugie Investments v Hackett
[1995] 1 WLR 713   262
Investors Compensation Scheme v
West Bromwich Building Society
[1998] 1 WLR 896   91–92, 94–95,
96–98, 99–103, 106
Isenberg v East India House Estate Co Ltd
(1863) 3 De GJ & S 263   240

*Islamic Republic of Iran Shipping Lines
v Steamship Mutual Underwriting
Association (Bermuda)* [2010] EWHC
2661 (Comm)   121

Jackson v Horizon Holidays [1975] 1
WLR 1468   266, 277–78
Jaggard v Sawyer [1995]
1 WLR 269   260
James Spencer v Tame Valley Padding
(CA 1998, unreported)   212
Jennings v Rice [2002] EWCA Civ 159   60
Jones v Lalic (2006) 197 FLR 27   61
Jones v Padavatton [1969]
1 WLR 328   42
Jones v Vernon's Pools [1938]
2 All ER 626   43
*Joseph Constantine Steamship Line v
Imperial Smelting Corp*
[1942] AC 154   122, 124
Joseph v Knox (1813) 3 Camp 320   278
Jumbo King v Faithful Properties
(1999) 2 HKCFAR 279   93

Keppel v Bailey (1834)
2 Myl & K 517   293
*King's Norton Metal Co v Edridge,
Merrett & Co* (1897) 14 TLR 98   172
Kingsford v Merry (1856)
11 Exch 577   172
*Kleinwort Benson Ltd v Malaysia Mining
Corp* [1989] 1 All ER 78   43
Krell v Henry [1903]
2 KB 740   120, 123, 129–30

The Laconia [1976] QB 835 and
[1977] AC 850   218, 219, 221
Laidlaw v Organ (1817)
15 US 178   156, 159–60
Lake River v Carborundum Co
(1985) 769 F.2d 1284   226, 227
*Larrinaga & Co v Societe Franco-
Americaine des Phosphates* (1923) 14
Ll L Rep 457   126, 176

Lee Chee Wei v Tan Hor Peow Victor
[2007] 3 SLR 537   80
The Leonidas D [1985] 1 WLR 925   9,
134
L'Estrange v F Graucob Ltd
[1934] 2 KB 394   75
Lewis v Averay [1972]
1 QB 198   168–69, 173
*Linden Gardens Trust v Linesta Sludge
Disposals* [1994] 1 AC 85   266, 277,
280, 281
Lipkin Gorman v Karpnale Ltd
[1991] AC 548   22, 143
Lister v Romford Ice [1956] AC 555   113
Liverpool City Council v Irwin
[1976] QB 319 and
[1977] AC 239   18, 111–13
London Drugs v Kuehne & Nagel
[1992] 3 SCR 299   274
*Lord Strathcona Steamship Co Ltd v
Dominion Coal Co Ltd*
[1926] AC 108   293
Lordsdale Finance v Bank of Zambia
[1996] QB 752   228
Low v Bouverie [1891] 3 Ch 82   58
Lumley v Gye (1853) 2 E & B 216   244,
253, 287–92, 294
Lynch v DPP of Northern Ireland
[1975] AC 653   186, 190–91

Mackay v Dick (1881)
6 App Cas 251   114
The Mahkutai [1996] AC 650   273, 274
Mainstream Properties v Young
[2005] EWCA Civ 861
(cf OBG v Allen)   291
Malik v BCCI [1998] AC 20   103, 114
Manchester Trust v Furness
[1895] 2 QB 539   293
*Mannai Investment Co Ltd v
Eagle Star Life Assurance Co Ltd*
[1997] AC 749   92
The Maratha Envoy [1978] AC 1 84–85,
94, 125

The Mary Nour [2007] EWHC
2070 (Comm) and [2008]
2 Lloyd's Rep. 526   123, 140
May and Butcher v Rex (1929)
[1934] 2 KB 17n   25
Maynard v Moseley (1676)
Swanst 651   181
McCutcheon v MacBrayne [1964]
1 WLR 125   77, 87
McRae v Commonwealth Disposals
Commission (1951) 84 CLR 377   176,
179
Mediterranean Salvage & Towage Ltd v
Seamar Trading [2009]
EWCA Civ 531   110–11
Merritt v Merritt [1970] 1 WLR 1211   42
Metrobus v UNITE [2009]
EWCA Civ 829   290
The Mihalos Angelos [1971]
1 QB 164   215
Miles v Wakefield Metropolitan DC
[1987] AC 539   277
Millar v Bassey [1994] EMLR 44   288,
291
Miller v Jackson [1977] QB 966   234
Mona Oil v Rhodesia Railways
[1949] 2 All ER 1014   114–15
The Moorcock (1889)
14 PD 64   107, 113
Moorgate Mercantile Co Ltd v
Twitchings [1976] QB 225   54
Multiservice Bookbinding Ltd v
Marden [1979] Ch 84   181
Munt v Beaseley [2006]
EWCA Civ 370   56
Murphy v Brentwood DC
[1991] 1 AC 398   274, 277
Murray v Leisureplay [2005]
EWCA Civ 963   228

National Carriers v Panalpina (Northern)
[1981] AC 675   124, 126, 140
Natwest Bank v Morgan [1985]
AC 686   198, 199

The Nema [1982] AC 724   121
Network Rail v RMT [2010]
EWHC 1084 (QB)   290
The New York Star [1979]
1 Lloyd's Rep 298 and [1981]
1 WLR 138   273
Newport City Council v Charles
[2008] EWCA Civ 1541   62
Nicholson & Venn v Smith Marriott
(1947) 177 LT 189   176
Nisshin Shipping v Cleaves & Co
[2004] 1 Lloyd's Rep 38   275
Nissho Iwai Petroleum v Cargill
International [1993]
1 Lloyd's Rep 80   114
Northern Indiana v Carbon County
Coal Co (1986) 799 F. 2d 265   126,
128, 129
Norwich City Council v Harvey
[1989] 1 WLR 828   274
Norwich Union Fire Insurance Society v
Price [1934] AC 455   179

OBG Ltd v Allan [2008] 1 AC 1   234,
287, 292
Oceanbulk Shipping v TMT Asia
[2010] UKSC 44   100
Office of Fair Trading v Abbey National
plc [2009] EWCA 116 and
[2009] UKSC 6   207–8
The Olympic Pride [1980]
2 Lloyd's Rep 67   100
Opera Co of Boston v Wolf Trap
Foundation (1987)
817 F.2d 1094   130
Orakpo v Manson Investments
[1978] AC 95   143

Panatown Ltd v Alfred McAlpine
Construction Ltd [2001]
1 AC 518   247, 248, 249, 266, 269,
272, 277–78, 279, 281–85
Pao On v Lau Yiu Long
[1980] AC 614   186

Paradine v Jane (1646) Al 26   112, 120,
    122, 136, 139, 178
Parker v SE Railway Co (1877)
    2 CPD 416   75
Partidge v Crittenden [1968]
    1 WLR 1204   11
Patel v Ali [1985] Ch 283   250
Peekay Intermark v Australia & New
    Zealand Banking Group [2006]
    2 Lloyd's Rep 511   78
Peevyhouse v Garland Coal &
    Mining Co (1962)
    382 P.2d 109   251
Pell Frischmann Engineering Ltd v Bow
    Valley Iran Ltd [2009] UKPC 45   259
Pepper v Hart [1993] AC 593   99
Peregrine Systems v Steria [2004]
    EWHC 275 (TCC)   220
Petromec v Petroleo Brasileiro
    [2006] 1 Lloyd's Rep 161   74
Pharmaceutical Society v Boots Cash
    Chemists [1953] 1 QB 401   13
Phillips v Brooks [1919] 2 KB 243   165,
    172
Philips Electronique Grand Public SA v
    British Sky Broadcasting Ltd
    [1995] EMLR 472   110, 111
Phillips Hong Kong v A-G of
    Hong Kong (1993) 61 BLR 41   228
Photo Production Ltd v Securicor
    Transport Ltd [1980] AC 827   102,
    112, 211, 213, 244
Pillans v Van Mierop (1765)
    3 Burrow 1663   30–31, 33
Pinnel's Case (1602) 5 Co Rep 117a   48
Planché v Colburn (1831) 8 Bing 14   24
The Playa Larga [1983]
    2 Lloyd's Rep. 171   138
Port Line v Ben Line [1958]
    2 QB 146   293
Premier Electricial Construction Co
    v National Electrical Contractors
    Association 814 F.2d 358,
    366 (7th Cir 1987)   135

Prenn v Simmonds [1971]
    1 WLR 1381   91, 97–98
Proforce Recruit Ltd v
    The Rugby Group Ltd [2006]
    EWCA Civ 69   96

Quadrant Visual Communications v
    Hutchison Telephone
    [1993] BCLC 442   246

Radford v de Froberville [1977]
    1 WLR 1262   248, 249, 252, 281
Radmacher v Granatino [2011]
    1 AC 534   42–43
Raffles v Wichelhaus (1864)
    2 H&C 906   164, 167
Raiffeisen Zentralbank Osterreich AG v
    The Royal Bank of Scotland plc
    [2011] 1 Lloyd's Rep 123   82–83
Raineri v Miles [1981] AC 1050   236
Rainy Sky SA v Kookmin Bank
    [2010] EWCA Civ 582 and
    [2011] UKSC 50   95, 105
Rann v Hughes (1778) 4 Bro PC 27   31
Re Castioni [1891] 1 QB 149   90
Re Moore and Landauer
    [1921] 2 KB 519   216
Re Selectmove [1995] 1 WLR 474   47
Redgrave v Hurd (1881)
    20 Ch.D. 1   8, 157
Regalian v LDDC [1995] Ch 212   26
Regina v Bunn (1872)
    12 Cox CC 316   291
Regina v Graham [1982]
    1 All ER 801   188
Regina v Hasan [2005] 2 AC 467   186,
    188
Regina v Howe [1987] AC 417   186, 188
Regina (Reprotech (Pebsham) Ltd) v East
    Sussex CC [2003] 1 WLR 348   54
Regina (Lumba) v Home Secretary
    [2011] UKSC 12   284
Reynell v Sprye (1852)
    1 De G M & G 660   56, 188

Rice v Great Yarmouth BC (2001) 3
LGLR 4   220–21
Riverlate Properties Ltd v Paul
[1975] Ch. 133   8, 158, 181
Riverside Housing Association v White
[2005] EWCA Civ 1385   62
Robbins v Jones (1863)
15 CB (NS) 221   156
Robinson v Harman (1848)
1 Ex Rep 850   254
Robophone Facilities v Blank
[1966] 1 WLR 1428   221, 223, 228
Rodocanachi v Milburn (1887)
18 QBD 67   247
Rookes v Barnard [1964]
AC 1129   253, 254
Rose & Frank v Crompton Bros
[1923] 2 KB 261 and
[1925] AC 445   41, 42, 43
Rose v Pim [1953] 2 QB 450   76
Royal Bank of Scotland v Etridge
(No 2) [2002] 2 AC 773   157, 199
The Rozel [1994] 2 Lloyd's Rep 161   249
RTS Flexible Systems Ltd v Müller
GmbH [2010] UKSC 14   26–27
Ruxley Electronics v Forsyth [1994]
1 WLR 650 and [1996] AC 344   248,
249, 250, 252, 269, 281, 283

Salkeld v Vernon (1758) 1 Eden 64   103
The Scaptrade [1983] 1 QB 529 and
[1983] 2 AC 694   84, 218–19, 221
Schroeder Music Publishing Co v
Macaulay [1974]
1 WLR 1308   85, 86
Schuler v Wickman Machine Tool Sales
[1974] AC 235   95, 105, 219–21
Scott & Sons v Del Sel 1922 SC 592   133
Scriven Bros & Co v Hindley & Co
[1913] 3 KB 564   3, 75
Scruttons v Midland Silicones
[1962] AC 446   266, 273
The Sea Angel [2007]
2 Lloyd's Rep 517   120, 125, 136

SERE Holdings v Volkswagen [2004]
EWHC 1551 (Ch)   81
Shelfer v City of London Electric
Lighting Co [1895] 1 Ch 287   234
Shepherd & Co Ltd v Jerrom
[1987] 1 QB 301   140
Shirlaw v Southern Foundries
[1939] 2 KB 206, 227   107
Shogun Finance v Hudson [2002]
QB 834 and [2003]
UKHL 62   3, 81, 167, 168, 169–72
The Siboen and The Sibotre
[1976] 1 Lloyd's Rep 293   185, 191,
194, 255
Sidemar [1961] 2 QB 278   134
Simpson v Simpson [1992]
1 FLR 601   197–98
The 'Sine Nomine' [2002]
1 Lloyd's Rep 805   255, 256
Sirius International v FAI Insurance
Ltd [2004] UKHL 54   93
Skeate v Beale (1841)
11 Ad & El 983   185
Slater v Hoyle & Smith
[1920] 2 KB 11   247
Smith v Hughes (1871)
LR 6 QB 597   2, 7–9, 155, 157, 163,
169
Smith v William Charlick
(1924) 34 CLR 38   191
Smith and Snipes Hall Farm v
River Douglas Catchment
Board [1949] 2 KB 500   268
Snepp v United States (1980)
444 US 507   254
Solle v Butcher [1950] 1 KB 671   125,
164, 175, 181–83
Somerfield Stores v Skanska [2006]
EWCA Civ 1732   94
Springwell Navigation Corp v
JP Morgan Chase Bank [2010]
EWCA Civ 1221   83
State Trading Corp of India v Golodetz
[1989] 2 Lloyd's Rep 277   215, 216

Stilk v Myrick (1809) 2 Camp 317
and 6 Esp 129   46, 49

Stocznia Gdanska SA v Latvian Shipping
Co [1998] 1 WLR 574   251

Stocznia Gdanska SA v
Latvian Shipping Co (No 2)
[2002] EWCA Civ 889   288

Suisse Atlantique Société d'Armement
Maritime SA v NV Rotterdamsche
Kolen Centrale [1967] 1 AC 361   102

The Super Servant Two,
J Lauritzen AS v Wijsmuller BV
[1990] 1 Lloyd's Rep 1   124, 136,
138, 140, 146

Surrey CC v Bredero Homes [1993]
1 WLR 1361   258

Swain v The Law Society [1983]
1 AC 598   266

Swiss Bank v Lloyds Bank [1979]
Ch 548   293

Tamplin v James (1880)
L.R. 15 Ch. D. 215   5, 181

Taylor v Caldwell (1863)
3 B & S 826   120, 122, 130–31, 145

Taylor v Johnson (1983)
151 CLR 422   163, 183

Teacher v Calder [1899] AC 451   254

Thomas Witter v TBP Industries
[1996] 2 All ER 573   81

Thoroughgood's Case (1582)
Co Rep 9b   173

Tilden Rent-A-Car Co v Clendenning
(1978) 83 DLR (3d) 400   76

Tinn v Hoffman (1873) 29 LT 271   9

Tito v Waddell [1977] Ch 106   251

Toll Pty Ltd v Alphapharm Pty Ltd
(2004) 211 ALR 342   77

Towne v Eisner (1918) 245 US 418   92

Tradax International SA v Goldschmidt
SA [1977] 2 Lloyd's Rep 604   215

Trident General Insurance Co Ltd v
McNiece Bros Pty Ltd (1988)
165 CLR 107   268

Trident Turboprop (Dublin) Ltd v
First Flight Couriers Ltd [2008]
EWHC 1686 (Comm)   83

Tulk v Moxhay (1848)
2 Phillips 774   292–93

Union Eagle v Golden
Achievement [1997] AC 514   93–94,
96, 219

United States v Dial (1985)
757 F.2d 163   160

United States v Stump Home
Specialties, Inc (1990)
905 F.2d 1117   49

The Universe Sentinel [1983]
1 AC 366   186, 187

Upton RDC v Powell [1942]
1 All ER 220   76

Vallejo v Wheeler (1774)
1 Cowp 143   214

Van der Garde v Force India
Formula One [2010]
EWHC 2373 (QB)   249, 251

Vercoe v Rutland Fund
Management [2010]
EWHC 424 (Ch)   256, 259–61

Walford v Miles [1992]
2 AC 128   74, 114, 146

Waltons Stores v Maher
(1988) 164 CLR 387   55, 57, 59–60

Ward v Byham [1956]
1 WLR 496   31, 65

Watford Electronics v Sanderson
[2001] 1 All ER Comm 696   82, 83

Watkins v Carrig (1941)
91 NH 459   52

Way v Latilla [1937]
3 All ER 759   25, 64

Webster v Cecil (1861)
30 Beavan 62   163, 165, 181

West Sussex Properties Ltd v
Chichester DC [2000] NPC 74   183

Weston v Downes (1778)
  1 Douglas 23   62
Whincup v Hughes (1871)
  LR 6 CP 78   270
White v Jones [1995] 2 AC 207   34, 283
White Arrow Express v Lamey's
  Distribution [1995] CLC 1251   250, 251
Whittle Movers Ltd v Hollywood Express
  Ltd [2009] EWCA Civ 1189   21
William Sindall plc v Cambridgeshire CC
  [1994] 1 WLR 1016   177
Williams v Agius [1914] AC 510   247
Williams v Bayly (1866)
  LR 1 HL 200   189, 197

Williams v Roffey Bros & Nicholls
  (Contractors) Ltd [1991]
  1 QB 1   44–47, 49, 51–52, 53, 62, 190, 193–94
Wolverhampton Corp v Emmons
  [1901] 1 QB 515   46
Woodar Investment Development Ltd v
  Wimpey Construction UK Ltd
  [1980] 1 WLR 277   278
World Wide Fund for Nature v
  World Wrestling Federation [2006]
  EWHC 184 (Ch) and [2007]
  EWCA Civ 286   258
Wrotham Park Estate v Parkside Homes
  [1974] 1 WLR 798   234, 256, 257–63

LEGISLATION

UK

Bills of Lading Act 1855   279

Carriage of Goods by Sea Act 1992,
   s. 2(1)   279
Conspiracy and Protection of
   Property Act 1875   291
Consumer Credit Act 1974,
   s.60   154
Consumer Protection
   from Unfair Trading
   Regulations 2008   154
Contracts (Rights of Third Parties)
   Act 1999   265–67, 271–72,
274–76, 279, 280, 282

Gambling Act 2005, s.335   43
Gaming Act 1845, s.18   43

Indian Contracts Act 1872, s.63   47
Industrial Relations Act 1971,
   s.334   43

Larceny Act 1861   172
Larceny Act 1916   172
Law Reform (Frustrated Contracts)
   Act 1943   140–45, 149, 150
   s.1(2)   142–43
   s.1(3)   143–45
   s.2(3)   149
Liabilities (War Time Adjustment)
   Acts 1941–1944   150
Law of Property (Miscellaneous
   Provisions) Act 1989, s.1(2)   39

Misrepresentation Act 1967
   s.1   180
   s.3   81, 82, 83
National Minimum Wage
   Act 1998   209

Sale of Goods Act 1893   172
Sale of Goods Act 1979
   s.6   176
   s.8(3)   19
   s.18(2)   19
   s.13   155, 216
   ss.14–15   112, 155
   s.15A   217–19
   s.53(3)   247
Statute of Frauds 1677, s.4   55
Surrogacy Arrangements
   Act 1985, s.1A   42

Third Parties (Rights Against
   Insurers) Act 2010   275
Torts (Interference with Goods)
   Act 1977, s.3   234
Trade Union and Labour
   Relations Consolidation Act
   1992, s.179   43, 290

Unfair Contract Terms Act 1977   77, 102
   S.2   82
   S.3   82, 138
   S.3(1)   87
   S.3(2)(b)(i)   82
   S.11(1)   81

Unfair Terms in Consumer Contracts
    Regulations 1999   138, 205–9
      Reg 3   208
      Reg 5(1)   87
      Reg 5(2)   76
      Reg 6(2)   207–9
      Sch 2   208
      Sch 2(e)   228
      Sch 2(g)   221

International
Australia
South Australian Frustrated
    Contracts Act 1988   149

France
Code Civil arts 953, 955, 960   37

Germany
Bürgerliches Gesetzbuch
    para 313   150
    paras 519, 530   37

New Zealand
Contractual Mistakes Act 1977   180

USA
Restatement (First) of Contracts (1932)
    para 90   59, 63
Restatement (Second) of Contracts
    (1981)
    para 90   37, 50, 59
    para 79   39
Uniform Commercial Code
    para 2–207   19

1
FORMATION OF CONTRACT

Debate 1

Does the law on offer and acceptance respect the parties' intentions?

Contracts are voluntarily assumed legal obligations. This seems so obvious that it is usually assumed to go without saying. Yet do the very rules which determine whether the parties have reached agreement respect the intentions of the parties? At the general theoretical level, the 'objective principle' may lead to contracts which diverge from the inner 'subjective' intentions of one (or even both) of the parties. At the technical doctrinal level, the rules on offer and acceptance may also apparently defeat the parties' 'true intentions'. In this debate we examine these claims. First, is it true that the law fails to respect the voluntariness principle? Secondly, if so, does this show that the rules ought to be changed to meet the principle – or should the principle be re-examined in the light of the rules?

A SUBJECTIVE OR OBJECTIVE APPROACH?

Classically, a contract is said to be a 'meeting of the minds' or *consensus ad idem*. But it is questionable whether English law has ever taken this particularly seriously. The modern law of contract is the product of nineteenth-century treatise-writers, who first attempted a 'full-blooded' theorization of the law, heavily influenced by the French jurist Pothier.[1] His central idea was that contractual obligation stems from the mutual assent of the parties. But as David Ibbetson comments, basing liability on the parties' minds was reasonably satisfactory in theory but problematic in practice. All too often 'what appeared to be a perfect agreement concealed a more ragged mixture of things on which the parties agreed, and things to which one or both of them had given no thought'.[2] Moreover, what of the party who

---

[1] D. J. Ibbetson, *A Historical Introduction to the Law of Obligations* (Oxford University Press 1999), p. 220; A. W. B. Simpson, 'Innovation in Nineteenth Century Contract Law' (1975) 91 *LQR* 247. Cf. R.-J. Pothier, *Traité des obligations* (1761).

[2] Ibid, p. 221.

gives every outward sign of assent but whose inner ('subjective') thoughts are quite different? How are such inner thoughts to be proved?

To avoid such practical problems, the common law has committed itself to an objective theory of contract formation, which John Wightman describes as a 'vehicle of compromise' between the will theory and commercial convenience.[3] Objectivity denies strength to any 'secret reservations' that the parties might have.[4] As Holmes put it, 'the making of a contract depends not on the agreement of two minds in one intention, but on the agreement of two sets of external signs – not on the parties having *meant* the same thing but on their having *said* the same thing'.[5] According to Joseph Perillo, this has been the basic approach since time immemorial, apart from 'a brief but almost inconsequential flirtation with subjective approaches in the mid-nineteenth century'.[6] It was memorably restated by Blackburn J in *Smith v Hughes*:[7]

> If, whatever a man's real intention may be, he so conducts himself that a reasonable man would believe that he was assenting to the terms proposed by the other party, and that other party upon that belief enters into the contract with him, the man thus conducting himself would be equally bound as if he had intended to agree to the other party's terms.

The clear rationale for the objective approach presented here is to protect the position of the other party, who may reasonably have relied on the outward appearance of willingness to contract. As Adam Smith had argued in his lectures of 1762–1763, an apparent promise should be binding (irrespective of the will of the promisor) because it produces 'the same degree of dependence' as one actually intended.[8] Thus, as J. R. Spencer argues, words or conduct are given the meaning that would be assigned by a reasonable person *in the position to whom they were addressed*.[9]

As J.P. Vorster notes,[10] this way of stating Spencer's argument rescues it from criticisms made by William Howarth. Howarth argues for a position of wholly detached objectivity, independent of either party's perspective – the 'fly on the wall'.[11] Howarth says there is nothing to choose between adopting the perspective of the 'promisor' or 'promisee'; this had led to uncertain law as the courts alternated between the indistinguishable options. Detached objectivity would resolve the debate, in Howarth's view. But as Vorster points out, the promisor/promisee terminology is unhelpful when in a bilateral contract, both parties will be *both* promisor and promisee. The rationale for objectivity being to protect reasonable

---

[3] J. Wightman, *Contract: A Critical Commentary* (Pluto Press, 1996) p. 78.

[4] H. Collins, *The Law of Contract* (Cambridge University Press, 4th edn, 2003) p. 118.

[5] O. W. Holmes, 'The Path of the Law' (1897) 10 *Harvard LR* 457, 464.

[6] J. M. Perillo, 'The Origins of the Objective Theory of Contract Formation and Interpretation' (2000) 69 *Fordham L Rev* 427.

[7] (1871) LR 6 QB 597.

[8] Adam Smith, *Lectures on Jurisprudence* [1762–63] (Clarendon Press, 1978) 93.

[9] J. R. Spencer, 'Signature, Consent and the Rule in *L'Estrange V. Graucob*' [1973] *CLJ* 104.

[10] J. P. Vorster, 'A Comment on the Meaning of Objectivity in Contract' (1987) 104 *LQR* 274.

[11] W. Howarth, 'The Meaning of Objectivity in Contract' (1984) 100 *LQR* 265.

reliance on outward appearances, the law must always take the perspective of the 'observer' rather than the 'actor', as Mindy Chen-Wishart puts it.[12] Howarth also fails to answer Spencer's main criticism of the fly-on-the-wall approach, that it could lead to the denial (or imposition) of a contract when *both* parties believed that they were (or were not) contracting – an 'absurd' situation.[13]

The 'reasonable observer' approach is said to require 'quite a complex amalgam of the objective and the subjective' in order to determine 'what each party intended, or must be deemed to have intended'.[14] The *reasonable* observer would not rely on the appearance of agreement when he ought to realize that the actor's true intentions did not go with the appearance. As Mindy Chen-Wishart points out, this is not a 'subjective exception' at all, but a simple application of observer objectivity. The observer will rely only when it would be reasonable to do so. Of course, if the observer actually knows that the actor's intention did not correspond with appearances it is *a fortiori*, but that does not mean the test becomes subjective. *Hartog v Colin & Shields* shows that *either* actual *or* deemed-because-reasonable knowledge will do.[15] A second point is that when the observer is responsible for the divergence between the actor's intention and appearance, he cannot hold the actor to the appearances. This is illustrated by *Scriven v Hindley*, where the auctioneer's misleading display of the auction lots induced a mistaken bid: as Lawrence J said, the auctioneer could not under such circumstances 'insist on a contract by estoppel'.[16]

It has often been observed that the objective principle ultimately rests on some kind of estoppel – preventing the denial of an apparent agreement. Lord Diplock argues that:

> The rule that neither party can rely upon his own failure to communicate accurately to the other party his own real intention by what he wrote or said or did, as negativing the *consensus ad idem*, is an example of a general principle of English law that injurious reliance on what another person did may be a source of legal rights against him.[17]

But if the principle were truly based on estoppel, then actual *action* in reliance on the outward appearances would be necessary. The fact that apparent agreement may always *potentially* generate reliance would be insufficient. Secondly, there would be important implications for remedies. It might seem more appropriate to compensate irreversible *detriment* incurred in reliance on the apparent agreement than to enforce it. But in fact, neither of these positions obtains in English law.

---

[12] M. Chen-Wishart, 'Objectivity and Mistake: The Oxymoron of *Smith v Hughes*' in J. Neyers, R. Bronough and S. G. A. Pitel (eds), *Exploring Contract Law* (Hart Publishing, 2009).
[13] Spencer, n.9 above.
[14] *Shogun Finance v Hudson* [2003] UKHL 62, [132] (Lord Phillips).
[15] [1939] 3 All ER 566.
[16] *Scriven Bros & Co. v Hindley & Co.* [1913] 3 KB 564.
[17] *The Hannah Blumenthal* [1983] 1 AC 854.

In *Centrovincial Estates v Merchant Investors Assurance* the plaintiffs by letter offered to lease premises to the defendants for £65,000 per annum.[18] But this figure was erroneous – the plaintiffs had intended to state £126,000. The defendants wrote back formally to accept the proposed £65,000 offer. The plaintiffs, realizing their mistake, immediately telephoned to inform the defendants that they had meant to say £126,000, but the defendants held them to the original offer. Before the Court of Appeal the plaintiffs argued that (on the assumption that the defendants had not realized the plaintiffs' mistake) there was no binding contract as a consequence of mere acceptance. In addition, they submitted, the defendants had to alter their position in reliance on the offer, to estop the plaintiffs from withdrawing it. This submission fell on very stony ground. Slade LJ held that as soon as the offer was accepted there was a binding contract, provided it was accompanied by good consideration. This could be satisfied by the offeree promising as to his future conduct, and therefore it was 'nothing to the point that the offeree may not have changed his position beyond giving the promise requested of him'.

The court rejected as irrelevant the question whether the statement had been relied upon.[19] Thus, *Centrovincial Estates* is authority for the proposition that contracts are binding from the outset, i.e. even when 'wholly executory'. It is a particularly strong statement of that classical position since the offer did not represent the offeror's true intention.[20] Yet the plaintiff was held to the contract, despite any detrimental reliance by the defendant.

P. S. Atiyah has criticized the general failure of contract theorists to distinguish between executory contracts and those where (partial) performance, reliance or the conferral of benefits have taken place.[21] In Atiyah's view, the law should (and generally does) set much more store by what people do than by bare intentions. Therefore, the law should prioritize the compensation of the reliance interest over the expectation interest. Atiyah is particularly critical of *Centrovincial Estates* ('clearly wrong').[22] The plaintiffs' liability cannot be justified by their intention or promise. Rather, the crux of the defendants' complaint is that they were *misled* by the apparent promise. But misleading someone, Atiyah argues, is akin to tort, and reliance damages would therefore be more appropriate than enforcement of the contract.

Daniel Friedmann notes such a solution in the Civilian tradition.[23] Under the doctrine of *culpa in contrahendo* (fault in contracting) in German law, parties are entitled to avoid a contract because of a subjective mistake of which the other party was not aware, but they must compensate that party for his reliance losses.[24] By contrast, the fully objective English approach (as seen above) holds the

---

[18] [1983] Com LR 158.

[19] P. S. Atiyah, *Essays on Contract* (Oxford University Press, 1990) p. 173.

[20] See also *Moran v University College Salford* (No 2) [1994] ELR 187.

[21] See, for example, *Essays on Contract*, ch 2.

[22] Ibid, pp. 172–75.

[23] D. Friedmann, 'The Objective Principle and Mistake and Involuntariness in Contract and Restitution' (2003) 119 *LQR* 68.

[24] Cf. R. von Jhering, '*Culpa in contrahendo, oder Schadensersatz bei nichtigen oder nicht zur Perfektion gelangten Verträgen*' (1861).

mistaken party to the contract itself, thus protecting the non-mistaken party's full expectation interest (like the defendant lessee's in *Centrovincial Estates*). Is this higher level of protection justified? For the Civilian, as Kessler and Fine point out, it is 'too harsh' on the ostensible promisor, and 'wasteful'.[25]

In similar vein, Hugh Collins points out problems with the characteristic all-or-nothing English position.[26] The court is faced with a stark choice, either to hold the parties to a full-blown contract, or to award no compensation at all. In cases where there has been considerable expenditure ('ancillary reliance') by one of the parties, the temptation will be for the court to 'manipulate and distort the classical rules' to find a contract. Might it not be preferable to compensate reliance? Collins cites American examples;[27] he argues that such a compromise would place the law on a more coherent doctrinal basis.

Therefore, while estoppel does provide the basic underlying reason for the 'observer objectivity' approach to contract formation in English law, it is not a perfect explanation. Actors are estopped from denying the outward appearance of agreement even when observers have not relied upon it. Critics like Atiyah and Collins argue that the estoppel rationale should be pursued to its conclusion and used only to protect detrimental reliance. On the other hand, the reliability of outward appearances generally is important to protect the whole institution of contracts, irrespective of actual reliance in a particular case. The experience of the playground provides a morality tale: if we can easily escape promissory obligation by secretly crossing our fingers behind our backs, people soon cease to bother to make (worthless) promises at all! The institution of promising falls into disrepute, followed by disuse.[28] The common law, to prevent this, provides powerful incentives to avoid careless manifestations of assent.[29]

English law is unusual in its fidelity to the objective principle. Are there any other justifications for it? Objectivity undoubtedly simplifies the factual inquiry. Proving inward intentions is difficult – lawyers invoke Bryan CJ's dictum that 'the devil himself knoweth not the mind of man'.[30] But this should not be over-exaggerated: trial for the most serious criminal offences daily requires lay jurors to decide defendants' intentions. However the courts have, clearly, been concerned about fraudulent denials of contractual intent, which would be difficult to disprove. Baggally LJ said in *Tamplin v James* that if simple mistake (in the absence of misrepresentation or ambiguity) were a good defence, 'the performance of a contract could rarely be enforced upon an unwilling party who was also unscrupulous'.[31] Short of outright fraud, unconscious self-interest could distort

---

[25] F. Kessler and E. Fine, '*Culpa in contrahendo*, Bargaining in Good Faith and Freedom of Contract: A Comparative Study' (1964) 77 *Harvard LR* 401, 429.

[26] Collins, n.4 above, pp. 176–77.

[27] E.g. *Drennan v Star Paving Co* (1958) 51 *Cal 2d* 409.

[28] D. Goddard, 'The Myth of Subjectivity' [1987] *Legal Studies* 263, 270.

[29] Kessler and Fine, n.25 above, p. 433.

[30] (1477) YB 17 Edw IV, Pasch, f2, pl2.

[31] (1880) L.R. 15 Ch. D. 215, 218.

recollections of what was intended.[32] Perillo argues that distrust of oral testimony has run throughout the history of the common law. The medieval courts prohibited parties from testifying in their own causes altogether. When this was relaxed by statute (1843–51), the courts (still fearing perjury) evolved the objective theory to make party testimony irrelevant.[33]

Perjury aside, the practical difficulties of a contract law based on the pure, inward intentions of the parties can hardly be exaggerated. In the light of this, even French law's official, codified commitment to the will theory has waned. Stefan Vogenauer comments that there is more rhetoric than substance of subjectivity in modern French law – having made their 'ceremonial bow in the direction' of the wills of the parties, the court turns to objective proof of what that will is.[34]

One major reason for the turn away from the will theory has been the rise of standard form contracts,[35] which meant 'ever greater weight' on the objective approach.[36] As Atiyah says, one who signs a printed form is 'almost invariably held bound in the teeth of his intentions and understandings except in some very exceptional cases of fraud or the like. The truth is he is bound not so much because of what he intends but because of what he does'. The signature binds because others are likely to rely on it in ways 'which are reasonable and even necessary by the standards of our society'.[37] Atiyah suggests that the fiction is so engrained in lawyers' habits of thought that they fail to notice it: 'When one lives in a culture and works in a professional tradition in which it is taken for granted that people who do or say certain things ought to come under certain obligations, it is very easy to convince oneself that these obligations have been voluntarily undertaken'.[38] For Atiyah, then, the objective approach undermines the paradigm of the executory contract founded solely in the intentions of the parties. Doing is much more important than merely promising.

Finally, we should note the argument that an objective approach is an unavoidable necessity. Contract is about agreement, which requires *communication*.[39] It is impossible to communicate in a wholly private language. David Goddard considers Humpty Dumpty saying 'I promise to meet Alice for tea': can Humpty claim that he did not mean to promise anything by saying these words?[40] (Humpty Dumpty famously told Alice, scornfully, that when he used a word it meant precisely what he wanted it to mean – neither more nor less.[41]) Of course not: to communicate we must use a language, which in turn relies on shared social conventions. In the

---

[32] Chen-Wishart, n.12 above.

[33] Perillo, n.6 above.

[34] S. Vogenauer, 'Interpretation of Contracts: Concluding Comparative Observations' in A. Burrows and E. Peel (eds), *Contract Terms* (Oxford University Press, 2007) p. 127.

[35] Cf. Ch.3 below.

[36] D. J. Ibbetson, *A Historical Introduction to the Law of Obligations* (Oxford University Press 1999) p. 246.

[37] Atiyah, n.19 above, p. 22.

[38] Ibid, p. 141.

[39] Chen-Wishart, n.12 above, p. 346.

[40] Goddard, n.28 above.

[41] L. Carroll, *Through the Looking-Glass* (1872).

absence of a linguistic convention, one cannot make a sound and mean anything by it.[42] When we do use language, we cannot coherently claim that it has some subjective meaning special to ourselves, different from its general objective meaning in the 'language game' necessary for communication. On this view, there is no choice but to assign meaning objectively, when considering formation and construction of contracts.

MISTAKES

Many contract textbooks contain a separate chapter about mistake, including cases where the parties have allegedly failed to reach agreement. For Pothier, the influential exponent of the will theory, mistake was 'the greatest defect that can occur in the contract'.[43] But some commentators argue that this treatment of the issue is itself mistaken. C.J. Slade denies that there is a separate doctrine of 'mistake' in English law at all: the question is simply whether 'offer and acceptance on their true interpretation are found to be divergent'.[44] Stephen Smith similarly argues that reference to agreement 'mistakes' is misleading: what matters is whether agreement is reached, and no principles other than those on formation are needed to answer that question.[45] This position, although perhaps unorthodox, arguably fits English law better.

As seen above, Blackburn J in *Smith v Hughes*[46] made an enduring statement of the objective principle. This was qualified where the seller made a mistake as to the terms. A mere mistake of fact or motive would be insufficient. The distinction is rather elusive. People do not 'habitually differentiate between such notions in their thoughts.'[47] Chen-Wishart says that the distinction 'seems paper-thin' and suggests that the average student's response is understandable disbelief.[48] Yet the distinction is a vital one.

There are all sorts of mistake which plainly do *not* invalidate a contract. James Gordley collects some 'textbook examples': a friend who buys a wedding gift and then learns that the engagement has been broken, a man who buys a new refrigerator and then learns that his wife hates the colour, a person who sells a valuable object falsely believing that he needs the money, and a person who buys property falsely believing he will inherit the money he needs to pay for it.[49] If such unilateral mistakes served to avoid contracts, what contract would ever be binding? With every bad bargain, the losing party can honestly point to a mistake (about present facts, or a misprediction of the future) at the root of his downfall.

---

[42] L. Wittgenstein, *Philosophical Investigations*, notes to para. 35.

[43] R.-J. Pothier, *Traité des Obligations* (1761) (trans. Sir W. Jones) 1.1.3 §1.

[44] C. J. Slade, 'The Myth of Mistake in the English Law of Contract' (1954) 70 *LQR* 385, 385. For 'common mistake' cf. Ch.6 below.

[45] S. A. Smith, *Contract Theory* (Oxford University Press 2004) p. 366.

[46] (1871) LR 6 QB 597.

[47] Wightman, n.3 above, p. 77.

[48] Chen-Wishart, n.12 above, pp. 343–44.

[49] J. Gordley, 'Mistake in Contract Formation' (2004) 52 *Am J Comp* L. 433.

As Collins puts it, despite the 'superficial logic' of allowing mistake to negative the intention to enter into a contract, this cannot be allowed to govern or it would provide 'an open-ended excuse to avoid any transaction which turns out to be unpalatable'.[50]

For this reason, *unilateral* mistakes avoid contracts *only* when induced by the other party – i.e. in cases of misrepresentation. Here, equity is fairly generous: even innocent misrepresentation justifies rescission of the contract, because it would be 'moral delinquency' to take advantage of a statement subsequently shown to be false.[51] But a sharp line is drawn between positive misrepresentation and a failure to disclose information. Again, *Smith v Hughes* illustrates this point. The underlying spirit of the decision was *caveat emptor* ("let the buyer beware"). The buyer's belief about the oats would gain legal protection only in two situations. First, if induced by the seller's positive misrepresentation. But there was no such misrepresentation in *Smith v Hughes*; the seller simply failed to rescue the buyer from his self-deception over the age of oats. This is not actionable.[52] Secondly, if there was a term of the contract whereby the seller promised (or 'warranted') that the oats were old. No such promise was made. If it had been, or if an appropriate term were implied,[53] then the buyer would have had a claim against the seller for breach of contract.

The crucial point is that the buyer's belief about the age of the oats is not by itself a term of the contract. Only if he believes that the seller was warranting their age (thus incorporating this as part of the seller's contractual obligation) might there be potential for *disagreement over the terms of the contract*. We have seen how the objective test deals with such agreement problems. If the buyer's conduct suggests that he is agreeing to the seller's proposal (which does not in fact contain any warranty about the age of the oats) the buyer is held to that outward appearance – unless the seller knows (or should have known) that the buyer was making a mistake as to the terms. Then the seller's reliance on apparent agreement would be unreasonable. It seems likely that there would be a contract on the *buyer's* terms, in this situation.[54] But such cases simply require application of the ordinary objective test: they don't require a special 'category' of mistake. For this reason, Mindy Chen-Wishart says that *Smith v Hughes* is 'oxymoronic'.[55]

To conclude, the law considers one party's unilateral misapprehension to be a potential obstacle to agreement only in narrowly defined situations. Daniel Friedmann comments that '*Smith v Hughes* whittled down the contents of the mistake category so that possibility of avoiding a contract on the ground of mistake was almost completely excluded'.[56] Mistake was 'marginalised', 'subordinate' to

---

[50] Collins, n.4 above, pp. 276–77.

[51] *Redgrave v Hurd* (1881) 20 Ch.D. 1, 12–13 per Jessel MR.

[52] Cf. pp. 153–156 below.

[53] Cf. now implied terms in Sale of Goods Act 1979, ss.13–14.

[54] Cf. *Riverlate Properties Ltd v Paul* [1975] Ch. 133, 140 (Russell LJ) – canvassing rectification for unilateral mistake where there has been 'sharp practice'.

[55] Chen-Wishart, n.12 above.

[56] Friedmann (2003), n.23 above.

the objective principle of formation and 'almost wiped out'. Instead, as Friedmann argues, much of the 'work' is done by rescission for misrepresentation. But the hapless buyer in *Smith v Hughes* was unprotected by a contractual term and unable to point to any misleading statement by the seller. John Wightman suggests that the *Smith v Hughes* approach to unilateral mistake enables due respect to the supposedly foundational principles of agreement, while severely restricting their scope so as not to subvert *caveat emptor*.[57]

OFFER AND ACCEPTANCE

In order to find an agreement, English law (usually) insists on an offer followed by an unconditional acceptance – possibly following a preliminary stage of negotiations consisting of offers, counter-offers and non-binding 'invitations to treat'. Whether there has been an offer, duly accepted, depends on the intentions of the parties, as deduced by objective interpretation of their words and conduct. Further complexity arises when the parties are communicating at a distance. The basic explanation for this complex set of rules is to provide clarity for the parties as to precisely when the moment of contractual responsibility arises. It is obviously important to know whether there is a contract or not, but *when* it is formed may be important in a situation of volatile prices. The main critique of the rules is that they are artificial, formalistic and complex, and may ultimately serve to defeat, not discern, the intentions of the parties.

Collins makes the bold claim that no other department of law displays the same august tradition of rigorous doctrinal reasoning as contract – and such 'sublime irrelevance'.[58] For Collins, the rules on offer and acceptance exemplify the point. While they purport to elaborate the requirements for agreement, this is a formalist mask for various policy choices.[59] Most dramatically, the rules sometimes deny force to actual agreements to ensure there is a clear answer to the question: was there a contract? Collins describes the rules' purpose as being 'to determine the moment at which both parties can rely upon the existence of a binding contract'.[60]

If party A writes to B offering to buy B's car, just as B is writing to A to offer to sell the car (for the same price), the parties are clearly in complete agreement. But (apparently) there would be no contract in such a case of simultaneous 'crossing offers'.[61] There is no offer followed by acceptance. Less dogmatically, the law considers this history an unsafe basis for the parties to conclude that a contract has been formed. Further communication is required to clarify this. Similarly, in *Felthouse v Bindley*, the parties were evidently in *consensus ad idem*.[62] Although silence is ambiguous,[63] the nephew withdrew the horse from

---

[57] Wightman, n.3 above, pp. 77–78.
[58] Collins, n.4 above, p. v.
[59] Ibid, pp. 159–61.
[60] Ibid, p. 164.
[61] *Tinn v Hoffman* (1873) 29 LT 271.
[62] (1862) 11 CBNS 869.
[63] Cf. *The Leonidas D* [1985] 1 WLR 925.

auction telling the auctioneer it had already been sold, on the strength of the uncle's offer. This was unambiguous, objective evidence of agreement. But still there was no contract because, Collins argues, 'the court could not accept that it was reasonable for the uncle to assume so without a further communication from the nephew'.[64] Most simply of all, if both parties manifest their willingness to be bound in some objective way but without telling each other about it (e.g. writing it in unposted letters), there is clearly agreement but for want of communication there is no contract.

The requirement of communication therefore ensures mutual certainty at the cost of recognizing true agreement in some cases. The artificiality is to the fore when parties are negotiating remotely, particularly in the postal rule which holds that an acceptance is effective as soon as the offeree posts it. This excites comparative lawyers who find it one of the characteristic curiosities of the common law when compared to continental systems. But as Stephen Smith argues, in some situations it is more important that there is *a* settled rule than what the rule is.[65] Like driving on the left (or right) of the road, the important thing is that everyone drives on the same side! It does not really matter which. The fact that English law has a different solution to the co-ordination problem, but one no more or less inherently suitable, is in the end unremarkable. The same can, no doubt, be said for the other rules, such as that withdrawals of offers must reach offerees to be effective, and that communication by instantaneous means is effective only on receipt.[66]

Simon Gardner agrees that the modern justification may simply be that any rules are preferable to no rules, for they remove 'what could otherwise be a costly muddle by letting people know where they stand'.[67] However, in an historical account Gardner points out that the nineteenth-century courts did not share this attitude of indifference. They evidently cared about the way the rules were settled. The notion of the post office as 'agent' for the parties enjoyed some popularity but was exploded by the Court of Appeal in *Henthorn v Fraser* in 1892.[68] The idea of 'business convenience' also cropped up in many decisions, but as Gardner says, it was one-sided since freedom of action for *offerees* seemed to be the unexplained assumption. In the end, Gardner suggests the courts were influenced by the prevailing social attitudes to new methods of communication. Posting a letter was equated in the popular mind with its arrival, after the postal reforms of c.1840. Pre-stamped mail would magically arrive in the addressee's house without any further agency outside the Royal Mail. When Lindley J came to decide that withdrawal of an offer took effect on receipt not posting in *Byrne v Van Tienhoven* in 1880, however, such a notion

---

[64] Collins, n.4 above, p. 164.

[65] S.A. Smith, *Contract Theory* (Oxford University Press, 2004) p. 188.

[66] *Entores Ltd v Miles Far East Corporation* [1955] 2 QB 327.

[67] S. Gardner, 'Trashing with Trollope: A Deconstruction of the Postal Rules in Contract' (1992) 12 *OJLS* 170.

[68] [1892] 2 Ch 27.

would have looked as fanciful as it does to twenty-first century eyes. The first telephone services had been introduced in London in 1878–79 – to public wonderment. Therefore Lindley J held that a postal withdrawal took effect only on arrival;[69] but the postal *acceptance* rule was by then too well entrenched to be overruled. It remains to this day – although it has attracted judicial hostility and is easily rebutted by the offer requiring 'notice' of the offeree's answer.

Even when the law requires 'communication', this does not mean that the message must come to the actual (subjective) attention of the other party. It has been suggested, for example, that posting through a letter-box is sufficient because the addressee has 'impliedly invited communication by use of an orifice in his front door designed to receive communications'![70] A telex arriving during ordinary business hours takes effect on arrival even though not read until the next morning – because the staff must have left the office early or neglected to check the telex machine.[71] In the end, according to Lord Wilberforce, there is and can be no universal rule: each dispute must be resolved 'by reference to the intentions of the parties, by sound business practice and in some cases by a judgment where the risks should lie'.[72]

These cases indicate a robustly pragmatic system. The Will Theory is readily sacrificed to provide clear and sensible solutions to contract formation problems. This is also evident in what Melvin Eisenberg calls 'expression rules' which attach standardized, objective meanings to the contract negotiation process.[73] For example, the rule that display of goods is usually only an 'invitation to treat,'[74] or that a counter-offer kills off the original offer.[75] These are not 'axiomatic truths'. Rather, such rules simplify the inquiry: the court does not need to interpret all the words and conduct afresh in each case, when such stock situations arise. But as Eisenberg says, that inevitably means that the 'expression rule' sometimes gives the wrong answer (i.e. not the one that objective interpretation would yield). How are the benefits (of simplification) to be weighed against the costs (of such errors)? Eisenberg says this will involve a complex 'prudential inquiry', balancing the costs and benefits. He chides lawyers for paying insufficient attention to the expression rules and how strong they should be (maxims, presumptions or strict rules?). In general, Eisenberg argues, expression rules should display 'high congru-ence' with the true interpretation of the situation, and actors' expectations. Many of the rules, he argues, fail to do this. Most people who saw goods advertised for a particular price would be outraged if on entering the shop they were told that the price had been raised, for example.

---

[69] (1880) LR 5 CPD 344.

[70] *Holwell Securities v Hughes* [1974] 1 WLR 155 (Russell LJ).

[71] *The Brimnes* [1975] QB 929.

[72] *Brinkibon v Stahag Stahl* [1982] 1 All ER 293.

[73] M. A. Eisenberg, 'Expression Rules in Contract Law and Problems of Offer and Acceptance' (1994) 82 *Cal L Rev* 1127.

[74] E.g. *Partidge v Crittenden* [1968] 1 WLR 1204.

[75] E.g. *Hyde v Wrench* (1840) 3 Beav. 334.

Such arguments do not seem to have made much of an impression on the English courts. In *Fisher v Bell*, Lord Parker CJ admitted that it seemed 'just nonsense' to say that displaying a knife in a shop window was not 'offering' it for sale, but nevertheless it was so clearly established that this was only an 'invitation to treat' that that rule must be applied.[76] There is dogmatism here, verging on the rule-fetishism that Simpson once described (in another context) as the 'theatre of the absurd'.[77] The courts take the view that it is preferable to have clear rules, consistently applied, than to attempt to find the parties' 'true intentions' (although in theory at least, whether a statement is an offer or invitation does depend on the speaker's intention). Again, this is Smith's point that a co-ordination problem is better solved by clear rules, irrespective of their actual content.

These points are well illustrated in the case of *Gibson v Manchester City Council*. Here, the judges differed over the application of the 'mirror image' rules of offer and acceptance – but more fundamentally, whether to apply those rules in the first place. Eisenberg treats these rules on offer–counter-offer–acceptance as stereotyped 'expression rules', suggesting that they can sometimes be discarded in favour of the general principles of interpretation. Lord Denning MR and Ormrod LJ followed that path in *Gibson*.[78] Lord Denning thought it was a mistake to apply 'strict offer and acceptance' – the court should instead examine all of the evidence (both written correspondence and what the parties actually did) to ascertain whether the parties were in agreement. He concluded that they were.

This approach was rejected in the House of Lords.[79] While there might be *exceptional* situations in which offer and acceptance analysis was inappropriate,[80] a case where negotiations had taken place by written correspondence was certainly not one of them. Applying the 'well-settled, indeed elementary, principles of English law' Lord Diplock found it impossible that the council had made an offer to sell the house to Mr Gibson: they stated that they '*may* be prepared to sell' and had invited him not to accept their offer but to 'make [a] formal application to buy'. Lord Edmund-Davies held that the parties' *conduct* did not unambiguously show there was a contract either. It was not clear whether certain improvements to the property had been made in reliance on the council's letter; the removal of the house from the council's list of maintained properties had predated the plaintiff's alleged acceptance of the offer to sell.

The House of Lords' decision in *Gibson* seems highly formalistic. If Lord Denning's interpretation of all the evidence was correct then the parties were, in fact, in agreement. The textual approach in Lord Diplock's leading speech gave priority to the formal letters exchanged to find that there was no 'mirror image' offer and acceptance, and therefore no contract. The case seems an excellent

---

[76] [1961] 1 Q.B. 394, 399.
[77] A. W. B. Simpson, 'Legal Science and Legal Absurdity: *Jee v. Audley*' in *Leading Cases in the Common Law* (Oxford University Press, 1995).
[78] [1978] 1 WLR 520.
[79] [1979] 1 WLR 294.
[80] Lord Edmund-Davies cited *Clarke v Earl of Dunraven, The Satanita* [1897] AC 59.

example of Collins's point that the law prefers clear answers to the question 'is there a contract?' to the messy reality of agreement. Parties may come to agreement gradually, indeed messily, rather than through the elegant dance of negotiations postulated by the law of offer and acceptance.

But Collins's argument is in some ways overstated. The law does not *always* insist on such a formalistic approach. Contrast the rules on offer and acceptance with the *stipulatio* in Roman law, where a precise, corresponding form of words had to be used for the obligation to arise, the question '*dare spondes?*' necessitating the answer '*spondeo*'.[81] There is no magic formula of words required in English law. Acceptance need not be made with the words 'I accept'. Moreover, agreement can be discerned through conduct as well as through speech.[82] Of course this brings much more flexibility to the process than in a formal contract like the *stipulatio*. The inevitable cost is uncertainty: Lord Cairns LC said that few cases gave rise to more disputes than those where the courts had to decide whether a contract had come into being (without 'the complete and formal shape of executed and solemn agreements').[83]

In the end, there is an eternal tension between the clear-cut formal rules applied by the House of Lords in *Gibson* and in the display of goods cases, and the more flexible approach preferred by Lord Denning and in cases of contracts formed by conduct. There may also be policy judgements involved in the rules. Winfield justified the display-of-goods rule on the basis that shops were forums for bargaining and not 'compulsory sales',[84] although with modern concerns about discrimination this seems out of date – and who ever tried to barter over the price of baked beans in Sainsburys? In the self-service chemist case, the court emphasized the statutory requirement for the pharmacist to supervise the sale: therefore the offer was made by the shopper presenting the goods at the till, not by the shop displaying them on the shelf.[85] Collins comments that the court may also have looked unfavourably on the Pharmaceutical Society's attempt to preserve 'restrictive practices', although this is not acknowledged in the judgments.[86] More generally, Collins identifies instrumentalism throughout this area – relevant policies include preserving room for manoeuvre, discouraging opportunism, and protecting reliance.[87]

Unilateral contracts are a good example. They are rather an anomalous category – offers that cannot be accepted by explicitly saying 'I accept!' but only by conduct. Must the person performing the condition even know of the promise, and must they contact the offeror first? What if the offeror tries to withdraw the

---

[81] In *The Owl and the Pussycat* (1871) the parties enter into a *stipulatio*, the question 'are you willing?...' being answered (by the piggy): 'I will'. Cf. D.J. Ibbetson, '*Ulula Felesque: Fabula de Stipulatione*' in *Old Crossum's Book of Placable Cats* [Festschrift for Tony Weir] (privately printed, Cambridge, 2003).

[82] *Brogden v Metropolitan Railway* (1877) 2 App Cas 666.

[83] Ibid, p. 672, quoted by Geoffrey Lane LJ (dissenting) in *Gibson v Manchester CC* [1978] 1 WLR 520.

[84] P. Winfield, 'Some Aspects of Offer and Acceptance' (1939) 55 *LQR* 499.

[85] *Pharmaceutical Society v Boots Cash Chemists* [1953] 1 QB 401.

[86] Collins, n.4 above, p. 173.

[87] Ibid, pp. 171–77.

offer once performance (i.e. acceptance) is under way? Smith suggests that the anomalies are so great that these cases should be located in another department of private law, such as conditional promises, rather than contract.[88] However, in *Carlill v Carbolic Smoke Ball Co* the Court of Appeal famously waved these difficulties aside.[89] The 'withdrawal' problem has been solved by conjuring up a collateral contract, or simply insisting that the offer may not be withdrawn once acceptance begins.[90] And unilateral contracts have proved very useful for giving effect to exclusion clauses intended to benefit third parties. A memorably pragmatic statement was made by Lord Wilberforce in the leading case.[91]

With so many competing policies, it seems unlikely that English law will ever commit itself wholeheartedly to the high formalism of the *stipulatio*, or the wide ranging flexibility favoured by Lord Denning. An unstable mixture of formalism tempered by pragmatism seems to be the prevailing approach. It is worth reiterating that Civilian systems endorse a compromise solution for cases like *Gibson*, through the doctrine of *culpa in contrahendo*.[92] Mr Gibson would have been able to recover any expenditure made in reliance on the Council but could not have held them to the contract and compelled them to sell the house to him. This approach would avoid the black-or-white choice that faced the courts in the *Gibson* litigation, although whether parties' freedom to negotiate should be limited by something like *culpa in contrahendo* is another matter.

Debate 2

How should the law resolve the 'battle of the forms'?

A problem with the strict 'mirror image' approach to offer and acceptance arises when two negotiating parties each use their own (different) standard terms of business during the negotiations. This would seem to obstruct 'mirrored' agreement, and so obstruct contract formation. The courts can often avoid this conclusion in practice, but there are serious criticisms of the traditional approach in this area nonetheless. Some have argued that the difficulties of resolving the problem within the framework of contract is so great that solutions should be sought in other areas of law, in particular restitutionary (gain-based) remedies.

THE TRADITIONAL 'MIRROR IMAGE' APPROACH

The majority of the Court of Appeal in *Butler Machine Tool Co v Ex-Cell-O Corp* applied the traditional rule that an offer must meet with a 'mirror image' acceptance

---

88 Smith, n.45 above, pp. 184–87.
89 [1893] 1 Q.B. 256. Cf. A.W.B. Simpson, 'Quackery and Contract Law: the Case of the Carbolic Smoke Ball' (1985) 14 *J Legal Stud* 345.
90 Collins, n.4 above, pp. 175–76.
91 *The Eurymedon* [1975] AC 154. Cf. p. 273 below.
92 M.M. Siems, '"Unevenly formed contracts": Ignoring the "mirror of offer and acceptance"' [2004] *European Review of Private Law* 771.

for a contract to be formed.[93] At first sight, this causes some difficulty on the facts. Butler (manufacturers) had offered to sell machinery to Ex-Cell-O Corpn for some £75,535; this was subject to Butler's enclosed standard terms of business, which included a price escalation clause. This allowed increased manufacturing costs to be passed on to the customer. Ex-Cell-O replied ordering the machinery subject to *their* standard terms, which did not contain a price escalation clause. Ex-Cell-O's terms included a tear-off slip, which Butler signed and returned. It stated 'We accept your order on the terms and conditions stated therein' but Butler also sent a letter referring back to its original offer (made on its standard terms). On delivery of the machinery, Butler sought to invoke the price escalation clause.

Lawton LJ said that the battle between the parties' standard forms should not be allowed to range over a wide area with the court doing its best to decide what had been in the parties' minds. Instead:

> the battle has to be conducted in accordance with set rules. It is a battle more on classical 18th century lines when convention decided who had the right to open fire first rather than in accordance with the modern concept of attrition.

Ex-Cell-O had not accepted Butler's offer by sending an order with different terms attached: this was a counter-offer which 'killed off' Butler's original offer.[94] Butler, by signing the tear-off slip, had accepted Ex-Cell-O's offer on their terms. The slip's wording was, according to Bridge LJ, 'perfectly clear and unambiguous'. Butler's accompanying letter was held to refer back only to the *price* of their original offer and not the 'small print conditions on the back' which had, consequently, 'disappeared from the story'. At best (according to Bridge LJ) the letter was 'equivocal' and could not override the plain acceptance in the tear-off slip. Therefore, there was a contract on the buyer's standard terms which did not include a price escalation clause.

How convincing is this judgment on the facts? It seems rather unlikely that Butler truly would have agreed to manufacture the machine tool without the protection of its standard price escalation clause. Indeed, it may be doubted whether the employees of Butler who processed the order had any authority to conclude a contract other than on Butler's standard terms.[95] Avery Katz points out that standard forms may be concerned as much with controlling discretion within an organization (lawyers controlling salesmen, etc.) as with imposing terms on trading partners.[96]

In the end, Butler lost the battle by *signing* something. Edward Jacobs refers to 'magical strength which the law gives to a signature'.[97] This is a general doctrine

---

[93] [1979] 1 WLR 401.

[94] *Hyde v Wrench* (1840) 3 Beav 334.

[95] E. J. Jacobs, 'The Battle of the Forms: Standard Term Contracts in Comparative Perspective' (1985) 34 *ICLQ* 297.

[96] A. Katz, 'On the Use of Practitioner Surveys in Commercial Law Research' (2000) 98 *Mich L Rev* 2748.

[97] Jacobs, n.95 above, p. 302.

of English contract law, and a controversial one.[98] Collins criticizes the 'plainly artificial' way that the tear-off slip was given priority over the standard terms to which Butler evidently remained committed. It was only this adept exclusion of part of the written evidence which enabled the court to find a contract.[99] Lawton LJ admitted that had Butler successfully reiterated their terms, there would have been no '*consensus ad idem*'.

This, it is often argued, is the root problem with the mirror-image approach to the battle of the forms. It seems to lead almost inevitably to the conclusion that there was no contract, since the parties were plainly not mirroring each other's proposals. Is it not absurd to conclude that the parties were not agreed when their conduct shows that they were (Butler manufactured the machinery at Ex-Cell-O's request – surely this indicates a contract)? In which case, the law of contract fails in its basic duty: to recognise and enforce agreements.

The critique has sociological support. There is ample evidence that businesses making contracts give no thought to contract *law*, or to the extent that they do think about it they are dismissive or actually hostile.[100] One commentator reported that having talked to more than 5,000 purchasing agents he had never found a manager who read printed terms; agents could not even explain the terms of their own forms![101] They had little understanding of what they perceived as the 'arcane science' of contract law. Thus, it is highly misleading to think of sales/purchasing departments deliberately setting out to impose their terms in a battle of the forms.[102] A more realistic explanation of the typical situation is that the parties believe that they *are* agreed and *do* have a contract – but the law fails to recognise this. The 'paper disagreement' at law diverges from the reality of agreement in practice.[103] Some commentators argue, therefore, that a more flexible approach to the formation of contract is necessary to reflect these business expectations.[104]

Others have debated the efficiency of the mirror image approach (on the assumption, however implausible, that real-life contractors consciously attempt to win the battle of the forms). The first point to note is that courts lean against the conclusion that there was no contract between the parties. What tends to happen is that the last form sent (the last 'shot fired' in the battle) prevails, because this is deemed to be accepted by conduct. The other party, by proceeding to perform (or accepting performance) is held thereby to have accepted the terms in that last

[98] Cf. pp. 75–78 below.

[99] Collins, n.4 above.

[100] S. Macaulay, 'Non-Contractual Relations in Business: A Preliminary Study' (1963) 28 *Am Soc Rev* 1; H. Beale and T. Dugdale, 'Contracts Between Businessmen: Planning and the Use of Contractual Remedies' (1975) 2 *Brit Jo L & Soc* 45.

[101] J.E. Murray, 'The Standardized Agreement Phenomena in the Restatement (Second) of Contracts' (1982) 67 *Cornell LR* 735, 778 n.207.

[102] D.G. Baird, 'Commercial Norms and the Fine Art of the Small Con' (2000) 98 *Mich L Rev* 2716.

[103] Cf. S. Macaulay, 'The Real and the Paper Deal: Empirical Pictures of Relationships, Complexity and the Urge for Transparent Simple Rules' (2003) 66 *MLR* 44.

[104] S.N. Ball, 'Work Carried Out in Pursuance of Letters of Intent – Contract Or Restitution?' (1983) 99 *LQR* 572.

form sent. Therefore, advertent parties can attempt to prevail by continuing to send forms, and re-send them, *ad infinitum,* to attempt to fire the 'last shot'. If this does not bring victory (because the opponent is doing the same) it may at least prevent defeat (there may be no contract – neither form prevails). *Pace* Lawton LJ, this would exactly resemble the trench warfare of the Western Front circa 1916. It is obviously undesirable for the law to encourage such a wasteful (and pointless) stalemate, an indefinite exchange of salvos. Baird and Weisberg have dismissed this account as unrealistic in practice: businesses have little interest in playing games with legal rules.[105] But it does seem that businesses do try to get in the last shot, by attaching their standard terms to all written correspondence.[106]

Baird and Weisberg defend the mirror-image approach.[107] They argue that it provides an incentive for negotiating parties to read each other's forms, otherwise there may be no contract at all. It is therefore said to encourage drafting that is more likely to be acceptable to the other side. But Murray dismisses the 'flagellant' theory that once burned by not reading standard terms, contractors will read them in future.[108] Experience shows that this simply does not happen. Moreover, such apparent indifference is entirely rational. As Victor Goldberg points out, much of the cost saving of standardizing terms in the first place would be lost if parties had to read each other's terms (and negotiate over them) in every case.[109] Therefore, encouraging actual negotiation would be very costly, and not obviously desirable. One survey of in-house corporate lawyers corroborates this, by showing concern about the costs of more frequent meaningful negotiations.[110] So Baird and Weisberg's proposal may be downright harmful, although the English experience suggests it would be simply futile because parties still don't read forms under a 'mirror-image' regime.

FLEXIBILITY IN FINDING CONTRACTS

In *Butler Machine Tool Co v Ex-Cell-O Corp*[111] Lord Denning MR took a different approach (although in the end agreed that the signature on the tear-off slip was decisive). Having set out the facts as summarized above, he said: 'No doubt a contract was then concluded. But on what terms?' As Edward Jacobs points out, this stands the traditional common law on its head.[112] The mirror-image approach of Lawton and Bridge LJJ simultaneously answers both questions: 'was there a contract?' and 'what were its terms?' Lord Denning expressly accepted that there

---

[105] D.G. Baird and R. Weisberg, 'Rules, Standards and the Battle of the Forms: A Reassessment of §2–207' (1982) 68 *Virginia LR* 1217, 1252.
[106] Beale and Dugdale, n.100 above, pp. 49–50; G.G. Murray, 'A Corporate Counsel's Perspective of the "Battle of the Forms"' (1980) 4 *Canadian Business LJ* 290, 293.
[107] Cf. n.105 above.
[108] J.E. Murray, 'The Chaos of the "Battle of the Forms": Solutions' (1986) 39 *Vand L Rev* 1307, 1383.
[109] V. P. Goldberg, 'The "Battle of the Forms": Fairness, Efficiency and the Best-Shot Rule' (1997) 76 *Oregon LR* 155.
[110] D. Keating 'Exploring the Battle of the Forms in Action' (2000) 98 *Mich L Rev* 2678.
[111] [1979] 1 WLR 401.
[112] Jacobs, n.95 above, p. 304.

might be 'a concluded contract [although] the terms vary'. This is irreconcilable with the mirror-image approach.

Lord Denning was well aware of this. The whole offer-and-acceptance approach was 'out of date', he said, citing Lord Wilberforce's judgment in *The Eurymedon*.[113] The battling forms should be 'construed together' to see whether a 'harmonious' synthesis is possible. If so,

> all well and good. If differences are irreconcilable – so that they are mutu-
> ally contradictory – then the conflicting terms may have to be scrapped
> and replaced by a reasonable implication.

Lord Denning's suggestion is characteristically radical. Supplying a 'reasonable implication' envisages a very wide role for the court in filling gaps in the contract. Only shortly before *Butler*, Lord Denning had claimed a power to imply terms in contracts on the basis of 'reasonableness', only to meet firm disapproval in the House of Lords.[114]

For present purposes, it should be noted that while default rules implied into a whole class of contracts might well depend on a judgment of reasonableness, an '*ad hoc* gap filler' for a particular contract is different in kind from such imposed terms.[115] Here, the courts insist on necessity, that the term 'went without saying', for good reason. It is surely impossible to maintain that anything went without saying in a battle-of-forms case. The problem is not the omission of something obvious, but the presence of mutually incompatible terms. For the court to choose between them or to conjure up some compromise position would be to make a contract for the parties. Indeed, the same may be said for Lord Denning's apparently innocuous suggestion of harmoniously construing the two sets of terms together. This will result in a set of terms to which neither party can have thought they were agreeing, either.[116]

Many kinds of contracts are governed (presumptively) by standardized default terms. For example, a bare sale contract will be extensively fleshed out by the implied terms in the Sale of Goods Act 1979. In such cases, it might appear that the law facilitates Lord Denning's proposal to 'knock out' inconsistent terms and then fill the gaps. But there are problems. First, the standard implied term may be very different from *both* parties' standard terms (what if they had intended two months or six weeks in which to bring a claim, whereas the implied term allows just seven days?). Secondly, the absence of an implied term on a particular subject may hand victory to one party, no less arbitrarily than the mirror-image approach. The Sale of Goods Act says nothing about price escalation clauses per se, so this approach (had not Lord Denning also used the signature as an 'escape') would have meant victory by default for the buyers in *Butler*. Whether terms implied by

---

[113] Cf. p. 273 below.
[114] *Liverpool CC v Irwin* [1976] QB 319; [1977] AC 239.
[115] Cf. pp. 107–111 below.
[116] Jacobs, n.95 above.

law will always provide the optimal solution to a battle of forms may, of course, be doubted.

It is true that some of the Sale of Goods Act implied terms are themselves flexible, and may be used by the court to impose a compromise. Section 18(2) states that when the price is not set by the contract 'the buyer must pay a reasonable price'; this is 'a question of fact dependent on the circumstances of each particular case'(s.8(3)). This found interesting application in *Glynwed Distribution v Koronka*.[117] The pursuers sold and delivered steel to the defenders, who accepted it. However, the sellers thought the agreed price was £149 per tonne, and the buyers thought the agreed price was £103 per tonne. The Court of Session held there was a contract, albeit with no agreement on the price. However, this could be supplied by the Sale of Goods Act 'reasonable price', which required a balancing of advantages so as to be fair to both parties. The court approved the trial judge's award of £135 per tonne (although the judge admitted that he had little evidence to go on, and the method by which he arrived at this sum was unknown). This shows a court willing to flesh out a contract in a fairly extreme case of parties being at cross-purposes, seemingly splitting the difference between them in an impressionistic way. If used in all cases, would this produce intolerable uncertainty? Or would imposed compromise better reflect business expectations?

The 'knockout' approach is the usual solution internationally.[118] The American Uniform Commercial Code contains famous §2–207 in which a 'definite and seasonable expression of acceptance' is effective even though it states different terms. The contract consists of 'the terms of the writings on which the parties agree,' plus terms implied by the Code. The provision has been much litigated. Murray comments that its drafting is 'murky' and 'a disaster' and its application 'chaotic'.[119] Grant Gilmore said it was 'arguably the greatest statutory mess of all time'.[120] It might be thought that these are parochial concerns. However, it seems likely that any 'knockout' provision will face severe interpretive difficulties. It is inevitably difficult to decide which terms must be agreed and which are of lesser importance and thus prone to being 'knocked out'. A case-by-case examination of what is 'important' or 'material' would seem the natural course.[121] But Jacobs thinks that this is an 'invitation to expensive litigation'; it would be better to have a rough and ready rule so that people can see where they stand.[122] Yet Jacobs's own suggestion (that terms printed on the front of the form are the ones that matter) show just how arbitrary this can be. Although the 'knockout' rule has wide international support and is said to conform better to business expectations,

---

[117] 1977 SLT 65.

[118] Cf. Jacobs, n.95 above; G. Rühl, 'The Battle of the Forms: Comparative and Economic Observations' (2003) 24 *U Pa J of Int Ec Law* 189.

[119] Murray, n.108 above.

[120] R.E. Speidel, R.S. Summers & J.J. White, *Teaching Materials on Commercial and Consumer Law* (West Publishing Co, 3rd edn, 1981) pp. 54–55.

[121] J Adams, 'The Battle of Forms' [1983] *JBL* 297.

[122] N.95 above, p. 315.

it clearly has costs. Moreover, some argue that rational businesses prefer clear-cut rules to uncertain standards reflecting the vaguer understandings of real life.[123]

Victor Goldberg makes a novel proposal. Faced with divergent forms but facts that suggest a contract was formed, the court should choose the *fairer* set of standard terms to govern the contract.[124] This provides incentives on all kinds of parties (buyers and sellers, etc.) to draft 'moderate' standard forms. The more one-sided the form, the less likely the court is to select it. Therefore, parties will be encouraged to fire the 'best shot' rather than simply the 'last shot'. Since both have this incentive, standard terms are likely to come closer together. This will automatically reduce the number of litigated disputes which forestalls one objection to Goldberg's proposal, that the uncertainty of the fairness criterion will foment disputes. But still, how is the court to choose which terms are 'fairer'? Goldberg suggests one useful guide is 'do as you would be done by': when assessing a seller's terms, the court should examine the terms used by that same company when it is acting as buyer. Is the seller attempting to impose on buyers terms that would be wholly unacceptable to itself, *qua* buyer? This would indicate unfairness.

It is nevertheless obvious that Goldberg is setting a difficult task for courts. Unpredictability of a standard makes dispute resolution more difficult (although as noted, the moderating incentives of the 'best shot' proposal mitigate this). In-house lawyers have been found to fear the inherent uncertainty of the approach.[125] Giesela Rühl prefers a modified version of the Goldberg proposal, in which the court should adopt the 'more efficient' rather than the fairer set of terms.[126] It is not clear that this is any easier for a court objectively to ascertain, however. Stewart Macaulay observes: 'It is easy to talk about efficiency, but it is hard to know whether any particular rule or approach will produce an efficient result in the real world.'[127] Rühl's solution to these problems is to ignore them: she simply asserts, in a casual way, that the advantages of the 'best shot' approach outweigh the costs – and that it is more efficient than the rival 'mirror-image' and 'knockout' rules in turn. A classic pitfall of economic analysis is to make things seem more clear-cut than they really are.

NON-CONTRACTUAL REMEDIES

It was noted above that courts lean in favour of finding a contract. It is embarrassing to suggest otherwise when the parties, believing that there was an agreement between them, partially (or totally) performed it. To say that 'the loss lies where it falls' would explode the logic of insisting on strict correspondence of terms for a contract formation.

---

[123] Cf. pp. 71–73 below.
[124] Goldberg, n.109 above.
[125] Keating, n.110 above.
[126] Rühl, n.118 above.
[127] S. Macaulay, 'Transcript of Panel Discussion' (2007) 49 *S Tex L Rev* 469, 476

However, several commentators have pointed out that the premise here does not justify the conclusion that there must be a contract. Ewan McKendrick influentially argues that courts need not force everything into the language of contract given the potential of restitutionary remedies.[128] Steven Smith makes the point more broadly. Contractual duties are onerous, and should not lightly be imposed. This justifies a strict approach to offer and acceptance (which Smith suggests accords with commercial expectations – you are not bound until you sign on the dotted line). Crucially, Smith argues, there is a range of other remedies to employ when negotiations fail to ripen into contract, including estoppel and *quantum meruit* as well as restitution of unjust enrichment.[129]

Estoppel may be dealt with briefly here,[130] since there is 'considerable doubt' over its applicability in battle of forms cases.[131] English law again differs from the Civilian tradition where such reliance losses are compensated through the concept of *culpa in contrahendo*.[132] The main remedy is, as McKendrick suggests, restitutionary.[133] Restitution (or 'unjust enrichment') is probably the underlying explanation of the venerable, but ill-defined, action for a *quantum meruit* ('as much as was deserved', i.e. a reasonable sum). Waller LJ has recently agreed that the courts need not 'strain' to find contracts when 'a restitutionary remedy can solve most if not all the problems'.[134] But is this too sanguine? In the next section we examine the restitutionary approach, along with its problems. These have led some to argue that the contractual route is superior, after all.

IS RESTITUTION THE SOLUTION?

The basic idea of unjust enrichment initially seems a promising fit with the battle of forms problem. Where (some) performance has taken place, one party may well have received a benefit at the hands of the other. If the recipient of performance kept that benefit without paying for it, he would be unjustly enriched. Therefore, he must make restitution of that benefit by paying for it (or literally by giving the thing back, which is possible with goods or money, but not when the benefit takes the form of services). More schematically, as McKendrick says, the court should analyse whether there was: (a) enrichment; (b) at the defendant's expense; (c) that was unjust; and (d) with no defences. McKendrick admits that the courts generally have not done this explicitly. This allows critics to claim that these cases are not

---

[128] E. McKendrick, 'The Battle of the Forms and the Law of Restitution' (1988) 8 *OJLS* 197.

[129] S.A. Smith, *Contract Theory* (Oxford University Press, 2004) pp. 193–94.

[130] Cf. M. Spence, *Protecting Reliance: The Emergent Doctrine of Equitable Estoppel* (Hart Publishing, 1999) pp. 114–16. Cf. pp. 54–66 below.

[131] *Countrywide Communications Ltd v ICL Pathway Ltd* (Unreported, QBD, 1999).

[132] Cf. L. Russi, *Cooperation Before Contract: The Law and Policy of Expenses Incurred During Negotiations in Comparative Perspective* (Vandeplas, 2009).

[133] Cf. wider argument in E. McKendrick, 'Work Done in Anticipation of a Contract Which Does Not Materialise' In W.R. Cornish et al., *Restitution: Past, Present and Future* (Hart Publishing, 1998). McKendrick comments at 186 that common lawyers should not look so enviously at *culpa in contrahendo* which even civilians think a 'grey area' between contract and tort.

[134] *Whittle Movers Ltd v Hollywood Express Ltd*. [2009] EWCA Civ 1189, [15].

about restitution at all,[135] although the courts have recognized unjust enrichment as a category fully distinct from implied or 'quasi' contract only since 1991.[136] So earlier cases might well use fictitious contractual language where today we would talk about unjust enrichment, it is said. Recent *quantum meruit* cases do just this.[137] This sharper definition of *quantum meruit* is probably an advance over the earlier case-law: one judge 'found it impossible to formulate a clear general principle which satisfactorily governs the different factual situations which have arisen' after a careful review of the authorities.[138] However, the narrower restitutionary focus arguably limits the utility of the remedy, and throws the correctness of some earlier decisions into serious doubt.

Various stages of the unjust enrichment inquiry cause difficulty in these cases where contracts fail to materialize, in particular, deciding whether (and by how much) the defendant was enriched, and whether that enrichment was 'unjust' (so as to trigger the obligation to make restitution). *British Steel v Cleveland Bridge & Engineering Co* is a highly influential authority.[139] British Steel agreed to manufacture steel nodes to the special order of Cleveland Bridge (CBE) for a building being erected by the latter in Saudi Arabia. The parties could not agree what British Steel's liability would be in the event of late delivery. Nevertheless, while negotiations actively continued on that point, British Steel began to manufacture and deliver the steel to CBE at their request (the nodes were urgently needed for the building). British Steel did not deliver the nodes in the correct order, which caused difficulties for CBE. Also, the final node was retained by British Steel owing to a payment dispute between the parties; it was then detained in their factory by a strike, before eventually arriving in Saudi Arabia. In sum, CBE suffered heavy losses from the disorderly and late delivery, and refused to pay for the steel. British Steel brought a claim for the price of the steel (agreed at £200,853). CBE counter-claimed over the late delivery, some £867,735.

Robert Goff J held that there was, and could be, no contract on the evidence. There was an 'unresolved dispute' as to which party's terms would govern the supply of steel, CBE's terms containing no limit to the seller's liability for delay and British Steel's terms excluding such liability altogether. It was impossible to predict how that dispute would be resolved when, in fact, it was ongoing. It would be 'extraordinary' to hold British Steel to an implied contract with unlimited liability for delay by dint of their manufacturing and delivering the steel, when they would never have agreed to such liability under an express contract.

What were the consequences? In the absence of a contract, the law simply imposed an obligation on CBE to pay a reasonable sum (*quantum meruit*) for the steel – the £200,853. Thus, the primary claim by British Steel was upheld.

---

[135] S. Hedley, 'A response [to McKendrick]' in W.R. Cornish et al., *Restitution: Past, Present and Future* (Hart Publishing, 1998).

[136] *Lipkin Gorman v Karpnale Ltd* [1991] AC 548.

[137] Eg *Benedetti v Sawiris* [2010] EWCA Civ 1427.

[138] Countrywide Communications, n.131 above (Nicholas Strauss QC).

[139] [1984] 1 All ER 504.

But CBE's (larger) counterclaim failed completely. This was a contractual claim or nothing. As there had been no contract, there were no obligations about the timing of delivery and 'no legal basis' for CBE's counterclaim.

British Steel has been criticized as a one-sided decision. As Ball notes, the sellers got everything that they wanted (payment for their goods at the going rate) whereas the buyers received no redress for their defeated expectation of better performance.[140] The only way the buyers could avoid their liability would be to reject the goods or services – impossible on the facts of *British Steel* since CBE urgently required the steel. Thus, Ball says, the case shows the limits of the restitutionary approach – it amounts to a 'modern-day version of *caveat emptor* [let the buyer beware]'.[141]

McKendrick criticizes Robert Goff J's reasoning for being insufficiently sensitive to unjust enrichment principles.[142] What CBE had requested was not any old steel, but these particular nodes *in the order stipulated*. As the nodes were not delivered in that order, the steel was less valuable to them. In other words, CBE's enrichment was considerably less than it would have been had their request been fulfilled. In restitution jargon, they should have been allowed to 'subjectively devalue' the steel.

There are difficulties with this proposal too. If the buyer can 'devalue' the steel to nothing, thus killing the seller's *quantum meruit* claim stone dead, is this not as harsh to the seller as *British Steel* is to the buyer? McKendrick admits that these questions might be answered more sensitively by asking, not whether the defendant was enriched, but how much restitution it would be just to require him to make.[143] This sounds dangerously close to the 'well meaning sloppiness of thought' that for decades led English judges to reject 'unjust enrichment' altogether.[144] Moreover, even the maximum 'subjective devaluation' can reduce the benefit only to zero. This would not satisfy CBE whose *net* counterclaim amounted to £666,882. So 'subjective valuation' cannot fill all of the gaps that the absence of a contract created for CBE. McKendrick recognizes a similar lacuna when he notes that in the absence of contract, there can be no recovery of consequential losses.[145] Like CBE's counterclaim for breach of contract, such damages must depend upon a contractual duty having been breached.

Another problem is that many of the *quantum meruit* cases are hard to rationalize as gain-based remedies at all. The old case of *Planché v Colburn* allowed a *quantum meruit* claim when the defendant wrongly refused to accept work done by the plaintiff at the defendant's request;[146] McKendrick has suggested that it does not lie in the mouth of the defendant to deny he has benefited in such a situation.[147]

---

[140] Ball, n.104 above.
[141] Ibid, p. 577.
[142] McKendrick, n.128 above, 212.
[143] Ibid, p. 213.
[144] Cf. *Holt v Markham* [1923] 1 KB 504, 513 (Scrutton LJ).
[145] McKendrick, n.128 above, 215.
[146] (1831) 8 Bing 14.
[147] McKendrick, n.128 above.

However, Gareth Jones doubts the propriety of using restitution as a disguised claim for wasted expenditure.[148] Similarly Nicholas Strauss QC comments that much of the difficulty in this area comes from attempts to classify as unjust enrichment what is really a loss unfairly sustained by the plaintiff.[149]

Graham Virgo concludes that *Planché v Colburn* was wrongly decided: if there is no enrichment, *quantum meruit* should be unavailable.[150] However, once the requirements of unjust enrichment have all been established, Virgo argues that the law's response via *quantum meruit* is properly a 'hybrid' remedy which may take both benefits and reliance losses into account.[151] Virgo admits that this may be seen as 'radical', but claims support from other areas of the law (in addition to *quantum meruit* cases): for example, the 'hypothetical bargain' approach to assessment of damages, when ordinary compensation is deemed inadequate. However, that claim is also controversial for the 'hypothetical bargain' cases are vigorously debated.[152] Moreover, Etherton LJ has (since Virgo's paper) held that *quantum meruit* cases are to be decided according to the objective value of the benefit and restitution ordered accordingly – there is no room for a discretionary approach.[153] *Quantum meruit* is concerned with the defendant's benefit and not the claimant's expenses or loss: with subtraction not compensation.[154] This shows that Virgo's wider approach has yet to gain judicial acceptance. The difficulties in explaining wasted expenditure cases using *quantum meruit* will persist.

CONTRACT, AFTER ALL, IS BEST?

It is clear that there are serious difficulties with using unjust enrichment (in the guise of *quantum meruit*) to solve these problems. The utility of contract as an alternative has been stressed by P.S. Atiyah, Steve Hedley and, most recently, Paul Davies. There are two positive prongs to the argument (in addition to the drawbacks of restitution). First, the potential for greater flexibility in assigning contractual responsibility. Secondly, the need to respect the parties' assignment of the risk of loss.

For Hedley not every implied contract must be denounced as a fiction, as some enthusiastic proponents of restitution think.[155] If services are requested in a commercial setting, when everyone knows that they are to be paid for, why not acknowledge the obvious – that there is a contract?

---

[148] G.H. Jones, 'Claims Arising Out of Anticipated Contracts Which Do Not Materialize' (1979) 18 *U W Ontario L Rev* 447.

[149] *Countrywide Communications*, n.131 above.

[150] G.J. Virgo, '*Quantum meruit*: Right or remedy?' (Conference Paper given at Obligations V, Oxford, July 2010).

[151] Compare *ERDC Group v Brunel University* [2006] EWHC 687 (TCC), [42]: 'there are no hard and fast rules for the assessment of a *quantum meruit*. All the factors have to be considered'.

[152] Cf. pp. 257–263 below.

[153] *Benedetti v Sawiris* [2010] EWCA Civ 1427, [140].

[154] Ibid, [142].

[155] S. Hedley, 'Implied Contract and Restitution' [2004] *CLJ* 435.

Why should the parties' hope that they would make a big contract prevent a conclusion that they have in fact made a more modest one? Why should the courts ignore good evidence of a contract? The court can simply enforce the agreement the parties actually made, vague though it might be, and leave aside the parties' fantasies as to agreements which they might have reached in other circumstances.[156]

It is significant that when parties have discussed the price to be paid for the goods or services, this will be important evidence in setting the 'reasonable sum'.[157] It is 'spurious' to give restitution and contract equal billing: the cases are nearly all contractual.

Before adopting such a flexible approach a vital question is whether performance has commenced on either side. It is evident that while the courts take a robust line on how certain a contract must be when it is purely executory, an executed contract is treated much more generously. This accords with Atiyah's refrain that what the parties actually do is much more important than their bare promises.[158] Hence where benefits have been conferred, or expenditure incurred, the law should strive to give effect to the contract. There is considerable judicial support for this. In *Foley v Classique Coaches* the Court of Appeal upheld a petrol supply agreement at prices to be agreed between the parties from time to time.[159] The courts lean in favour of upholding contracts;[160] for a contract to be rendered unenforceable, 'indefiniteness must reach the point where construction becomes futile'.[161] However, an 'agreement to agree' has traditionally been held void for uncertainty.[162] The crucial distinction in *Foley* was that both parties had acted in reliance on the agreement's validity for some three years. Steyn LJ puts the matter generally:

> The fact that the transaction was performed on both sides will often make it unrealistic to argue that there was no intention to enter into legal relations. It will often make it difficult to submit that the contract is void for vagueness or uncertainty. Specifically, the fact that the transaction is executed makes it easier to imply a term resolving any uncertainty, or, alternatively, it may make it possible to treat a matter not finalised in negotiations as inessential.[163]

Ball notes the 'alacrity' with which courts find contracts when the agreement is executed.[164]

---

[156] Hedley, n.135 above, p. 197.
[157] Cf. *Way v Latilla* [1937] 3 All ER 759.
[158] Cf. nn.21–22 above.
[159] [1934] 2 KB 1.
[160] Cf. *Hillas v Arcos* [1932] 43 LlL Rep 359.
[161] *Cohen & Sons v M. Lurie Woolen Co* (1921) 232 NY 112, 114 (Cardozo J).
[162] *May and Butcher v Rex* (1929) [1934] 2 KB 17n.
[163] *G Percy Trentham Ltd v Archital Luxfer Ltd* [1993] 1 Lloyd's Rep. 25, 27.
[164] Ball, n.104 above, p. 586.

What if a contract cannot be upheld, even on such a flexible approach? Is there room outside contract for remedies such as *quantum meruit*? Classically, the answer was 'no'. As Atiyah observes, nineteenth-century freedom of contract was not just a positive principle (upholding agreements) but an exclusionary one – no liability in the absence of agreement. This was not mere formalism but an ideological commitment to autonomy. Liability could arise only through consent.[165] Such a position sounds extreme today but in 2010 the Supreme Court, considering a stalled negotiations case, observed: 'The moral of the story is to agree first and to start work later'.[166] Davies supports this admonition: 'If there is no agreement, the claimant should not recover anything, and should suffer the consequences of performing without the security of a contract.'[167] However, the experience with such 'flagellant' approaches suggests that the incentives have little effect.[168] Should the law tolerate unjust enrichment (or unconscionably induced reliance) merely because there was no contract?

A more nuanced approach may be necessary. There is considerable emphasis in the authorities on the concept of 'taking the risk'. For example, a firm tendering for a job will know that it is taking a risk that its expenditure in preparing the tender will be wasted, for it may not be awarded the contract. When parties declare themselves to be agreed in principle but 'subject to contract' that is taken to be shorthand for each bearing the risk of wasting any expenditure in preparation for the contract, should full agreement not be reached.[169] There will be no contract in such cases, and no claim in unjust enrichment can succeed: 'there is nothing unjust about being visited with the consequences of a risk which one has consciously run.'[170] But nothing is absolute. If a tenderer is encouraged to do work that is wholly exceptional, for the defendant's benefit, he may successfully claim payment.[171] A 'subject to contract' clause may be overtaken by events. In *RTS Flexible Systems v Müller*, parties negotiating 'subject to contract' had agreed, but never signed, a detailed written contract. RTS went on to provide the services required of them under that contract. The Supreme Court held that on the facts, the parties had impliedly agreed to waive the 'subject to contract' term.[172] This accorded better with commercial reality and the standard of the 'honest reasonable businessman'; the parties had simply decided to let sleeping dogs lie rather than formally sign the contract.[173] Therefore, a contract had arisen by conduct. It was unrealistic to suppose

---

[165] Atiyah, n.19 above, p. 143.
[166] *RTS Flexible Systems Ltd v Müller GmbH* [2010] UKSC 14, [1].
[167] P. S. Davies, 'Anticipated Contracts: Room for Agreement' [2010] *CLJ* 467.
[168] Cf. p. 17 above.
[169] E.g. *Regalian v LDDC* [1995] Ch 212.
[170] *Stephen Donald Architects Ltd. v King* [2003] EWHC 1867 (TCC), [79].
[171] *William Lacey (Hounslow) Ltd v Davis* [1957] 1 W.L.R. 932.
[172] [2010] UKSC 14, [55], [56], [86].
[173] Ibid, [86]–[87]. Contrast the importance of the signature in *Butler*, p. 16 above and cf. generally pp. 75–78 below.

that RTS would agree to complete an entire contract of detailed work 'on a non-contractual basis subject to no terms at all'.[174]

Paul Davies supports this flexible approach to the discovery of a contract, deploring the rigid approach to contract (and consequent invocation of *quantum meruit*) by Waller LJ in the court below. The very wide notion of contract is what makes Davies's rigid approach to non-contractual liability tolerable.[175] It also shows that there is a reflexive quality to the opponents in this debate: those who favour restitution tend to take a stricter view of contractual obligation,[176] and vice versa. But in the end, are these anything more than barren debates about classification of obligations? Atiyah asserts that the categories of contract, tort and restitution are much less watertight than is often supposed.[177] Hedley notes that concerns about 'making deals for the parties', often expressed by contract lawyers, should be taken no less seriously in restitutionary claims: if it is nannyish to impose liability in contract, it is nannyish to do it in restitution![178] Switching the labels round on fundamentally similar obligations does not make the problems go away.

In conclusion, a failure to reach complete 'mirror-image' agreement will continue to pose severe problems for legal analysis, whether the failure occurs through the battle of forms, through 'active' failure to agree terms as in *British Steel v Cleveland Bridge & Engineering Co*[179], or other situations like *RTS v Müller*.

Further Reading

Agreement, mistake and the objective principle

J. R. Spencer, 'Signature, Consent and the Rule in *L'Estrange v Graucob*' [1973] *CLJ* 104.

D. Friedmann, 'The Objective Principle and Mistake and Involuntariness in Contract and Restitution' (2003) 119 *LQR* 68.

M. Chen-Wishart, 'Objectivity and Mistake: The Oxymoron of *Smith v Hughes*' in J. Neyers, R. Bronough and S.G.A. Pitel (eds), *Exploring Contract Law* (Hart Publishing, 2009).

Offer and acceptance

S. Gardner, 'Trashing with Trollope: A Deconstruction of the Postal Rules in Contract' (1992) 12 *OJLS* 170.

M. A. Eisenberg, 'Expression Rules in Contract Law and Problems of Offer and Acceptance' (1994) 82 *Cal L Rev* 1127.

---

[174] Ibid, [59].

[175] P.S. Davies, 'Contract and Unjust Enrichment: A Blurry Divide' (2010) 126 *LQR* 175.

[176] Cf. Smith, n.129 above.

[177] Cf. Atiyah, n.19 above, pp. 52–56.

[178] Hedley, n.135 above.

[179] [1984] 1 All ER 504.

Battle of the forms

S. N. Ball, 'Work Carried Out in Pursuance of Letters of Intent—Contract Or Restitution?' (1983) 99 *LQR* 572.

E. J. Jacobs, 'The Battle of the Forms: Standard Term Contracts in Comparative Perspective' (1985) 34 *ICLQ* 297.

E. McKendrick, 'The Battle of the Forms and the Law of Restitution' (1988) 8 *OJLS* 197.

V. P. Goldberg, '"The 'Battle of the Forms'": Fairness, Efficiency and the Best-Shot Rule' (1997) 76 *Oregon LR* 155.

P. S. Davies, 'Anticipated Contracts: Room for Agreement' [2010] *CLJ* 467.

2

ENFORCEABILITY: CONSIDERATION, INTENTION AND ESTOPPEL

INTRODUCTION

The law must decide when agreement has been reached. In England, the rules on offer and acceptance (and 'certainty') perform this function (see Chapter 1). We now examine the requirements for agreement to be a legally enforceable *contract*. The English rules are complex to the point of eccentricity. The cornerstone of the common law approach, historically and (probably) still today, is the doctrine of consideration, which appears 'surprising, even shocking' to Civilian eyes.[1] We examine whether the doctrine serves any useful purpose in the modern law of contract. A possible alternative is the doctrine of 'intention to create legal relations'. Consideration has proved especially controversial as a requirement for the modification of contracts, where its retention is the subject of Debate 3. Finally, we examine calls for an expanded, reliance-based form of liability – and in particular the debate about whether 'estoppel' is truly distinct from contract law, or a branch of it.

Debate 1

Does the doctrine of consideration serve any useful purpose?

In 1936, Lord Wright extrajudicially called for consideration to be abolished.[2] The following year, his Lordship chaired a committee which recommended that consideration should no longer be required where a promise was in writing or gave rise to detrimental reliance.[3] The report has never been implemented. Is that a cause for regret? Many would think so. Defenders of the doctrine of consideration are rare.[4] Most commentators seem to agree either with Lord Wright's view

---

[1] K. Zweigert and H. Kotz, *An Introduction to Comparative Law* (trans. J.A. Weir) (Oxford University Press, 3rd edn, 1998) p. 392.

[2] Wright, 'Ought the Doctrine of Consideration to Be Abolished from the Common Law?' (1936) 49 *Harvard LR* 1225.

[3] Law Revision Committee, *Sixth Interim Report: Statute of Frauds and the Doctrine of Consideration* (1937).

[4] Cf. C.J. Hamson, 'The Reform of Consideration' (1938) 54 *LQR* 233.

that the only requirement for an enforceable promise is that it should seriously be intended as legally binding, or with the alternative test of the 1937 Committee: that reliance on the promise is enough. The doctrine is typically dismissed as a parcel of 'absurdities, inconsistencies, and anomalies'.[5] Holmes said it was a remnant of earlier law whose reason had long been forgotten – like the 'clavicle [collarbone] in the cat'.[6]

To assess this position, we first need to ascertain what, if anything, the doctrine means in the modern law. This requires an overview of the legal history (consideration is not infrequently assumed to be a barbarous historical relic). One can tentatively propose the hypothesis that consideration still excludes purely gratuitous promises from legal enforcement. Assuming that is so, the wisdom of that exclusion will be considered separately for commercial and non-commercial situations. Finally, the continued existence of special formalities as a way of rendering gift promises enforceable must be noted.

CONSIDERATION: A BRIEF HISTORY

The medieval law of contract enforced all kinds of agreements (covenants) contained in deeds, i.e. documents formally signed, sealed and delivered. Additionally, debts could be recovered, even when informal.[7] By the fourteenth century 'the opposition between formal and informal contracts was aligned directly with the opposition between gratuitous and reciprocal arrangements'.[8] With the rise of the modern law of contract (the action for *assumpsit* – 'undertakings'), lawyers spoke of the 'consideration' (linguistically just the reason or motive) for a promise. There was a 'near-deafening clamour of cases' discussing the meaning of this new doctrine in the second half of the sixteenth century.[9] The result of these Elizabethan debates was a doctrine at whose core lay the same idea of reciprocity or *quid pro quo* as in the medieval action of debt.[10]

The need for something valuable 'in exchange' meant that promising to pay in reward for a past service lacked consideration, for nothing further was gained by the promise. Also, 'natural love and affection' was not good consideration (would this not mean that 'every promise would bind every man because this natural love should be between everyone'?[11]). These are two situations where there is clearly good reason for a serious promise to be made (gratitude, love) but because there is no economic exchange, there is no enforceable contract. This suggests an inchoate division between commercial and private/social/moral obligations.

The bargain theory of contract was attacked by Lord Mansfield CJ. In *Pillans v Van Mierop*, Lord Mansfield held that all written contracts between merchants

---

[5] Wright, n.2 above, p. 1251.
[6] O.W. Holmes, *The Common Law* (1881) p. 35.
[7] Cf. generally D.J. Ibbetson, *A Historical Introduction to the Law of Obligations* (Oxford, 1999) chs 2 and 5.
[8] Ibid, p. 80.
[9] Ibid, p. 143
[10] Ibid, p. 144
[11] *Harford v Gardiner* (1589).

were binding without consideration: 'it would be very destructive to trade' to hold otherwise.[12] Wilmot J concurred that writing was 'a sufficient guard against surprise [sic]'. However, the House of Lords subsequently overruled this, holding that a formally executed deed was the only permissible exception to the consideration requirement.[13] Undeterred, Lord Mansfield CJ held that a moral duty to pay, although unenforceable in itself, was consideration for a *promise* to make the payment, through 'the honesty and rectitude of the thing'.[14] Buller J, concurring, said: 'The true rule is, that wherever a defendant is under a moral obligation, or is liable in conscience and equity to pay, that is a sufficient consideration.'

While this view lasted longer, it was firmly repudiated in *Eastwood v Kenyon*, a past services case.[15] Counsel for the plaintiff argued: 'A stronger case of moral obligation can hardly arise.' But rejecting this submission, and Lord Mansfield's approach generally, Lord Kenyon CJ reasoned that it would 'annihilate the requirement of consideration, inasmuch as every promise creates a moral obligation to perform it'. Thus was the bargain theory of consideration (and contract) reaffirmed. The courts paid lip service to it throughout the nineteenth century, although they were astute to 'discover' consideration in meritorious cases (even when the parties had omitted the usual incantation, 'for value received').[16] Lord Dunedin restated the doctrine (using Pollock's definition) in 1915. Consideration was 'the price for which the promise of the other is bought'.[17]

CONSIDERATION TODAY

Consideration came in for weighty criticism in the twentieth century. As seen, Lord Wright called for its abolition on the (Mansfieldian) basis that a seriously intended promise should be sufficient.[18] P.S. Atiyah used an inaugural lecture in 1971 to call for a 'fundamental restatement' of the doctrine.[19] Atiyah's central argument seems to be that as consideration is the main test of enforceability in English contract law, it must rationally mean 'the reason for enforcing promises'. He criticizes the orthodox, bargain doctrine for ossifying into rigid rules, divorced from such substantive reasoning. However, Atiyah argues that despite this, in practice the courts reach decisions in accordance with their view of justice and public policy. He suggests (for example) that the presence of children explains the different results in *Ward v Byham* and *Combe v Combe*.[20] Atiyah is particularly

---

[12] (1765) 3 Burrow 1663. Cf. G. McMeel in C. Mitchell and P. Mitchell (eds), *Landmark Cases in the Law of Contract* (Hart Publishing, 2008).

[13] *Rann v Hughes* (1778) 4 Bro PC 27.

[14] *Hawkes v Saunders* (1782) 1 Cowper 289.

[15] (1840) 11 Ad & El 438.

[16] Ibbetson, n.7 above, pp. 238–39.

[17] *Dunlop Pneumatic Tyre Co v Selfridge & Co* [1915] AC 847, 855.

[18] Cf. n.2 above.

[19] Cf. (revised version) P.S. Atiyah, 'Consideration: A Restatement' in *Essays on Contract* (Oxford University Press, 1990).

[20] [1956] 1 WLR 496 and [1951] 2 KB 215 (respectively).

concerned to emphasize the courts' protection of relied-upon promises.[21] The bargain theory is 'manifestly inconsistent with a mass of case law'.[22] He concludes that lawyers should concentrate on the reasons that make it 'just or desirable' to enforce promises, instead of the formal doctrine of consideration.[23]

In a well-known reply G.H. Treitel argued that Atiyah's 'restatement' fails because in the end, it is nothing more than a vague recommendation to enforce contracts when 'just' to do so. Far from restating the doctrine this is a 'negation of the existence of any applicable rules of law'.[24] On Atiyah's critique of the rigidity of the orthodox doctrine, Treitel responds that the courts have the power to 'invent' consideration where necessary. In portraying the doctrine as 'hidebound', Atiyah had underestimated this source of flexibility. Treitel is no doubt correct – as seen above, Victorian judges did this too, and Grant Gilmore describes Cardozo J's benevolent imposition of contracts in 1920s New York by discovering 'gossamer spider webs of consideration'.[25] On the other hand, as Atiyah drily says, the fact that 'our most distinguished and orthodox interpreter of the modern law of contract' admits that the courts indulge in fictions suggests 'there is something pretty strange going on'.[26] David Campbell is more brutal: the 'utter absurdity' of Treitel's argument leads to 'a downward spiral where further ad hoc strategies are needed to cope with … lack of theoretical integrity'. Such desperate attempts to maintain orthodoxy show a degenerating theory – but one that its defenders simply will not give up, however many counter-examples Atiyah might provide.[27]

Treitel admits that the 'invention' of consideration might mask the courts' real reasons for their decisions. His argument is that Atiyah does not lead us much closer to unmasking those reasons. Atiyah would presumably reply that it is better to face the problem openly than to perpetuate the classical theory by manifest pretence. A pessimistic conclusion from this famous exchange of views may be that consideration is now agreed to be meaningless, but nobody knows how to replace it.

Is that too despairing? If consideration has a core meaning, surely it is that purely gratuitous promises, i.e. promises to make gifts, unrelied upon, are not binding. Is this still true? And if so, should the doctrine be abolished in line with Lord Wright's conclusions?

> There is no public policy that I can see against enforcing gratuitous obligations. The most vital element of public policy in this regard is that people should keep their plighted word.[28]

---

[21] Cf. further 'Contracts, Promises and the Law of Obligations' in *Essays on Contract* (Oxford University Press, 1990) and pp. 63–66 below.

[22] P.S. Atiyah, *Essays on Contract*, p. 127.

[23] Atiyah, 'Consideration: A Restatement', p. 243.

[24] G.H. Treitel, 'Consideration: A Critical Analysis of Professor Atiyah's Fundamental Restatement' (1976) 50 Australian LJ 439, 449.

[25] G. Gilmore, *The Death of Contract* (Ohio State University Press, 1974) p. 69.

[26] Atiyah, 'Consideration: A Restatement', p. 179.

[27] D. Campbell, 'The Undeath of Contract: A Study in the Degeneration of a Research Programme' (1992) 22 Hong Kong LJ 20, 35–37.

[28] Wright, n.2 above, p. 1253.

GRATUITOUS PROMISES IN COMMERCIAL LAW

The fundamental challenge to consideration here is whether it is *ever* plausible to describe a business promise as truly 'gratuitous'. As Atiyah observes, it 'may appear gratuitous [but] the promisor expects some return in a rather more indirect way than the present doctrine of consideration recognizes'.[29] As the saying goes: there's no such thing as a free lunch! Carol Rose argues that people in business make gifts all the time, in order to create and foster the trust that is essential in good working relationships.[30] Thus, Rose (paradoxically) concludes, *'giving lies at the heart of exchange'*.[31] Daniel Farber and John Matheson also focus on trust, and argue that within ongoing commercial relationships 'exchange is a continuing rather than a discrete event'.[32] In other words, businesses are engaged in ongoing, mutually beneficial trading, but not necessarily through the isolated bargains presupposed by the classical doctrine of consideration. It is a 'fundamental fact' that promises are constantly made to promote economic activity 'without any specific bargained-for exchange'.[33] Farber and Matheson conclude from this insight that consideration should be replaced with a simple rule: *all* promises made in furtherance of economic activity should be enforced. Otherwise, by breaching such promises businesses will 'pollute the pool of trust' to the detriment of society and the economy.

This seems like a radical change indeed. But if the arguments above are correct, it would be quite consistent with the logic of consideration. The claim is that all commercial promises are in fact, in the long run, reciprocal. Even if there is no immediate 'price' attached, a reciprocal benefit is expected. Businesses, after all, act to make profits – and companies have a *duty* to do so in the interests of their shareholders. Therefore according to a classic authority on directors' duties, ostensibly charitable decisions are permitted only to the (admittedly 'not very philanthropic') extent that they are in the interests of the company.[34] Therefore it hardly seems likely – and it might even be illegal – for a company to act with truly disinterested benevolence. If, then, business promises are always reciprocal, they must all satisfy the bargain theory of consideration.

English law probably adopts this approach in practice, tacitly at least. In commercial cases the courts will strain to find consideration – 'the least spark of a consideration will be sufficient'[35]– or even invent it outright. According to distinguished German commentators, the English judges are 'astute ... at snuf-

---

[29] Atiyah, 'Consideration: A Restatement', pp. 241–42. At p. 193 Atiyah claims *Chappell v Nestle* [1960] AC 87 as an 'indirect benefit' case.
[30] Cf. generally pp. 69–71 below.
[31] C.M. Rose, 'Giving, Trading, Thieving and Trusting: How and Why Gifts Become Exchanges and (More Importantly) Vice Versa' (1992) 44 Florida LR 295, 313 (emphasis in original).
[32] D.A. Farber & J.H. Matheson, 'Beyond Promissory Estoppel: Contract Law and the "Invisible Handshake"' (1985) 52 *U Chi L Rev* 903, 925.
[33] Ibid, p. 929.
[34] *Hutton v West Cork Railway* (1883) LR 23 Ch D 654 (Bowen LJ).
[35] *Pillans v Van Mierop* (1765) 3 Burrow 1663, 1666 (Wilmot J).

fling out some consideration lurking in the background'.[36] In modification of commercial contracts, it has been said to be 'utterly fictional to describe what has been conceded as a gift' – there should be a 'strong presumption that good commercial "considerations" underlie any seemingly detrimental modification'.[37] Lord Wilberforce famously said in *The Eurymedon* that it was 'paradoxical' and 'implausible' to identify promises in 'commercial relations entered into for business reasons of ultimate profit' as being gratuitous.[38]

Perhaps such boldness is not always possible. Lord Wright argued that although it had been said that an ingenious person can devise a consideration for any transaction, cases existed where 'no ingenuity could avail'.[39] But such obstructions seem to be rare. Gerard McMeel argues that while Lord Mansfield's critique of consideration failed, his lasting legacy (across the law of contract) has been a determination to adapt doctrine to meet the needs of commerce.[40] McMeel discusses the development of payment mechanism such as letters of credit, adopting Sir Roy Goode's argument that these are enforceable notwithstanding absence of consideration.[41] McMeel concludes that 'consideration fundamentalism is eschewed where commercial necessity demands it'.[42] He uses Bagehot's distinction between the 'dignified' and 'efficient' parts of the constitution to illuminate the law of contract: the doctrine of consideration is part of the 'venerable façade,'[43] whereas the 'efficient secret' is an incredibly flexible approach to ascertaining the content and ambit of agreements.[44] Such pragmatism would allay fears that English contract law is 'deficient' because 'hampered' by the 'unnecessary' doctrine of consideration.[45]

GRATUITOUS PROMISES IN PRIVATE LIFE

What then of *non-commercial* gratuitous promises? The economic arguments implicit in the above are inapplicable. Where a promise is made for reasons of 'love, affection, friendship, comradeship, gratitude, … benevolence or generosity', awarding damages to the promisee cannot be justified to see that he gets the price for performance rendered, or to enable him to plan future cost of materials, or to allocate the risk of price changes.[46] Is the common law right to deny protection to a bare expectation of something-for-nothing?

---

[36] Zweigert & Kotz, n.1 above, p. 399.
[37] *Antons Trawling v Smith* [2003] 2 NZLR 23, [92].
[38] [1975] AC 154, 167.
[39] Wright, n.2 above, p. 1251.
[40] McMeel, n.12 above.
[41] Cf. R. Goode, 'Abstract payment obligations' in P. Cane & J. Stapleton, *Essays for Patrick Atiyah* (Oxford, 1991).
[42] McMeel, p. 58.
[43] With its doctrinal twin, privity of contract: cf. pp. 265–276 below.
[44] McMeel, p. 24. Cf. W. Bagehot, *The English Constitution* (1867).
[45] Cf. *White v Jones* [1995] 2 AC 207, 262–63 (Lord Goff).
[46] M.A. Eisenberg, 'The World of Contract and the World of Gift' (1997) 85 *California LR* 821.

A moral critique readily occurs. Those who believe that contract law rests on the morality of promise keeping do not discriminate between donative and bargain promises. Charles Fried admits that the traditional doctrine of consideration is inconsistent with his promissory theory. But he attempts to dismiss it as 'too internally inconsistent to offer an alternative at all'.[47] This is not, perhaps, adequate to dispose of the core of the doctrine – that truly gratuitous promises are unenforceable. *Eastwood v Kenyon* explicitly rejected the challenge to consideration from promissory morality.[48] Fried's theory entails complete abolition of consideration, as Lord Kenyon feared. Similarly, Seana Shiffrin complains that the consideration doctrine diverges from 'the moral rules of promise [which] typically require that one keep a unilateral promise, even if nothing is received in exchange'.[49]

To these moralistic arguments we could raise the general objection of standard liberal political theory – that we are justified in imposing legal sanctions only where necessary to protect other people from harm.[50] To say that non-receipt of a promised gift is 'harm' requires us to assume an entitlement to that gift (rather than a bare expectation of gain) – but that would beg the question. Even if we ignore the libertarian objection, it is not clear that the duty justifies enforcement. Andrew Gold argues that a promise to make a gift imposes only a weak moral duty (breach of which justifies criticism) rather than a strong moral duty (which would justify compulsion to perform, by force).[51] If so, it would be unjust to interfere with the autonomy of the gratuitous promisor by coercing him to make the gift. Gold also criticizes Shiffrin's claim that absence of *legal* enforcement of gift promises undermines the *moral* duty to perform them. This is ultimately an empirical question which 'is not only uncertain, [but] may actually be unanswerable'.[52] The effect, if any, of the doctrine of consideration on the culture of promising must then remain 'obscure'.

What of economic arguments for enforcing gratuitous promises? It was long common to dismiss them as 'sterile transmissions' of wealth.[53] But Andrew Kull says this was always an odd position to take, and based on little more than 'mercantilist prejudice'.[54] No transaction will take place unless it is beneficial to both parties (gifts may be rejected); in which case, why condemn it as 'sterile'? 'All gratuitous promises are presumptively beneficial to the promisor at the time the promise is made.'[55] Melvin Eisenberg suggests (somewhat speculatively, perhaps)

---

[47] C. Fried, *Contract as Promise* (Harvard University Press, 1981) p. 35.
[48] (1840) 11 Ad & El 438.
[49] S. Shiffrin, 'The Divergence of Contract and Promise' (2007) 120 *Harvard LR* 708, 709–10.
[50] J.S. Mill, *On Liberty* (1859). Cf. D. Kimel, 'The Morality of Contract and Moral Culpability in Breach' [2010] *King's LJ* 213.
[51] A.S. Gold, 'Consideration and the Morality of Promising' in J.W. Neyers et al. (eds), *Exploring Contract Law* (Hart Publishing, 2009).
[52] Ibid, p. 136.
[53] Cf. L.L. Fuller, 'Consideration and Form' (1941) 41 *Columbia LR* 799, 815.
[54] A. Kull, 'Reconsidering Gratuitous Promises' (1992) 21 *JLS* 39, 49.
[55] Ibid, p. 65.

that gifts as a class 'tend to move assets from persons with more wealth to persons with less'.[56]

Richard Posner considers why people would make a binding promise to make a gift in the future, rather than just making the gift when the time comes (the law is entirely happy with gift giving: it is *promising* to make gifts that is problematic).[57] Posner considers a philanthropist wishing to give an orchestra $1,000 a year, for twenty years. (There may be good reasons not to give the entire sum at once, e.g. liquidity or taxation.) If he *promises* to make the future gifts, they will have *present* value to the orchestra – an additional benefit compared with 'surprising' them with each annual donation. However, if his promise is not enforceable, the orchestra will 'discount' that present value to take account of the fact that the gifts may not be received (e.g. the donor may change his mind). Thus the non-binding promise is worth very considerably less. Therefore, the philanthropist will have to promise much more than $1,000 to confer on the orchestra the same value as a binding promise to give $1,000, or make a large one-off gift instead (which, as seen, may also be inefficient). Or to put it a different way, enabling the philanthropist to make a *binding* commitment enables him to increase the size of the gift (in present value terms) at no cost to himself.[58] As Kull says, the benefit of contract law is that it gives to every person's words the reliability that would otherwise be accorded only to the most trustworthy of us.[59]

Kull notes the influential contribution of Lon Fuller in 1941.[60] Fuller's concerns fall under three headings: promises that were not made at all (evidentiary), that should not have been made (cautionary), or were not intended to be made (channelling). Fuller argues that formality requirements (such as the old-fashioned sealed deed) solve these problems. A deed provides excellent evidence of what was agreed; sealing wax ('symbol in the popular mind of legalism and weightiness') was an 'excellent device' to induce a 'circumspective frame of mind'. The deed also 'channels' the promisor's intention, i.e. can be used to signify, through a simple external badge, an unequivocal intention to be legally bound. Consideration (bargain) serves these functions to a limited degree also. But an informal promise, if lacking consideration, should not be enforced as it lacks any of the necessary safeguards.

Kull attacks this conclusion. He claims there is no evidence that the existence and terms of gift promises are any harder to prove than those of bargain promises.[61] Moreover, he questions the paternalist assumptions of Fuller's 'cautionary' requirement. It is often claimed that gifts are 'lightly made ... often by ruinous prodigality'.[62] Such impulsiveness is, indeed, a literary commonplace. But the idea

---

[56] Eisenberg, n.46 above, p. 828.
[57] R.A. Posner, 'Gratuitous promises in economics and law' (1977) 6 *JLS* 411.
[58] Ibid, p. 412.
[59] Kull, n.54 above, pp. 60–61.
[60] Fuller, n.53 above.
[61] Kull, n.54 above, p. 53.
[62] *Davis & Co v Morgan* (1903) 117 Ga 504.

that this applies to all (and only) gift promises 'will not withstand examination. The gift promise that is not only calculated but calculating is as well known as the spontaneous one'.[63] An incautious bid at an exhilarating auction is enforceable (because it is an exchange) whereas a deliberate, long-meditated gift promise is not! So the cautionary concern does not fit the bargain/gift distinction.

Kull describes the channelling problem as distinguishing 'tentative and exploratory expressions of intention' from legally binding promises. He dismisses the need for special protection of gratuitous promisors. They have at their disposal 'precisely the same means as the commercial negotiator to distinguish a promise from a statement of intent: the vast resources of the spoken and written language'.[64] In other words, they simply need to state their intentions clearly. However, C.J. Hamson argues that to intend a binding gratuitous promises is wholly exceptional.[65] The usual construction of a gift promise implies a certain leeway: that the promisor will do his best to fulfil the promise, but reserves some discretion to vary performance (e.g. because of changed circumstances). Only exceptionally could he intend to be strictly bound in law, rather than as a matter of honour. Michael Trebilcock points out that this is very different from bargain promises where firm commitments are usually expected, required and given.[66] This difference in (presumptive) intention means a sharp and systematic difference between bargain and non-bargain promises, providing 'some semblance of a rationale for the traditional requirement of consideration'.

So Hamson notes that while many people subscribe to charities, few will formally bind themselves to make future donations by executing a deed. Trebilcock suggests that this may show a judgment on the part of charities that they can actually raise more money by not seeking to bind donors in law. People may not promise to donate in the first place if they will lose their freedom of action (for the donor's circumstances might change, or he could disapprove of changes in the charity's operations). On the other hand, in the United States a non-deed charitable promise is enforceable even without consideration or reliance.[67] Thus, Trebilcock suggests, the across-the-board effect of legal enforcement on charitable giving is not clear.[68]

It has been suggested that a *via media* between full enforcement and non-enforcement of gift promises might be optimal. French and German law allow revocation in specified instances of changed circumstances of the donor (e.g. financial hardship), or misconduct or ingratitude by the donee.[69] Kull argues that it would be better to allow gift promises to be discharged in such circumstances

---

[63] Kull, p. 54.

[64] Ibid.

[65] Hamson, n.4 above.

[66] M.J. Trebilcock, *The Limits of Freedom of Contract* (Harvard University Press, 1993) p. 183.

[67] § 90(2), Restatement (Second) of Contracts (1981). For reliance rendering a charitable promise enforceable in England cf. *Re Soames* (1897) 13 TLR 439.

[68] Trebilcock, n.66, p. 176.

[69] Cf. French Code Civil arts 953, 955, 960; Bürgerliches Gesetzbuch §§ 519, 530.

than not to enforce them at all.[70] Atiyah adds the suggestion of a shorter time limit in which to bring enforcement proceedings.[71] Eisenberg notes the symmetry between giving effect to the moral obligation to keep a gift promise, and recognizing moral excuses as defences. But he argues that the content of those defences would be 'inherently messy' and 'extremely fluid' – should the donor be able to keep the promised gift for his medical bills or a new business venture? Eisenberg argues that the dynamics of the personal relationships within which these promises are made are 'too subtle' for effective handling by the law.[72] Mindy Chen-Wishart declares that the 'internal coherence' of the law of contract would be undermined by a recalibration of 'excuses and remedies' to cater for gratuitous promising.[73]

Eisenberg's main reason for opposing the enforcement of non-commercial gift promises is that this would 'impoverish' them. If performance were backed up by legal sanctions, how could the promisee (or indeed the promisor) be sure that a gift was fulfilled 'in a spirit of love, friendship, affection' rather than to avoid legal action? The donor's motives would inevitably become mixed. Enforceability would translate the promise into cash terms, whereas gifts are important for their intrinsic value (it would be inappropriate to give your lover cash on Valentine's Day!). 'Simple donative promises would be degraded into bills of exchange, and the gifts made to keep such promises would be degraded into redemptions of the bills.'[74] The worlds of commercial contract and love and friendship ('our better selves') are quite separate and must remain so. Moreover, those who emphasize the moral duty of the gift promisor have ignored the equally important moral obligation of a gift *promisee* – to release a repenting promisor.[75]

Eisenberg mounts a powerful defence of the traditional consideration requirement in family and close social situations. Whether it applies to all 'non-commercial activities' is more questionable, and indeed the boundaries of that concept are hazy. What of charitable giving? Here the arguments are more finely balanced. What is perhaps most interesting of all is to find that the non-enforcement of gratuitous promises, entailed by consideration, is not as destitute of merit as many, following Lord Wright, would assume.

FORMAL CONTRACTS

Many legal systems demand the observation of formalities for promises to be binding. In the Roman *stipulatio*, a particular formula of corresponding words was required.[76] European systems today typically require authorization by a

---

[70] Kull, n.54 above, pp. 63–64.
[71] Atiyah, n.22 above, p. 242.
[72] Eisenberg, n.46 above, pp. 828–29.
[73] M. Chen-Wishart, 'A bird in the hand: Consideration and contract modification' in A. Burrows and E. Peel (eds), *Contract Formation and Parties* (Oxford University Press, 2010) p.110.
[74] Eisenberg, n.46 above, p. 848.
[75] Ibid, pp. 849–50.
[76] Cf. p. 13 n.81 above.

legally qualified official, the notary. Ancient Scythian contractors filled a bowl with wine and mixed it with the blood of the parties, before dipping in 'a sword, some arrows, a battle-axe and a javelin' and drinking it![77] In England, a promise contained in a deed is still enforceable without consideration, a survival from medieval law. It is no longer accurate to talk of a promise 'under seal', for sealing has been replaced with a formulaic declaration that a document is intended by a deed; Lord Wilberforce informed Parliament in 1971 that sealing had become 'completely fictitious' (save perhaps for 'some noble Dukes ... who get a seal off their watch chain and put down a piece of wax').[78]

Less obviously, 'nominal consideration' is best seen as a second type of formal contract.[79] Lord Somervell once observed that: 'A peppercorn does not cease to be good consideration if it is established that the promisee does not like pepper and will throw away the corn'.[80] Treitel argues that this follows logically from the proposition that the courts do not concern themselves with the 'adequacy' of consideration. Provided what is given in exchange is of *some* value, the promise binds.[81] However, Atiyah maintains that the conclusion cannot be logically entailed by the premise.[82] For he notes that in the United States, the 'adequacy' rule is observed but *not* if the bargain is 'a mere formality or pretence'.[83] Such 'sham or "nominal" consideration' is not good. Atiyah defends the English rule not through (spurious?) doctrinal 'logic', but because going to the trouble of stipulating the peppercorn is the 'clearest possible indication that the promisor intended his promise seriously and intended to give the promisee a legally enforceable right'. Fuller too said that such a promise should be enforceable for the same reasons as a deed.[84]

Lord Wright argued that the logical next step was simply to examine whether the promisor intended to be bound. This was 'simpler and juster' than the 'solemn pretence' of the peppercorn.[85] As seen, this view has been acted upon in the US where 'nominal consideration' is ignored. Also, the deed has been abolished in most American states. But many point to the difficulties of a 'simple' intention-based approach. As seen, C.J. Hamson, criticizing Lord Wright's committee's report,[86] argued that it was highly unusual for gift promisors to intend to be contractually bound. Furthermore, useful evidence rarely exists for courts to discover whether there was, exceptionally, such an intention. Hamson therefore defended the deed or peppercorn promise as the *only* exception to the presump-

---

[77] Herodotus, *Histories* iv.70.
[78] Ibbetson, n.7 above, p. 241; Law of Property (Miscellaneous Provisions) Act 1989, s.1(2).
[79] Hamson, n.4 above, p. 241.
[80] *Chappell & Co Ltd v Nestle Co Ltd* [1960] AC 87, 114. The picturesque medieval equivalent was 'a rose at midsummer'.
[81] Treitel, n.24 above.
[82] Atiyah, n.19 above, p. 194.
[83] § 79, Restatement (Second) of Contracts (1981), Note d.
[84] Fuller, n.53 above, p. 820.
[85] Wright, n.2 above, p. 1231.
[86] Cf. nn.3–4 above.

tion against enforcement. That pains had been taken to execute a deed, or to cast the gift in the form of a bargain, was 'conclusive' of the promisor's intention to be bound. Hamson commended Roman law (the *stipulatio*) as well as English law for embodying a 'decisive external test' of intention. The Law Revision Committee was wrong to dismiss these formalities as 'pretence'.[87] Richard Posner agrees that formalities relieve courts of the major administrative cost related to gift promises – determining whether they were intended to be binding. Thus, he says, the abolition of the deed in America is a 'mysterious development from the standpoint of efficiency'.[88]

Formal contracts may therefore be seen as facilitative. One wishing to bind herself to make a gift in future has a ready way to do it. This meets Eisenberg's concern that the law will commodify and subvert 'the world of (private) gift': employment of legal formalities deliberately takes the promise outside it and into 'the world of (legal) contract'.[89] A failure to make use of the deed (or peppercorn consideration) route may suggest, at least, ambiguity in the promisor's intentions.[90] This supports Hamson's presumption against intention to be legally bound to make a gift. Moreover, Hamson argues, the onus should be on the prospective donee to secure a binding obligation. This requires a difficult tactical choice, for by asking for a binding promise he may receive nothing at all.[91] But if the promisee believes the promisor would refuse to execute a deed 'surely it is dishonest of him subsequently to attempt to foist upon the promisor that very obligation for which he may have judged it prudent not expressly to ask'.[92] Trebilcock agrees that because of the ambiguity of intention in gift promises it is essential to provide a clear signalling mechanism for donors who do wish to make legally binding promises, and that where such a mechanism exists (as in England), *informal* gratuitous promises should be unenforceable.[93]

One may debate what level of formality is optimal. In the late eighteenth century Lord Mansfield unsuccessfully argued that every commercial contract in writing should be enforceable. Lord Wright's committee in 1937 revived the proposal.[94] But Hamson objected. Mere writing was not enough to bring home the gravity of a gift promise. Written correspondence had become as casual as conversation, and an ordinary person did not take the same care over letter writing as he did sealing a deed.[95] With texts, tweets and email, this argument rings truer still. Few would deem the Scythian formation ceremony appropriate in modern times, but something that can only be done *deliberately* is necessary if formality is

---

[87] Hamson, n.4 above.
[88] Posner, n.57 above, p. 420.
[89] Eisenberg, n.46 above, p. 850.
[90] Trebilcock, n.66 above, p. 174.
[91] Cf. discussion of incentives on charitable giving, n.68 above.
[92] Hamson, n.4 above, p. 256.
[93] Trebilcock, n.66 above, p. 186.
[94] Cf. n.3 above, para 29.
[95] Hamson, n.4 above, p. 247.

to provide unequivocal evidence of intention to be bound. Writing per se is not distinctive enough.

Debate 2

Should 'intention to create legal relations' take over as the hallmark of enforceability?

The debate here is a brief one. Theorists who subscribe to the will theory of contract require only that it should be seriously intended to be legally binding. This was first claimed as a separate requirement (in England) by Leake's treatise of 1867.[96] There was then no judicial authority for the view and Leake relied on the French jurist Pothier. But in the early twentieth century, the courts recognized the doctrine.[97] On the assumption that its presence merely indicates a serious intention to be bound, it is therefore argued that consideration has been rendered entirely redundant by the 'unanimous' adoption of the (separate) need for proof of serious intention.[98]

If that assumption is correct, then there is everything to be said for such assimilation. Simpson comments that having offer and acceptance, consideration, estoppel *and* 'intention to create legal relations' seems like 'rather too many doctrines chasing a limited number of problems'; Simpson recommends discarding old doctrines (consideration?) when importing new ones ('intention to create…').[99] But there are two objections to this simplifying proposal. First, as seen in Debate 1, it is possible to stake out a distinct role for consideration. It is not merely evidence of intention, as the historical rules on past consideration (gratitude) and 'natural love and affection' show. Rather, the doctrine excludes gratuitous promises from legal enforcement (at least outside the commercial context). While not uncontroversial, these arguments make it unsafe to assume that consideration is the equivalent of the 'intention to create…' doctrine. The second objection is that that doctrine is not what it seems. Arguably it has little to do with intention! Rather, it is an instrument to draw the boundaries of contractual obligation.

Steve Hedley makes the case forcefully.[100] Save when the parties have (exceptionally) made them explicitly clear, there is very little evidence of actual intentions as to legal enforceability. For commercial parties as much as for lovers or families, litigation is literally the last thing on their minds when making an agreement, since few relationships survive a court case.[101] Therefore courts

---

[96] S.M. Leake, *Elements of the Law of Contracts* (Stevens, 1867).

[97] *Balfour v Balfour* [1919] 2 KB 571; *Rose & Frank v Crompton Bros* [1925] AC 445.

[98] A.G. Chloros, 'The Doctrine of Consideration and the Reform of the Law of Contract: A Comparative Analysis' (1968) 17 ICLQ 137, 140.

[99] A.W.B. Simpson, 'Innovation in Nineteenth Century Contract Law' (1975) 91 *LQR* 247.

[100] S. Hedley, 'Keeping Contract in Its Place – *Balfour v Balfour* and the Enforceability of Informal Agreements' (1985) 5 *OJLS* 391.

[101] Cf. S. Macaulay, 'Non-Contractual Relations in Business: A Preliminary Study' (1963) 28 American Sociological Rev 1; H. Beale and T. Dugdale, 'Contracts between Businessmen: Planning and the Use of Contractual Remedies' (1975) 2 *BJL&S* 45.

trying to uncover intention are 'inevitably driven to impose their own view of whether the agreement *ought* to be enforced'.[102] And this, Hedley argues, was the very point of the synthesis of the doctrine by Atkin LJ in *Balfour v Balfour*.[103] The courts wished to control the novel reliance on contracts in domestic litigation (e.g. between separated spouses). The idea of 'intention' could be used to keep contract in its place. It was this imperative rather than 'any sudden conversion to the academic view that all contracts required an intention to create legal relations' that explained the reception of the doctrine.[104] Consideration could not be used as the control device since some domestic promises are unquestionably bilateral, but the courts still hold them to be based on trust and unenforceable.[105] Where one person says to another, '"I will meet you at 7.30; you bring the food; I will bring the drink", neither party of course envisages any action in the county court if either commodity is not forthcoming'.[106]

Hedley identifies positive rules laid down by the courts, bearing no relation to any actual party intention (Hedley has no time for the mealy-mouthed invocation of 'presumptions' or the 'reasonable man'). Business contracts are nearly always enforceable.[107] Conversely, parties not 'at arm's length' do *not* enter into legally enforceable commitments except where one party has performed. That other party will be required to shoulder the burden of performance having received the benefit of the consideration.[108] Purely executory social arrangements will be unenforceable. But none of this is truly dependent on intention, save when this is *express*.[109]

It is one thing to 'keep contract in its place', but what *is* its proper 'place'? Atiyah notes the everyday observation that the market has no place in social relations, citing the abolition of liability for breach of promise of marriage and the unenforceability of surrogate motherhood agreements.[110] On the other hand, Fried objects to the idea that legal contracts should be the exclusive preserve of some 'separate merchant class'.[111] Michael Freeman argues that the boundaries of the 'private' in family life have shifted so that the presumption against contractual obligation should be removed: this would allow greater autonomy in regulating the incidents of marriage and relationships.[112] But this is a highly controversial proposition. When the Supreme Court recently decided to enforce pre-nuptial agreements Baroness Hale vigorously dissented. She argued that giving

---

[102] Hedley, p. 393.
[103] n.97 above; cf. Ibbetson, n.7 above, pp. 233–34.
[104] Hedley, p. 403.
[105] Eg *Jones v Padavatton* [1969] 1 WLR 328.
[106] *Ford Motor Co v Amalgamated Union of Engineering and Foundry Workers* [1969] 2 QB 303 (Geoffrey Lane J).
[107] Cf. *Edwards v Skyways* [1964] 1 WLR 349.
[108] Cf. *Merritt v Merritt* [1970] 1 WLR 1211.
[109] Cf. *Rose & Frank v Crompton*, n.97 above.
[110] Atiyah, *Essays on Contract* (1990) p. 18. Cf. now Surrogacy Arrangements Act 1985, s.1A.
[111] Fried, n.47 above at 37.
[112] M.D.A. Freeman 'Contracting in the Haven: *Balfour v Balfour* Revisited' in R. Halson (ed.), *Exploring the Boundaries of Contract* (Dartmouth, 1996).

effect to freedom of contract under such circumstances disadvantages economically weaker spouses, usually (although not *in casu*) wives, and that such a socially important change should be made by Parliament rather than the male-dominated judiciary.[113] Hugh Collins warns, more generally, that enforcing contracts between cohabiting partners forces relationships into the currency of exchange rather than 'more open-ended commitments of sharing, reciprocity and loyalty'.[114]

Hedley recognizes that delicate policy questions may also arise over (e.g.) whether to enforce a 'collective bargaining agreement' between trade unions and an employer.[115] But as Hepple observes, the 'intention' doctrine means these questions are 'cloak[ed] ... in the mantle of private contractual autonomy'.[116] Hepple remarked that the status of collective bargaining was so important and politically controversial that it should be determined by Parliament; subsequently it has been.[117] It is abundantly clear that these questions are not, and could not be, determined simply by reflecting on the parties' 'intentions'. It is not surprising that, as David Ibbetson comments, 'intention to create legal relations' has proved wholly unsuccessful as a new organizing principle or 'metwand' for contractual liability.[118]

The strong presumption that commercial agreements are legally enforceable may be rebutted by clear words to that effect. This is generally accepted in Western legal systems.[119] However, Rudden notes 'dark suspicion' from jurists who cannot understand why anyone would prefer *vacuum juris* to *vinculum juris*.[120] In fact there are good reasons for this. For example, Scrutton LJ suggests in the leading English case that parties may prefer settling disputes among themselves to avoid the 'necessity of expressing themselves so precisely that outsiders may have no difficulty in understanding what they mean' (i.e. to adjudicate between them).[121] Given the presence of effective social sanctions,[122] rational parties might well prefer an 'honourable' obligation to the costs and delays of the law. Entire industries flourish in that way.[123] Sometimes indeed, the courts have recognized that the very nature of the agreement is that it is to be unenforceable, as with 'letters of comfort'. The consequences of the 'comforter' refusing to honour its 'moral obligation' under the letter are not the court's concern.[124] On the other hand, to

---

[113] *Radmacher v Granatino* [2011] 1 AC 534, [132]–[137].

[114] H. Collins, *The Law of Contract* (4th edn, Cambridge University Press, 2003) p. 111.

[115] Cf. *Ford v AUEFW*, n.106 above.

[116] B.A. Hepple, 'Intention to create legal relations' [1970] CLJ 122.

[117] Industrial Relations Act 1971, s.334; cf. Trade Union and Labour Relations Consolidation Act 1992, s.179.

[118] Ibbetson, n.7 above, p. 247.

[119] B. Rudden, 'The Gentleman's Agreement in Legal Theory and in Modern Practice' [1999] *Eur Rev Private Law* 199.

[120] Ibid, p. 220 (a legal vacuum to a legal bond).

[121] *Rose & Frank v Crompton* [1923] 2 KB 261.

[122] Cf. D. Charny, 'Nonlegal sanctions in commercial relationships' (1990) 104 *Harvard LR* 373.

[123] Traditionally betting (Gaming Act 1845, s.18 but cf. now Gambling Act 2005, s.335). See also *Jones v Vernon's Pools* [1938] 2 All ER 626.

[124] *Kleinwort Benson Ltd v Malaysia Mining Corp* [1989] 1 All ER 78.

the extent that the legal obligations in contracts have a protective (paternalist) function, such clauses may see weaker parties bargaining away their protection.[125] So some limit may, in these cases, be necessary.

But such express 'intention *not* to create legal relations' cases aside, the brocard has limited connection with actual intentions. Some jurisdictional policing function is, no doubt, necessary. Should the tenuous link with intention not be severed and the limits of the law of contract considered directly?

Debate 3

Should consideration be necessary to modify contracts?

The common law requires consideration to validate the modification as well as the initial creation of contractual obligations. The doctrine here has notable bite. It invalidates 'one-sided' modifications, as when greater payment is promised for timely completion of the initially specified services, or where a creditor agrees to accept less than is due, in full settlement of a debt. Since the promisee undertakes, in return, only what he is already bound to the promisor to do, there is logically no 'fresh consideration'.[126]

The rule is controversial. In 1856 its 'vicious reasoning' was criticized for defeating contractors' intentions.[127] John Dawson describes it as a 'distortion' which has done most to discredit the bargain principle.[128] In England, the rule has come under heavy fire, first from 'outside' via promissory estoppel in the *High Trees* case,[129] and latterly crumbling from within, in *Williams v Roffey Bros & Nicholls (Contractors) Ltd*.[130] These developments have been much debated. The issues fall roughly into two types. First we discuss the doctrinal coherence of the developments. Secondly, we go more deeply into the underlying question: whether (and when) the law should be welcoming, or suspicious, of contract modification.

THE DOCTRINAL QUESTION

In the *Williams v Roffey Bros & Nicholls (Contractors) Ltd*,[131] Williams fell behind schedule with carpentry work sub-contracted out to him by Roffey Bros, main building contractors on a block of flats. With 18 flats still to be finished by Williams, Roffey Bros feared that his delays meant the entire project would be

---

125 Rudden, p. 206.

126 *Foakes v Beer* (1884) L.R. 9 App Cas 605.

127 Cf. M. Lobban, '*Foakes v Beer* (1884)' in C. Mitchell and P. Mitchell (eds), *Landmark Cases in the Law of Contract* (Hart Publishing, 2008) p. 229.

128 J. Dawson, *Gifts and Promises: American and Continental Law Compared* (Yale University Press, 1980) p. 4. Cf. E.W. Patterson, 'An apology for consideration' (1958) 58 *Columbia LR* 929, 936.

129 *Central London Property Trust v High Trees House* [1947] KB 130.

130 [1991] 1 QB 1.

131 Ibid.

late. Therefore, they promised to pay him an extra £575 per flat to ensure timely completion of the carpentry. However, Roffey Bros made only one further payment of £1,500 and after substantially completing eight further flats, Williams ceased work altogether.

The main question for the Court of Appeal was whether Roffey's promise to pay the £575 extra was supported by consideration, since Williams had not promised to do anything that he was not already obliged to do under the original contract. Not without 'some hesitation',[132] the court held that Roffey Bros received the 'practical benefit' of Williams's continued performance in exchange for their promise to pay more. There had 'clearly' been 'a commercial advantage to both sides from a pragmatic point of view in reaching the [variation] agreement'.[133] Thus Williams recovered £575 for each of the eight flats (less amounts already received and deductions for incomplete work).

The 'practical benefit' notion has been heavily criticized.[134] Mindy Chen-Wishart once dismissed it as an Emperor's New Clothes (transparent) fiction.[135] The increased payment may have bought an objectively better chance of performance of the existing contract, given doubts about Williams's cash flow and staffing levels. But Brian Coote points out that this is nothing to which Roffey Bros were not already entitled.[136] Janet O'Sullivan doubts the wisdom of an ill-defined, discretionary concept of 'benefit' – a test of commercial convenience or social morality will be highly unpredictable.[137] Zweigert and Kötz criticize the 'implausibility' of practical benefit, so strenuously hunted in *Roffey*. For these Civilian observers, the fuss 'merely shows how useless' is the requirement of consideration for modifications.[138]

But perhaps such arguments prioritize doctrinal logic over practical realities. In Victorian times Lord Blackburn, in a famous near-dissent on the related issue of creditors accepting part of a due debt, was convinced that:

> all men of business, whether merchants or tradesmen, do every day recognize and act on the ground that prompt payment of a part of their demand may be more beneficial to them than it would be to insist on their rights and enforce payment of the whole. Even where the debtor is perfectly solvent, and sure to pay at last, this often is so. Where the credit of the debtor is doubtful it must be more so.[139]

---

[132] Ibid, p. 23 (Purchas LJ).

[133] Ibid, p. 22.

[134] Cf. M. Spence, *Protecting Reliance: The Emergent Doctrine of Equitable Estoppel* (Hart Publishing, 1999) p. 130, 'vacuous'.

[135] M. Chen-Wishart, 'Consideration, practical benefit and the Emperor's New Clothes' in J. Beatson and D. Friedmann (eds), *Good Faith and Fault in Contract Law* (Oxford University Press, 1995).

[136] B. Coote, 'Consideration and Benefit in Fact and in Law' (1990) 3 *JCL* 23, 28.

[137] J.A. O'Sullivan, 'In Defence of *Foakes v Beer*' [1996] CLJ 219.

[138] n.1 above, p. 394.

[139] *Foakes v Beer* (1884) LR 9 App Cas 605, 622.

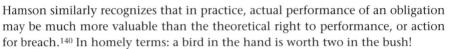

Hamson similarly recognizes that in practice, actual performance of an obligation may be much more valuable than the theoretical right to performance, or action for breach.[140] In homely terms: a bird in the hand is worth two in the bush!

Chen-Wishart now accepts this maxim.[141] The reason for birds in the hand (actual performance) being so valuable is the limit on both the right to perform-ance and damages for breach of contract.[142] In *Roffey* itself, a court order for specific performance would probably have been unobtainable,[143] and it is questionable whether Roffey Bros could have recovered all of their consequential losses in the event of Williams's breach (e.g. triggering a penalty clause in Roffey's contract with the building owner and damage to Roffey's own reputation for punctual comple-tion). All of this assuming that Williams was good for the money (if damages were sought), and ignoring the inevitable cost and delay of legal proceedings. With such legal and practical obstacles, it is clear why rational parties in the position of Roffey Bros value actual performance over their legal entitlement to it – and are willing to pay extra to ensure they get it.

This is something of an embarrassment for the law. Holding a *legal right* to £100 (or prompt carpentry) is not equivalent to having the cash or service itself. This shows the law's weakness. To anticipate the Debate in Chapter 9, the remedial deficiencies that allow this gap to open up support Holmes's provocative claim that there is actually no duty to perform a contract – the promisor has a choice to perform, or breach and pay damages.[144] Purchas LJ in *Roffey* commented that it had been open to Williams deliberately to breach the contract in order to 'cut his losses'.[145] Roffey Bros promised him £575 extra per flat to see that he did not.

One of the difficulties with *Roffey* is the treatment of the classic case of *Stilk v Myrick*.[146] Although treated as a 'pillar stone' of the law that the court could not contemplate overruling,[147] *Stilk* was re-interpreted as a 'public policy' case, i.e. an economic duress case before that defence had received separate recognition. This is more compatible with the report of *Stilk* by Espinasse, usually thought an unreli-able reporter,[148] than with its accepted basis, the existing duty rule, as in Campbell's report.[149] This clumsy circumvention is unconvincing as a matter of precedent. But the more interesting question is whether economic duress does indeed provide a better answer to 'the question of policy which has troubled the courts since before *Stilk v Myrick*, and no doubt led at the date of that decision to a rigid adherence to the doctrine of consideration'.[150] This is considered in the next section below.

---
[140] Hamson, n.4 above.
[141] M. Chen-Wishart, 'A Bird in the Hand: Consideration and Contract Modification' in A. Burrows and E. Peel (eds), *Contract Formation and Parties* (Oxford, 2010).
[142] Ibid, p. 94 ('trite law').
[143] Cf. *Wolverhampton Corp v Emmons* [1901] 1 QB 515.
[144] Cf. pp. 235–238 below.
[145] [1991] 1 QB 1, 23.
[146] (1809) 2 Camp 317; 6 Esp 129.
[147] [1991] 1 QB 1, 20.
[148] Although he was counsel for the plaintiff in *Stilk v Myrick*.
[149] Cf. Gilmore, n.25 above, pp. 25–30.
[150] [1991] 1 QB 1, 13–14 (Glidewell LJ).

Another doctrinal curiosity is that *Roffey's* 'practical benefit' approach does not extend to a creditor accepting a lesser sum in full satisfaction of a due debt, even though Lord Blackburn's observations about the practical realities of debt collection were made in that context. Moreover, Michael Lobban argues, the mid-nineteenth-century courts had stretched consideration to accommodate business needs.[151] In the end however, Lord Blackburn did not press his doubts to a full dissent, and so the rule in *Foakes v Beer* was entrenched.[152] Hence for reasons of stark binding precedent, English law currently treats two functionally identical situations differently.[153]

Janet O'Sullivan has attempted (in her own words) to 'defend the indefensible' (i.e. *Foakes v Beer*), in part by maintaining the rule's distinctiveness from the *Roffey* situation. First, she points out that in the action for debt, creditors are entitled to what they are owed – they do not claim damages for breach of the debtor's promise to pay, and so the various limitations on the assessment of damages are simply inapplicable. Secondly, O'Sullivan suggests that it would undermine the legal principle that money has an incontrovertible, universal objective value if creditors were allowed to value £100 (in cash) more than £200 (a debt). But neither of these points is fully convincing. It is true that the creditor is at much less of a disadvantage, legally speaking, than a party like Roffey Bros seeking damages for breach of a non-monetary obligation. But it is still expensive to collect debts, and the law's delays may prove fatal to recovery where the debtor's solvency is precarious. For similar reasons, while it clearly would be lunacy to prefer £100 to £200, to prefer £100 cash to a £200 I.O.U. may be extremely sensible. Therefore, the *Roffey* and *Foakes v Beer* situations ought rationally to be treated in the same way.

Finally, we should note that even orthodoxy allows exceptions to the pre-existing duty rule. First, by bringing the old contract to an end and entering into a new one. Provided there are still outstanding duties on both sides,[154] such rescission of the old contract will be supported by consideration. At which point there are simply no pre-existing duties left to raise the rule. The parties can enter into a new contract which (effectively) re-imposes the same duties on one party, but for a higher price, with orthodox consideration on (re-)formation. This seems an obvious 'dodge' around the pre-existing duty rule, but the courts will only accept that this has happened when the parties have *expressly* cast the variation as a rescission and new contract.[155]

Secondly, the usual exceptions to consideration are all available. A variation made by deed cannot fail for want of consideration. An alteration in performance from the variation promisee will be consideration for the promise to pay

---

[151] Lobban, n.127 above, p. 235.
[152] (1884) LR 9 App Cas 605. NB it had been expressly reversed in the British Indian codification: Indian Contracts Act 1872, s.63.
[153] *Re Selectmove* [1995] 1 WLR 474.
[154] Unlikely with debts, i.e. if the creditor has already advanced the loan.
[155] Cf. *Cie Noga d'Importation v Abacha* [2003] EWCA Civ 1100, [44]–[61].

more (or accept less). The courts' refusal to examine the 'adequacy' of such 'new consideration' means that a nominal addition, the proverbial peppercorn, is enough. This explains Coke CJ's observation that while a creditor cannot accept a lesser sum of money in satisfaction of a debt, 'a horse, a hawk, or a robe, &c.' is good consideration, for this 'might be more beneficial to the [creditor] than the money'.[156] This respects the 'subjectivity of value', as soon as we move away from hard currency. Nevertheless, the great Equity judge Sir George Jessel MR satirized the 'mystery' that:

> a creditor might accept anything in satisfaction of his debt except a less amount of money. He might take a horse, or a canary, or a tomtit if he chose, ... but, by a most extraordinary peculiarity of the English Common Law, he could not take 19s. 6d. in the pound;[157] that was *nudum pactum*.[158]

So there are routes available for legally knowledgeable parties to side-step the pre-existing duty rule. Most are straightforward enough (although as Jessel MR remarked, debtors tend not to possess 'a stock of canary-birds or tomtits, or rubbish of that kind').[159] But to the extent that one-sided modifications should remain unenforceable as a matter of policy, such devices ought to be carefully scrutinized.

WHAT IS THE CORRECT POLICY TOWARDS CONTRACT MODIFICATION?

The law faces a dilemma when it comes to enforcing modifications (other than straightforward cases where payment is increased for a true increase in services provided). On one hand, the party said to be making a 'gift' (like Roffey Bros) is actually acting rationally in its own self-interest. The modification is not truly gratuitous: it is to *both* parties' advantage.[160] Therefore, on ordinary principles, it should be enforced. But on the other hand, there is an ever-present danger that such modifications will be extracted through economic opportunism. Any party threatened with breach of contract but with no alternative supplier of the goods or services will *par excellence* receive a 'practical benefit' from continued performance.[161] The question is whether the law can satisfactorily separate the 'good' modifications from (coerced) 'bad' ones, or whether as a prophylactic to opportunism they should not be enforced at all (effectively the old common law position – *Stilk v Myrick* and *Foakes v Beer*).[162]

Richard Posner considers an employer whose builder demands payment over the contract price. The employer may wish to pay more to gain a reputation for fair dealing, to prevent driving the builder into bankruptcy or even from genuine

---

[156] *Pinnel's Case* (1602) 5 Co Rep 117a.
[157] 97½p.
[158] *Couldery v Bartrum* (1880) LR 19 Ch D 394, 399.
[159] Ibid, p. 400.
[160] Cf. nn.31 and 32 above.
[161] Chen-Wishart, n.135, p. 145.
[162] nn.146 and 152 above.

altruism. For the gains to be realized, the promise must be enforceable – if the builder knows the employer is free to renege he may decide to down tools and take his chances in the bankruptcy court after all. Yet the employer will want to make a *promise* rather than handing over any money when there is financial shakiness – any prepayments may end up with the trustee in bankruptcy leaving the employer an unsecured creditor. 'This is a clear case where the enforcement of a promise not supported by fresh consideration enhances the welfare of the promisor.'[163]

But Posner has pointed out judicially that such promises may frequently be extracted through opportunistic pressure.

> [T]here is often an interval in the life of a contract during which one party is at the mercy of the other. A may have ordered a machine from B that A wants to place in operation on a given date [and] may have made commitments to his customers that it would be costly to renege on. As the date of scheduled delivery approaches, B may be tempted to demand that A agree to renegotiate the contract price, knowing that A will incur heavy expenses if B fails to deliver on time. A can always refuse to renegotiate, relying instead on his right to sue B for breach of contract if B fails to make delivery by the agreed date. But legal remedies are always costly and uncertain.[164]

Thus may B hold A 'over a barrel'.[165] Enforcing such modifications is undesirable as although it will certainly be in A's interest to have B perform punctually, enforcement will encourage such opportunism in future. Conversely, if B knows that A's promise to pay more will be unenforceable (or that any payment made by A will be recoverable from B), there will be no incentive for B to attempt to take advantage like this in the first place.

As seen above, the approach in *Williams v Roffey Bros & Nicholls (Contractors) Ltd*[166] was to recognize 'good consideration' and rely on the relatively new doctrine of economic duress to police opportunism.[167] There is certainly much to be said for this view. The classic existing duty rule (*Stilk v Myrick*) was too wide, indiscriminately invalidating mutually beneficial, *non-coerced* promises (as in *Roffey* itself). But the rule is simultaneously too narrow. Since 'slight consideration' satisfies the rule, the protection it grants to A is 'feeble': surrendering contractual rights in exchange for a peppercorn is not functionally different from giving them up for nothing.[168] Duress focuses directly on the question of coercion.

However, doubts have been expressed. Chen-Wishart comments that economic duress is 'too coarsely calibrated' to deal with the problem.[169] If a threat to breach a

---

[163] Posner, n.57 above, p. 421.
[164] *United States v Stump Home Specialties, Inc* (1990) 905 F.2d 1117, [12].
[165] Cf. *Atlas Express v Kafco* [1989] QB 833, 838.
[166] [1991] 1 QB 1.
[167] See now *Adam Opel GmbH v Mitras Automotive UK Ltd* [2007] EWHC 3205 (QB).
[168] *US v Stump Home Specialities* at [13].
[169] Chen-Wishart, n.135 above, p. 144.

contract (including an implicit threat from inability to perform) were sufficient to constitute duress then *no* modification would be enforceable.[170] The emphasis on ensuring free 'volition' in the early duress cases has been criticized as a 'slippery, even metaphysical, concept [and] devoid of readily ascertainable content'.[171] The requirement of 'illegitimate' pressure is also 'conclusory [and] unilluminating'.[172] Janet O'Sullivan suggested in 1996 that blanket non-enforcement (i.e. *Foakes v Beer*) was preferable to economic duress while the rules of that defence were still being worked out.[173] It is arguable that nothing has happened since to bring about the necessary clarity and precision.[174]

The problem of dividing the mutually beneficial from the opportunistically coerced modification seems an intractable one. But it must be faced directly, to 'break out of [the] vicious circle of inventing new language to restate old problems'.[175] A workable definition of opportunism pure and simple is Posner's.[176] It is where the only thing that has changed between the original contract and the modification is the bargaining power between the parties, i.e. B's power over A increases because A becomes dependent on B's performance.[177] B gains monopoly power over A, because nobody else will be able to make the machine for A at such short notice. (For this reason, A will not be adequately compensated by allowing B to breach and pay damages – the presupposition of damages is that they can 'make the promisee whole' by enabling him to buy perfect substitute performance.) Such a renegotiation is wasteful – a pure 'zero sum' transfer, in which B's gain exactly mirrors A's loss, but there is no wealth increase (as there is when resources are moved to those who value them most). The parties will waste resources in 'gaming' the renegotiation and perhaps designing the original contract to forestall such opportunism. All of these costs will be avoided if opportunistic renegotiations are unenforceable. The original contract should not be viewed solely as a starting point for future negotiation.[178]

Posner contrasts situations in which an unexpected event makes it impossible for a (willing) promisor to perform at the originally agreed contract price. That is, there is a real risk of breach (or bankruptcy) if there is no modification (contrast the previous category). In *Goebel v Linn* it became uneconomic to supply ice at the contract price because the ice 'crop' had failed in an unusually mild winter (at this time, ice was 'harvested' from the American Great Lakes).[179] The customer agreed to pay more to the supplier, and the court upheld the modification. It was in both parties' interest that the modification should be made in such 'very extraordinary'

---

[170] Ibid, p. 146.
[171] V.A. Aivazian, M.J. Trebilcock & M. Penny, 'The Law of Contract Modifications: the Uncertain Quest for a Bench Mark of Enforceability' (1984) 22 *Osgoode Hall LJ* 173, 184.
[172] Ibid, p. 185.
[173] n.137 above.
[174] Cf. pp. 185–196 below.
[175] Aivazian, Trebilcock & Penny, n.171 above, p. 187.
[176] n.57 above (1977).
[177] Cf. *D&C Builders v Rees* [1965] 2 QB 617.
[178] P.B.H. Birks, 'The Travails of Duress' [1990] LMCLQ 342, 346.
[179] (1882) 47 Mich 489.

circumstances – it was surely not in the customer's interests that the ice supplier should be 'ruined' by insistence on the original contract price. Posner comments that there was no exploitation of a monopoly position and so the court was right to uphold the modification.

But Posner's neat dichotomy between external changes in circumstances and purely 'internal' exploitation of an intra-party monopoly seems too simplistic. Take *Roffey*. There is no suggestion that Williams was exploiting his hold over Roffey Bros. He was *unable*, rather than cynically *unwilling*, to complete the carpentry punctually at the original contract price. However, those circumstances were largely Williams's own fault. The court found two reasons for the delays. First, the contract was seriously underpriced (£20,000 instead of a reasonable £23,783). Secondly, Williams failed to supervise his workforce adequately. If we think about future cases with similar facts, we can see that the incentive for someone like Williams to manage his workforce efficiently will be considerably weakened if he knows that the employer may be forced to make a (legally enforceable) promise to pay more than the agreed price. The point is a general one. Might the ice supplier in *Goebel v Linn* have invested further in (e.g.) insulation to ensure an adequate ice crop? There is a 'moral hazard' problem: if the party who can take precautions against an adverse event is relieved of the consequences, precautions are less likely to be taken.[180]

What of under pricing? It has been suggested that where the original contract was 'unfairly' underpriced, modifications to it should be enforced.[181] There are obvious problems with this. English law shuns assessment of the fairness of contracts or, technically speaking, the 'adequacy of consideration'. But even assuming that the underpricing in *Roffey* (almost 20 per cent) was severe enough to be unfair (perhaps driving Williams to ruin as in *Goebel v Linn*), other complications emerge. Should Williams have been able to escape from a bad bargain in this way? Responsibility in contract formation (not to mention the sanctity of contract) will be undermined.[182] Those submitting tenders might even be encouraged cynically to bid at an undervalue knowing that the price would have to be increased later, once the tender was secured.[183] Allowing such modifications turns a fixed-cost building contract into one for 'costs plus', effectively transferring all risks from builder to employer, a form of contract that the parties could have agreed if they wished but manifestly did not (presumably for good reasons).[184]

In other words, there is the danger of upsetting the initial contractual allocation of risks. This applies even to truly unforeseen events outside the parties' control (like the weather in *Goebel v Linn*, or the solid rock encountered by the

---

[180] Cf. Aivazian, Trebilcock & Penny, n.171 above.
[181] G.H. Treitel & F.M.B. Reynolds, 'Consideration for the Modification of Contracts' (1965) 7 *Malaya LR* 1, 20.
[182] Chen-Wishart, n.135 above, p. 144.
[183] Birks, n.178 above.
[184] Aivazian, Trebilcock & Penny, n.171 above, p. 201.

builder employed to dig a cellar in *Watkins v Carrig*).[185] Through the common law doctrine of strict liability (including an extremely narrow doctrine of frustration), the risks of such events fall on the party who stands to lose by them.[186] Allowing modifications when such risks ripen into losses 'deprives the frustration principle of its sting'.[187] This will be inefficient when the risk was initially placed on the party best able to bear it.[188] A rule against modifications will (like a narrow frustration doctrine) encourage the parties to write efficient allocation of risks into the original contract.[189] Therefore, Aivazian, Trebilcock and Penny conclude that modifications should *not* generally be upheld.[190] Even when not purely opportunistic, they upset the allocation of risks and increase moral hazard (such as Williams's lax contract pricing and working practices in *Roffey*).

However, the same authors concede that when the identity of the initial 'superior risk bearer' is unclear,[191] and when the risk was so remote that it was unlikely to be expressly allocated in the contract, enforcing a modification will not have these effects. They illustrate this by considering the case of the cellar excavation hampered by solid rock. If the builder is a large firm engaged in numerous commercial construction projects, it is likely that it will be the superior bearer of this risk. The building company will have better information to assess the likelihood of such problems in the first place, and be better placed to absorb the losses by diversifying its projects. Therefore, the risk should remain on the builder and a modification to increase the price should be unenforceable. It is different if the builder is a small concern engaged in a domestic project, as in *Watkins v Carrig* itself. It will be far from clear whether builder or employer is better able to assess the risk of encountering solid rock, and to insure against it, whereas it is clearly in both parties' interest to see that the excavation continues at a realistic price. Therefore, the modification should be enforced.

With debts, Aivazian, Trebilcock and Penny hold that a creditor's promise to accept less should be unenforceable where the debtor opportunistically offers less to take advantage of the creditor's cash flow problems,[192] or simply of the fact that enforcing debts is costly so that £100 cash is worth more than a right to £200. But it may be different where the debtor cannot repay owing to (e.g.) illness or unemployment. Arguably, debtors have little control over these events, whereas (commercial) lenders have good information about the default rate from such causes, and may diversify the risk (and set their interest rates accordingly) because they are dealing with a large number of loans. In such a situation, enforcing the modification will be mutually beneficial without providing incentives for future

---

[185] (1941) 91 NH 459.
[186] Cf. pp. 126–128, 131–140 below.
[187] Chen-Wishart, n.135 above, p. 139.
[188] Aivazian, Trebilcock & Penny, n.171 above. Cf. generally R.A. Posner & A.M. Rosenfield, 'Impossibility and related doctrines in contract law: An economic analysis' (1977) 6 *JLS* 83.
[189] Aivazian, Trebilcock & Penny, n.171 above, p. 196.
[190] Ibid.
[191] Which is typically the case: pp. 128–131 below.
[192] *D&C Builders v Rees* [1965] 2 QB 617.

bad behaviour. Indeed, if it can be shown by empirical evidence that this is the usual reason for consumer debt default, it would simplify the court's task to rule that all such modifications are enforceable.

Aivazian, Trebilcock and Penny accept that their analysis requires difficult case-by-case assessment. The court must balance the benefit to the immediate parties in enforcing a mutually beneficial modification against the incentive for future contractors. It does seem that there is no easy answer to the modification problem. The number of conflicting factors to be weighed up means that a 'delicate' task is unavoidable.[193]

ALTERNATIVES?

It has been suggested that the modification problem could better be solved by addressing remedies for breach of contract, or the doctrine of promissory estoppel. As noted above, the fundamental reason why promisors are willing to pay more to ensure performance is the weakness of remedies. This incomplete protection also explains their vulnerability. Faced with a threat to breach, only the foolhardy promisee would exclaim 'Breach, and be damned!' when contract law's damnification is insufficient to deter breach, or even to compensate the promisee. It has therefore been argued that boosting remedies would be the 'first best' solution to coerced contract modifications (whereas the discussion in the previous section concerns 'second best' amelioration of problems).[194] For now, we simply note this view. There is heated controversy whether the primary remedy for breach of contract should be specific performance and whether punitive or restitutionary damages should be available to deter breach.[195]

Some commentators argue that promissory estoppel should be used for modifications in the *Williams v Roffey Bros & Nicholls (Contractors) Ltd*[196] situation (as in the *Foakes v Beer* cases).[197] Reservations exist about enforcing purely *executory* promises to pay more in exchange for a promise to continue with performance. After all, if actual performance is not thereafter rendered, how has the additional payment benefited the employer? The bird is not in the hand – it is still in the bush! Hence a preference for estoppel's protection of *relied-upon* promises. However, more recently Chen-Wishart has criticized the court's use of estoppel in *Collier v Wright* for 'undermining' *Foakes v Beer*.[198] The better explanation of *Roffey*, she now argues, is that the promise to pay extra (or accept less) is conditional on actual performance (or payment) by the other side. Or in formal analysis, there is a unilateral offer which can be accepted (only) by the actual performance/payment.

[193] Treitel & Reynolds, n.181 above, p. 22.
[194] Aivazian, Trebilcock & Penny, n.171 above, p. 212.
[195] Cf. Ch. 9 below; Chen-Wishart, n.141 above, p. 95.
[196] [1991] 1 QB 1.
[197] Cf. Chen-Wihart, n.135 above; O'Sullivan, n.137 above; Spence, n.134 above, pp. 135–38; (1884) LR 9 App Cas 605.
[198] Chen-Wishart, n.141 above; [2008] 1 WLR 643.

But Spence claims that it would be artificial to imply a condition that the payment is due only when the work is completed.[199]

Whether the analysis is couched in terms of estoppel or unilateral contract, however, the concern is the same. Only when the promise to pay more (or accept less) has been acted upon should it become enforceable. In one sense this is entailed by the reason for giving effect to the 'one-sided' modifications, actual performance being more valuable than a contractual *right* to performance. At a deeper theoretical level, the argument lends support to Atiyah's claim that the law should – and does – enforce promises more readily when they have actually been detrimentally relied upon, or conferred a valuable benefit, or both.[200] This argument is further supported by the estoppel principle.

Debate 4

How does estoppel fit into contract law?

Lord Neuberger MR tells us that estoppel 'simply amounts to putting legal cloth-ing on the adage that you should not lead people up the garden path'.[201] Lord Hoffmann has referred to its underlying 'moral values',[202] and Lord Denning MR says it is a 'principle of justice and of equity' under which 'when a man, by his words or conduct, has led another to believe in a particular state of affairs, he will not be allowed to go back on it when it would be unjust or inequitable for him to do so'.[203]

Yet despite these eminent claims for ethical simplicity, there is hardly a more controversial or complex area of the law of obligations. Twelve subspecies of estoppels have been listed – non-exhaustively.[204] James Edelman writes that the influential Australian doctrine is an 'orphan among causes of action' that 'defies taxonomy'.[205] There has been considerable debate whether the 'species' should be merged. Oliver LJ describes the distinction between proprietary and (other) promissory estoppels as 'both archaic and arcane'.[206] But Sir Guenter Treitel notes that interbreeding may cause sterilization as well as cross-fertilization.[207] We will not consider this further when 'to many, the naming and categorising of different

---

[199] Spence, n.134 above, p. 132.

[200] P.S. Atiyah, 'Contracts, Promises and the Law of Obligations', n.21 above.

[201] Neuberger of Abbotsbury, 'Thoughts on the Law of Equitable Estoppel' (2010) 84 *Australian LJ* 225, 238.

[202] *Regina (Reprotech (Pebsham) Ltd) v East Sussex CC* [2003] 1 WLR 348, [35].

[203] *Moorgate Mercantile Co Ltd v Twitchings* [1976] QB 225, 241.

[204] A. Leopold, 'Estoppel: A Practical Appraisal of Recent Developments' (1991) 7 *Australian Bar Review* 47 at 71–73.

[205] J. Edelman, 'Remedial Certainty Or Remedial Discretion in Estoppel after *Giumelli*?' (1999) 15 *JCL* 179.

[206] *Habib Bank v Habib Bank Zurich* [1981] 1 WLR 1265, 1285.

[207] G.H. Treitel, *Some Landmarks of 20th Century Contract Law* (Oxford University Press, 2001).

estoppels is a parlour game for legal academics, which obfuscates rather than illuminates'.[208]

For present purposes the important question is the relationship of estoppel to the law of contract. Some, such as Atiyah, argue that estoppel is fundamentally a contractual principle, although this is obscured by the difference in nomenclature.[209] United States law includes promissory estoppel in the famous §90 of the *Restatement of Contracts*. Others take the view that estoppel is a wholly distinct branch of the law, concerned with protecting detrimental reliance rather than enforcing agreements.[210] This is the approach in the equally celebrated Australian cases of *Waltons Stores v Maher*[211] and *Commonwealth v Verwayen*.[212]

This debate is not merely (in the pejorative sense) academic. The law in England is that estoppel cannot enforce promises 'positively', but can only be invoked 'defensively'.[213] (For reasons inadequately explained this limitation does not apply to promises concerning property rights.) The courts fear that allowing estoppel to establish rights would threaten the law of contract (by providing a way of enforcing promises lacking consideration).[214] If, however, estoppel has an entirely different rationale then it should be allowed its own space – it is not a threat to contract to have intersecting obligations of a different nature.[215] This is the Australian rationale for rejecting the 'defensive' limitation. Also, some legal rules apply to contracts (e.g. requirements for them to be in writing) but not to estoppel.[216] Therefore, the question of the doctrine's theoretical basis has real practical importance.

The comparison between estoppel and contract will take place on two levels. First, the criteria necessary to establish an estoppel. Secondly, the remedial effect of estoppel. 'Separationists' argue that either or both of these are quite different from the rules in contract, thereby laying the foundations for an expansion of promissory estoppel. We ask whether the offensive/defensive distinction has any redeeming qualities before considering the more general debate about protecting reliance in contract law. The discussion will include US and (especially) Australian law, since non-proprietary 'promissory' estoppel in England has been given such a narrow compass.

---

[208] Neuberger, n.201 above, p. 237.

[209] P.S. Atiyah, 'When Is An Enforceable Agreement Not a Contract? Answer: When It Is An Equity' (1976) 92 *LQR* 174.

[210] E.g. N.J. McBride, 'A Fifth Common Law Obligation' (1994) 14 *LS* 35; A. Robertson, 'Reliance and Expectation in Estoppel Remedies' [1998] LS 360; M. Spence, *Protecting Reliance: The Emergent Doctrine of Equitable Estoppel* (Hart Publishing, 1999).

[211] (1988) 164 CLR 387.

[212] (1990) 170 CLR 394.

[213] *Combe v Combe* [1951] 2 KB 215.

[214] Ibid.

[215] For overlapping tort and contract, cf. *Henderson v Merrett Syndicates* [1995] 2 AC 145.

[216] E.g. contract to guarantee another's debts (cf. Statute of Frauds 1677, s.4 and *Actionstrength Ltd v International Glass Engineering* [2003] 2 AC 541).

ESTABLISHING ESTOPPELS

The law of contract enforces promises from the time of formation. Even before any action in reliance has taken place, a purely executory contract is binding in full.[217] It is argued that estoppel is very different. It does not depend on a promise as such and, moreover, it is not binding from the outset but only from the time that it has been *relied upon* to the promisee's detriment. It is this 'change of position' that makes it 'unconscionable' for the defendant to disappoint the relying party's belief.[218] Spence formulates estoppel as a duty to protect the reliability of induced expectations by preventing harm to the relying party.[219]

Stephen Smith doubts the distinctiveness of estoppel on these points.[220] First, Smith argues that a promise is required for estoppel just as much as in contract; it would not be reasonable for the estoppel claimant to rely upon anything short of a promise. As Andrew Robertson points out, however, there has always been a minority of successful claims in 'proprietary' estoppel without anything resembling a promise.[221] Typically, the defendant has stood by while the claimant acted on a false belief, doing nothing to correct the claimant's error; he is held to be estopped by his 'acquiescence' in the relied-upon mistake.[222]

Smith further argues that the courts never in practice dismiss an estoppel claim on the basis that it was not relied upon.[223] Again, Robertson responds. It is true that the courts do not insist upon proof of reliance, i.e. demonstration of causation (that but for the belief induced by the defendant, the claimant would not have acted the way he did). But this is because there is a strong presumption of such reliance once the statement is one 'calculated to influence the judgment of a reasonable man'.[224] This is a similar presumption to that in cases of fraud and undue influence, where the court will not 'speculate' whether the deception or pressure 'caused' the contract, since it is 'impossible to analyse the operations of the human mind' so minutely.[225] But the presumption is rebuttable, and so if it is positively shown that there was no detrimental reliance on the belief induced by the defendant, the estoppel claim will fail. This clearly shows estoppel's basis in reliance, in Robertson's view.

For Atiyah, action in reliance is the fundamental basis of liability. A promise is not, he argues, strictly necessary. It serves a 'useful evidential role' in deciding whether the claimant did rely on the defendant (rather than on his own judgment) and whether that reliance was reasonable. These inquiries will be 'greatly

---

[217] Cf. pp. 3–5 above.

[218] Neuberger of Abbotsbury, 'The Stuffing of Minerva's Owl? Taxonomy and Taxidermy in Equity' [2009] CLJ 537, 547–48.

[219] n.210 above.

[220] S.A. Smith, *Contract Theory* (Oxford University Press, 2004), p. 244.

[221] A. Robertson, 'Estoppels and Rights-Creating Events: beyond Wrongs and Promises' in J. Neyers et al. (eds), *Exploring Contract Law* (Hart Publishing, 2009).

[222] Eg *Munt v Beaseley* [2006] EWCA Civ 370.

[223] Smith, n.220 above, pp. 237–38.

[224] *Brikom Investments v Carr* [1979] QB 467.

[225] *Reynell v Sprye* (1852) 1 De G M & G 660, 708 (Lord Cranworth).

assisted' by the presence of an express promise. But it does not follow that the promise itself created liability.[226]

But a further problem with detrimental reliance is that it is a threshold so easily crossed that it is not a serious 'test' of liability at all. All members of society constantly depend on the actions of others being consistent and non-harmful: 'life would be impossible in modern conditions unless … we were entitled to rely on the other man behaving like a reasonable man'.[227] Moreover, 'reliance' may always be presumed 'detrimental' because when we commit ourselves to one course of action, we sacrifice the opportunity to engage in other valuable activities. In economic jargon, reliance will always incur 'opportunity costs'. Therefore something beyond reliance is needed. The element stressed in proprietary estoppel and the Australian cases is 'unconscionability'. According to Dawson J, this requirement is 'the protection against undue intrusion upon the law of contract'.[228]

Now 'unconscionability' seems a word pregnant with mysteries. James Edelman, who relies on it (as well as reliance) to show the distinctiveness of estoppel from contract, has to admit that this 'elusive element … has still to be precisely determined'.[229] We are more often warned what 'unconscionability' isn't than told what it actually is. Mason CJ observes that 'the breaking of a promise, without more, is morally reprehensible, but not unconscionable'.[230] Does detrimental reliance turn the 'reprehensible' into the 'unconscionable'? Apparently 'something more is required'.[231] But what? In *Collier v Wright*, Arden LJ held that payment of part of a debt in reliance on a creditor's promise not to enforce the whole made it inequitable, in itself, for the creditor to go back on the promise and claim the balance of the debt.[232] Mindy Chen-Wishart criticizes this for removing all content from the requirement of unconscionability – but again, without stating positively what unconscionability *does* require.[233]

Another warning comes from Lord Neuberger MR. Particularly in the commercial context where certainty is at a premium and parties can protect themselves by entering into legally binding agreements, estoppel must not be used by the court to punish 'dishonourable' conduct: 'equity is not a sort of moral US Fifth Cavalry riding to the rescue any time a court thinks that a defendant has behaved badly and the common law affords the plaintiff no remedy'.[234] This echoes the general warning that unconscionability is not a 'panacea' for rewriting the contracts of 'competent persons'.[235]

---

[226] P.S. Atiyah, *The Rise and Fall of Freedom of Contract* (Oxford, 1979) p. 2.

[227] *Gollins v Gollins* [1964] AC 644, 664 (Lord Reid).

[228] *Commonwealth v Verwayen* (1990) 170 CLR 394, 453.

[229] Edelman, n.205 above.

[230] *Verwayen*, n.212 above, p. 416.

[231] *Waltons Stores v Maher* (1988) 164 CLR 387, 406 (Mason CJ).

[232] [2008] 1 WLR 643.

[233] Chen-Wishart, n.141 above.

[234] Neuberger, n.201 above (hailing 'the death of estoppel' in commercial cases as 'probably all to the good'; cf. B. Macfarlane and A. Robertson [2008] *LMCLQ* 449).

[235] *Bridge v Campbell Discount Co* [1962] AC 600, 626 (Lord Radcliffe).

Perhaps the 'unconscionability' requirement should merely be seen as a cipher for 'all other relevant considerations'. Spence identifies seven factors for the courts to weigh up, concerning the parties' conduct and the relationship between them.[236] But there must be a concern about uncertainty. Ewan McKendrick worries that courts will use the 'largely unstructured discretion' to duck hard questions about the basis of liability.[237] Spence maintains that courts are 'quite accustomed to making decisions by the balancing of clear criteria', quoting Sir Thomas Bingham's claim that the 'dragon of discretion' can be 'domesticated' thereby.[238]

It is difficult to pin down precisely what makes it unconscionable (or 'inequitable') to disappoint expectations, so that the defendant is estopped from acting inconsistently with them. A number of factors must be balanced, and the most important of these are the claimant's reliance, whether it is detrimental, and whether it is reversible. All of this differs sharply from contracts, which are enforceable as of right from the outset without any need for reliance. Estoppel's rather ill-defined nature is arguably its greatest point of distinction from the crisp rules of commercial contract law. The flexibility is carried over into estoppel remedies, another highly controversial area.

ESTOPPEL REMEDIES

The greatest controversy about estoppel concerns its effect. Does it enforce the expectations of the relying party, or does it only prevent her being made worse off through that reliance? This gets to the heart of the purpose of the doctrine and its relationship with contract. If estoppel protects the 'expectation interest' it moves much closer to contract law. It might well be seen as a different route to contractual obligation, based in reliance and 'unconscionability' rather than orthodox agreement and consideration.

The traditional form of estoppel by representation of fact lends support to this 'enforcement' view. When one party leads the other to believe that a certain state of affairs obtains and that party relies on that belief, the court proceeds as if those facts did in fact exist. In other words, the defendant is estopped from denying the represented facts.[239] If translated into cases of relied-on promises, being prevented from going back is equivalent to being made to keep the promise – viz. enforcement of it. On this traditional approach, estoppel logically leads to enforcement.

However, in proprietary estoppel (and in Australia and America) a more flexible approach is taken.[240] Lord Neuberger sums up the effect of estoppel as preventing disappointment of the claimant's expectations 'at least without giving … some compensation'.[241] But on what basis should this compensation be assessed? In the

---

[236] M. Spence, 'Australian Estoppel and the Protection of Reliance' (1997) 11 *JCL* 203.

[237] E. McKendrick, 'Work Done in Anticipation of a Contract Which Does Not Materialise' in W.R .Cornish et al., *Restitution: Past, Present and Future* (Hart Publishing, 1998) p. 189.

[238] Bingham, 'The Discretion of the Judge' (The Royal Bank of Scotland Law Lecture, 1990) p. 2.

[239] *Low v Bouverie* [1891] 3 Ch 82.

[240] S. Gardner, 'The Remedial Discretion in Proprietary Estoppel' (1999) 115 *LQR* 438.

[241] n.218 above.

United States it seems that the expectation measure is favoured: to put the claimant in the position she would have been in had the promise been performed.[242] §90 of the first *Restatement of Contracts* (1932) said that a relied-upon promise could be binding when justice required it. As Grant Gilmore argued, this was a sensible solution for hard cases but left an 'entirely unresolved' tension between §90 and the orthodox requirement of consideration for a binding promise; the result (by 1970) was that reliance had 'swallowed' the bargain principle of contract.[243] But as S.F.C. Milsom points out, the animals might coexist happily in separate cages rather than one devouring the other, i.e. §90 might be seen as non-contractual.[244] In the second *Restatement* (1981), §90 carries the important qualification: 'The remedy granted for breach may be limited as justice requires.' However (*pace* Milsom) the obligation is still defined in commentary as 'contractual' (albeit the *Restatement* has a broader view of contracts than English law – viz. they do not necessarily result in enforcement remedies).[245] As Donal Nolan comments, this classification seems to influence the dominant practice of American courts to award expectation damages.[246]

Milsom himself notes a particular need for reliance-based enforcement of promises in the US: the abolition of the deed promise. So in England, it is easy to render a promise to make a gift binding by use of the relevant formalities. In America this is not possible where (as in most States) the deed has been abolished. Therefore, US courts are considerably more sympathetic towards those relying on donative promises. They cannot hold, as in England, that 'the benefactor could have made a binding promise under seal, and [so] the beneficiary relied on anything less at his own risk'.[247]

The High Court of Australia has attempted to keep estoppel in a separate compartment, to prevent it swallowing contract law. The argument developed by Brennan J in *Waltons Stores v Maher*[248] is that the aim of 'equitable estoppel' is to eliminate the detriment that the relying party would otherwise suffer. Contractual remedies depend on the terms of the contract whereas 'estoppel varies according to what is necessary to prevent detriment resulting from unconscionable conduct'. Provided this object was 'kept steadily in mind', Brennan J argued, any conflict between contract and estoppel could be avoided. Therefore, there was no need to draw the 'illogical' distinction between using estoppel defensively (to extinguish a right) and offensively (to create a new one). This reasoning was echoed in *Commonwealth v Verwayen*.[249] Mason CJ said that in devising a remedy, the court should award what was necessary to prevent the relying party suffering a detriment, 'and no more'. It was essential that there be proportionality between

---

[242] Yorio and Thel, 'The Promissory Basis of Section 90' (1991) 101 *Yale LJ* 111.

[243] Gilmore, n.25 above, pp. 70–71, 79–80.

[244] S.F.C. Milsom, 'A pageant in modern dress' (1975) 84 Yale LJ 1585.

[245] D. Nolan, 'Following in Their Footsteps: Equitable Estoppel in Australia and the United States' (2000) 11 *KCLJ* 202.

[246] Ibid.

[247] Milsom, n.244 above. Cf. pp. 39–40 above.

[248] (1988) 164 CLR 387.

[249] (1990) 170 CLR 394.

the detriment and the remedy awarded, a requirement that has been echoed by Aldous LJ in a leading English proprietary estoppel decision.[250] Equity had discarded the view that the purpose of estoppel was 'to make good the relevant assumption'.

This seems a firm repudiation of the American view of estoppel as an alternative means of *enforcing* promises. Instead, reliance generates a reliance-focused remedy. But things are not all they seem. Mason CJ admits that avoiding detriment might require nothing short of enforcement of the promise, 'in appropriate cases'. Spence agrees that this will sometimes be the *'only* or *only satisfactory* way in which to put the relying party in the position in which she would have been had the assumption never been induced'.[251] Spence claims that this should be done 'only as a last resort'. But the Australian case law reveals a different practice. In *Waltons Stores* and *Verwayen* themselves the expectation measure was used (although there were dissents in *Verwayen*, and in *Waltons Stores* the defendants did not argue that their liability should be limited to reversing the plaintiff's detriment). Moreover, Andrew Robertson found that in the first 24 Australian cases since *Verwayen* expectations had been compensated in *every single case*.[252] This was also true in the next leading decision of the High Court of Australia,[253] and in 2008 Robertson confirms that in Australian (and English proprietary estoppel) cases expectation relief is now granted in most cases.[254] How can this be explained?

Nolan suggests, in effect, that old habits die hard. He says that the lower Australian courts have shown a continuing 'predilection' to hold parties to their promises, derived from classic estoppel reasoning, which the 'signals from on high' have not been strong enough to overcome.[255] This may well be right, although it is troubling if judges are guided by their 'psyches' and impervious to new ideas! Robertson has a more intellectually appealing explanation.[256] He argues that expectation remedies are usually the best way to protect detrimental reliance adequately. This seems 'paradoxical' but the reason is that reliance is typically difficult to quantify.[257] In many 'family homes' cases there is reliance of an intrinsically non-pecuniary kind, such as a decision to have children or move home, on the strength of promised land. Even in commercial cases, detriment tends to come in the form of lost opportunities. Quantifying a lost commercial venture will be 'highly speculative'.[258] While the courts could put rough figures

---

[250] *Jennings v Rice* [2002] EWCA Civ 159 at [36].

[251] M. Spence, 'Australian Estoppel and the Protection of Reliance' (1997) 11 *JCL* 203 (original emphasis).

[252] A. Robertson, 'Satisfying the Minimum Equity: Equitable Estoppel Remedies after *Verwayen*' (1996) 20 *Melbourne LR* 805, 829.

[253] *Giumelli v Giumelli* (1999) 73 ALJR 547.

[254] A. Robertson, 'The Reliance Basis of Proprietary Estoppel Remedies' [2008] *Conv* 295.

[255] Nolan, n.245 above, p. 223.

[256] nn. 252 and 254 above.

[257] Cf. generally L.L. Fuller and W.R. Purdue, 'The Reliance Interest in Contract Damages' (1936) 46 *Yale LJ* 52 and 373.

[258] *Cobbe v Yeoman's Row* [2006] EWCA Civ 1139, [95].

on such non-pecuniary or imponderable losses, there would be a real danger of failing fully to reverse the detriment. Rather than risk such under-compensation, it is better simply to enforce the expectation.

In effect, Robertson argues, the onus is placed on the representor to show that there would be disproportionality between the detriment and the expectation. Only if this is clearly demonstrated will the remedy be limited to the former. In *Jones v Lalic* the plaintiff had made expenditure of $50,000 in expectation of half interest in a house worth $800,000. The court held that it would be disproportionate to award him a half share ($400,000) and awarded $50,000 instead.[259] Robertson suggests it will be 'comparatively rare' neatly to reverse reliance losses in this way.[260] His account is therefore contrary to Spence's (although both support the reliance basis of estoppel remedies). Far from being a 'last resort', enforcing expectation will be the usual remedy.

Of course, some would argue that this consistent practice shows that dicta aside, Australian estoppel is really committed to enforcing promises. That does seem a less convoluted way of explaining the practice. James Edelman takes this position. He defines the 'detriment' suffered in estoppel cases 'purely' by reference to the lost expectation.[261] Obviously, if you promise me £10 and don't pay, there is a sense that I am £10 worse off. As Edelman observes, this makes it 'inevitable' that the courts will award expectation damages. That is surely correct, for Edelman's definition of 'detriment' in terms of 'expectation' entirely collapses the distinction between them! It is not clear why we should make this move (or, if the courts have done so, whether it is correct). Edelman (as seen) argues that 'unconscionability' makes estoppel distinct from contract as a way of enforcing promises. But even if that is true, it does not compel us to reject reliance remedies (as defended by Robertson). Elizabeth Cooke's argument that estoppel is most 'useful' when enforcing expectations might also appear circular.[262] Isn't this what contract law is for? And Cooke's claim that expectation is a more certain approach looks questionable in light of her own agreement that this is only the starting point, for the equitable remedy is a flexible one.

In conclusion, it seems that the 'once and for all' settlement of the basis of estoppel remedies demanded by Andrew Burrows is still awaited.[263] The reliance argument enjoys powerful support from the High Court of Australia and Andrew Robertson, although its adoption may, it seems, make surprisingly little difference in practice. But by stressing the separate theoretical basis from orthodox accounts of contract, it would defuse the perceived threat posed by estoppel to contractual obligation.

---

[259] (2006) 197 FLR 27 (NSWSC).

[260] Robertson, n.254 above, 367–68.

[261] Edelman, n.205 above, replying on Giumelli, n.253 above.

[262] E. Cooke, 'Estoppel and the Protection of Expectations' [1997] *Legal Studies* 258.

[263] Cf. A. Burrows, 'Contract, Tort and Restitution: A Satisfactory Division Or Not?' (1983) 99 LQR 217 at 243.

ESTOPPEL: A SWORD OR A SHIELD?

In England, estoppel cannot (outside the proprietary context) be used as a cause of action. It can only be used defensively, i.e. when a promise not to enforce certain rights has been relied upon. The reason given is basically pragmatic, or prudential. In *Combe v Combe* Denning LJ did not wish the nascent doctrine of promissory estoppel (of which he had recently been midwife in the *High Trees* case) to be endangered by over-extension.[264] In particular, he declared that the doctrine of consideration remained a 'cardinal necessity' for contract formation (although not its modification or discharge). Denning LJ clearly feared that a direct conflict between contract and estoppel could only mean the defeat for the latter. Hence the 'vivid' metaphor that estoppel can be used as a shield but not a sword.[265]

This reasoning seems questionable. First, the distinction is difficult to draw. Clearly, it cannot depend on the position of the litigants: would *High Trees* be decided differently according to whether the landlord brought an action to recover the full rent or the tenant sought a declaration that he was not liable for it?[266] Surely not. But the distinction between bringing an action 'on the promise' and using the estoppel to supply the missing element of 'another cause of action' also seems difficult.[267] Arguably, in *Combe* itself the plaintiff pled estoppel to establish the missing element of her contractual claim against her husband (viz. consideration).[268]

Even where the distinction can be easily applied,[269] its rationale is not very convincing. Why is it acceptable for consideration to be 'overthrown by a side-wind' in modification cases?[270] In *Collier v Wright*, Arden LJ considered that *High Trees* had, in effect, implemented the 1937 report of the Law Reform Committee recommending that *Foakes v Beer* be overruled.[271] How is this any less a challenge to the doctrine of consideration than permitting estoppel to enforce 'increasing modifications' (*Stilk v Myrick*[272] or *Williams v Roffey Bros & Nicholls (Contractors) Ltd*[273])? Obviously the rule in *Combe v Combe* does limit the clash between contract and estoppel to some extent, but fails to eliminate it entirely while drawing the line in a pretty arbitrary way. Recent cases have applied the rule with notable reluctance.[274]

---

[264] [1951] 2 KB 215, 219. Cf. similar comments (in a different context) *Weston v Downes* (1778) 1 Douglas 23, 24 (Lord Mansfield CJ); *Central London Property Trust v High Trees House* [1947] KB 130.

[265] [1951] 2 KB 215, 224 (Birkett LJ).

[266] M Barnes, 'Estoppel as a Sword' [2011] *LMCLQ* 372.

[267] [1951] 2 K.B. 215, 225–26 (Asquith LJ). Cf. *Robertson v Minister of Pensions* [1949] 1 KB 227 (Denning J).

[268] Barnes, n.266 above, p. 390.

[269] Cf. R. Halson, 'The Offensive Limits of Promissory Estoppel' [1999] *LMCLQ* 256.

[270] [1951] 2 K.B. 215, 200 (Denning LJ).

[271] [2008] 1 WLR 643; cf. nn.3 and 264 above; (1884) LR 9 App Cas 605.

[272] n.146 above.

[273] [1991] 1 QB 1.

[274] *Riverside Housing Association* v *White* [2005] EWCA Civ 1385; *Newport City Council* v *Charles* [2008] EWCA Civ 1541.

Roger Halson has attempted to defend the limitation by stating that contract modifications pose such important and difficult questions that a 'dedicated' estoppel doctrine is required. The limitation on estoppel in *Combe v Combe* preserves the necessary 'expertise'.[275] As seen in Debate 3, modification is undoubtedly a knotty problem, but it is questionable whether its analysis is helped at all by confining promissory estoppel only to 'decreasing' modifications. Halson, secondly, argues that *Combe* prevents conflict between estoppel and contract. But as seen, it does this rather erratically and moreover, if the Australian approach is well founded no fundamental clash between contract and estoppel exists.

Halson explains that most proprietary estoppel cases are concerned with a different problem: not lack of consideration but failure to comply with the necessary formalities. No doubt this is true, but since consideration difficulties can arise with the creation of rights as well as their variation, it is difficult to see that the formalities point really explains the difference between proprietary and other estoppels. The incidence of that question does not map onto the sword/shield distinction.

Michael Barnes has recently argued that the sword/shield distinction does not fit with the moral precepts that underlie estoppel.[276] Nevertheless, he accepts (as a sheer matter of authority) that only *proprietary* estoppel may be the sole factor that founds a cause of action. This may be true as a statement of the positive law, but is of limited use in deciding how the law should develop. If Barnes had worked through the law with his moral values, he may perhaps have reached the conclusion that there is no distinction of logic or principle between 'offensive' and 'defensive' cases, and between proprietary and other promissory estoppel claims. If this blurring of distinctions is still thought to threaten the law of contract, than asserting the distinctiveness of estoppel in the Australian fashion could provide reassurance.

THE DEATH OF CONTRACT?

English and Australian judges have therefore attempted, in different ways, to protect contract from the threat of contamination (even destruction) by promissory estoppel. Finally, we consider whether such a separation is necessary. Would infusion of estoppel, reliance-based reasoning into contract be such a bad thing after all?

In US law, as seen, Gilmore argued that promissory estoppel had led to the 'death of contract'. The 'unwanted stepchild' in the first *Restatement of Contracts* (1932) had become a basic principle of contract law by 1970. Even executory contracts were now viewed as enforceable because they *invited reliance*.[277] The title of Gilmore's lectures was deliberately apocalyptic: he compared the pronounce-

---

[275] Halson, n.269 above, p. 276.
[276] Barnes, n.266 above.
[277] Gilmore, n.25 above, pp. 79–80.

ment that 'God is dead'.[278] It may be that reports of contract's death, like Mark Twain's (and indeed God's) have been exaggerated – later commentators note its resurgence and even 'undeath'.[279] It was always a melodramatic way of describing the influence of the reliance principle in contract law.

Atiyah has famously welcomed that change.[280] He argues that legal obligations should arise primarily from what people do rather than what they intend (i.e. promise). Action in reliance (or conferring a benefit) is more deserving of legal protection than the bare expectation of gain. By 'no definitional jugglery' can we equate one who 'suffers a diminution of his assets in reliance on a promise' with one who is simply disappointed (without relying).[281] Lawyers and philosophers are equally at fault for failing to draw 'the all important distinction between promises and contracts which rest purely in intention, and promises and contracts which depend partly on action'.[282] Who can deny that the latter are more deserving?

Atiyah would not discard the idea of promising, and voluntary undertaking, altogether. We do not perform transactions like shopping or boarding a bus in our sleep. But there is much more to liability than voluntary conduct alone. The man on the Oxford omnibus is required to pay the fare irrespective of his actual intentions – because he is gaining the benefit of travel. People decide whether to rely (and which benefits to accept), and here promises play an important role. But one that is ultimately secondary, and *evidential*. So, a promise to pay back a loan makes clear that it was not a gift. Agreement about remuneration aids quantification in *quantum meruit* cases.[283] A clear promise can also show that action in reliance upon was reasonable.[284] Such evidence is 'an indispensable tool of efficient administration in a free market society'.[285] However the role of the promise is not a 'wholly independent source of obligation' but 'is frequently to bolster up an already existing duty'.[286] The underlying basis of liability is actions – incurring detriment or conferring a benefit – not words.

Accordingly, Atiyah attacks the paradigm of contract law which places the executory contract, the full enforcement of pure intention, at its heart.[287] They are 'nothing like as binding in practice as legal theory might suggest' and do not deserve their central place in contract theory.[288] Consistent with this, Atiyah argues that intellectual honesty requires lawyers to accept that when agreements lacking consideration are enforced by the courts under the guise of 'proprietary

---

[278] Eg Nietzsche, *Die fröhliche Wissenschaft* (1882) §108.

[279] Cf. P.S. Atiyah, 'Freedom of Contract and the New Right' in *Essays on Contract* (Oxford University Press, 1990); Campbell, n.27 above.

[280] Atiyah, 'Contracts, Promises and the Law of Obligations', n.21 above.

[281] *Essays on Contract*, pp. 20–21.

[282] Ibid, p. 39.

[283] *Way v Latilla* [1937] 3 All ER 759. Cf. pp. 24–25 above.

[284] Cf. n.221 above.

[285] Atiyah, *Essays on Contract*, p. 27.

[286] Ibid, p. 39.

[287] Ibid, pp. 12–13.

[288] Ibid, p. 30.

estoppel', this is really a species of contractual liability.[289] The problem of whether relied-upon agreements should be enforceable cannot be 'magically wafted away' by changing the label of liability.[290] Might not the pretence that estoppel is non-contractual serve to conceal 'vitally important changes in judicial attitudes to contractual ideas?'[291] Reliance is treated as a badge of enforceability alternative to consideration – it is only the 'hardening of the arteries' of classical contract theory which prevents the recognition of this.[292] It would relieve the 'unnecessarily cumbrous' duplication of doctrines to subsume estoppel under contract.[293] The courts could consider whether protection of expectations or reliance was appropriate without the distraction of the contract/estoppel distinction.

Recognizing estoppel as part of contract law would greatly support Atiyah's emphasis on the protection of reliance rather than bare expectations. It follows that Atiyah is no friend of the rule in *Combe v Combe*.[294] He argues that the court could easily have found 'bargain' consideration (an implied request by the husband to the wife not to apply to the court for maintenance) had they wished to enforce the promise, but the changing social attitude towards maintenance of an estranged spouse with no children underlay the decision.[295] *Combe* stands for nothing more than: if there is foreseeable reliance the promise is not enforceable *if the justice of the case does not require it.*[296]

How should we respond to Atiyah's radical proposal? Donal Nolan warns that the US experience does not support Atiyah's view that merging contract and estoppel would mean greater emphasis on detriment-protecting remedies.[297] As seen above, the usual practice in estoppel cases seems to protect expectations. Nolan suggests that the pull of the contract tradition has strongly influenced estoppel. To stand Gilmore on his head, we could argue that the contractual classification of US estoppel has actually meant 'the death of estoppel'! Ironically, the separate-category approach to estoppel that Atiyah deplores has meant much greater emphasis on detrimental reliance in Australia.

Now Atiyah might accept the point, since he does not argue that the remedy in contract (or 'estoppel') should *never* be expectation damages. Rather, that the protection of expectations or detriment does not properly correspond to the distinction between contract and estoppel.[298] Atiyah explicitly allows that there are reasons to enforce executory contracts (i.e. in the absence of reliance).[299] Moreover, in the introduction to his magnum opus *The Decline and Fall of Freedom*

---

[289] Atiyah, n.209 above. Cf. 'Riposte' by P.J. Millett (1976) 92 *LQR* 342.
[290] Ibid, p. 178.
[291] Ibid, p. 179.
[292] P.S. Atiyah, 'Consideration: A Restatement' in *Essays on Contract* (Oxford University Press, 1990) p. 187.
[293] Ibid, p. 240.
[294] [1951] 2 KB 215.
[295] n.292 above, p. 197; 231 (contrasting *Ward v Byham* [1956] 1 WLR 496).
[296] Ibid, p. 232.
[297] Nolan, n.245 above.
[298] Atiyah, n.292 above, p. 240.
[299] Ibid, pp. 33–36, 45.

of Contract Atiyah paid tribute to the influence of Fuller and Purdue's seminal account of the reliance interest in contract damages.[300] Fuller and Purdue argue that because reliance is so difficult to prove and quantify, the award of expectation damages is a good proxy, especially given reliance via 'foregone opportunities'. This is the kernel of Andrew Robertson's reconciliation of the theory of reliance and the practice of expectation relief in estoppel, of course.[301] Perhaps when it comes to what really matters – the remedy – the classification as contract or estoppel is not vitally important. Legal terminology is important, but the tail should not wag the dog. An estoppel by any other name would smell as sweet.[302]

Further Reading

Consideration and gratuitous promises

Lord Wright, 'Ought the Doctrine of Consideration to Be Abolished from the Common Law?' (1936) 49 *Harvard LR* 1225.

C.J. Hamson, 'The Reform of Consideration' (1938) 54 *LQR* 233.

L.L. Fuller, 'Consideration and Form' (1941) 41 *Columbia LR* 799.

P.S. Atiyah, 'Consideration: A Restatement' in *Essays on Contract* (Oxford University Press, 1990).

G.H. Treitel, 'Consideration: A Critical Analysis of Professor Atiyah's Fundamental Restatement' (1976) 50 *Australian LJ* 439.

R.A. Posner, 'Gratuitous Promises in Economics and Law' (1977) 6 *JLS* 411.

A.Kull, 'Reconsidering Gratuitous Promises' (1992) 21 *JLS* 39.

M.A. Eisenberg, 'The World of Contract and the World of Gift' (1997) 85 *California LR* 821.

Intention to create legal relations

S. Hedley, 'Keeping Contract in Its Place – *Balfour v Balfour* and the Enforceability of Informal Agreements' (1985) 5 *OJLS* 391.

M.D.A. Freeman, 'Contracting in the Haven: *Balfour v Balfour* Revisited' In R Halson (ed.), *Exploring the Boundaries of Contract* (Dartmouth, 1996).

B. Rudden, 'The Gentleman's Agreement in Legal Theory and in Modern Practice' [1999] *Eur Rev Private Law* 199.

Contract modification

V.A. Aivazian, M.J. Trebilcock & M. Penny, 'The Law of Contract Modifications: the Uncertain Quest for a Bench Mark of Enforceability' (1984) 22 *Osgoode Hall LJ* 173.

M. Chen-Wishart, 'Consideration, Practical Benefit and the Emperor's New Clothes' In J. Beatson and D. Friedmann (eds), *Good Faith and Fault in Contract Law* (Oxford University Press, 1995).

---

[300] Atiyah, n.226; Fuller and Purdue n.257 above.
[301] Cf. pp. 60–61 above.
[302] Cf. Coke on Littleton (1628): 'estoppels are odious'.

J.A. O'Sullivan, 'In Defence of *Foakes v. Beer*' [1996] *CLJ* 219.

M. Chen-Wishart, 'A Bird in the Hand: Consideration and Contract Modification' In A. Burrows and E. Peel (eds), *Contract Formation and Parties* (Oxford University Press, 2010).

Estoppel and reliance

P.S. Atiyah, 'When Is An Enforceable Agreement Not a Contract? Answer: When It Is An Equity' (1976) 92 *LQR* 174.

P.S. Atiyah, 'Contracts, Promises and the Law of Obligations' In *Essays on Contract* (Oxford University Press, 1990).

R. Halson, 'The Offensive Limits of Promissory Estoppel' [1999] *LMCLQ* 256

D. Nolan, 'Following in Their Footsteps: Equitable Estoppel in Australia and the United States' (2000) 11 *KCLJ* 202.

A. Robertson, 'The Reliance Basis of Proprietary Estoppel Remedies' [2008] *Conv* 295.

Lord Neuberger of Abbotsbury, 'Thoughts on the Law of Equitable Estoppel' (2010) 84 *Australian LJ* 225.

3

STANDARD FORMS AND WRITTEN CONTRACTS

INTRODUCTION

This chapter will not be found in every contract textbook, or indeed every contract course (or not in so many words). But standard form contracts are enormously important in practice. Also, some of the trickiest doctrinal issues arise in this area. It is, furthermore, the setting for a truly great debate over the way we should think about contract law generally.

Although there is, outside special categories such as sales of land, no requirement that contracts should be made in writing in English law, in practice most agreements are to be found in documents. Most will not have been individually negotiated. The standard form is an inevitable fact of modern contracting.[1] It reduces the otherwise prohibitive cost of negotiations in an economy based on mass transactions. Its very prevalence shows its indispensability.[2] Nevertheless, the standard form has received much criticism: denounced as a 'contract of adhesion' presented on a take-it-or-leave-it basis, allowing enterprises to impose their will on consumers (resembling legislative *fiat* not contractual *agreement*).[3]

Notwithstanding such critiques, English law traditionally seems very welcoming of the written contract. This may be seen in the signature rule and the parol evidence rule, discussed below. Contracting parties (or at any rate, those who draft contracts) frequently set out to re-affirm the exclusive status of written agreements through 'entire agreement clauses', which will also be considered. We also examine the utility of, and problems with, standard forms generally.

First we examine a more fundamental disagreement over the nature of contracts. Many authors have argued that contracts can only properly be understood *contextually*. The formal contract (and the formal law that goes with it) is only part of

---

[1] Cf. O. Prausnitz, *The Standardization of Commercial Contracts in English and Continental Law* (London, 1937).

[2] W. David Slawson, 'Standard Form Contracts and the Democratic Control of Lawmaking Power' (1971) 84 *Harvard LR* 529.

[3] Friedrich Kessler, 'Contracts of Adhesion – Some Thoughts about Freedom of Contract' (1943) 43 *Columbia LR* 629.

the story. The critique builds on sociological findings that in practice, contracting parties rely much more on implicit relations of trust and co-operation than formal legal enforcement. Some argue that contract law must be transformed to take into account these insights – to give effect to the parties' actual expectations rather than the fictitious 'intentions' embalmed in the written contract. But in response, 'formalists' doubt the feasibility, and indeed the desirability, of this revisionist stance. This Debate has wide-ranging significance across the field of contract law.

Debate 1

Contract law versus the reality of contracting?

THE SOCIO-LEGAL CRITIQUE: REGULATORY AND RELATIONAL CONTRACT LAW

A fundamental critique of orthodox contract law uses empirical research which suggests that law is, generally speaking, remote from deal-making in the real world – remote to the point of irrelevance.[4] The leading scholar of socio-legal contract studies, Stewart Macaulay, accordingly identifies a large gap between 'the real and the paper deal'.[5] The 'paper deal' (the written contract) tends to consist of clear, formal rules which are straightforward to enforce. But these rules are very different from the 'real deal' which actually governs the transaction. The *relationship* between the parties is key here.[6]

As Tom Palay puts it, 'parties who have, or anticipate, strong relational ties with their contracting opposites are not particularly worried about initial terms of agreement'.[7] They expect to work out any problems co-operatively as they arise, rather than standing on the letter of their contractual rights as contained in the document.[8] Economists such as Oliver Williamson and 'relational contract' theorists led by Ian Macneil have stressed the central importance of trust, co-operation and long-term relationships in commerce.[9] David Campbell comments that co-operative norms are dominant even in commercial situations – not through generosity but out of 'deep economic self-interest'.[10] Such concepts are more familiar to the family lawyer than the traditional contract lawyer, and indeed

---

[4] See, seminally, S. Macaulay, 'Non-Contractual Relations in Business: A Preliminary Study' (1963) 28 *American Sociological Rev* 1. Cf. also H. Beale & T. Dugdale, 'Contracts between Businessmen: Planning and the Use of Contractual Remedies' (1975) 2 *BJL&S* 45; R. Lewis, 'Contracts between Businessmen: Reform of the Law of Firm Offers and an Empirical Study of Tendering Practice in the Building Industry' (1982) 9 *BJL&S* 153.

[5] S. Macaulay, 'The Real and the Paper Deal: Empirical Pictures of Relationships, Complexity and the Urge for Transparent Simple Rules' (2003) 66 *MLR* 44.

[6] See, generally, H. Collins, *Regulating Contracts* (Oxford University Press, 1999) pp. 128–36.

[7] T.M. Palay, 'A Contract Does Not a Contract Make' [1985] *Wisconsin LR* 561, 562.

[8] Cf. Macaulay (2003) 66 *MLR* 44, 46 n.6.

[9] O.E. Williamson, *The Economic Institutions of Capitalism: Firms, Markets, Relational Contracting* (New York: Free Press, 1985); D. Campbell (ed.) & I.R. Macneil, *The Relational Theory of Contract: Selected Works of Ian Macneil* (Sweet & Maxwell, 2001).

[10] D. Campbell, 'Macneil and the Relational Theory' in Campbell & Macneil, ibid.

Robert Gordon rather earthily observes that contract is more like marriage than a one-night stand![11] Marriages, obviously enough, could not hope to be governed successfully by the terms of a formal contract executed at the time of the wedding.[12] But on this critical account, neither can a healthy commercial relationship.

In sum, as Macaulay says: 'Contracts are always more than the contract document'.[13] According to Gordon, they inhabit separate 'moral universes'.[14] It is accordingly mistaken for courts to enforce strictly the terms of the document. It will surely defeat the parties' reasonable expectations of trust and co-operation. Hugh Collins similarly argues that the courts should not limit themselves to the traditional 'contract law perspective', which sees 'absolute undertakings, firm commitments' and is marked not by collaboration but the 'demand for entitlements without compromise'.[15] If the law is to do its job of supporting commerce, it should enforce the implicit dimension of trust in every contractual relationship.[16]

To some extent, this has been achieved in the US through the Uniform Commercial Code. Legal Realist academic Karl Llewellyn was in charge of drafting and it reflects his belief that commercial law should employ flexible standards rather than rigid rules, absorbing and applying trade usages to give content to those standards.[17] But Collins's work suggests that far-reaching changes would be needed to produce similar results in England. Generally, he warns the courts not to be 'mesmerized' by the terms of the formal written contract.[18] So, should unexpected change of circumstances occur, courts should establish and apply business norms and the parties' expectations, rather than just 'referee the quality of the lawyers' (i.e. the drafters). If there is a discrepancy between written contract and reasonable expectations, courts 'should then not hesitate to engage in suitable measures of judicial revision of the planning documents'.[19] More generally, in long-term contracts 'the duty to co-operate should supplement *and even override* express terms of the contract, in order to provide legal support for wealth-maximizing potential for this type of transaction'.[20] Not surprisingly, Collins is dismissive of 'entire agreement clauses',[21] stating that they should be treated 'with scepticism' when the written terms diverge from the parties' actual (oral) discussions.[22]

---

[11] R. Gordon, 'Macaulay, Macneil, and the Discovery of Solidarity and Power in Contract Law' [1985] *Wisconsin LR* 565.

[12] Cf. R. Scott & E. Scott 'Marriage as Relational Contract' (1998) 84 *Virginia LR* 1225.

[13] (2003) 66 MLR 44, 45.

[14] Gordon, n.11 above, 572.

[15] Collins, n.6 above, pp. 132–35.

[16] H. Collins, 'The Research Agenda' in D. Campbell, H. Collins & J. Wightman, *Implicit Dimensions of Contract* (Hart Publishing, 2003).

[17] Cf. Z.B. Wiseman, 'The Limits of Vision: Karl Llewellyn and the Merchant Rules' (1987) 100 *Harvard LR* 465.

[18] Collins, *Regulating Contracts*, n.6 above, p. 173.

[19] Collins, *Regulating Contracts*, p. 165.

[20] Collins, *Regulating Contracts*, pp. 171–72 (emphasis added).

[21] Cf. pp. 79–84 below.

[22] Collins, *Regulating Contracts*, p. 159.

In short, Collins calls for the gap between the 'real and paper deals' to be closed. The formal contract perspective should take on board the actual expectations of the parties. Indeed, those actual expectations are to be privileged over the terms of the written contract. If it defeats the reasonable expectations of the parties, they should prevail over the drafter's words.

Of course, the protection of party expectations is a truism of contract law.[23] However, it seems unlikely that the courts would go as far as Collins recommends, ignoring the written contract as a kind of legal fiction to uphold 'reasonable expectations'. There is the obvious problem of freedom of contract: the parties (and not the courts) make agreements. But in this context at least, this seems a circular argument with which to respond to Collins. His central point is that the implicit dimensions of the commercial relationship represent the true agreement between the parties – the document does not, and so need not be treated with the respect properly due to party autonomy. Further responses to the Collins school of relational/regulatory contract law are available. First, that it is beyond the capacity of the courts. Secondly, that it may be actively harmful to the very trust and co-operation that Collins would seek to promote.

IN DEFENCE OF FORMALISM

Macaulay admits that we cannot have our cake and eat it: there are costs in focusing on the real deal as there are for strict enforcement of the contract document.[24] One obvious loss would be the predictable enforcement of contracts according to their terms. When English contract law traditionally places such high value on certainty and predictability, this must be counted a significant cost of taking a more realistic, relational approach.

Others criticize the demands that it would place upon courts if they had to identify and enforce implicit understandings rather than written contract terms. Enforcing written contracts is relatively straightforward, whereas Collins's contextual, regulatory approach would tax even a superhuman judge 'made up of Oliver Williamson, Max Weber, Ronald Dworkin's Hercules and Sir Humphrey Appleby'![25]

The most wide-ranging reaction to the calls for relational contract law is the so-called 'neo-formalist' school. In an important article, Alan Schwartz and Robert Scott emphasize the limits of judicial capacity to uncover and enforce implicit norms between contracting parties, or indeed to design economically efficient 'default rules' to supplement the contract terms.[26] Moreover, Scott argues that even if this were possible, it would be undesirable.[27] One cannot *force* contract-

---

[23] Cf. Lord Steyn, 'Contract Law: Fulfilling the Reasonable Expectations of Honest Men' (1997) 113 *LQR* 433.

[24] (2003) 66 *MLR* 44, 45.

[25] J. Gava & J. Greene, 'Do We Need a Hybrid Law of Contract? Why Hugh Collins Is Wrong and Why It Matters' [2004] *CLJ* 605, 620.

[26] A. Schwartz and R.E. Scott, 'Contract Theory and the Limits of Contract Law' (2003) 113 *Yale LJ* 541.

[27] R.E. Scott, 'The Death of Contract Law' (2004) 54 *University of Toronto LJ* 369.

ing parties to trust each other, and attempting this might be damaging as well as futile. Compelled 'trust' is only a simulation of the real thing; it may also corrode it, 'crowding out' true trust and co-operation.[28] The conclusion to be drawn from such arguments is that traditional, rule-based contract law may be the most effective after all. Hence neo-formalism, as a reaction to contextualism.

Interestingly, something strikingly similar to Macaulay's metaphor was used in argument in a recent 'battle of the forms' case.[29] But the court was unmoved by the suggestion that the objective approach to formation should be discarded.[30] Counsel submitted that there were 'in effect two parallel universes', and only in the artificial 'universe' of contract law were there 'battling terms' causing an obstacle for agreement. The problem arose 'only when the lawyers came on the scene' at which point 'the parties were transposed to an artificial world where reliance was placed on standard terms'. In the real world, neither had read the other's standard terms, and so neither set of terms was incorporated into the contract. Christopher Clarke J, however, decided the case using ordinary objective principles; the 'real world' perspective was given short shrift. English law, at least for the moment, remains committed to a formal, objective approach to formation of contracts.

RESOLVING THE DEBATE THROUGH EMPIRICAL RESEARCH?

How are we to choose between the relational/contextual and the neo-formalist approaches? Each camp is in effect making the claim that this is what contract law should look like – and is what contracting parties want. These claims should, in principle, be capable of proof by empirical evidence. But such evidence about what happens in the real world, and what parties really do want from the law of contract, seems thin on the ground. Therefore, each side in this debate should proceed cautiously: Avery Katz notes that the limited information stressed by the neo-formalist account of contract applies equally to neo-formalism itself.[31]

Nevertheless, some empirical research has been done, and may be adduced for both sides of the debate. For 'contextualism' there are many studies showing that people doing business together rely much more on 'social norms' of trust and co-operation than they do upon the clear rules of formal contract law.[32] By contrast, the research of Lisa Bernstein favours neo-formalism. Bernstein shows that the cotton trade, for example, has contracted out of publicly available US contract law with its emphasis on flexible contextual standards. Instead, disputes are resolved by arbitrators applying the rules of the cotton trade association – and these rules (and the arbitrators' approach to them) are considerably stricter

---

[28] Cf. B. Frey & R. Jegen, 'Motivation Crowding Theory: A Survey of Empirical Evidence' (2001) 15 *Journal of Economic Surveys* 589.

[29] *Balmoral Group Ltd v Borealis (UK) Ltd* [2006] EWHC 1900 (Comm).

[30] Cf. pp. 14–20 above.

[31] A.W. Katz, 'The Economics of Form and Substance in Contract Interpretation' (2004) 104 *Columbia LR* 496, 505–6.

[32] Cf. n.4 above.

and more formal than those of the Uniform Commercial Code.[33] Bernstein's hypothesis is that at the end of a commercial relationship, parties prefer clear-cut 'end game norms' to resolve their disputes quickly and effectively; these rules are quite different from the 'relationship preserving norms' that prevail during the currency of the deal.[34]

This is direct evidence for 'what parties want' from one sector of commerce. However, Macaulay doubts whether it is possible to come up with a theory applicable to all kinds of contracts without a great deal of oversimplification.[35] He accepts that in specific industries, parties may withdraw from the publicly available law through arbitration. But this may be to take advantage of the trade knowledge of an expert arbitrator, to facilitate the contextual approach, as much as to opt for formalism.[36] Macaulay argues that while a case may be made for formal contract law, we must face up to its costs. Parties' reasonable expectations will inevitably be defeated. There is a legitimacy problem if 'contract rests on manipulations of forms and courts reject the substance of the real deal of the parties'.[37] Such costs have to be balanced against the advantages of greater efficiency and lower prices for goods and services.

It seems that more research needs to be done (which is the academic's typical response to every legal problem!). But even then, can the trade-off between costs and benefits identified by Macaulay ever be resolved?

CONCLUSION

This debate seems as insoluble as it is important. It has ramifications right across contract law. Collins describes a fissure in contract scholarship, between those who emphasize the certainty of literal interpretations of express terms, and those who accept the importance (the inevitability) of taking the implicit dimensions of contracts into account.[38] The positions have little common ground. Yet clear victory for either side in the debate seems a long way off and either synthesis or compromise impossible.

Is it possible to avoid these treacherous controversies? Can the parties themselves make the choice between contextual and formal approaches, according priority to either the real or the paper deal? There is no good reason (except, perhaps, the doctrine of certainty) why the parties should not expressly incorporate broad and flexible norms into their contracts. Although the House of Lords has refused to imply a duty to negotiate in good faith on the grounds that this lacked sufficient

---

[33] Lisa Bernstein 'Private Commercial Law in the Cotton Industry: Creating Cooperation Through Rules, Norms, and Institutions' (2001) 99 *Michigan LR* 1724.

[34] Cf. Lisa Berstein 'Merchant Law in a Merchant Court: Rethinking the Code's Search for Immanent Business Norms' (1996) 144 *Univ Pennsylvania LR* 1765.

[35] (2003) 66 MLR 44, 45 n.3.

[36] Ibid, p. 51 n.25.

[37] Ibid, p. 79.

[38] Collins, 'The Research Agenda', n.16 above.

certainty,[39] the Court of Appeal has indicated that an *express* good faith clause may well be given effect.[40] It is possible (although apparently very uncommon in practice) to empower arbitrators to decide according to broad notions of 'equity and good conscience'.[41] Thus can the hard edges of the formal document – and formal doctrine – be softened, should the parties wish it, although we may question how frequently they do.

It is a fallacy to assume that the converse position obtains automatically by the same logic. A formalist tribunal wedded to the signature rule and standard form contracts will have to give effect to an 'equity and good conscience' clause as best it can; respect for the document requires it. But can a contextualist tribunal be forced to accord sanctity to a document by a clause declaring that it is the entire agreement between the parties – or that the contract is to be interpreted strictly according to its letter? Catherine Mitchell argues that courts should give effect to such clauses. Parties may have very good reason to prefer formalist approaches; why should they not be able to contract out of contextualism?[42] But the argument approaches circularity. If a signed standard form is (at least presumptively) not a true reflection of the parties' real expectations, then how can a clause in the signed standard form *of itself* exclude the recognition of those expectations? In Macaulay's terminology, an entire agreement clause in the 'paper deal' does not make it any less subversive of the 'real deal'. If anything it increases the divergence. It is hardly surprising that Collins expresses scepticism of entire agreement clauses.[43] Contextualists will not readily accept that parties have agreed to exclude contextualism when the supposed 'agreement' is a standard form.

Therefore, it seems that the Debate remains intractable, and cannot necessarily be avoided by careful contract drafting. One possible compromise would be for the courts to use formalism as the default approach, combined with a willing acceptance of party-designated relational standards where appropriate. If, as suggested, it is easier to contract out of formalism than it is out of contextualism, then this approach maximizes freedom of contract, whereas it seems difficult for parties that really do want to prioritize the written terms over unwritten understandings to do so, if the court is determinedly contextualist in its outlook.

If the contextualist/relational perspective is indeed the better one for understanding contracts, this stands as a radical critique of the existing English law on written contracts that we consider in Debate 2. Alternatively, it may be said that the current law provides considerable support to the neo-formalist position.

---

[39] *Walford v Miles* [1992] 2 AC 128.

[40] *Petromec v Petroleo Brasileiro* [2006] 1 Lloyd's Rep 161. See E. Peel, 'Agreements to Negotiate in Good Faith' in A. Burrows and E. Peel (eds), *Contract Formation and Parties* (Oxford University Press, 2010).

[41] M.J. Mustill and S.C. Boyd, *The Law and Practice of Commercial Arbitration in England* (Butterworths, 2nd edn, 1989) pp. 75–76.

[42] C. Mitchell, 'Entire Agreement Clauses: Contracting Out of Contextualism' (2006) 22 *JCL* 222.

[43] Cf. n.22 above.

Debate 2

Does the law over-privilege documents?

THE SIGNATURE RULE

As stated in the leading case of *L'Estrange v F Graucob Ltd*, 'Where a document containing contractual terms is signed, ... the party signing it is bound, and it is wholly immaterial whether he has read the document or not'.[44] It is not necessary to show that reasonable notice has been given of the terms therein to incorporate them into the contract.[45] That requirement may prove exacting: the degree of notice required increases with the unusual or onerous nature of the terms.[46] Thus, the signature, or its electronic equivalent,[47] is of enormous importance for excluding the notice requirement. But whether this is a matter for condemnation or praise has sharply divided courts and commentators.

J.R. Spencer is the leading critic of *L'Estrange*.[48] He views the outcome of the case itself as harsh (Miss L'Estrange was held bound by a wide exclusion of liability – a vending machine she had bought from Graucob Ltd for her café did not work).[49] Spencer identifies a fundamental flaw in legal analysis. Not only was there no actual 'subjective' agreement to the exclusion clause by Miss L'Estrange, but on the correct approach there was no objective agreement either.[50] The point of the objective approach is to protect reasonable reliance on the appearance of assent. As Lord Diplock once put it, the test is 'impersonal': what a reasonable person in the position of the promisee would have understood by what the promisor said and did.[51] But there are well-known exceptions to the principle: where the promisee actually knows, or should have known, that the promisor was not actually assenting, there is no agreement on those terms.[52] There is simply no reliance on outward appearances to protect, when the other party knows the truth (or should have done). Also, if the promisee is responsible for an erroneous signification of assent, he cannot rely on it to hold the promisor bound.[53]

These exceptions should govern *L'Estrange*, according to Spencer. Arguably, Graucob had induced Miss L'Estrange's ignorance of the exclusion clause by printing it in small print on brown paper, on the back of a poorly laid-out form. But in any event, Graucob must have realized that she did not assent to the term: 'Who

[44] [1934] 2 KB 394, 403 per Scrutton LJ.
[45] Cf. *Parker v SE Railway Co* (1877) 2 CPD 416.
[46] *Interfoto v Stiletto* [1989] 1 QB 433.
[47] Cf. E. Macdonald, 'Incorporation of Standard Terms in Website Contracting – Clicking "I agree"' (2011) 27 *JCL* 198.
[48] J.R. Spencer, 'Signature, Consent and the Rule in *L'Estrange v. Graucob*' [1973] *CLJ* 104.
[49] Spencer endorses the contemporary criticism that *L'Estrange* was 'a menace to the community': P. A. Landon (1935) 51 *LQR* 272.
[50] Cf. pp. 1–7 above.
[51] *Ashington Piggeries v Christopher Hill* [1972] AC 441, 502.
[52] *Hartog v Colin & Shields* [1939] 3 All ER 566.
[53] *Scriven v Hindley* [1913] 3 KB 564.

in their right mind would sign a document headed "I agree to pay for your goods even if they are useless…"?'[54] The parties might appear to be in agreement to an entirely detached observer, the 'reasonable fly on the wall'. But such a theory of detached objectivity is mistaken.[55] Thus for Spencer, *L'Estrange* is to be 'attacked on the ground that it contradicts the settled theory of agreement which underlies the law of contract generally'.

Matthew Chapman broadly agrees with Spencer.[56] *L'Estrange* is a harsh decision that stifles inquiry into the reality of agreement – 'the theoretical premises upon which contract law itself is based'.[57] It is used by powerful bargainers to impose their terms. In this connexion, Chapman welcomes the European Directive on Unfair Terms in Consumer Contracts, which applies to terms that have not been individually negotiated.[58] He notes the presence in the 'greylist' of terms that may be deemed unfair the following provision: terms 'irrevocably binding the consumer to terms with which he had no real opportunity of becoming acquainted before the conclusion of the contract'.[59] Chapman expresses the hope that this provision might embolden the judges to reject *L'Estrange*.

However, Chapman wonders whether swatting the 'fly on the wall' is enough to see off the signature rule. Might not Graucob, like the notional fly, reasonably believe that Miss L'Estrange was assenting to the terms in the document that she signed, whatever they might be?[60] Asking what the party proffering the form knew, or should have known, about the signer's state of mind will frequently be difficult and elusive. Therefore Chapman suggests that it would be more straightforward to apply the ordinary requirement of notice of terms to signed documents in the same way as to unsigned ones. Information, he declares, gives moral content to consent, and consent is the moral component of agreement.[61]

These criticisms have born fruit in Canada. In *Tilden Rent-A-Car Co v Clendenning* the court reasoned that the objective principle only protects *reasonable* reliance on what the other party appears to be assenting to.[62] At least with consumer transactions that are 'invariably carried out in a hurried, informal manner', it would be quite *un*reasonable to suppose that the signature represented true assent to any unusual and onerous terms contained within the document. Thus reasonable notice must be given.

In dissent, Lacourcière J.A. approved 'the wisdom of the common law' embodied in the signature rule, and said that unfair consumer contracts would better be

[54] [1973] CLJ 104, 115.
[55] Spencer criticizes the 'ridiculous' implications of *Rose v Pim* [1953] 2 QB 450 and explains *Upton RDC v Powell* [1942] 1 All ER 220 as a case of unjust enrichment.
[56] Matthew Chapman, 'Common Law Contract and Consent: Signature and Objectivity' (1998) 49 *N Ir Legal Q* 363.
[57] Ibid, p. 377.
[58] Unfair Terms in Consumer Contracts Regulations 1999, reg 5(2).
[59] Ibid, sch 2(1)(i).
[60] Chapman cites J.C. Smith, *Smith and Thomas: A Casebook on Contract* (10th edn, 1996) p. 133.
[61] (1998) 49 N Ir Legal Q 363, 380.
[62] (1978) 83 DLR (3d) 400.

regulated directly by statute. The High Court of Australia has, similarly, re-affirmed *L'Estrange* as 'fundamental principle based on sound legal policy'.[63] The court noted the Australian legislation giving relief against unfair contracts: there was no reason to depart from the signature rule, and indeed every reason to apply it, in cases where the legislation was inapplicable (or not invoked).[64] It should be noted that the (English) Unfair Contract Terms Act 1977 has been the foundation for similar reasoning in a different context. The courts have accepted that there is no longer need to go through 'gymnastic contortions' when interpreting exclusion clauses, because UCTA provides a direct means of regulating them.[65] To the extent that the criticisms of *L'Estrange* have rested on its baleful effect on consumers, therefore, the advent of such statutory regulation will have blunted their force.[66] Elizabeth Macdonald has recently argued, however, that since there are some gaps in the statutory scheme,[67] a rule with such 'capacity for unfairness' should not be extended to the internet age, i.e. clicking a button on a website should not, for these purposes, be treated as a signature.[68] As yet, there is no authority on this issue.

As for the critique based on the consensual nature of contracting, this has cut little ice. The courts are very well aware of the likely absence of full, subjective assent behind a signature. This is plain from Scrutton LJ's statement that 'it is wholly immaterial whether [the signer] has read the document or not'. It was memorably underlined in a case where a ferry company had failed to obtain a customer's signature to their standard terms (as was their usual practice). Asking what difference this made, Lord Devlin said:

> If it were possible for your Lordships to escape from the world of make-believe, which the law has created, into the real world in which trans-actions of this sort are actually done, the answer would be short and simple. It should make no difference whatever. This sort of document is not meant to be read, still less to be understood. Its signature is in truth about as significant as a handshake that marks the formal conclusion of a bargain.[69]

But whatever the 'reality' of the matter, in law the absence of the signature did make all the difference. Just as the customer would be bound by the terms (of which he was wholly ignorant) if he had signed, so he was not be bound by them as he had not. But despite recognizing the 'make-believe' at the heart of the signature rule, Lord Devlin was not prepared to question *L'Estrange*.[70]

---

[63] *Toll Pty Ltd v Alphapharm Pty Ltd* (2004) 211 ALR 342, [54].
[64] Ibid, [48].
[65] *George Mitchell v Finney Lock Seeds* [1983] QB 284, 299 per Lord Denning MR. See pp. 101–103 below.
[66] Spencer wrote before UCTA and the Unfair Terms in Consumer Contracts Regulations.
[67] E.g. the protection of small business (as in *L'Estrange* itself).
[68] Macdonald, n.47 above.
[69] *McCutcheon v MacBrayne* [1964] 1 WLR 125, 133.
[70] Ibid, p. 134.

In the end, it may be that, as P.S. Atiyah says, 'the practical convenience of treating signed printed forms as binding on the parties is so great' that the law is willing to accept the violence that this does to principle.[71] Macaulay complains, however, that the rule 'turns contract law's claim to rest on choice into pure magic'.[72] Nevertheless, it been praised by Moore-Bick LJ as 'an important principle of English law which underpins the whole of commercial life; any erosion of it would have serious repercussions far beyond the business community'.[73] Although Atiyah stated that the law is far too ready to accept signatures as conclusive evidence,[74] elsewhere he admits that:

> A signature is, and is widely recognized even by the general public as being a formal device, and its value would be greatly reduced if it could not be treated as a conclusive ground of contractual liability at least in all ordinary circumstances.[75]

Most people recognize the legal significance of signing a document (even if they have no very precise idea what they are signing). They are taken to do so when they seek to plead '*non est factum*'.[76] Furthermore, if the matter is financially important enough then reading before signing, or even obtaining professional legal advice, may well become worthwhile. Moringiello states that the signature has 'alerting power' – signalling the need to read the terms.[77] In the end, it may not be entirely unreasonable to take a signature as assent to all of the terms in a document, whatever they may be. This is certainly the position in English law; its practical convenience cannot be doubted.

THE PAROL EVIDENCE RULE

Where the parties intend a document to be a complete and exhaustive statement of the terms of the contract between them, extrinsic evidence cannot be adduced 'to add to or subtract from, or in any manner to vary or qualify the written contract'.[78] This applies equally to oral or written evidence. Stephen Waddams has noted the confusion caused by the lack of an agreed formulation of the 'parol evidence rule'.[79] The 'scare quotes' here signify that there is probably no 'rule' strictly speaking since the exclusionary approach depends on *the intentions of the*

---

[71] P.S. Atiyah, 'Freedom of Contract and the New Right' in *Essays on Contract* (Oxford University Press, 1990).

[72] S. Macaulay, 'The Real and the Paper Deal: Empirical Pictures of Relationships, Complexity and the Urge for Transparent Simple Rules' (2003) 66 MLR 44, 47.

[73] *Peekay Intermark v Australia & New Zealand Banking Group* [2006] 2 Lloyd's Rep 511, [43].

[74] Atiyah, n.71 above.

[75] P.S. Atiyah, 'Form and Substance in Legal Reasoning: The Case of Contract' in N. MacCormick and P.B.H. Birks (eds), *The Legal Mind: Essays for Tony Honoré* (Clarendon Press, 1986) p. 34.

[76] Cf. *Gallie v Lee* [1970] AC 1004; pp. 173–174 below.

[77] J.M. Moringiello, 'Signals, Assent and Internet Contracting' (2005) 57 *Rutgers LR* 1307, 1313. For doubts whether this justifies applying *L'Estrange v Graucob* to 'click button' agreement on the internet, cf. Elizabeth Macdonald, 'Incorporation of Standard Terms in Website Contracting – Clicking "I agree"' (2011) 27 *JCL* 198.

[78] *Goss v Lord Nugent* (1833) 5 B & Ad 58, 64–65 (Denman CJ).

[79] S.M. Waddams, 'Do We Need a Parol Evidence Rule?' (1991) 19 *Can Bus LJ* 385.

parties and not on any rule of law.[80] It is not even limited to 'parol' (oral) evidence as such. Nevertheless, the terminology is traditional (and ineradicable), so we will use it with the necessary disclaimers. The definition of the parol evidence rule adopted here does not cause major controversy. But this section will serve to introduce some of the wider debates about the correct approach to the interpretation of contracts.

The Law Commission has dismissed the alleged 'rule' as no more than a circular statement, viz. when the parties intend a document to be an exhaustive statement of the contract between them, terms extrinsic to the document are irrelevant.[81] Robert Stevens describes the rule's 'irresistible logic'.[82] This is, in one sense, obviously true. But in consequence, the really important question becomes: what *are* the parties' intentions? Here, the parol evidence rule is not entirely pointless. It has 'bequeathed to the modern law a presumption – namely that a document which *looks* like a contract is to be treated as the *whole* contract'.[83] However, 'although when the parties arrive at a definite written contract the implication or presumption is very strong that such contract is intended to contain all the terms of their bargain, it is a presumption only'.[84] It remains possible for the parties to show additional obligations, collateral to the main written contract, or variations to its terms.[85] As the leading case teaches, however, courts must view alleged collateral contracts 'with suspicion' and insist upon clear proof of their existence: 'Any laxity ... would have the effect of lessening the authority of written contracts'.[86]

It may be questioned whether Lord Moulton's warning has been sufficient to protect 'the authority of written contracts'.[87] Evidence to the contrary comes from the wide usage of 'entire agreement clauses'. These are frequently found in written commercial contracts, as in the typical formulation: 'The parties acknowledge that this Agreement constitutes the entire Agreement between the parties'. Their effect will be considered fully in the next section. Lightman J says:

> The purpose of an entire agreement clause is to preclude a party to a written agreement from threshing through the undergrowth and finding in the course of negotiations some (chance) remark or statement (often long forgotten or difficult to recall or explain) on which to found a claim such as the present to the existence of a collateral warranty. The entire agreement clause obviates the occasion for any such search and the peril to

---

[80] Law Com Report No 154, 'Law of Contract: The Parol Evidence Rule' (1986) 2.17.

[81] Law Com Report No 154, 2.7.

[82] Robert Stevens, 'Objectivity, Mistake and the Parol Evidence Rule' in A. Burrows and E. Peel (eds), *Contract Terms* (Oxford University Press, 2007).

[83] K.W. Wedderburn, 'Collateral Contracts' [1959] *CLJ* 58, 62.

[84] *Gillespie Bros & Co v Cheney, Eggar & Co* [1896] 2 QB 59, 62 (Lord Russell CJ).

[85] Eg *Evans & Son v Merzario Ltd* [1976] 2 All ER 930.

[86] *Heilbut, Symonds & Co v Buckleton* [1913] AC 30, 47, per Lord Moulton.

[87] Lord Denning MR admitted that before *Hedley Byrne v Heller* [1964] AC 465, the courts invariably treated innocent misrepresentations as collateral warranties to give a remedy in damages: *Esso Petroleum v Mardon* [1976] QB 801, 817.

> the contracting parties posed by the need which may arise in its absence to conduct such a search ... The operation of the clause is ... to denude what would otherwise constitute a collateral warranty of legal effect ... [It] provides in law a complete answer to any claim ... based on the alleged collateral warranty.[88]

Peden and Carter comment that the presence of an entire agreement clause dispenses with the need to search for an implied or inferred intention to treat the written contract as exclusive source of the parties' obligations: it proves that the document was adopted with that intention. The routine use of such clauses 'reflects the general commercial understanding that a negotiated document is executed with the object of crystallising the bargain and superseding all prior negotiations. In other words, the entire agreement clause is intended to underline the fact that the document *is* the contract.'[89]

Thus, as the parol evidence 'rule' has softened into, at best, a presumption, commercial draftsmen have reacted to re-affirm that rule through entire agreement clauses. As McKendrick says, this does suggest that watering down the parol evidence rule in the first place 'might not necessarily have been a desirable development'.[90] Commercial practice seems to desire a very high degree of documentary security. We consider in the next section the extent to which these entire agreement clauses should be given legal effect.

ENTIRE AGREEMENT CLAUSES

The debate over entire agreement clauses (EACs) is complicated by the fact that there is a 'smorgasbord of variously worded provisions'.[91] Some have quite well understood standard names (e.g. 'non-reliance clauses') but these are not terms of art, and we must accordingly examine the substance rather than the nomenclature, in assessing whether the courts ought to enforce them. The common feature is that all of the clauses are included in written contracts to preserve their 'authority', by seeking to exclude obligations derived from outside the document.

The simple entire agreement clause declares that the document is an exhaustive definition of the contract between the parties. Thus, as seen above, it may be seen as a deliberate invocation of the parol evidence rule. The courts have accepted that the inclusion of such a clause excludes the finding of collateral contractual obligations.[92] Some commentators dissent. Gerard McMeel complains that this is to 'resuscitate the now discredited parol evidence rule'.[93] But the

---

[88] *Inntrepreneur v East Crown Ltd* [2000] 2 Lloyd's Rep. 611, [7]–[8].

[89] E. Peden & J.W. Carter, 'Entire Agreement – and Similar – Clauses' (2006) 22 *JCL* 1.

[90] E. McKendrick, *Contract Law: Text, Cases and Materials* (Oxford University Press, 2nd edn, 2004) p. 340.

[91] *Lee Chee Wei v Tan Hor Peow Victor* [2007] 3 SLR 537, [25] (Rajah JA).

[92] *Inntrepreneur v East Crown Ltd* [2000] 2 Lloyd's Rep 611.

[93] G. McMeel, 'Prior Negotiations and Subsequent Conduct –The Next Step Forward for Contractual Interpretation' (2003) 119 *LQR* 272 at n 97.

criticism seems unconvincing. The whole *point* of these clauses is to affirm (or 'resuscitate') the parol evidence rule. Moreover, the 'rule' cannot be dismissed so readily when it has recently been described as 'fundamental to the mercantile law of this country' by Lord Hobhouse.[94] As stated in *Phipson on Evidence*, there is considerable advantage to the parties in having the document as 'a full and final statement of their intentions ... beyond the reach of future controversy, bad faith or treacherous memory'.[95] Finally, from the straightforward freedom of contract perspective, enforcing EACs makes 'eminent sense', especially in the commercial context.[96] The parties have chosen, by inserting an EAC in the final contract, to make any collateral agreements unenforceable; it is 'elementary' to give effect to this choice.[97]

A much debated variant is the 'non-reliance clause'. After it was ruled that a simple EAC did not exclude liability for misrepresentation (as opposed to nullifying statements with *contractual* effect, i.e. collateral warranties),[98] drafters began to include clauses declaring that neither party had 'relied on' statements made by the other in agreeing to enter into the contract. Since reliance upon the statement is essential, should the courts give effect to such non-reliance clauses misrepresentation logically cannot be made out. Jacob J insisted that one who seeks to evade liability for 'falsehoods' 'cannot be mealy-mouthed in his clause' – the limitation of liability must be brought home to the other side.[99] However, non-reliance clauses have generally been successful in barring misrepresentation claims. Debate has centred on the basis of their effectiveness and the applicability of unfair terms legislation.

Section 3 of the Misrepresentation Act 1967 requires those who would 'exclude or restrict' liability or remedies for misrepresentation to prove this 'reasonable'.[100] But it has been argued that non-reliance clauses do not *exclude* liability – rather, they prevent it from arising in the first place. This approach accords with Brian Coote's general critique of exclusion clause regulation.[101] Coote identified a fallacy going to the heart of the law's approach. He argued that all so-called 'exclusion clauses' are simply *defining* liability, determining the obligations assumed under the contract in the first place. 'Instead of being mere shields to claims based on breach of accrued rights, exception clauses substantially delimit the rights themselves.'

There is, on this argument, no stable distinction between 'exclusions' and any other clauses in the contract.

---

[94] *Shogun Finance v Hudson* [2004] 1 AC 919, [49].

[95] M.N. Howard (ed.), *Phipson on Evidence* (Sweet & Maxwell,15th edn, 2000) pp. 1165–66 (quoted ibid).

[96] *Lee Chee Wei v Tan Hor Peow Victor* [2007] 3 SLR 537, [27].

[97] *SERE Holdings v Volkswagen* [2004] EWHC 1551 (Ch), [22] (Nugee QC).

[98] *Alman and Benson v Associated Newspapers Group Ltd* (1980, unreported).

[99] *Thomas Witter v TBP Industries* [1996] 2 All ER 573, 596. See further *Axa Sun Life Services plc v Campbell Martin Ltd* [2011] EWCA Civ 133, [80]–[81], [94].

[100] Cf. UCTA, s.11(1).

[101] B. Coote, *Exception Clauses* (Sweet & Maxwell, 1964).

> Sophie employs a party planner, Olivia, to organize a lavish party. Sophie is very keen to have ageing boy band *Take That* as the star attraction, but Olivia fears that this may be difficult. The contract is drafted with the following term: 'Olivia shall make all reasonable efforts to secure *Take That's* performance but if they are unavailable she will engage a professional *Take That* tribute act.'

Looked at from one perspective, Olivia is excluding potential liability to a disappointed Sophie if *Take That* are unavailable (provided a tribute band appears).[102] But viewed differently, Olivia never guaranteed *Take That's* appearance. The only obligation that she assumed (or was willing to assume) was a duty of care ('reasonable efforts') rather than an absolute duty. There was never any stricter liability there to exclude.

Tony Weir gives qualified approval to Coote's thesis.[103] Weir agrees that refusing to assume a contractual obligation does not entail the avoidance of a duty. Thus, there is no 'exclusion' of liability in the example of Sophie and Olivia. Accordingly, we could question the wisdom of provisions such as UCTA 1977, s.3, which strike at the exclusion of contractual liabilities. If one is not under a duty to contract on particular terms (or indeed, of course, to contract at all) in the first place, then how can refusing to assume particular contractual liabilities sensibly be deemed an 'exclusion'? But Weir argues that Coote runs into difficulties when a clause seeks to avoid a tortious duty. Such liability is imposed by law, independent of the terms of the contract. Thus, it is hard to accept that the contract is *in these cases* merely creating – and defining the limits of – the parties' obligations. It is indeed excluding liabilities that would otherwise be there. This distinction sees provisions such as UCTA, s.2 (exclusion of liability for negligence) on much safer ground. The same goes for s.3 of the Misrepresentation Act 1967, since misrepresentation liability arises by operation of law.

Nevertheless, the argument that 'non-reliance' clauses prevent and do not exclude misrepresentation liability was accepted by Chadwick LJ in *Watford Electronics v Sanderson*, who commented that it would be 'bizarre' to say that the parties intended 'to exclude a liability which they must have thought could never arise'.[104] But later courts have not followed this analysis. Christopher Clarke J contrasts 'sophisticated commercial parties' who should be entitled to define which statements made in negotiations have been relied upon, and 'the man in the street': 'to tell [him] that the car you are selling him is perfect and then agree that the basis of your contract is that no representations have been

---

[102] The clause might fall foul of UCTA, s.3(2)(b)(i), if it allows for performance different from that reasonably expected.
[103] J.A. Weir [1965] CLJ 801.
[104] [2001] 1 All ER Comm 696, [41].

made or relied on, may be nothing more than an attempt retrospectively to alter the character and effect of what has gone before, and in substance an attempt to exclude or restrict liability'.[105] Alexander Trukhtanov also advocates such a distinction, since only consumers require protection.[106] Presumably Chadwick LJ might also find this acceptable, since *Watford Electronics* was a commercial case, and he was impressed by the usefulness of non-reliance clauses in the commercial context (by promoting certainty and allocating risks efficiently).[107] Christopher Clarke J thought it 'obviously advantageous that commercial parties of equal bargaining power should be able to agree what responsibility they are taking (or not taking) towards each other without having to satisfy some reasonableness test'.[108]

On the other hand, the Misrepresentation Act 1967 does not draw a distinction between business and consumer contracts so it is difficult to see how s.3 might apply only to consumer non-reliance clauses. It is hard to believe that non-reliance clauses alter their juridical basis with the context, however pragmatically desirable this might be. The Court of Appeal has now accepted that s.3 applies to non-reliance clauses even in commercial contracts. While Stanley Burnton LJ approved the 'logic' behind the submission that such clauses prevent misrepresentation liability from arising in the first place rather than excluding it, he held it was 'too formalistic'.[109] To the extent that this result is commercially undesirable, the blame lies with the undifferentiated scope of the Misrepresentation Act. Note that s.3 confers considerable power on trial courts – appellate courts can intervene only when the judge has proceeded on an erroneous basis or was plainly wrong.[110] The Court of Appeal recently refused to correct the judge's disapproval of an EAC that they thought was perfectly fair given the 'commercial autonomy' of the parties.[111]

It has been suggested that EACs may have a more far-reaching effect on the courts' approach to written contracts, by controlling the principles of interpretation.[112] As will be seen in the next chapter, there has been a decisive shift towards purposive, contextual interpretation in recent years. Might not parties who wish for a more traditional, 'strict' textual approach include clauses in their contracts to that effect? Scott cites a contract which requires the parties' obligations 'to be determined from [its] precise and literal language', not by 'additional duties of

---

[105] *Raiffeisen Zentralbank Osterreich AG v The Royal Bank of Scotland plc* [2011] 1 Lloyd's Rep 123, [314]–[315].

[106] Alexander Trukhtanov, 'Misrepresentation: Acknowledgement of Non-Reliance as a Defence' (2009) 125 LQR 648.

[107] n. 104, [39].

[108] [2011] 1 Lloyd's Rep 123, [313].

[109] *Axa Sun Life Services plc v Campbell Martin Ltd* [2011] EWCA Civ 133, [51]. See further *Trident Turboprop (Dublin) Ltd v First Flight Couriers Ltd* [2008] EWHC 1686 (Comm); *Springwell Navigation Corp v JP Morgan Chase Bank* [2010] EWCA Civ 1221 [181]–[182].

[110] *George Mitchell v Finney Lock Seeds* [1983] 2 AC 803.

[111] *Cleaver v Schyde Investment Ltd* [2011] EWCA Civ 929.

[112] Mitchell, n.42 above.

good faith, fair dealing or fiduciary obligation'.[113] Again, this may be seen as a commercial reaction to changes in the law, intended to protect the authority of the contractual documents. Consideration of this wider effect of EACs, and the desirability of giving effect to it, must be postponed until we have discussed the principles of interpretation themselves.[114]

In conclusion, English law does give effect, in principle, to EACs. In their various forms they will, if properly drafted, be apt to uphold the formal contractual document as the exhaustive source of obligations. On the other hand, the statutory controls will generally apply. Therefore, an EAC's 'reasonableness' will have to be demonstrated. While this will often be easy in contracts between commercial parties of roughly equal bargaining skill, the need to satisfy the statutory controls does tend to undermine the certainty that the clauses are intended to ensure. The ability to raise a statutory defence complicates and lengthens litigation, seriously compromising the enforceability of the contract.[115]

STANDARD FORMS: VIRTUE OR VICE?

Finally, we return to the general question of standard forms. They have often been criticized as 'contracts of adhesion' used to impose unfair terms on weaker parties. Moreover, as seen in Debate 1, it is said that standard forms routinely defeat the reasonable expectations of the parties. The 'real deal' lies elsewhere. But against these points, the usefulness of the standard form should be pointed out, especially but not only in the commercial context. It may be that rather than rejecting the standard form altogether, as a pale imitation of true contractual accord, we should accept its utility while guarding against its abuse.

Ross Cranston emphasizes the importance of industry-wide standard forms for the development of commodity trading.[116] For example, the London Corn Trade Association was founded in 1878 partly to provide standard contract terms for its members. Standardization reduces the costs of doing business, as Lord Diplock has explained.[117] First, if the 'small print' is standardized it makes price comparison much easier. Secondly, where standard forms are used over long periods of time, they become the subject of exposition by the courts. Lord Diplock referred to the charterparty: 'Its form and nearly all the phrases used in it have evolved over many years, in some cases running into centuries, in the course of which their meaning in the special context of this kind of contract has acquired legal certainty by judicial exegesis'. While charterparties were 'not notorious for stylistic elegance or easy intelligibility by those whose

---

[113] R.E. Scott, 'In (Partial) Defence of Strict Liability in Contract' in O. Ben-Shahar & A. Porat (eds), *Fault in American Contract Law* (Cambridge University Press, 2010).

[114] See pp. 89–106 below.

[115] Cf. *The Scaptrade* [1983] 1 QB 529.

[116] R. Cranston, 'The Rise and Rise of Standard Form Contracts: International Commodity Sales 1800–1970' in *Jan Hellner in Memoriam – Commercial Law Challenges in the 21st Century* (Stockholm Centre for Commercial Law, 2007).

[117] *The Maratha Envoy* [1978] AC 1, 13–14.

business does not lie in the freight market,' for the shipping trade certainty as to their meaning had been achieved by years of 'costly litigation'. The need for settled and certain interpretation of standard forms was Lord Diplock's central message.

Such standard forms may often provide a fair balance between the interests of the parties. The members of a commodity trade association will likely be both buyers and sellers, and so demand balanced standard forms. Michael Bridge refers to such trade forms as the result of 'private legislation'.[118] In the construction industry, the Joint Contracts Tribunal (JCT) has since 1870 contained representatives from the various constituencies (employers, builders etc.) in order to draft contracts acceptable to them all. These JCT forms are widely employed in practice. Where different standard terms are available, there will be a 'market for contracts' which should mean that more efficient form will be the most popular.[119] The House of Lords has accepted that a widely adopted standard form, 'moulded under the pressures of negotiation, competition and public opinion' was at least presumptively fair (i.e. did not fall foul of the common law doctrine against restraint of trade).[120] The common standard forms for mercantile transactions 'have been settled over the years by negotiation by representatives of the commercial interests involved and have been widely adopted because experience has shown that they facilitate the conduct of trade'; their wide usage raises a strong presumption that the terms are fair and reasonable.[121]

Therefore in the charterparty case Lord Diplock warned courts that they should not attempt to dictate the terms on which the shipping trade made its contracts. The fact that the contract might seem 'unwise ... or unlucky' was irrelevant:

> The only merits of the case are that parties who have bargained on equal terms in a free market should stick to their agreements. Justice is done by seeing that they do so or compensating the party who has kept his promise for any loss he has sustained by the failure of the other party to keep his.[122]

Bridge points out that trade associations can and do amend standard forms to deal with perceived abuses of their terms. Such quasi-legislative activity is prospective and effective, although possibly lacks the 'ethical tingle' of judicial intervention![123]

However, the courts have taken a very different view of standard form *consumer* contracts. Lord Diplock explained that where one party could impose terms on a take-it-or-leave-it basis on the other, there could be no presumption that the

---

[118] M. Bridge, 'Good Faith in Commercial Contracts' in R. Brownsword, N. Hird and G. Howells (eds), *Good Faith in Contract: Concept and Context* (Ashgate, 1999) p. 151.

[119] For doubts over whether such competition generally exists cf. Slawson, n.2 above.

[120] *Esso Petroleum Co Ltd v Harper's Garage (Stourport) Ltd* [1968] AC 269, 333 per Lord Wilberforce.

[121] *Schroeder Music Publishing Co v Macaulay* [1974] 1 WLR 1308, 1316 per Lord Diplock.

[122] *The Maratha Envoy* [1978] AC 1, 8.

[123] Bridge, n.118 above, p. 162.

terms were fair. On the contrary, there was a presumption of unconscionable conduct which 'calls for vigilance on the part of the court'.[124] Friedrich Kessler made the point long ago that such 'contracts of adhesion' were not based upon agreement/consent at all. Standard forms were the imposition of a new 'feudal order' drafted by commercial overlords; authoritarian control without its outward appearance.[125] Against this it is argued that so long as some consumers do read forms, firms will be obliged to moderate their terms to attract such consumers and this will benefit all consumers.[126] Nevertheless, it is now generally accepted that standard forms require some kind of legal control, in addition to this discipline of the market.

Todd Rakoff defends intervention on the simple ground that courts have a broader view of the public good than those drafting the contracts of adhesion.[127] Slawson even describes them as 'mass fraud' and a one-sided dictatorship; only to the extent that there is actual consent should contracts be enforceable. This would appear to be very limited: standard forms do not satisfy the principles either of mutual assent (the consumer doesn't read, or can't understand them) or the parties' expectations (which are influenced by advertising and other sales pitches, rather than the form).[128]

There are a number of problems with these arguments. First, it is entirely unrealistic to expect consumers actually to read the forms; as even Ian Macneil pointed out, if they attempted to do 'such a foolish thing' the modern economy would 'come to a screeching halt'.[129] Michael Trebilcock points out that 'take it or leave it' (a refusal to negotiate) is logically required for the – wholly benign – reduction in the cost of contracting which is the forms' principal rationale.[130] Thus, realistically, we must accept that forms are binding although unread, or scrap them entirely and replace with implied terms. Obviously the courts are not *parti pris* when implying terms. But is there ever an Archimedean point of absolute neutrality? It seems odd to discard the undoubted intentions of one (if only one) of the contracting parties and replace its terms with terms imposed by law. These are terms to which neither party has agreed! This really is 'take it or leave it' – businesses might well contract out of the public law of contract altogether if such a drastic stance were adopted.[131]

Moreover, although Rakoff takes a sanguine view of the courts' ability to supply the missing terms – little short of writing the entire contract for the

[124] *Schroeder Music Publishing Co v Macaulay* [1974] 1 WLR 1308.

[125] F. Kessler, 'Contracts of Adhesion – Some Thoughts about Freedom of Contract' (1943) 43 *Columbia LR* 629.

[126] A. Schwartz & L.L. Wilde, 'Intervening in Markets on the Basis of Imperfect Information: A Legal and Economic Analysis' (1979) 127 *Univ Pennsylvania LR* 630.

[127] T.D. Rakoff, 'Contracts of Adhesion: An Essay in Reconstruction' (1983) 96 *Harvard LR* 1174.

[128] W.D. Slawson, 'Mass Contracts: Lawful Fraud in California' (1974) 48 *Southern California LR* 1.

[129] I.R. Macneil, 'Bureaucracy and Contracts of Adhesion' (1984) 22 *Osgoode Hall LJ* 5, 6.

[130] M.J. Trebilcock, *The Limits of Freedom of Contract* (Harvard University Press, 1993) p.119.

[131] Cf. S. Macaulay, 'Freedom From Contract: Solutions in Search of a Problem?' [2004] *Wisconsin LR* 777.

parties, in his robust account[132] – this too may be challenged. As will be seen in the next chapter, it makes huge demands upon the courts' capacity to require them to imply terms so as to make contracts more efficient, or fairer or for any other policy reason.[133] To discard standard forms altogether would require such an approach writ large.

Characteristically, English law has settled for a compromise. Signed standard forms are prima facie enforceable even though they are 'not meant to be read, still less to be understood'.[134] On the other hand, there is legislative control – effectively, judicial review – of terms in standard form contracts. The Unfair Terms in Consumer Contracts Regulations 1999 (UTCCR) apply to terms that have 'not been individually negotiated';[135] UCTA applies even to business – business contracts when there is an exclusion clause in the 'written standard terms of business'.[136] This is regulation on a case-by-case (or term-by-term) approach, rather than outright rejection of standard forms. English law pragmatically recognizes that forms are literally indispensable in contractual planning, whatever violence they might do to contract law's theoretical foundation in assent.

Further Reading

Empirical and relational contract

S. Macaulay, 'Non-Contractual Relations in Business: A Preliminary Study' (1963) 28 *American Sociological Rev* 1.

H. Beale & T. Dugdale, 'Contracts between Businessmen: Planning and the Use of Contractual Remedies' (1975) 2 *BJL&S* 45.

R. Gordon, 'Macaulay, Macneil, and the Discovery of Solidarity and Power in Contract Law' [1985] *Wisconsin LR* 565.

H. Collins, *Regulating Contracts* (Oxford University Press, 1999).

S. Macaulay, 'The Real and the Paper Deal: Empirical Pictures of Relationships, Complexity and the Urge for Transparent Simple Rules' (2003) 66 *MLR* 44.

Neoformalism

L. Bernstein 'Private Commercial Law in the Cotton Industry: Creating Cooperation Through Rules, Norms, and Institutions' (2001) 99 *Michigan LR* 1724.

A. Schwartz & RE Scott, 'Contract Theory and the Limits of Contract Law' (2003) 113 *Yale LJ* 541.

J. Gava & J. Greene, 'Do We Need a Hybrid Law of Contract? Why Hugh Collins Is Wrong and Why It Matters' [2004] *CLJ* 605.

---

[132] See further T.D. Rakoff, 'Implied Terms: of "Default Rules" and "Situation Sense"' in J. Beatson and D. Friedmann (eds), *Good Faith and Fault in Contract Law* (Oxford University Press, 1995).

[133] Cf. pp. 111–119 below.

[134] *McCutcheon v MacBrayne* [1964] 1 WLR 125, 133.

[135] Reg 5(1).

[136] S. 3(1).

Standard form and written contracts

F. Kessler, 'Contracts of Adhesion – Some Thoughts about Freedom of Contract' (1943) 43 *Columbia LR* 629.

C. Mitchell, 'Entire Agreement Clauses: Contracting Out of Contextualism' (2006) 22 *JCL* 222.

4

CONTRACTUAL CONTENT: TERMS AND THEIR MEANING

INTRODUCTION

By far the most important question that contract lawyers face in legal practice is the meaning of the words in the contract. Courts spend considerable time resolving disputes about the correct interpretation of contracts. This has a mundane ring to it. Yet the subject is surprisingly controversial, and has been much debated in recent years, both in the courts and outside them. With its practical importance and topical theoretical interest, contract interpretation is the subject of Debate 1 in this chapter. Secondly, we examine the implication of terms. According to one influential (but still unorthodox) argument, implication 'in fact' is an extended version of interpretation rather than an entirely different process. This must be distinguished from terms implied 'by law' which is a sensitive area, clearly in conflict with the basic notion of obligations being assumed by the parties. The basis on which such terms should be implied is also, unsurprisingly, controversial.

Debate 1

How should contracts be interpreted?

The subject of contract interpretation ('construction') typically receives little attention in undergraduate contract courses. This is unfortunate. A Court of Appeal judge told a student audience that: 'For anyone who intends to practise commercial law, the interpretation of contracts is a topic of vital importance', whereas he declared that the subjects that he had learned as an undergraduate, such as formation, misrepresentation and privity, had barely featured since![1] Certainly, a high proportion of commercial contract cases are about interpreting the meaning of the terms.

---

[1] Sir Christopher Staughton, 'How Do the Courts Interpret Commercial Contracts?' [1999] *CLJ* 303.

This is not entirely surprising. Terms, and their interpretation, cover a surprising amount of 'contract law'. Contracting parties can with certain legal limits make provision for monetary payments, or cancelling the contract, in the event of breach (liquidated damages and termination clauses), for the impact of changed circumstances on the contract (hardship, price variation and *force majeure* clauses), and so forth. Stephen Smith comments that the rules on 'excuses' and even remedies can all be viewed as the contract's 'content', whether terms implied by law or agreed by the parties.[2]

Disputes are bound to arise about the meaning of even the most carefully drafted contract. Words are inevitably a fallible means of communication, shot through with ambiguity (are feathers 'light' in colour or weight?), and vagueness (precisely when is a ripening tomato 'red'?).[3] Furthermore, those who draft contracts cannot foresee every possible problem that may arise; or they might consciously decide not to raise awkward questions during negotiations, for fear of endangering the deal.[4] This leaves fertile ground for disputes later on. Drafting a watertight contract is near impossible:[5] it is worth quoting the words of Stephen J on the difficulty of the *parliamentary* draftsman's task: 'It is not enough to attain a degree of precision which a person reading in good faith can understand, but it is necessary to attain if possible to a degree of precision which a person reading in bad faith cannot misunderstand'.[6] When liability depends upon it, parties may do their best to 'misunderstand' the language of the contract. It is then necessary for the court to referee the 'true meaning'.

The one area in which every undergraduate typically encounters contractual construction is in the area of exclusion clauses. This is unfortunate. The rules are *atypical*, distorted by the judicial desire to control exclusion clauses prior to the unfair terms legislation. In fact, the courts' approach to these clauses has relaxed considerably, and will probably be assimilated with the approach to interpretation more generally. This will be considered below.

It is sensible to examine the general approach first. In recent years the courts have placed considerable emphasis on 'contextual' as opposed to 'literal' interpretation. Although generally welcomed, some judges and commentators have criticized the unpredictability of the new approach. A particular controversy over 'contextualism' is whether it is appropriate to examine the negotiations between the parties prior to the final agreement, to shed light upon the meaning of its terms. The House of Lords has reaffirmed the rule that this is inadmissible, pointing to the action for rectification as a way of easing any injustice that this might cause.[7] The extent to which rectification remains distinct from 'interpretation' is another matter considered further below.

---

[2] S.A. Smith, *Contract Theory* (Oxford University Press, 2004) p. 269.
[3] E.A. Farnsworth, '"Meaning" in the Law of Contracts' (1967) 76 *Yale LJ* 939.
[4] Ibid, p. 954.
[5] Cf. I.R. Macneil, 'A Primer of Contract Planning' (1975) 48 *Southern Calif L Rev* 627.
[6] *Re Castioni* [1891] 1 QB 149, 167.
[7] *Chartbrook Ltd v Persimmon Homes Ltd* [2009] 1 AC 1101.

THE MODERN APPROACH: CONTEXT AND PURPOSE

The first cardinal principle of contract interpretation today is that the words must be understood in their context. The second, related, cardinal principle is that the interpretation must advance the commercial sense and purpose of the contract (which is obviously a key feature of the 'context'). This is contrasted with 'narrow, literal' construction, which gives effect to words according to their 'dictionary' meanings, taking no account of what they are designed to achieve. It has been said that the 'history of the law of interpretation is the history of a progress from a stiff and superstitious formalism to a flexible rationalism'.[8] In this section we outline this approach and the leading authorities, along with some of the favourable commentary upon them. The next section will consider counter-arguments.

The leading authority is Lord Hoffmann's speech in *Investors Compensation Scheme v West Bromwich Building Society* (or '*ICS*').[9] Lord Hoffmann built on an important dictum of Lord Wilberforce deploring 'internal linguistic' interpretations 'isolated from the matrix of facts'.[10] Lord Hoffmann thought that this 'matrix' includes 'absolutely anything' that would affect the meaning of the contract – with the policy-based exception of the negotiations leading up to the contract. In summary: 'Interpretation is the ascertainment of the meaning which the document would convey to a reasonable person having all the background knowledge which would reasonably have been available to the parties...'. This is not a special 'legal' exercise. It is the same process as giving meaning to language in everyday life. Just as in ordinary conversation, we may sometimes conclude that the contracting parties 'must, for whatever reason, have used the wrong words or syntax', although it is not lightly to be assumed that the wording of a formal legal document is mistaken.[11]

On the facts of *ICS*, Lord Hoffmann re-arranged the wording of the contract. But this was not 'doing violence' to the language as Leggatt LJ had claimed. That was an 'over-energetic' description of the process of interpretation. It was clear that the parties could not have intended the literal meaning of the contract since it made no legal or commercial sense. 'Many people, including politicians, celebrities and Mrs. Malaprop, mangle meanings and syntax but nevertheless communicate tolerably clearly what they are using the words to mean.' Lord Hoffmann's point is that when Sheridan's character refers to 'an allegory on the banks of the Nile' we know she means 'alligator', and for 'the very pine-apple of politeness' we substitute 'pinnacle'.[12]

Lord Hoffmann's emphasis upon contextual interpretation reflects linguistic philosophy, where it is argued that the intelligibility of most utterances depends

---

[8] *Wigmore on Evidence* quoted by Lord Nicholls, 'My Kingdom for a Horse: The Meaning of Words' (2005) 121 LQR 577.

[9] [1998] 1 WLR 896, 912–13.

[10] *Prenn v Simmonds* [1971] 1 WLR 1381, 1384.

[11] Grabiner, 'The Iterative Process of Contractual Interpretation' (2012) 128 LQR 41.

[12] *The Rivals* (1775).

on a shared background of knowledge, and understanding of the context.[13] Some deny that literal acontextual meanings of words are even possible.[14] Lord Hoffmann, prior to *ICS*, had described the idea of the 'natural meaning' of words as 'unhelpful' since their meaning always depends upon syntax (the arrangement of words in a sentence) and context.[15] Stanley Fish claims that: 'A sentence that seems to need no interpretation is already the product of one'.[16] Arthur Corbin states that every interpreter must draw upon the background knowledge of his linguistic experience.[17]

Thus it seems that a contextual approach of some sort is inevitable. Holmes J once put the point poetically: 'A word is not a crystal, transparent and unchanged, it is the skin of a living thought and may vary greatly in color and content according to the circumstances and the time in which it is used.'[18] Lord Bingham has suggested that the 'sober truth' is that interpretation is 'a composite exercise, neither uncompromisingly literal nor unswervingly purposive'.[19] The real question becomes how far towards the contextual and purposive end of the spectrum this should go. May the background override the text, as Lord Hoffmann thinks (and as his decision in *ICS* shows)? This suggestion has produced considerable disquiet, as we will see in the following section.

The other *leitmotif* of interpretation today is the purpose of the contract. An array of dicta can be collected. Much quoted is Lord Diplock's observation that 'if detailed semantic and syntactical analysis of a word in a commercial contract is going to lead to a conclusion that flouts business common sense, it must be made to yield to business common sense'.[20] Lord Bingham approved this approach: contract law should be the 'handmaid' of commerce and 'not its dominatrix'![21] Lord Steyn argues that Lord Diplock's dictum gives effect to the intentions of the parties since 'the reasonable commercial person is hostile to technical interpretations and undue emphasis on niceties of language'.[22] Similarly, Rogers J has warned that it would be inimical to the resolution of commercial disputes for the courts to approach contracts with 'a finely tuned linguistic fork'.[23] On the other hand, the text of the contract does impose some limits: 'business commonsense' does not allow the court to rewrite its language.[24]

---

[13] Adam Kramer, 'Common Sense Principles of Contract Interpretation (and How We've Been Using Them All along)' (2003) 23 *OJLS* 173. Cf. Hoffmann, 'The Intolerable Wrestle with Words and Meanings' (1997) 114 *South African LJ* 656.

[14] Cf. J.P. McBaine, 'The Rule against Disturbing Plain Meaning of Writings' (1943) 31 *California LR* 145.

[15] *Charter Reinsurance v Fagan* [1997] AC 313, 391.

[16] S.E. Fish, 'Normal Circumstances, Literal Language, Direct Speech Acts, the Ordinary, the Everyday, the Obvious, What Goes without Saying, and Other Special Cases' (1978) 4 *Critical Inquiry* 625.

[17] A.K. Corbin, 'The Interpretation of Words and the Parol Evidence Rule' (1965) 50 *Cornell LQ* 161.

[18] *Towne v Eisner* (1918) 245 US 418, 425.

[19] Bingham, 'A New Thing Under the Sun? The Interpretation of Contracts and the *ICS* Decision' (2008) 12 *Edinburgh LR* 374.

[20] *The Antaios* [1985] AC 191, 201.

[21] Bingham, n.19 above.

[22] *Mannai Investment Co Ltd v Eagle Star Life Assurance Co Ltd* [1997] AC 749, 771.

[23] *Banque Brussels Lambert v Australian National Industries* (1989) 21 NSWLR 502.

[24] *Co-operative Wholesale Society Ltd v National Westminster Bank plc* [1995] 1 EGLR 97.

Elsewhere Lord Steyn defines the antonym of the purposive approach, literalism, as follows:

> The tyrant Temures promised the garrison of Sebastia that no blood would be shed if they surrendered to him. They surrendered. He shed no blood. He buried them all alive. This is literalism.

Defined thus, it is hardly surprising that Lord Steyn said that literalism should be 'resisted in the interpretative process'.[25] But joining in the game of literary allusions, we could cite *The Merchant of Venice* in rejoinder to Temures (and Lord Steyn). Portia uses a highly literalistic interpretation of the condition in Shylock's penal bond (the 'pound of flesh') to save the merchant Antonio's life. In life as well as art, strict interpretations of criminal statutes are important to preserve the liberty of the subject. So 'literalism' is not necessarily evil. The 'pedantic lawyer'[26] may after all be a force for good.

CRITICISMS OF THE MODERN APPROACH

The great concern is that contextual/purposive interpretation is less predictable than a textual/literal approach. Thus, it makes contractual planning more hazardous because the meaning that the courts will ultimately assign to the words is harder to foresee.[27] Unpredictability in interpretation also provides greater scope for disputes about the meaning of the contract. These are undoubtedly significant costs. But can they fairly be attributed to the modern approach to interpretation?

Context may helpfully resolve some kinds of linguistic disputes, particularly ambiguity. On the other hand, as Catherine Mitchell observes, 'Context is no more determinate and unequivocal than language'.[28] Mitchell makes an important clarification. It is little use talking about 'context' in the abstract: the question is *which* context.[29] The court may choose to place the contract text in the broad context of its commercial (or other) purpose. Alternatively, it might view the contract as a technically drafted instrument, written by lawyers for lawyers, and to be understood accordingly (i.e. narrowly, even 'pedantically').[30] A good example of the latter approach is *Union Eagle v Golden Achievement* where a ten-minute delay in completing a land sale meant that the purchaser forfeited its deposit.[31] Lord Hoffmann himself referred to the need for speedy certainty in the particular commercial context, the Hong Kong real estate market. This indicated a

---

[25] *Sirius International v FAI Insurance Ltd* [2004] UKHL 54, [19], citing *The Works of William Paley* (1838 ed.), Vol III, 60.

[26] Cf. *Jumbo King v Faithful Properties* (1999) 2 HKCFAR 279 per Lord Hoffmann.

[27] M. Bridge, 'The Future of English Private Transactional Law' [2002] *CLP* 191.

[28] C. Mitchell, *Interpretation of Contracts* (Routledge-Cavendish, 2007) 68.

[29] Ibid, ch. 3.

[30] Also recognised by John Wightman in 'Beyond Custom: Contract, Contexts, and the Recognition of Implicit Understandings' in D. Campbell, H. Collins and J. Wightman (eds), *Implicit Dimensions of Contract* (Hart Publishing, 2003).

[31] [1997] AC 514.

93

rigid insistence on the time provision in the contract.[32] So a contextual approach need not spell broad flexibility. But it *may* do so.

The question becomes: when should the courts use a relatively formal 'context' and when is broader contextual interpretation appropriate? Mitchell stresses that these are points on a gradual spectrum from the more formal to the more contextual. Neither pure formalism nor pure contextualism is possible. The latter would mean discarding the text of the contract altogether, which is not supported in any of the English jurisprudence.[33] If pure formalism supposes that words have acontextual self-announcing meanings, not requiring interpretation at all, then it is doomed to failure. So there is not a binary choice between absolutes. How should the courts proceed?

Contextual interpretation is now the current default interpretive position in England.[34] However in *ICS* itself Lord Lloyd dissented, holding that Lord Hoffmann's reading did violence to the language of the contract and had crossed the line from purposive into 'creative' interpretation.[35] Even Lord Hoffmann has admitted that concerns about *ICS* might depend on a 'sound practical intuition' (rather than 'the fallacy that words have inherent or "available" meanings'), namely that 'the more one allows conventional meanings or syntax to be displaced by inferences drawn from background, the less predictable the outcome is likely to be'.[36] Hence the longstanding view in the legal profession that 'the less one has to resort to any form of background in aid of interpretation, the better'.[37]

Neuberger LJ warns that reference to the surrounding circumstances should not encourage the courts to re-write a contract 'merely because its terms seem somewhat unexpected, a little unreasonable, or not commercially very wise'. Whereas the parties control the text of the contract, they have considerably less control over its context; moreover, judges are 'not always the most commercially-minded, let alone the most commercially experienced, of people' and must beware over-confident determinations of what is commercially reasonable.[38] There is arguably a higher risk of judicial error with a contextual approach, since the court must grapple with frameworks of analysis whose conventions may be wholly unfamiliar.

If judges (who have usually been independent practitioners at the Bar) are commercially inexperienced, what can we say about academics? There is a tangible divide between academic and professional positions in the current Debate. Writing after a colloquium between the Oxford law faculty and Norton Rose solicitors, Richard Calnan (a partner at the firm) registered his dismay at the 'willingness of the court to ignore what the contract said and to impose its own view of what it

---

[32] Cf. also *Arcos Ltd v Ronaasen & Son* [1933] AC 470.
[33] Cf. Collins's arguments, pp. 70–71 above.
[34] Mitchell, n.28 above, ch. 5.
[35] [1998] 1 WLR 896.
[36] *Ali v BCCI* [2002] 1 AC 251, [37].
[37] Ibid, [36] citing *The Countess of Rutland's Case* (1604) 5 Co Rep 25b, 26a.
[38] *Somerfield Stores v Skanska* [2006] EWCA Civ 1732, [21]-[22]. See also *The Maratha Envoy* [1978] AC 1, 8 (Lord Diplock) quoted p. 125 below [sic].

thought was meant' since *ICS*.[39] Yet Lord Hoffmann's approach had been widely welcomed by the academic participants at the colloquium. In Calnan's view, a broad contextual approach makes it difficult to draft contracts and to advise clients. It increases complexity, cost and time taken in litigation. He fears that the international esteem of English commercial law might be impaired.[40] This practical perspective is an important counterweight to the general enthusiasm for contextual interpretation.

Similar points can be made about purposive construction. The courts cannot construe 'purposively' in the abstract: the question is *what* purpose the particular contract was intended to serve. This gives room for ample disagreement, between the parties and between judges. A well-known example is *Schuler v Wickman Machine Tool Sales*.[41] More recently in *Rainy Sky SA v Kookmin Bank* there was disagreement within the Court of Appeal and between that court and the Supreme Court over a guarantee's applicability upon insolvency of the guaranteed company. The wording indicated that it did not apply but the Supreme Court decided that this made no commercial sense, holding the guarantee enforceable.[42] However, Patten LJ had held that the words were clear and the results were neither irrational nor absurd. There were any number of reasons why insolvency was omitted from the bond; the court was not privy to the commercial pressures on the parties and it was impermissible to speculate. Patten LJ argued that the purposive approach risked the court substituting its own commercial judgment.[43]

One could point also to the leading *Chartbrook* case, where the House of Lords held that a definition clause made 'no commercial sense' read in accordance with the ordinary rules of syntax. It was not just a bad bargain but 'arbitrary and irrational'; it was clear that something had gone wrong with the language, and the contract should be understood as reasonable parties must have intended.[44] But the Court of Appeal had decided that the words of the contract were clear and commercial arguments did not justify departure from those words.[45]

Paul Davies notes how many interpretation cases now seem to be troubling the courts and proceeding to the ultimate tribunal, and suggests that this is evidence of the unsettling effect of *ICS* upon contract law.[46] For Lord Grabiner QC the focus must be on 'the meaning of the contract as recorded in the words used'; construction must not become 'speculative'.[47] Recently the Supreme Court rejected Martin Hogg's argument that contracts should be given their plain meaning and parties to badly drafted contracts not rescued from their fecklessness by 'commercially

---

[39] R. Calnan, 'Construction of Commercial Contract: A Practitioner's Perspective' in A. Burrows and E. Peel (eds), *Contract Terms* (Oxford University Press, 2007) p.18.

[40] Ibid, p. 20.

[41] [1974] AC 235. Discussed at pp. 219–220 below.

[42] [2011] UKSC 50.

[43] [2010] EWCA Civ 582 [42], [51].

[44] *Chartbrook Ltd v Persimmon Homes Ltd* [2009] 1 AC 1101, [16], [20], [25] (Lord Hoffmann).

[45] [2008] EWCA Civ 183.

[46] (2011) 127 LQR 185.

[47] Grabiner, n.11 above.

sensible interpretations'.[48] The fears about uncertainty do not seem entirely imaginary. On the other hand, Lord Bingham argues that although certainty is highly desirable in commercial law, the ultimate task of the interpreter is to ascertain the intention of the parties. The courts should not ascribe 'rather literal' meanings in the interests of certainty if reasonable parties are unlikely to have intended those meanings.[49] But how are we to decide, without circularity, whether reasonable parties would intend the 'literal' meaning or not?

FRAMING THE CONTEXT

We have seen above how the commercial context, such as the commercial property market in *Union Eagle v Golden Achievement*,[50] can mandate a narrow textual approach to construction. Equally, the drafting of the contract may indicate whether a broader or narrower approach is appropriate. Where the drafting is technical, detailed and precise, this strongly suggests, *pace* Lord Steyn and Rogers J, that it is meant to be understood with 'a finely tuned linguistic fork', paying full attention to the 'niceties of language'. Commercial contracts typically fall into this category, whereas a less detailed contract, or one making express use of broad notions such as good faith and reasonableness, indicates that broader contextual interpretation is required. In other words, the choice of context (interpretive approach) depends upon both the text and context of the contract.

There seems no good reason why drafters should not *expressly* control the interpretive approach used by the courts. If freedom of contract allows parties to choose the terms of their contract, then why not the way that those terms are interpreted and given effect?[51] Mitchell states, however, that direct 'interpretation clauses' are not encountered in practice.[52] The Court of Appeal has held that an 'entire agreement clause' was designed to prevent incorporation of further terms or representations into the contract and was therefore 'not apt to govern the construction of the written terms that the parties had included or to exclude evidence relevant to the ascertainment of their meaning'.[53] This suggests that if parties do not want the prevailing contextual/purposive interpretative approach to apply to their contract, they will have to say so expressly.[54] Should they do so, the court should respect that choice. For if the court were to insist on the contextual approach against the parties' declared wishes, *ICS*[55] would after all be open to the one criticism that is 'truly damaging' – that it does not reflect the commercial intentions of the parties.[56]

---

[48] M Hogg, "Fundamental Issues for Reform of the Law of Contractual Interpretation" (2011) 15 *Edinburgh LR* 406; *Aberdeen CC v Stewart Milne Group* [2011] UKSC 56, [21] (Lord Hope).

[49] Bingham, n.19 above.

[50] [1997] AC 514.

[51] Mitchell, n.28 above, p. 148.

[52] Cf. n.54 below.

[53] *Proforce Recruit Ltd v The Rugby Group Ltd* [2006] EWCA Civ 69, [40] per Mummery LJ.

[54] Cf. C. Mitchell, 'Entire Agreement Clauses: Contracting Out of Contextualism' (2006) 22 *JCL* 222.

[55] *Investors Compensation Scheme v West Bromwich Building Society* [1998] 1 WLR 896.

[56] Cf. Bingham, n.19 above.

LIMITING THE CONTEXT: PRIOR NEGOTIATIONS

Lord Hoffmann in *ICS* created an exception to the general proposition that the 'factual matrix' includes 'absolutely anything' that is relevant for interpreting the contract.[57] He excluded the negotiations preceding the agreement. Lord Hoffmann said that there were sensible practical reasons for this. After considerable debate, the House of Lords has reaffirmed the exception.[58] Again, it should be noted that academic opinion had strongly favoured the abrogation of the exclusionary rule while practitioners strongly supported it.[59]

In the seminal case of *Prenn v Simmonds* Lord Wilberforce held that prior negotiations were irrelevant not on technical or convenience grounds, but simply because they were unhelpful.[60] It was only at the point of agreement that a consensus came into being; prior to this, each party had its own objectives that it was trying to advance.[61] Of course, each might have to compromise to achieve agreement: 'in a world of give and take, men often have to be satisfied with less than they want... [and] it would be a matter of speculation how far the common intention was that the particular objective should be realised'.[62] Lord Hoffmann seemed to have a similar objection in mind when he described the excluded category as 'the previous negotiations of the parties *and their declarations of subjective intent*'.[63]

Nevertheless, the exception came under heavy attack after *ICS*. While evidence of prior negotiations might frequently reveal nothing more than 'subjective declarations' it could on occasion show exactly what the parties had understood by a particular word or phrase. In which case (as Lord Macnaghten said in a different context), 'Why should [the judge] listen to conjecture on a matter which has become an accomplished fact? ... With the light before him, why should he shut his eyes and grope in the dark?'[64] McMeel argued that the exclusionary rule was inconsistent with the whole *ICS* philosophy of considering anything contextually relevant.[65] The rational approach was to examine the evidence to decide whether it was helpful, not to condemn all negotiations as necessarily unhelpful (subjective and inconclusive). Firm use of the courts' case management powers could prevent the cost and length of litigation spiralling upwards. Arden LJ was also critical of the exclusionary rule, commenting that it would be 'unattractive' to ignore a clear definition in the negotiations which was not to be found in the final contract.[66] She also pointed out that all relevant context, including negotiations,

---

[57] *Investors Compensation Scheme v West Bromwich Building Society* [1998] 1 WLR 896.

[58] *Chartbrook Ltd v Persimmon Homes Ltd* [2009] 1 AC 1101.

[59] 'Overview' in A. Burrows and E. Peel (eds), *Contract Terms* (Oxford University Press, 2007).

[60] [1971] 1 WLR 1381, 1384.

[61] English law views such negotiations as 'inherently adversarial': *Walford v Miles* [1992] 2 AC 128.

[62] [1971] 1 WLR 1381, 1385.

[63] [1998] 1 WLR 896, 913 (emphasis added).

[64] *Bwllfa and Merthyr Dare Steam Collieries (1891) Ltd. v Pontypridd Waterworks Co* [1903] AC 426, 431.

[65] G. McMeel, 'Prior Negotiations and Subsequent Conduct – The Next Step Forward for Contractual Interpretation?' (2003) 121 LQR 577.

[66] *Proforce Recruit Ltd v The Rugby Group Ltd* [2006] EWCA Civ 69, [57]. Cf. trial stage of the same case: [2007] EWHC 1621 (QB).

was admissible under international contract instruments such as the UNIDROIT principles and the Vienna Convention.[67]

Lord Nicholls also argued that if the negotiations had been conclusive enough to help the notional reasonable person understand the meaning of the contract, the evidence should be admissible.[68] The more information the court has, the better the quality of the decision. It may be that frequently, or even usually, the negotiations are unhelpful, as in *Prenn v Simmonds* itself. But that could not justify a rule that they were *never* to be taken into account. Such rigidity was unjust. Judges are well able to recognize and ignore self-serving evidence. When negotiations clarified the meaning of a provision it would fulfil rather than obstruct the objective approach to make use of them. Moreover, Lord Nicholls argued this would make the law more 'transparent'. A familiar tactic to circumvent the exclusionary rule was for counsel to include a parallel claim for rectification (again as in *Prenn v Simmonds*). In rectification claims, evidence of prior negotiations *is* admissible, and pleaders hope that the judge would be influenced by it, whether consciously or not, when *interpreting* the contract. Allowing the evidence to be admissible at the interpretation stage would therefore regularize what was happening in any event. It was unlikely that greater complexity, expense or delay would result from abolition of the exclusion as the evidence was already admissible under separate but linked claims.

On the other hand, Lord Bingham (also extrajudicially) aligned himself with 'the judicial dinosaurs' by endorsing the exclusionary rule.[69] He had two main reasons. First, that it would tend to undermine the objective approach to contracts if the court considered the exchanges between the parties, consisting of competing and fluctuating aims that may not ultimately have been achieved. It would mean 'excessive emphasis on what the parties wanted to agree and too little on what they actually did agree'. Secondly, and more practically, removing the exception would lead to a huge increase in the complexity and expense of litigation, since any important contractual negotiation generates a 'huge' amount of material, much of which is 'entirely inconclusive'.

The debate has been settled for the foreseeable future by Lord Hoffmann's speech (although strictly speaking obiter) in *Chartbrook v Persimmon Homes Ltd*.[70] The rule was not a tautology stating that irrelevant evidence was to be excluded; it applied even when 'among the dirt of aspirations, proposals and counterproposals there may gleam the gold of a genuine consensus'.[71] Such evidence, however rare, would be helpful (*pace* Lord Wilberforce in *Prenn v Simmonds*). Moreover, it might restore 'intellectual honesty' to admit such evidence for interpretation purposes when it was 'almost invariably tendered in support of an alternative claim for rectification'.[72]

---

[67] UN Convention on Contracts for the International Sale of Goods (1980).
[68] Nicholls, n.8 above.
[69] Bingham, n.19 above.
[70] [2009] 1 AC 1101.
[71] Ibid, [32].
[72] Ibid, [35].

Nevertheless, there were weighty practical reasons to uphold the exclusionary rule. It remained extremely difficult to distinguish statements embodying at least a provisional consensus from the parties' purely unilateral aspirations, 'drenched in subjectivity'.[73] Indeed, in parallel with the effect of *Pepper v Hart* upon ministerial statements in Parliament, parties might attempt to impose their preferred meaning through statements in negotiations rather than the wording of the contract.[74] The international rules were heavily influenced by the French view that contract is a matter of the purely subjective intentions of the parties; this philosophy could not simply be transposed into English law.[75] In the end, whether the advantages of the rule outweighed the one clear disadvantage (that sometimes the parties' meaning would not be given effect by the court) was an empirical question. But this was not suitable for judicial decision.[76] So in the end, the case for change had not been made out.

Some see *Chartbrook* as a disappointing decision. It does appear timid. The courts are often not so shy about weighing essentially empirical arguments; if they routinely refused, the common law would never develop at all. On the other hand, such bold development is typically found in tort law leading to great fluctuations that would be unacceptable in commercial contract law. Lord Hoffmann perhaps thinks *ICS* quite unsettling enough, without permitting consideration of contractual negotiations. He noted in *Chartbrook* that there are 'safety nets' whereby such negotiations can be given effect where necessary: estoppel and rectification. We now consider the role of rectification.

RECTIFICATION AND INTERPRETATION

A written contract which fails accurately to record the agreement reached between the parties may be 'rectified' by the court to do so. This is an area of law that is 'in some respects surprisingly unclear'.[77] The basic idea is that there must be an outwardly manifested common intention that the contract has failed to express.[78] Rectification is about correcting the mistakes in defectively drafted documents.

It will at once be appreciated that there is an overlap between rectification and *ICS*-style 'interpretation' of contracts.[79] *ICS* requires the court to go beyond the wording of the contract, and if the court concludes from this background that something has gone wrong with the drafting, it may 'interpret' the contract to mean something different from its literal meaning. In the light of this, Andrew Burrows inquires whether the *ICS* approach to construction has made rectification

---

[73] Ibid, [38].

[74] Ibid, cf. *Pepper v Hart* [1993] AC 593.

[75] *Chartbrook* [39]

[76] Ibid, [41]; cf. [70] (Lord Rodger). Cf. [99] (Baroness Hale doubts reform of a common law rule by Law Commission-inspired legislation).

[77] A. Burrows, 'Construction and Rectification' in A. Burrows and E. Peel (eds), *Contract Terms* (Oxford University Press, 2007) p. 84.

[78] Although where one party knowingly ('unconscionably') takes advantage of a mistake by the other there may be 'unilateral rectification': *Commission for the New Towns v Cooper* [1995] Ch 259.

[79] *Investors Compensation Scheme v West Bromwich Building Society* [1998] 1 WLR 896.

redundant.[80] He considers that some cases that would classically have been occasions for rectification can now be decided through interpretation. *ICS* itself is a prime example. A 'radical decision on the facts',[81] Lord Hoffmann altered the wording in a way that Evans-Lombe J at trial thought might more appropriately be achieved by rectification (but no rectification claim was made, in contrast with *Prenn v Simmonds*[82] and *Chartbrook v Persimmon Homes Ltd*[83]).

Sir Richard Buxton argues that this aspect of *ICS* is revolutionary. It is not about the meaning of what was said ('interpretation') at all, but rather addresses what the parties meant to but did not actually say: 'in reality, even though not in form, what is thereafter enforced is the original consensus, and not the written agreement that purported, wrongly, to set out that consensus'. This is, in effect if not in form, identical to rectification.[84]

The one great difference is that evidence of prior negotiations is (as seen) excluded from 'interpretation' but admissible in 'rectification'. It will be important evidence in any rectification claim. Its admissibility eased Lord Hoffmann's conscience when he reaffirmed the exclusionary rule in *Chartbrook*. Buxton takes a different view. If interpretation and rectification are structurally the same, and address the same problem of incompetent drafting, then there is no justification for the discrepancy ('dissonance') between them over prior negotiations. Since *ICS* occupies no ground distinct from rectification, but has the handicap of non-admissibility of evidence, parties will rationally prefer rectification. This will be pled in the alternative by 'all but the most negligent of counsel'.

However, Buxton argues that *Chartbrook* has unsettled rectification itself. If one of the reasons for excluding prior negotiations from interpretation is that they are 'drenched in subjectivity',[85] then this makes them dubious evidence for rectification too. Rectification is allowed only when there is an objectively manifested common intention, shown by the parties' 'words and acts', not their 'inward thoughts'.[86]

One other important feature of rectification is noted by Burrows.[87] Rectification is historically an equitable remedy in the court's discretion and one of the bars to rectification is third party rights. If a contractual document has been assigned to a third party, that party will likely rely on the words of the document, knowing nothing of any prior consensus between the initial parties, or the document's failure to record that consensus accurately. It would adversely affect the third party's reliance on the document if it were rectified to reflect a consensus to which he was not privy and of which he was wholly ignorant when it was assigned to him. Accordingly, the courts refuse relief.

---

[80] Burrows, n.77 above.

[81] Ibid, p. 93.

[82] [1971] 1 WLR 1381.

[83] [2009] 1 AC 1101.

[84] R. Buxton, '"Construction" and Rectification after *Chartbrook*' [2010] CLJ 253. Cf. *Oceanbulk Shipping v TMT Asia* [2010] UKSC 44, [44]–[45] (Lord Clarke).

[85] See n.73 above (Lord Hoffmann).

[86] *The Olympic Pride* [1980] 2 Lloyd's Rep 67, 72 (Mustill J).

[87] Burrows, n.77 above.

This is potentially a concern about contextual interpretation generally: assignees (third parties) may be quite unaware of the 'factual matrix' in which the document that they hold was drafted. Contextual rather than literal/textual interpretation of it may, therefore, produce results that would unfairly surprise them. As Burrows says, this is a reason why *ICS*-style 'amending' construction rather than rectification may be argued tactically when a third party is involved – precisely to outflank the limits on rectification. Burrows suggests that courts should refuse to interpret 'contextually' in such cases.

Distinguished judges have doubted whether the third party problem is a real concern. Lord Nicholls points out that 'when interpreting a document intended for commercial circulation it may be reasonable to attach added weight to the meaning the words bear on their face'.[88] This is, in effect, to argue for textualism in such cases, which would seem to undermine Lord Nicholls's support for pre-contractual negotiations to be taken into account. It is notable that in *Chartbrook* at first instance, Briggs J thought that the effect on third parties was the strongest reason for excluding that evidence.[89] Lord Bingham similarly argues that where the courts are dealing with a kind of contract that is typically assignable in the market, this mandates 'a more or less literal approach' to construction.[90] In *Chartbrook* Lord Hoffmann simply commented that it was difficult to say whether contextual interpretation generally, and the admissibility of prior negotiations in particular, caused problems in practice in three-party cases.[91]

In sum, the remedy of rectification and post-*ICS* interpretation have an uneasy coexistence. To the extent that they are similar in function and effect, it is questionable whether the different approach to admissible evidence is entirely rational. The limits on rectification in three-party situations also raises questions about contextual interpretation generally. On the other hand, there are clearly limits on how much 'correction' can be done by 'construction'. Rix LJ warns that *Chartbrook* must not be viewed as an 'open sesame' for rewriting contracts; only 'a clear error of language which could not have been intended' may properly be interpreted away.[92] The fact that the contract is a bad bargain for one of the parties does not show that something must have gone wrong with its drafting.[93]

PACKING UP THE 'BAGGAGE' OF OLD-STYLE LEGAL INTERPRETATION?

Lord Hoffmann stated in *ICS* that: 'Almost all the old intellectual baggage of "legal" interpretation has been discarded'.[94] Strict, artificial rules of construction are to be shunned and avoided. Legal instruments are instead to be given the

---

[88] Nicholls, n.8 above.
[89] [2007] 1 All ER (Comm) 1083.
[90] Bingham, 'A New Thing Under the Sun? The Interpretation of Contract and the *ICS* Decision' (2008) 12 *Edinburgh LR* 374.
[91] [2009] 1 AC 1101, [40].
[92] *ING Bank NV v Ros Roca SA* [2011] EWCA Civ 353, [110].
[93] *Bashir v Ali* [2011] EWCA Civ 707.
[94] *Investors Compensation Scheme v West Bromwich Building Society* [1998] 1 WLR 896, 912.

ordinary meaning that they would as seriously intended utterances in everyday speech. We consider in this section whether Lord Hoffmann's claim is entirely correct. It seems that at least with some kinds of clauses which have traditionally attracted the disfavour of the courts, a trace of the old philosophy lingers on. It has been said that while the great cabin trunks of 'the canons of construction' have been packed up, some 'airline suitcases' still remain.[95]

The best known redoubt of artificially narrow construction is exclusion clauses. These are traditionally construed *'contra proferentem'*, i.e. against the party relying on them, in case of doubt. Here we find entirely counter-intuitive rules such as that in *Canada Steamships*: when an exclusion clause is wide enough to cover damage both through negligence and through other causes, it will be held *not* to exclude liability for negligence.[96] In other words, negligence must be *expressly* excluded. The rule is repellent to our understanding. The natural sense of a clause excluding 'any claim for damage to goods' (*Canada Steamships* itself) means any claim, including negligence.

The reason for this artificial rule was the judicial hostility to exclusion clauses. While the judges were not willing to recognize a common law doctrine of outright unenforceability of exclusion clauses,[97] they were prepared to construe them very narrowly at whatever cost to the ordinary objective meaning. But with direct statutory control inaugurated by the Unfair Contract Terms Act 1977 (UCTA), such common law stratagems have been rendered unnecessary. Shortly after it was enacted, Lord Diplock declared that UCTA had 'banished' any need for 'judicial distortion of the English language' and the 'very strained constructions' hitherto placed on exclusion clauses.[98] Similarly Lord Denning MR admitted that 'strained and unnatural construction' had previously been used by the courts as a 'secret weapon' to 'stab the idol' of freedom of contract, in exclusion clause cases. But the need for such 'gymnastic contortions' had gone when UCTA 'shattered' the idol![99]

Also, of course, such an approach is inconsistent with Lord Hoffmann's 'ordinary language' approach to construction in *ICS*. *Canada Steamships* has therefore been downgraded to a mere presumption, at least in commercial cases. In *HIH Casualty Insurance v Chase Manhattan Bank* a clause was held sufficient to exclude the defendants' liability for their agents' negligence although it simply disclaimed responsibility for disclosure of information, without mentioning negligence.[100] The plain commercial purpose of the clause was to exclude liability for the agents' negligence; *Canada Steamships* was not to be treated as a rigid rule and mechanically applied to defeat the purpose.[101] It was a presumption drawn from

---

[95] *BOC Group plc v Centeon LLC* [1999] 1 All ER (Comm) 970 (Evans LJ).
[96] *Canada Steamship Lines v R* [1952] AC 192.
[97] Cf. *Suisse Atlantique Société d'Armement Maritime SA v NV Rotterdamsche Kolen Centrale* [1967] 1 AC 361.
[98] *Photo Production Ltd v Securicor Transport Ltd* [1980] AC 827.
[99] *George Mitchell v Finney Lock Seeds* [1983] QB 284, 299.
[100] [2003] UKHL 6.
[101] Ibid, [116] (Lord Scott).

the 'inherent improbability' of a party waiving its claims in negligence.[102] While this presumption was ordinarily a sound one,[103] on the facts of *HIH Casualty* there was no inherent improbability in the exclusion extending to negligence – on the contrary, the commercial sense of the contract required it.[104]

The approach to exclusion clauses now seems purposive. If the exclusion is commercially sensible then it will be given its natural width. The suggestion that *Canada Steamships* lives on as the starting point is surely questionable, however, when there are statutory tools with which to regulate unfair exclusion clauses – UCTA and (for consumers) the Unfair Terms in Consumer Contracts Regulations 1999. It would simplify the interpretation stage to give the wording its ordinary meaning and limit its effect through the statutory jurisdiction, when necessary.

Lord Hoffmann warmed to his theme of 'discarding the baggage' in a case subsequent to *ICS*, but in a dissenting speech. In *Ali v BCCI* employees who had been made redundant waived 'any or all claims' they might have had against their employer, in exchange for compensation.[105] Subsequent to those agreements, it was discovered that the employer had conducted its business illegally and dishonestly and, accordingly, former employees would be entitled to damages for the 'stigma' (reputational damage) of having worked there.[106] The question was whether the compromise agreements barred the claims for 'stigma' damages, which neither party could have foreseen as a realistic possibility at the time that they were entered into.

The majority of the House of Lords held that while it was legally possible to surrender claims of which one was unaware through a compromise agreement by using suitably clear words,[107] the court would be 'very slow to infer' such a surrender.[108] This was established by a long line of authority. The compromise at issue in *Ali* was not worded emphatically enough to rebut the presumption, and accordingly the claim for 'stigma' damages was not barred by it.

Lord Hoffmann dissented. He argued that the terms of the compromise were comprehensive and 'very wide': 'the draftsman meant business'. Accordingly, given their plain meaning, they would extend to claims of which the parties could not have been aware.[109] He thought that refusing to give effect to this plain meaning was unfortunate for a number of reasons. First, it recalled the rigid nineteenth-century 'canons of construction' which often defeated party intentions in the 'pursuit of certainty'.[110] Secondly, in reaction to this, those drafting compromise agreements would be required by the majority decision 'to add verbiage to the form of release in order to attain the comprehensiveness which it is obviously

---

[102] *Ailsa Craig Fishing Co Ltd v Malvern Fishing Co Ltd* [1983] 1 WLR 964, 970 (Lord Fraser).
[103] [2003] UKHL 6 [11] (Lord Bingham).
[104] Ibid [67] (Lord Hoffmann).
[105] [2002] 1 AC 251.
[106] Cf. *Malik v BCCI* [1998] AC 20.
[107] *Salkeld v Vernon* (1758) 1 Eden 64 (Lord Keeper Henley).
[108] [2002] 1 AC 251 [10] (Lord Bingham).
[109] Ibid, [38].
[110] Ibid, [54]–[57].

intended to achieve'.[111] Thirdly, the decision reflected the one striking 'canon of construction' evolved in the twentieth century, that on exclusion clauses.[112] But this was regrettable. The exclusion clause jurisprudence had been 'a desperate remedy', 'bordering on judicial legislation' that could only be justified to remedy a widespread injustice. Otherwise, there was 'much to be said' for giving effect to the parties' intentions as revealed through ordinary interpretation.[113] In conclusion, the majority decision was an 'unfortunate retreat into formalism' against the modern trend in interpretation (*ICS*), and retrieved 'a substantial piece of the baggage' of old-style 'legal' interpretation.[114] 'Lord Keeper Henley's ghost' had struck back.[115]

There is certainly much to be said for Lord Hoffmann's dissent, which will hopefully guide future development on interpretative controversies less overlaid with authorities than compromise agreements. His fears about verbose drafting are well founded. McMeel points out that a suspicious draftsman, fearing a hostile court, will draft defensively.[116] *Ali* may well encourage the elaborate American-style release clauses, extending into pages in length, that Lord Hoffmann noted.[117] As he said, such 'grosser excesses of verbiage' should be discouraged, by making draftsmen believe that judges will use common sense to get the message.[118]

Lord Hoffmann commented that even in the nineteenth century, the strict 'canons of construction' had been applied to formal documents such as wills and deeds, but not usually to commercial contracts, where giving effect to purpose trumped the quest for certainty.[119] It might be questioned whether such certainty was ever achieved. The American Legal Realists criticized the supposed determinacy of formal rules of law in general. Karl Llewellyn attacked 'canons of construction' in particular, noting that for every 'rule' there was usually a counter-rule which could be used to justify the precisely opposite result. Accordingly, the court was able to determine the meaning of the instrument as it pleased. Lord Hoffmann allows that the settled meanings ascribed to particular words and phrases would reflect the parties' intentions – at least where documents were skilfully drafted by lawyers able to navigate 'the reefs and shoals' of the rules. But even this was not guaranteed: Lord Hoffmann referred to books on wills as 'a melancholy record of the occasions on which [the rules] have defeated the intentions of testators'.[120]

These comments lead to familiar conclusions. Formal approaches to construction are rigid and artificial. They encourage, and depend upon, precise and technical

---

[111] Ibid, [62].

[112] Ibid, [57].

[113] Ibid, [60].

[114] Ibid, [62].

[115] Cf. *Salkeld v Vernon* (1758) 1 Eden 64.

[116] G. McMeel, 'The Principles and Policies of Contractual Construction' in A. Burrows and E. Peel (eds), *Contract Terms* (Oxford University Press, 2007).

[117] [2002] 1 AC 251 [38].

[118] Ibid.

[119] [2002] 1 AC 251 [57]

[120] [2002] 1 AC 251 [55].

drafting. But such old-style 'legal' interpretation may lead to greater predictability of outcome. The alternative 'plain language' approach of Lord Hoffmann is to be welcomed insofar as it disposes with the highly artificial constructions familiar from exclusion clause cases. But in one sense, such approaches are consistent with the modern purposive approach to interpretation. The courts have to decide whether the parties' purpose was to exclude a given liability, compromise a claim, etc. As *Ali v BCCI* shows (like *Schuler v Wickman Machine Tool Sales*[121] and *Rainy Sky SA v Kookmin Bank*[122]),[123] courts may differ over the purpose to be attributed to the parties. The purpose will usually be determinative, for the court will demand very clear words before it is driven to decide that the contract's true meaning thwarts its own purpose. Thus, the 'linguistic gymnastics' of the exclusion clause jurisprudence lives on today, in cases where the court assigns a purpose to the contract which is inconsistent with its wording. And of course, such judicial assignments of purpose (on a more or less open policy basis) are open to the criticism that 'business men would prefer a general rule that words mean what they say in ordinary English, rather than a rule that contracts shall mean what the House of Lords, or some of it members, think they ought to mean'.[124]

CONCLUSION

We have seen that the interpretation of contracts is not only important but highly controversial. The competing positions may be portrayed as follows. First there is old-fashioned, narrow, textual, literal, formal interpretation. Secondly, modern, broad, contextual, purposive interpretation. But both of these are caricatures. In the end, there is a spectrum of approaches and the task for the court is to decide how textually, or how purposively, to approach the contract. This question must be answered by taking both the text and context of the contract fully into account. So, for example, a need for commercial certainty might be a contextual reason for narrow, textual interpretation. Conversely, the contract text might implicitly or explicitly require broad, purposive interpretation. Each approach has costs. Formal approaches may maximize certainty but sacrifice the parties' true intentions. Contextual/purposive approaches may conversely ensure realism at the cost of unpredictability, and place considerable demands upon the interpreting court. Formal interpretation may ease dispute resolution, but front-load costs onto the drafting stage: it is expensive for the parties to translate their entire agreement into the precise, non-idiosyncratic language suitable for textual interpretation.[125]

The costs and benefits need to be weighed up, both for the parties and for the system of contract generally. So the need for formalist certainty is greater when the court is dealing with an industry-wide standard form than with an *ad hoc*

---

[121] [1974] AC 235.
[122] [2011] UKSC 50.
[123] See pp. 103–104 above.
[124] Staughton, n.1 above.
[125] S.A. Smith, *Contract Theory* (Oxford University Press, 2004) pp. 275–76.

contract; third parties may be adversely affected by contextual interpretations, again requiring formal approaches to contracts which are typically 'marketable'. But the 'committed contextualist' may be unconvinced by this.[126] The ultimate question is what the parties meant, and this can only properly be understood contextually.

The courts' response to the debate may be to steer a middle course, 'neither uncompromisingly literal nor unswervingly purposive'.[127] Lord Hoffmann's much-debated restatement in *ICS*[128] may be seen, in historical perspective, as more a change of emphasis or rhetoric.[129] Stefan Vogenauer, comparing English law with the interpretation of contracts in France and Germany, finds that the apparently 'subjective' stance of the French (in particular) is a difference of theory and values, but in practice has results very similar to those in England.[130] So interpretation is not an either/or binary choice. But the degree to which a judge emphasizes the formal or contextual pole of interpretation, *how* formal or *which* purpose, will continue to be highly significant. Understanding this Debate is vital for understanding the disagreement underlying a whole range of contractual disputes.

Debate 2

How should terms be implied into contracts?

The implication of terms attracts controversy over both its theoretical basis and its practical application. Michael Trebilcock comments that it poses 'one of the most daunting challenges' for both instrumental and non-instrumental approaches to contract law.[131] Even the taxonomy of the field causes difficulties. It is as well to clarify this at the outset.

The well-known distinction is between terms implied 'by law' and those implied 'in fact'. This is not, perhaps, a very illuminating description of the distinction between them. Much better is Lord Steyn's classification, contrasting 'standardized implied terms ... general default rules' and '*ad hoc* gap fillers' respectively.[132] We will use the traditional terminology here, but with Lord Steyn's meaning. Other commentators deny that there is any common ground between these 'species' of implied terms. Adam Kramer argues that 'implication in fact' is actually an offshoot of interpretation, and that terms implied by law would more

---

[126] Cf. H. Collins, 'Objectivity and Committed Contextualism in Interpretation' in S. Worthington (ed.), *Commercial Law and Commercial Practice* (Hart Publishing, 2003).

[127] Cf. Bingham, n.19 above.

[128] *Investors Compensation Scheme v West Bromwich Building Society* [1998] 1 WLR 896.

[129] McMeel (2007), n.116 above, 29.

[130] S. Vogenauer, 'Interpretation of Contracts: Concluding Comparative Observations' in A. Burrows and E. Peel (eds), *Contract Terms* (Oxford Universtiy Press, 2007).

[131] M.J. Trebilcock, *The Limits of Freedom of Contract* (Harvard University Press, 1993) p.126.

[132] *Equitable Life v Hyman* [2002] 1 AC 408, 458–59.

accurately be described as 'imposed' or 'constructive' terms.[133] These are important arguments that we consider below.

FILLING THE GAPS: TERMS IMPLIED 'IN FACT'

Traditionally, contract lawyers have distinguished express terms (their identification and interpretation) from implied terms. However, a new view sees implication of terms 'in fact' as a variant of 'interpretation' of the contract. The argument is a powerful one, and it will be discussed below. It turns on certain basic propositions about intention and communication, and the assignment of meaning to contracts.

There are well-known traditional tests for an implied term (Lord Steyn's 'ad hoc gap filler') in a one-off dispute.[134] What need not be expressed is that which is so obvious that it goes without saying, so that

> if, while the parties were making their bargain, an officious bystander were to suggest some express provision for it in their agreement, they would testily suppress him with a common 'Oh, of course!'[135]

In *The Moorcock*, it was said that the parties' intention 'must obviously have been' to include terms necessary for the 'business efficacy' of the transaction.[136] This seems to be a particular application (*avant la lettre*) of the general 'officious bystander' test.

In *A-G of Belize v Belize Telecom* Lord Hoffmann, in another seminal judgment, has stressed that the ultimate issue is, simply, what the agreement means.[137] The court has no power to supply additional terms to make the contract better or fairer. If the contract is silent on a given matter, the usual inference is that nothing is to happen. But in some cases, 'the only meaning consistent with the other provisions of the instrument, read against the relevant background, is that something is to happen'. Accordingly, the court gives effect to that meaning. The court is sometimes said to be 'implying' a term, but in fact it is only spelling out, in express words, what the contract means. *The Moorcock* and 'officious bystander' may be useful guides but are not ends in themselves. The latter, in particular, creates the danger of 'barren speculation' about how the parties themselves would have reacted to the proposed term; it is not necessary that it be immediately apparent (so their response to the bystander may have been 'Could you please explain that again?'). The ultimate question remains the meaning of the contract, *objectively* ascertained.

---

[133] A. Kramer, 'Implication in Fact as An Instance of Contractual Interpretation' [2004] *CLJ* 384.
[134] Where each case turns on its own facts and the precise wording of the agreement: *BJ Aviation Limited v Pool Aviation Limited* [2002] P&CR 25, [20].
[135] *Shirlaw v Southern Foundries* [1939] 2 KB 206, 227.
[136] (1889) 14 PD 64.
[137] [2009] 1 WLR 1988.

View of an expert

Adam Kramer

Lord Hoffmann's judgment is about rendering explicit what is otherwise implicit. Adam Kramer has presented a sophisticated argument for the assimilation of interpretation and 'implication of terms in fact'.[138] It runs on similar lines. Kramer argues that much of 'interpretation' in the traditional sense is about supplementing the linguistic meaning of the words used. A process of pragmatic inference is always needed for successful communication because it is prohibitively costly (and probably impossible) to convey all intended meaning by 'encoding' it linguistically. In brief, not everything is said explicitly in so many words. Nor could it be. Where it is clear that the communicator's intended meaning goes beyond the linguistic meaning, therefore, the interpreter must construct the full meaning by using the broader context (community standards, reasonable expectations, past dealings between the parties).[139]

Kramer stresses the insight from linguistic philosophy that a communicator can intend what goes without saying and what does not cross his mind.[140] As Lord Hoffmann puts it, 'We use words in daily life against a background of knowledge which we assume that our listeners share and we need not therefore specifically mention'.[141] This does not even depend on conscious thought. The formulation of thoughts into words is an unconscious, reflex process.[142] Kramer uses a famous example of the philosopher Ludwig Wittgenstein: if someone asks me to 'teach the children a game' they do not intend me to show them how to gamble with dice. This is true even though excluding unsuitable games with dice was not present in the speaker's mind when he made the request.[143] Every communicator *intends* his utterances to be interpreted using the background of social norms, understandings and expectations. 'This is not a fiction, or a diluted form of intention, it is the way communication and the mind works.'[144]

With this insight, Kramer argues that the distinction between interpretation and implication breaks down. Both set out to ascertain what would reasonably be intended in the situation that has arisen, which is what the parties' (objectively ascertained) intention *is*.

---

[138] Kramer, n.133 above.
[139] Trade custom of sufficient 'notoriety, certainty and reasonableness' is a well-known source of implicit contractual obligations: *Hutton v Warren* (1836) 1 M&W 460.
[140] Kramer, n.13 above.
[141] Hoffmann, n.13 above, p. 658.
[142] D. Cooper, *Knowledge of Language* (Prism Press, 1975) ch. 7.
[143] L. Wittgenstein, *Philosophical Investigations* (trans. G.E.M. Anscombe, Basil Blackwell, 3rd edn, 1972) p. 33.
[144] Kramer, n.133 above, p. 385.

This does not, however, give the interpreter *carte blanche*. The question in each case is whether there is a 'licence to supplement the terms by inference'. That is, whether it would be normal to leave a matter to go without saying rather than actually 'encoding' it in 'linguistic meaning'. Faced with a commercial contract, there will be limited licence to supplement its terms. Certainty is of great importance in such a form of communication, so it is likely that the communicator will have conveyed meaning through the more secure (albeit more costly) explicit linguistic medium, instead of relying on implicit meanings. This point applies with heightened force the more complete (and professionally drafted) the contract appears to be. Since language is frequently indeterminate (e.g. vague or ambiguous), however, the court may nonetheless need to supplement the linguistic meaning.

There are also different levels of supplemental meanings that the interpreter might be invited to infer. The greater the degree of inference required, the more demanding the test becomes. This, explains Kramer, is the reason for a stiffer test of *necessity* in the 'implied term' cases, whereas in ordinary 'interpretation' the question is simply what the contract is reasonably taken to mean. Kramer refers to 'primary information' that is wholly independent of other parts of the communication ('an entirely new thread in an utterance'). Primary information defines a distinct and fundamental aspect of the communication (or transaction). It is determined by the communicator's personal preferences, and is accordingly very difficult to *infer*.

This corresponds to the law's notion of an implied term, namely, a separate positive obligation in a contract, rather than merely a supplementary clarification of an existing term. Implied terms consist of primary information. But it is unlikely that such important matters would be left to 'go without saying'.

> The greater the primariness of an issue, the greater the probability of unsuccessful communication of a determination of the issue and the greater the importance of the issue, and so the greater the benefit of linguistic encoding of such a determination and the lesser the likelihood that such a determination was intended to go without saying.[145]

The fact that it is unlikely that an entire term would be left implicit, especially in a commercial contract, explains Lord Hoffmann's point that the usual inference when the contract is silent is that nothing is to happen. The courts rightly approach an allegedly implicit term with the 'scepticism' inherent in the officious bystander test: it is only likely that

---

[145] Ibid, p. 392.

something will be left to go without saying when it is too obvious to need saying!

But still, the process remains the same one of determining the tacit intentions of the parties. There is no sharp line between 'interpretation' and 'implication'. 'As the primariness of information sits on a spectrum, the strictness of the test for supplementation should be a question of degree.'[146] Kramer's conclusion, therefore, is that 'terms implied in fact' should be abandoned as a separate category. Its continued existence suggests that at some point along the spectrum from implication of terms to construction of express terms, there must be 'a radical change in approach'.[147] But there is no such discontinuity. It is a fundamentally similar exercise, differing in emphasis with the degree of 'licence to supplement' claimed.

This is an important and interesting theoretical clarification. But the practical implications may be small. Kramer's argument justifies a demanding test for discovering a whole new term implicit in the contract. Lord Clarke MR observes that Lord Hoffmann's assimilation of implication and construction in *Belize Telecom* did not abolish the test of necessity for a term to be added to the contract.[148] He cited with approval Bingham MR's warning that it is 'difficult to infer with confidence' what the parties must have intended regarding some crisis in performance about which their 'lengthy and carefully-drafted contract' is silent.[149] It might be tempting for the court to fill the gap with the benefit of hindsight using the merits of the case: 'Tempting, but wrong'.[150]

In the *Mediterranean Salvage* case, the Court of Appeal refused to recognize as 'implicit' what the parties easily could, but had not, made explicit.[151] A ship was damaged by an underwater projection while chartered to the defendants; the claimant ship-owners argued that it was implicit in the contract that the charterers would ensure that the ship had a safe berth. But the basic risk of damage to the vessel lay on the owners, and if they wanted to shift it to the charterers the 'time-honoured way' was to extract a warranty of safety. These are commonly seen in ship charters of all kinds. The fact that the owners had failed to do so here meant that the risk remained with them.[152] The usual inference from silence applied, i.e. the loss lay where it fell.[153] The allegedly implicit term would be rejected when

---

[146] Ibid, p. 385.
[147] Cf. K. Lewison, *The Interpretation of Contracts* (Sweet & Maxwell, 3rd edn, 2004) p. 156.
[148] Cf. n.151 below.
[149] *Philips Electronique Grand Public SA v British Sky Broadcasting Ltd* [1995] EMLR 472.
[150] Ibid.
[151] *Mediterranean Salvage & Towage Ltd v Seamar Trading* [2009] EWCA Civ 531 [15].
[152] [2009] EWCA Civ 531 [61] (Rix LJ).
[153] [10] (Lord Clarke MR).

it 'would at best lie uneasily beside the express terms of the charter'.[154] Although Paul Davies has expressed concern that *Belize Telecom* will unsettle the law, giving the courts too much scope to rewrite contracts,[155] there is little evidence of this happening to date. Lord Hoffmann expressly warned that there is no judicial power to 'improve' the terms of the contract. Both Kramer and the courts recognize the need for a very strong case before a whole new term can be read in as implicit.

In conclusion, it seems hard to maintain that 'implication of terms in fact' is wholly different in nature from 'interpretation'. Both exercises aim to discover the implicit meanings of the contract. On the other hand, there is an important difference (albeit only a difference of degree) between clarifying or supplementing the meaning of an express term, and discovering an entirely new implicit obligation. The latter exercise is, as Bingham MR once observed, an 'altogether more ambitious undertaking', which is why the law places 'strict constraints' on this 'potentially intrusive' and 'extraordinary' power.[156] Adam Kramer's argument is to abandon the bright-line distinction between techniques that actually shade into each other, and this seems correct. But differences of degree remain, and must not be overlooked.

DEFAULT RULES: TERMS IMPLIED 'BY LAW'

Some terms are implied into an entire category of contracts. Lord Steyn referred to them as 'standardized implied terms' or 'general default rules'.[157] The standardization or generality is obvious enough. 'Default rules' are those that will apply in the absence of any expression by the parties to the contrary. In principle, and subject to certain statutory controls,[158] the parties are free to contract out of the default rules. But they are significant as the starting point, framing the process of negotiation, and will of course govern the contract unless otherwise stated.

The first problem is to clarify their relationship with 'terms implied in fact'. We could argue that the distinction between them is basically a difference between the general and the specific. If a term is implied into a one-off contract *ad hoc*, it is 'fact' but if it is adopted as prima facie suitable for a whole category of transactions this is a matter of 'law'. This would mean that there was a continuum rather than a sharp disjunction. Mance LJ recognizes that by sub-dividing the categories into more and smaller units with less general application, the line between the two blurs.[159] The view that there are 'shades on a continuous spectrum' appealed to Lord Wilberforce in the leading case *Liverpool City Council v Irwin*.[160] The House of Lords implied a term into a tenancy agreement with a local authority landlord

---

[154] *The APJ Priti* at 42 (Bingham MR) quoted at [48].
[155] P.S. Davies 'Recent Developments in the Law of Implied Terms' [2010] *LMCLQ* 140.
[156] *Philips Electronique Grand Public SA v British Sky Broadcasting Ltd* [1995] EMLR 472.
[157] Cf. n.132 above.
[158] Cf. UCTA 1977 s.6 (regarding terms implied by Sale of Goods Act 1979, ss.12–15).
[159] *Crossley v Faithful & Gould Holdings* [2004] EWCA Civ 293.
[160] [1977] AC 239.

of a high-rise block of flats, requiring that the landlord maintain the lifts and common parts of the building. Their Lordships upheld the decision of the Court of Appeal, but condemned the approach of Lord Denning MR. Lord Denning had implied the term on the simple basis that it was a fair and reasonable one in the circumstances (which he admitted was 'blasphemy'). The House of Lords declared this to be dangerous. The test was not whether the term was reasonable but whether it was *necessary*.

This seems to unify the approach to terms implied in fact and by law. However, Atiyah doubts whether there was much difference in substance (as opposed to rhetorically) between Lord Denning and Lord Wilberforce in *Irwin*.¹⁶¹ The House of Lords claimed to reach the same result by a safer route. But is it really necessary, in the strict sense, for the landlord to maintain the lifts of a block of flats? Even were the lifts themselves strictly necessary, the tenants could employ a lift mainte-nance company (and, crucially, pay for this service). No doubt there were practical advantages in leaving it to one landlord rather than requiring many tenants to organize themselves, as Collins suggests.¹⁶² But that hardly proves necessity – at best, the term was 'reasonably necessary', which is essentially Lord Denning's position.

Karl Llewellyn once referred to implied terms as 'the *minimum decencies* ... which the court will insist upon as essential to [or] inherent in a bargain of that type'.¹⁶³ This sounds a more promising approach to 'necessity'. We can hardly envisage a contract with no remedies for breach, for example. It would, legally speaking, be unenforceable. The law accordingly supplies remedies. Lord Diplock famously described the promisor's 'secondary obligations' to pay damages for breach as 'aris[ing] by implication of law, generally common law'. Yet since the contract was the source of these secondary (remedial) obligations, they could be modified by agreement between the parties.¹⁶⁴ In other words, the 'remedies for breach of contract' are merely default rules, terms implied by law.¹⁶⁵ Their pres-ence is necessary in any system of contract law, as a minimum requirement. If there are no agreed remedies defined in the contract, the law supplies them.

But remedies may be a special case. A binding legal contract without sanctions for breach is an oxymoron. But we can imagine contract law without, for example, the doctrine of frustration.¹⁶⁶ We can certainly imagine sales contracts without implied terms as to the quality of the subject matter: *caveat emptor* (let the buyer beware) remains the rule in real property sales.¹⁶⁷ No doubt Llewellyn would have thought such a stripped-down contract law to be indecently exposed. But strict necessity is a hard test to satisfy.

---

¹⁶¹ S.A. Smith, *Atiyah's An Introduction to the Law of Contract* (Oxford University Press, 6th edn, 2006).
¹⁶² H. Collins, *The Law of Contract* (4th ed, Cambridge University Press, 2003) p.245.
¹⁶³ K. Llewellyn 'Book Review' (1938–9) 52 *Harvard LR* 701, 703.
¹⁶⁴ *Photo Production v Securicor* [1980] AC 827, 848–49.
¹⁶⁵ Cf. Chapter 9 below.
¹⁶⁶ *Paradine v Jane* (1646) Al 26, cf. pp. 131–140 below.
¹⁶⁷ Cf. Sale of Goods Act 1979, ss. 14–15.

The aptness of necessity may, furthermore, be questioned (quite apart from its narrowness and/or indistinctiveness). In *Irwin*, necessity is clearly being read across from cases such as *The Moorcock* where, as seen above, it is useful to show what 'goes without saying'.[168] But Adam Kramer argues that terms 'implied by law' have nothing to do with the process of interpretation. Such terms are not implicit within the contract, and therefore attributable to the parties' intentions. Rather, they are being *imposed* on the contract – Kramer suggests 'constructive' terms as a more accurate description.[169] It can hardly be *necessary* to impose a term on a whole category of cases, nor can it go without saying. The basis for such terms is in legal policy, external to the contract, rather than the contract itself (including inferred meanings).

In *Irwin* Lord Cross correctly recognized that what the court was being invited to do was to insert a prima facie rule suitable for an entire category of cases (local authority tenancies). This depended on what was reasonable (as Lord Denning MR had rightly held). The necessity test of the officious bystander was useful for the different purpose of ascertaining the parties' unexpressed intentions so as to 'rectify' a particular contract.[170] Mance LJ has carefully drawn the same distinction, when invited to imply a general duty on employers to protect their employees' economic well-being.[171] His Lordship doubted the utility of the 'elusive' and 'somewhat protean' concept of necessity for implying a standardized term. Mance LJ suggested it was

> better to recognise that, to some extent at least, the existence and scope of standardised implied terms raise questions of reasonableness, fairness and the balancing of competing policy considerations.[172]

The leading analysis of the policies behind implied terms is Elisabeth Peden's. It was relied on by Mance LJ in the passage just quoted.[173] There is no such thing as one single 'public policy'. Peden therefore describes the variety of policy arguments that are used. These include the following: analogies with tort (especially where there is concurrent liability in tort and contract); analogies with legislative implied terms; deciding which of the parties is best placed to insure against, or to bear, the loss; the wider social effects of the implied term;[174] the parties' relative bargaining strength.

It will be seen without further argument that many of these policy factors are likely to give rise to controversy, and some will be wholly intractable. Peden provides little reassurance about the difficulty of the task in her portmanteau

---

[168] (1889) 14 PD 64.

[169] Kramer, n.133 above, p. 402, n.58.

[170] [1977] AC 239, 257–58.

[171] *Crossley v Faithful & Gould Holdings* [2004] EWCA Civ 293, [33].

[172] Ibid, [34], [36].

[173] Elisabeth Peden, 'Policy Concerns behind Implication of Terms in Law' (2001) 117 LQR 459.

[174] Eg *Lister v Romford Ice* [1956] AC 555 – employer's implied right to seek indemnity from employee against vicarious liability (employee's negligent driving) would increase incentives for careful driving by employees.

descriptions: 'the essence of the test is a consideration of the nature of the contract and of how to maximise the social utility of the relationship'. 'The underlying notion is always fairness or reasonableness, which requires a consideration of all the issues and a balancing of competing interests.' This is no doubt accurate, but underlines the indeterminacy of the exercise. Requiring consistency with the general principles of contract law does not help much, either. It first requires their identification and this too is highly controversial. As Peden notes, freedom of contract may be set against more 'progressive' notions of co-operation and good faith. But the correct balance between them is one of the most difficult and urgent questions facing contract lawyers today. It provides no sure guide for a court invited to impose a default rule on a category of contracts.

In the end, Peden aligns herself firmly with the proponents of good faith. Underlying all of the various policy factors, she claims, is 'a general overarching principle of co-operation'. This renders the 'otherwise vague element of policy concerns' relevant to imposition of terms 'more certain'. There are two problems with this argument. One is authority and the other is principle.

Peden relies heavily on *Malik v BCCI* where the House of Lords recognized mutual duties of good faith between employer and employee, in all contracts of employment.[175] Notably, Lord Steyn argued that this was rooted in the general duty of co-operation that exists between all contracting parties.[176] But it is elementary that there is no general duty of good faith between negotiating parties.[177] Although positive obstruction of performance may attract legal sanction,[178] the law is much less ready to impose positive duties of co-operation upon contractors. Devlin J once said that

> in the ordinary business contract, and apart, of course, from express terms, the law can enforce co-operation only in a limited degree – to the extent that is necessary to make the contract workable. For any higher degree of co-operation the parties must rely on the desire that both of them usually have that the business should get done.[179]

This is a clear recognition of the limits of *legal* enforcement of co-operation.

There is, moreover, a fierce debate about whether English law should recognize general duties of trust, co-operation and good faith.[180] Whether or not morality requires it,[181] some commentators argue that attempting to enforce social norms of trust through the legal process will be counterproductive.[182] No doubt some degree of co-operation, the minimum required for the contract to be workable,

---

[175] [1998] AC 20.

[176] See further *Mackay v Dick* (1881) 6 App Cas 251, discussed in E. Peden, 'Co-Operation in English Contract Law – To Construe Or Imply?' (2000) 16 *JCL* 56.

[177] *Walford v Miles* [1992] 2 AC 128.

[178] See e.g. *Nissho Iwai Petroleum v Cargill International* [1993] 1 Lloyd's Rep 80.

[179] *Mona Oil v Rhodesia Railways* [1949] 2 All ER 1014.

[180] See pp. 69–74 above.

[181] Cf. P. Finn, 'Commerce, the Common Law and Morality' (1989) 17 *Melbourne University LR* 87; G. Brennan, 'Commercial Law and Morality' (1989) 17 *Melbourne University LR* 100.

[182] See e.g. R.E. Scott, 'The death of contract law' (2004) 54 *Univ Toronto LJ* 369.

is implicit in every contract, as Devlin J accepted. But Peden moves from this uncontroversial minimal position to a pervasive norm of co-operation across the law of contract. This is a *non sequitur*. There is a defensible case for trust and co-operation in contract law, but Peden does not make that case, nor seem to recognize that it is necessary to do so.

Elisabeth Peden's work is valuable because it brings into the open the policy factors that lie behind the imposition or 'implication' of terms by law. The courts should not hide behind the 'necessity' test. It is confused to do so, because this is appropriate only for the inference of the parties' unexpressed intentions – and the imposition of standardized default rules has nothing to do with those intentions. It is welcome that Lord Cross and Mance LJ have recognized this. It may be inevitable that policy reasoning will be indeterminate, unless we can find an overall 'organizing policy' with which to rank the priority of the others. Peden suggests that co-operation may provide this organizing policy, but that is open to question. We will now examine another influential attempt to formulate a guiding criterion for default rules.

LAW AND ECONOMICS: EFFICIENT DEFAULT RULES

In this section we will consider the economist's approach to the implication of terms. The pursuit of economic efficiency provides an attractive organizing principle. The arguments are elegant and at the theoretical level would seem to provide useful guidance for legal development. But we will see that their practical implementation presents formidable difficulties.

The central idea of economic analysis of contract law is to 'maximise the social utility of the relationship', in Elizabeth Peden's phrase. Economists are interested in ways the law can reduce the cost of making contracts ('transaction costs') and so maximize the economic wealth of society: resources find their way into the hands of those who value them most through exchange. One important way for law to lower transaction costs is by supplying default rules (i.e. those that apply in the absence of agreement to the contrary). If the law can provide a set of 'efficient' default rules that mimic what the parties themselves would agree, this will minimize the cost of negotiation. The parties will not need to negotiate – they will be content for the default position to govern their contract.[183] A further possible advantage to relying on the default terms is that, being formulated by the courts, there is presumably little danger of judicial misinterpretation, whereas the parties' own express terms 'are always subject to an additional dimension of interpretation error'.[184]

An ideal term would maximize the overall value of the transaction, while providing for an acceptable division of the profits. This is what the parties would agree upon if there were no costs involved in negotiation. If the law can supply

---

[183] See eg R. Cooter & T. Ulen, *Law and Economics* (Addison Wesley, 4th edn, 2003) pp. 211–17.
[184] C.J. Goetz & R.E. Scott, 'The Limits of Expanded Choice: An Analysis of the Interactions Between Express and Implied Contract Terms' (1985) 73 *California LR* 261, 283.

such a term most contracting parties will presumably be very happy with it. Hence these terms are often described as 'majoritarian defaults'. As Goetz and Scott put it, 'implied terms expand contractors' choices by providing standardized and widely suitable "preformulations", thus eliminating the cost of negotiating every detail of the proposed arrangement'.[185] Note that standardization does not harm 'atypical' parties, who can of course contract out of the default rules.

This sounds marvellous in theory. But how, precisely, is the court to decide what the parties would have wanted? There may be evidence from trade practice, but not always. There seems to be no alternative but to inquire from first principles what rational parties would want. In brief, they demand efficient rules. But discerning what is 'efficient' proves difficult.

The 'remoteness of damage' test in *Hadley v Baxendale* has been extensively analysed as a default rule.[186] We will use it as the main example of economic analysis, although other doctrines such as frustration could also be used to illustrate the point.[187] Judge Richard Posner argues that untoward consequences should be allocated to the party 'who was able to avert the consequence at least cost and failed to do so'.[188] He identifies this as the 'animating principle' of *Hadley*. In *Hadley* itself the plaintiff mill-owner was, according to Posner, able to avert the consequential loss at least cost. His lost profits were attributable to his 'lack of prudence' in not having a spare mill-shaft. Hence his claim failed.

This would therefore be the efficient default rule that a majority of rational parties may be taken to want. Their joint costs are minimized (and therefore joint profits maximized) if the 'cheapest cost avoider' bears the relevant risk. However, Melvin Eisenberg argues that Posner reaches his blithe (and convenient) conclusion about *Hadley* far too readily. Calculations about the optimum level of spare parts are enormously complex, depending on their availability, cost, the probability of failure and so forth. Eisenberg finds no clear evidence that the plaintiff had acted imprudently.[189] The wider point is that the efficiency theory is much more complex to apply than first appears.[190]

A further complication is that *Hadley* has been explained by quite a different economic rationale. Instead of being a 'majoritarian default' that parties are presumed to want, it has been argued that *Hadley* is a 'penalty default'.[191] That is, a rule that the parties would *not* want, to encourage them to contract out of it. So, the restricted liability under the first, 'ordinary course of things' limb of *Hadley* serves to encourage a party who will suffer unusually large consequential losses on breach to reveal this fact, to ensure their recoverability. This tackles problems

---

[185] Ibid, 262.
[186] (1854) 9 Ex 341. Cf. *The Achilleas* [2008] UKHL 48 (Lord Hoffmann).
[187] Cf. pp. 128–131 below.
[188] *EVRA Corp v Swiss Bank Corp* 673 F.2d 951 (1982).
[189] M.A. Eisenberg, 'The Principle of *Hadley v. Baxendale*' (1992) 80 *California LR* 563.
[190] For criticism of *The Heron II* [1969] 1 AC 350 on efficiency grounds, cf. R.A. Epstein, 'Beyond Foreseeability: Consequential Damages in the Law of Contract' (1989) 18 *JLS* 105.
[191] I. Ayres & R. Gertner, 'Filling Gaps in Incomplete Contracts: An Economic Theory of Default Rules' (1989) 99 *Yale LJ* 87.

of strategic withholding of information. Such non-disclosure may lead to overall inefficiency (a smaller 'pie') through a party's efforts to gain a larger share of the surplus (a bigger slice of that (smaller) 'pie'). In *Hadley* itself, if the defendant carrier knew the true (high) value of the plaintiff's mill-shaft, he would take an appropriate (i.e. higher) level of care. He might also charge a premium price over his usual rates. The disclosure of information therefore leads to optimal behaviour on both sides.

But again, in practice, difficult questions arise, as Ayres and Gertner admit in their seminal article.[192] Are the gaps in a contract explicable by 'strategic incompleteness' or because negotiating a totally gapless contract is prohibitively expensive? Penalty defaults create incentives for further party negotiations – but is the cost of such negotiations lower than the court filling the gap through an efficient implied term? The most promising situation for a penalty default is where it will lead to the revelation of valuable information, at low cost (but how valuable, and at what cost?).

There are obvious difficulties in finding the empirical data necessary for these calculations, and Ayres and Gertner's analysis, path-breaking though it was, seems rather impressionistic. J.S. Johnson argues that their penalty defaults model is oversimplified.[193] If parties are withholding information strategically, they will also react strategically to rules designed to overcome this! Johnson notes that in game theory, used to model the behaviour of economic actors, the problem of withheld information is a central one. But a rich and realistic account of real-world haggling is beyond the reach of current game-theoretical models. This defeats any truly general account of the problem. In a later article, Ayres and Gertner seem to admit defeat: the introduction of even slight real-world elements to the model (such as strategic bargaining behaviour) makes the determination of efficient rules 'dramatically more difficult'.[194] While efficiency can be demonstrated in theory, 'our model suggests that there is small hope that lawmakers will be able to divine the efficient rule in practice'. They conclude that lawyer-economists should be more circumspect in claiming to find efficient rules when parties behave strategically.

Eisenberg anyway doubts the usefulness of the information 'induced' by *Hadley*.[195] Theoretically, the service provider will be able 'to efficiently stratify prices and precautions for buyers who present varying risks of liability'. But the conceivable efficiency gains will be severely curtailed, because it is very expensive to employ the information revealed: 'the cost of processing the information, stratifying precaution, or both will exceed the expected value of the stratifica-

---

[192] Ibid.
[193] J.S. Johnson, 'Strategic Bargaining and the Economic Theory of Contract Default Rules' (1990) 100 *Yale LJ* 615.
[194] I. Ayres & R. Gertner, 'Strategic Contractual Inefficiency and the Optimal Choice of Legal Rules' (1992) 101 *Yale LJ* 729.
[195] Eisenberg, n.189 above.

tion'. This is especially so when the chance of breach occurring is very low, as it usually is.

Eric Posner concludes, starkly, that economic analysis of contract law has largely failed.[196] The information with which to decide on the most efficient default rule is wholly lacking. So with *Hadley*, it matters whether the population of consigners is predominantly low-value (so would be content with the default rule) or high-value (with incentive to contract out of it). But there are not enough empirical data even to guess at the actual distribution. The normative prescriptions of economic analysis are therefore implausible or radically indeterminate. Duncan Kennedy claims the appeal of efficiency arguments is their – wholly spurious – objectivity. Economic analysis depends on 'probably unknowable social science data that no one would ever try to collect but which provides ample room for fanciful hypotheses'. Economics is in truth no more scientific than distributive justice arguments which are usually dismissed for their subjectivity.[197] On the other hand, Richard Posner argues that parties' reactions to default rules – whether they contract around them or not – provides an empirical test of the efficiency of the rule. But this is undermined by his admission that parties may passively adopt the default rule for other reasons, whether a psychological 'status quo bias' or a rational decision that renegotiation is not cost-effective when litigation is so rare.[198]

Richard Craswell admits much of Eric Posner's critique, when responding to it. The point of law and economics is not to provide all the answers, but to view the problems in the right way (identifying the costs and benefits of various proposed solutions).[199] But surely this represents a serious weakening of ambition.

The verdict on economic analysis of default terms is a pessimistic one. It provides a strong theoretical framework for the analysis of the problem. But it seems impossible to apply in practice; certainly for judges with limited data at their disposal.[200] Both the approach and the problems with it are shown well in the debate over the remoteness rule in *Hadley*. It can be rationalized as a majoritarian default that would maximize wealth in most cases, or as a penalty default providing incentives to reveal information by contracting out of the rule. The costs involved in such negotiation are very hard to estimate, as is the value of the information that would be produced. If trained economists have difficulty in answering such questions, it may be doubted whether the courts should even try. Alan Schwartz's comments may serve as our conclusion:

---

[196] E.A. Posner, 'Economic Analysis of Contract Law after Three Decades: Success Or Failure?' (2003) 112 *Yale LJ* 829.

[197] D. Kennedy, 'Distributive and Paternalist Motives in Contract and Tort Law' (1982) 41 *Maryland LR* 563.

[198] R.A. Posner, 'Let Us Never Blame a Contract Breaker' in O. Ben-Shahar & A. Porat (eds), *Fault in American Contract Law* (Cambridge University Press, 2010) p. 17.

[199] R. Craswell, 'Economics and the Demands of Contract Theory' (2003) 112 *Yale LJ* 903. See similarly A.A. Leff, 'Economic Analysis of Law: Some Realism about Nominalism' (1974) 60 *Virginia LR* 451.

[200] Cf. Chief Judge Wald, 'Limits on the Use of Economic Analysis in Judicial Decision-Making' (1987) 50 *Law & Contemporary Problems* 225.

State supplied defaults are seldom cost justified. This is due to high costs of state rule creation, party heterogeneity (too many contractual solutions are needed), the inability of the state to know what the benefits of good defaults are, and the state's relative lack of expertise in creating efficient contract terms.[201]

It seems that there is no alternative but to weigh up the various competing policies, when the court or legislature is deciding whether to imply (or rather impose) a term into a whole category of contracts. But if Schwartz is right about public institutions' capacity to do this well, it might be better for them not to supply terms on policy grounds at all.

Further Reading

Contract interpretation

A. Kramer, 'Common Sense Principles of Contract Interpretation (and How We've Been Using Them All along)' (2003) 23 *OJLS* 173.

C. Mitchell, *Interpretation of Contracts* (Routledge-Cavendish, 2007).

R. Calnan, 'Construction of Commercial Contract: A Practitioner's Perspective' in A. Burrows and E. Peel (eds), *Contract Terms* (Oxford University Press, 2007).

Lord Bingham, 'A New Thing Under the Sun? The Interpretation of Contracts and the *ICS* Decision' (2008) 12 *Edinburgh LR* 374.

Lord Grabiner QC, 'The Iterative Process of Contractual Interpretation' (2012) 128 *LQR* 41.

Implication of terms

I. Ayres & R. Gertner, 'Filling Gaps in Incomplete Contracts: An Economic Theory of Default Rules' (1989) 99 *Yale LJ* 87.

E. Peden, 'Policy Concerns behind Implication of Terms in Law' (2001) 117 *LQR* 459.

A. Kramer, 'Implication in Fact as An Instance of Contractual Interpretation' [2004] *CLJ* 384.

---

[201] A. Schwartz, 'Incomplete Contracts' in Newman (ed.) *New Palgrave Dictionary of Economics and the Law* (Macmillan, 1998) p. 282.

5

FRUSTRATION

Debate 1

What is the basis of the doctrine of frustration?

It is usually accepted that English law today has a doctrine of frustration of contracts, dating from *Taylor v Caldwell*.[1] Prior to 1863, the general rule was that contracts remained binding even in the face of radical change of circumstances. In the words of the classic authority *Paradine v Jane*, the parties could have made provision in their contract if they wanted it not to apply.[2] Even at the turn of the twentieth century *Paradine v Jane* was still treated as the general principle (to which *Taylor v Caldwell* was an exception) by contract lawyers such as Anson.[3] Catherine Macmillan finds that frustration was finally cemented in place by the Coronation Cases such as *Krell v Henry*[4] and the spate of litigation caused by the interruptions of the First World War.[5] The leading definition of frustration is Lord Radcliffe's in the *Davis Contractors* case: the change of circumstances would make performance 'a thing radically different from that which was undertaken by the contract. *Non haec in foedera veni.*[6] It was not this that I promised to do.'[7]

This sounds well, but placing the test in the 'decent obscurity of a learned language' hardly makes it clearer.[8] Lord Radcliffe admitted that the assessment must be an impressionistic one: 'In the nature of things there is often no room for any elaborate inquiry. The court must act on a general impression of what its rule requires.' Also, as Rix LJ notes, it is ironic that Aeneas's 'shabby excuse' for deserting Dido, Queen of Carthage, has become the watchword for frustration.[9]

---

[1] (1863) 3 B & S 826.

[2] (1648) Aleyn 26.

[3] Cf. 'The Ballad of Subsequent Impossibility' in W.R. Anson, *Ballads en Termes de la Ley* (Oxford, 1914).

[4] [1903] 2 KB 740.

[5] C Macmillan, '*Taylor v. Caldwell* (1863)' in C. Mitchell & P. Mitchell (eds), *Landmark Cases in the Law of Contract* (Hart Publishing, 2008).

[6] Virgil, *Aeneid* IV, 338–39.

[7] *Davis Contractors Ltd v Fareham UDC* [1956] AC 696, 728.

[8] B. Nicholas, 'Impracticability and Impossibility in the U.N. Convention on Contracts for the International Sale of Goods' in Galston & Smit (eds), *International Sales* (Matthew Bender, 1984).

[9] *The Sea Angel* [2007] 2 Lloyd's Rep 517, [84].

Nonetheless, Lord Radcliffe's test has been approved as canonical by the House of Lords: 'always remembering that the doctrine is not lightly to be invoked to relieve contracting parties of the normal consequences of imprudent commercial bargains.'[10]

The existence and definition of frustration are, therefore, now widely accepted. However, the theoretical basis for the doctrine remains controversial. Lord Radcliffe famously held that frustration was not based on the parties' intentions. The court decided the question as spokesman for that 'anthropomorphic conception of justice', the reasonable man.[11] Admitting that frustration is an imposed solution only puts the question back a stage, however. When should the court exercise this power? One popular justification is some form of justice or fairness, in mitigation of the usual strict liability for breach of contract. Or, alternatively, frustration may be conceived as an exercise in risk allocation, with the most developed argument here coming from economic analysis. Before examining these contentions, however, it is necessary to examine the situations in which the law may hold contracts to be frustrated in further detail.

SUPERVENING ILLEGALITY

There can be no doubt that where contractual performance is rendered illegal by some change in the law subsequent to the agreement, it is discharged by operation of law from that point. This is the explanation for many frustration cases arising out of the two world wars – all Anglo-German contracts became illegal to perform on the outbreak of war (the crime of trading with the enemy). But in many ways this is an atypical situation within the law of frustration. It is really a branch of the public policy doctrine, the 'illegality defence' (*ex turpi causa non oritur actio*). That is not an area of law that we examine in this book. But the idea is simple enough. A contract to commit a crime is unenforceable from the outset. A contract which is lawful at the time of agreement is not caught by this rule, but if the law subsequently changes to render the performance illegal it becomes unenforceable from that point – both parties are discharged from further performance. The rationale, in both cases, is for contract law to be consistent with other branches of the law.

As Beatson J recently observed,[12] it is usual to treat supervening illegality within the conception and terminology of frustration,[13] although Lord McNair had deplored this tendency as long ago as 1948.[14] There is much to be said for McNair's view. While elsewhere, there is no room for frustration when the parties have (or should have) catered for the situation in their contract, it is irrelevant that an alteration in the law was foreseeable, foreseen or even expressly provided

---

[10] *The Nema* [1982] AC 724 (Lord Roskill).
[11] *Davis Contractors*, n.7 above.
[12] *Islamic Republic of Iran Shipping Lines v Steamship Mutual Underwriting Association (Bermuda)* [2010] EWHC 2661 (Comm) at [100].
[13] *Chitty on Contracts* 30th edn, pp. 23–24.
[14] A.D. McNair, *Legal Effects of War* (3rd edn, 1948) p. 134.

for by the parties. In *Ertel Bieber v Rio Tinto* a clause suspending a contract between British and German companies for the duration of the war was invalid, as it would tend to hamper the trade of the British seller while increasing the freedom of action of the German buyer.[15] It is clear that public policy (when strong enough to invalidate the contract) takes precedence over the allocation of risks by the parties. It is significant that supervening illegality discharged contracts even during the *Paradine v Jane*[16] era of 'absolute contracts', prior to *Taylor v Caldwell*.[17] It is strongly arguable that supervening illegality is entirely separate from other areas of frustration, with such a distinctive rationale that it should be viewed as an unrelated doctrine.

IMPOSSIBILITY, IMPRACTICABILITY AND FRUSTRATION OF PURPOSE

As suggested in the previous section, the really important division in the taxonomy of frustration is between supervening illegality (a head of public policy) and other grounds for discharge. In brief, the law seems to be that impossibility of performance may sometimes discharge a contract; but it is rare for impracticability or frustration of purpose to do so.

Some believe, on the strength of *Taylor v Caldwell*,[18] that destruction of the subject matter of the contract automatically leads to its frustration. But it is not necessarily so. As Sir Guenter Treitel says,[19] while destruction of essential subject matter is generally sufficient for frustration, 'destruction' is a relative concept – the walls of the Surrey Music Hall remained standing after the fire in *Taylor v Caldwell* (not to mention the attached Pleasure Gardens with their fireworks, 'Chinese and Parisian games', 'wizard' and (weather permitting) 'aquatic sport'!). Was the Parthenon in Athens 'destroyed' by the explosion of 1687? Also, destruction does not equate to absolute impossibility – perhaps the Music Hall could have been reconstructed in time for the concerts, with superhuman efforts (and at vast expense).

More fundamentally, there is no general doctrine of supervening impossibility equivalent to that of supervening illegality.[20] Such a general proposition is both too broad and too narrow: some contracts are not frustrated even when performance becomes impossible; conversely, contracts have been discharged even though performance remained physically possible. We turn to the latter presently. What of cases where the contract remains fully in force (and the promisor liable for breach) even though performance has become impossible?

In *Blackburn Bobbin v TW Allen & Sons* the impossibility of importing timber from Finland during the First World War did not frustrate a contract for sale of such

---

15 [1918] AC 260.
16 (1648) Aleyn 26.
17 (1863) 3 B & S 826.
18 Ibid.
19 G.H. Treitel, *Frustration and Force Majeure* (2nd edn, Sweet & Maxwell, 2004) Ch. 3 (hereafter 'Treitel').
20 *Joseph Constantine Steamship Line v Imperial Smelting Corp* [1942] AC 154 (Viscount Simon LC).

timber.[21] It was 'of the utmost importance to a commercial nation that vendors should be held to their business contracts', unless they had inserted a term to excuse themselves. A more recent example is *The Mary Nour*.[22] The buyer desired cement to break a Mexican cartel operated by a third party company, Cemtex. But the seller was unable to fulfil the contract because Cemtex managed to place Asian cement suppliers under pressure too. There was no doubt that the seller did all that it could; it was simply impossible to purchase sufficient Asian cement to perform. Nevertheless, the court held that the contract was not frustrated by the failure of the ultimate source of supply. A seller assumes the risk of his supplier's failure. The rationale was explained very clearly by Field J at first instance. There is always a risk of supplier failure and as between the buyer and seller, the seller is clearly in a better position to guard against it. He may enter into a binding and enforceable contract with the supplier, or make his promise to the buyer conditional on the goods' continued availability.[23]

These cases show that impossibility is not sufficient for frustration. Nor is it necessary. *Krell v Henry* is a leading case in which performance of the contract was perfectly possible, i.e. letting the rooms and paying the hire charge. However, the court held that the purpose of the contract had been frustrated by the cancellation of King Edward VII's coronation.[24] While it was still perfectly possible for Mr Henry to pay the hire charge, the change of circumstances meant that the rooms were now virtually worthless for him. Treitel points out that the Coronation Cases have rarely been applied in England – indeed, he states that there is no clear example of a decision directly following *Krell*,[25] whereas many cases show a striking reluctance to release parties who have paid over the odds (in the light of experience). In *Amalgamated Investment & Property v John Walker*,[26] government 'listing' of a building shortly after the contract of sale reduced its value from £1.7m to £0.2m. The buyer's plea of frustration was unsuccessful. The possibility of buildings becoming listed was inherent in property ownership. Therefore, this was a known risk for buyers to evaluate 'in considering whether to buy and at what price'. Should the risk mature into loss, that loss must lie where it falls (i.e. on the buyer). As Treitel says, the courts display caution in the face of bad bargains, to protect the sanctity of contract.[27]

The courts have displayed no more sympathy in the converse situation, where performance remains physically possible but financially impracticable. The law of insurance, through the concept of a constructive total loss, recognizes that repairs at unreasonable or prohibitive cost are treated as commercially impossible.[28] But in contract law, unexpected increases in expense are rarely sufficient to discharge

---

[21] [1918] 1 KB 540; [1918] 2 KB 467.
[22] [2008] 2 Lloyd's Rep. 526.
[23] [2007] EWHC 2070 (Comm).
[24] [1903] 2 KB 740.
[25] Treitel, Ch. 7 (conclusion).
[26] [1976] 3 All ER 509.
[27] Treitel, 7–004.
[28] *Moss v Smith* (1850) 9 CB 94.

the contract. In the leading case of *Davis Contractors*, performance of a building contract was rendered more onerous by shortages of labour in the period after the Second World War. This was insufficient to frustrate the contract.[29] According to Lord Reid, 'the contractor undertakes to do the work for a definite sum and he takes the risk of the cost being greater or less than he expected'. Lord Radcliffe held that the shortage of labour had been readily foreseeable and the contractors could have protected themselves through suitable clauses and pricing in the original tender. As Lord Denning MR summed it up in *The Eugenia*, for performance to become 'a thing radically different' it was not sufficient for it to be more onerous or expensive: 'It must be positively unjust to hold the parties bound'.[30] But as Lord Denning noted, it will often be difficult to draw the line.

Treitel notes that in 1918, a Board of Trade committee examined the 'harsh' position at common law whereby increased costs did not frustrate contracts 'unless to an enormous and extravagant extent, ... [or] so great as to amount to physical prevention'. Nevertheless, the committee did not recommend any change in the law – the desire for certainty and to uphold sanctity of contract prevailed, even at the cost of harshness.[31]

How is the discharge of contracts by frustration to be explained – whatever the precise contours of the doctrine? The explanations fall into two camps. First, those that appeal to notions of fairness, external to the contract. Secondly, explanations that examine the allocation of risks, where possible within the contract, although accepting that the parties' intentions may need to be supplemented by legal implication. We examine these in turn.

JUSTICE

Frustration is often explained by pointing to notions of fairness and justice.[32] The difficulty comes in defining these inevitably nebulous terms. Furthermore, why is it thought proper to modify contracts when circumstances change, but not otherwise?

Many leading judicial statements place fairness at the heart of the doctrine.[33] Lord Sumner declared that frustration was 'really a device, by which the rules as to absolute contracts are reconciled with a special exception which justice demands'.[34] Lord Simon of Glaisdale said that the doctrine was 'an expedient to escape from injustice' which justifies departure from the literal terms of the contract in order to 'vindicate justice'.[35] In an influential summary, Bingham LJ said that the proposition that frustration existed to 'mitigate the rigour' of absolute liability was 'not open to question'.[36] Rix LJ has recently held that although

---

[29] [1956] AC 696.

[30] [1964] 2 QB 226.

[31] Treitel, Ch. 6.

[32] E.g. G.J. Webber, 'Frustration of Contract' (1951) 4 *CLP* 283.

[33] Cf. Lord Denning, n.30 above; *Joseph Constantine v Imperial Smelting Corp* [1942] AC 154 (Lord Wright).

[34] *Hirji Mulji v Cheong Yue Steamship Co Ltd* [1926] AC 497.

[35] *National Carriers v Panalpina (Northern)* [1981] AC 675, 701.

[36] *J Lauritzen AS v Wijsmuller BV ('The Super Servant Two')* [1990] 1 Lloyd's Rep 1, 8.

the court has no 'broad absolving power', justice provides frustration's 'ultimate rationale'.[37]

But in none of the copious statements about justice do the eminent judges attempt to define what they say is the basis of the doctrine. Is this not a major flaw in the explanation? Hard-nosed commercial lawyers would disagree that there is anything 'unjust' in holding parties to the unqualified words of their contract. Lord Diplock memorably observed that: 'The only merits of the case are that parties who have bargained on equal terms in a free market should stick to their agreements. Justice is done by seeing that they do so.'[38] To opposite effect, Denning LJ once said of interpretation in a frustration case that the words of the contract must not become the court's 'tyrannical masters': 'The old maxim reminds us that … He who clings to the letter, clings to the dry and barren shell, and misses the truth and substance of the matter'.[39] But this simply revives the question of what 'the truth and substance' is, and assumes that holding the parties to the word of the contract is 'barren'.

Another problem arises from the fact that 'frustration brings the contract to an end forthwith, without more and automatically'.[40] The effect of frustration will be considered in Debate 3. But the stark nature of its operation is evident. A court intent on 'doing justice' might well find such a rigid, automatic rule insufficiently flexible for the task. Denning LJ, indeed, once suggested that the court should exercise a qualifying power 'in order to do what is just and reasonable in the new situation'.[41] However, this was expressly disapproved by Lord Simonds on appeal.[42] Lord Denning later complained that the parties would never have agreed to an automatic discharge of the contract, had they given their minds to the change of circumstances. Rather, each side would have sought 'reservations or qualifications of one kind or another'.[43] Lord Denning argued that this discredited the 'implied term' theory of frustration – the parties would never have desired the absolute discharge that the law imposes. But the same rigidity counts against the 'fairness' explanation of frustration.

A final problem is to explain why judicial interference with contracts is justified in this situation only. It appears inconsistent for the common law to rediscover a concern with fairness and justice in the singular situation of change of circumstances. Indeed, as George Trianitis asks, why regulate the unfairness of unusual losses when there is judicial unconcern over unexpected windfall *gains*?[44]

---

[37] *The Sea Angel* [2007] 2 Lloyd's Rep 517, [113], [132].

[38] *The Maratha Envoy* [1978] AC 1.

[39] *British Movietonews v London and District Cinemas* [1951] 1 KB 190.

[40] *Hirji Mulji v Cheong Yue Steamship Co Ltd* [1926] AC 497.

[41] *British Movietonews v London and District Cinemas* [1951] 1 KB 190, 200. Cf. also *Solle v Butcher* [1950] 1 KB 671, pp. 180–183 below.

[42] [1952] AC 166, 188.

[43] *The Eugenia* [1964] 2 QB 226. Cf. *Denny, Mott & Dickson v Fraser* [1944] AC 265, 273–76: 'As to that, the court cannot guess' (Lord Wright).

[44] G.G. Trianis 'Contractual Allocations of Unknown Risks: A Critique of the Doctrine of Commercial Impracticability' (1992) 42 *Univ Toronto LJ* 450.

Treitel observes that there has been unusually elaborate judicial discussion of the basis of frustration,[45] compared with other important areas such as termination for breach.[46] Treitel suggests that this betrays uneasiness about the effect of the doctrine on the binding nature ('sanctity') of contracts. It might also suggest a continuing inability to formulate the emotionally appealing idea of a 'concession to justice' in intellectually satisfying terms. Lord Hailsham LC once commented that this might admirably express the purpose of frustration but leaves the doctrine with no theoretical basis at all.[47] Ewan McKendrick notes that the 'justice' formulation means that 'uncertainty [is] inherent in the doctrine of frustration'.[48] This is worrying in any sphere of commercial law.

RISK ALLOCATION

Risk allocation is at the heart of contract law. This was understood long ago by Oliver Wendell Holmes. It explains why we can make valid legal promises in respect of things that are entirely outside our control, such as the 'promise' that it will rain tomorrow.[49] Really what this means is that the promisor is taking the risk of the weather being fine, and promising to pay damages if it does not rain. Why should a promisor unconditionally assume such a risk? As Judge Richard Posner says, it is not because the promisor believes he has 'superhuman powers' but because he can 'insure against the risk of nonperformance better than the promisee, or obtain a substitute performance more easily than the promisee'.[50] Judge Learned Hand makes clear the reason why even impossibility should not usually lead to the discharge of the contract: every promise involves the risk of difficult or even impossible performance, but the 'very purpose [of the contract] is to give assurance to the promisee against hazards of the future'.[51] As Lord Sumner once observed:

> In effect, most forward contracts can be regarded as a form of commercial insurance in which every event is intended to be at the risk of one party or another. Each party is likely most to need the maintenance of such a contract exactly when the other would most wish to be rid of it.[52]

In other words, the whole point of the contract may be to place the risk of nonperformance because of external causes onto the promisor. This is clearly the case with insurance contracts. It might seem, at first sight, grossly unfair that an insurer should bear a multi-million-pound loss from a freak accident when the

---

[45] E.g. *National Carriers Ltd v Panalpina (Northern) Ltd* [1981] AC 675.

[46] Treitel, ch. 16.

[47] *Panalpina*, n.45 above.

[48] E. McKendrick, 'Force Majeure and Frustration – Their Relationship and a Comparative Assessment' in E. McKendrick (ed.), *Force Majeure and Frustration of Contract* (2nd edn, Lloyd's of London Press, 1994) p. 39.

[49] O.W. Holmes, *The Common Law* (1881) pp. 299–300.

[50] *Northern Indiana v Carbon County Coal Co* (1986) 799 F. 2d 265.

[51] *Companhia de Navegaceo Lloyd Brasilerio v Blake* (1929) 34 F 2d 616, 619.

[52] *Larrinaga & Co v Societe Franco-Americaine des Phosphates* (1923) 14 Ll L Rep 457, 464.

policyholder had paid only a ten-pound premium. But, of course, the sole purpose of such a contract is precisely to allocate such risks to the insurer.[53]

The point is not limited to the special situation of insurance per se. As John Swan says: 'The making of any bargain necessarily involves the creation of a risk that subsequent events will cause the bargain to turn out to be less advantageous to one party than might have been hoped at the time it was made'.[54] Often the way that parties choose between different forms of contract determines where the risk will lie. A good example is in the charter of ships. Someone needing to convey a cargo from Liverpool to Shanghai may charter a vessel either for that *voyage* for a fixed sum, or on a *time* basis. The choice between these contracts will affect the location of the risk of delays caused by the closure of a shipping lane such as the Suez Canal. Such closure will extend the length of the voyage in both miles and days. If the charterer is paying a fixed price for the voyage, however, he will be financially unaffected. On the other hand, where there is a time charter the freight is payable by the day, and the cost of delays will now fall upon the charterer rather than the owner.

At least as a starting point, therefore, an unqualified contractual obligation implicitly allocates risks to the party who has agreed to perform for a fixed price (in voyage charters, the shipowner).[55] Should the risk eventuate, ripening into loss, the loss will fall upon that party. As Judge Posner says, 'a fixed-price [sale] contract is an explicit assignment of the risk of market price increases to the seller and the risk of market price decreases to the buyer'.[56] Where does frustration fit into this?

The beginning of wisdom, according to Edwin Patterson, is to recognize that risk-bearing is a perpetual question of business activity, and that frustration is a device for addressing it: 'Merely getting the obligation stated as one of risk-taking is … a considerable advance over the old statement of the will theory'.[57] Holding the contract frustrated shifts the loss (or viewed *ex ante*, the risk) from the promisor, who would otherwise be in breach of his obligations, onto the promisee. It may be questioned whether English law has yet reached the point of development that Patterson identified in 1924 – as seen above, a mysterious and indefinable sense of 'justice' seems to be the most popular judicial explanation. Patterson criticized the unhelpfulness of frustration doctrine, too. Its concepts 'do not guide us to a solution of risk-apportioning problems; they merely lead us by devious paths to the point we started from'. Patterson had no time for Aristotelian and Stoic metaphysical distinctions about the 'substance' of vinegar and (sour) wine, familiar from the law on mistake (*'error in substantia'*). Abstract approaches excluded the

---

[53] J. Gordley, *Foundations of Private Law* (Oxford University Press, 2006) p. 345.

[54] J. Swan, 'The Allocation of Risk in the Analysis of Mistake and Frustration' in B.J. Reiter and J. Swan (eds), *Studies in Contract Law* (Butterworths, 1980).

[55] Cf. P.S. Atiyah, *Essays on Contract* (Oxford University Press, 1990) pp. 169–70 (the risk-allocation function of contract has been exaggerated).

[56] *Northern Indiana*, n.50 above.

[57] E.W. Patterson, 'The Apportionment of Business Risks through Legal Devices' (1924) 24 *Columbia LR* 335.

most important consideration, i.e. risk allocation, in favour of physical and 'other adventitious factors'. In such a state, doctrinal analysis alone could not answer questions about risk. John Swan similarly warns that the traditional doctrine, vague and manipulable, must be replaced by open discussion of the allocation of risk. Only then can the courts evolve useful rules.[58]

Patterson accepted that courts were not well placed to make decisions about the allocation of risk. This explained their retreat into 'an attempted logical development of legal rules and concepts rather than a formulation of social policies as to the ultimate incidence of the burden of risk'. But ultimately, the task of formulating such policies is unavoidable. Patterson himself was vague about what they should be. Economists have attempted to provide the answer.

ECONOMIC EFFICIENCY AND THE 'SUPERIOR RISK BEARER'

The seminal economic analysis of frustration is by Richard Posner and Andrew Rosenfield.[59] The basic problem in every case, they say, is the same: 'to decide who should bear the loss from an event that has rendered performance by one party uneconomical'. They are critical of the 'pointless subcategories' into which the legal doctrine has fragmented. They also deplore the contention that 'a broad and undefined judicial discretion, the result of such amorphous *ad hoc* concepts as fairness, equity and justice, is all that is required to handle the discharge issue adequately'.[60] Nor are they impressed by authors such as Corbin who recognize that frustration is about risk allocation but provide no useful guidance how to do it – Corbin said the court must 'exercise its equity powers and pray for the wisdom of Solomon'![61]

What is the correct approach, according to Posner and Rosenfield? In a nutshell, the court should *shift the loss to the promisee when he is better able to bear it*, 'either because he is in a better position to prevent the risk from materializing or because he can better reduce the disutility of the risk (as by insuring) if the risk does occur'.[62] Posner and Rosenfield refer to such a party as the 'superior risk bearer'. Where the promisor is the superior risk bearer, frustration should not of course apply. In the ordinary way, the risk of non-performance will then remain on the promisor. The parties would *both* want the risk to lie on the party best able to bear it, as this minimizes their joint costs, thus maximizing the profit from the contract to be divided between them.[63] Posner and Rosenfield suggest that inefficient contract rules are futile, since parties will contract out of them.

[58] Swan, n.54 above, 232. See also W. Swadling, 'The Judicial Construction of *Force Majeure* Clauses' in McKendrick (ed.), n.48 above.
[59] R.A. Posner & A.M. Rosenfield, 'Impossibility and Related Doctrines in Contract Law: An Economic Analysis' (1977) 6 *JLS* 83.
[60] Ibid, p. 87.
[61] A.L. Corbin, *Contracts* (1962) p. 372.
[62] *Northern Indiana*, n.50 above, 278 (Posner J).
[63] For an argument that the loss should be divided between the parties in proportion to their ability to bear it, cf. L.E. Trakman, 'Winner Take Some: Loss Sharing and Commercial Impracticability' (1985) 69 *Minn L Rev* 471.

The two criteria for a superior risk bearer are being able to prevent the risk from occurring or being able to insure against it (since many risks are not preventable). To assess the ability to insure, the relevant factors are the parties' relative knowledge of the magnitude of the loss and the chance of its occurring, and other costs of self- or market insurance. Posner and Rosenfield admit that when the key parameters point in different directions, the analysis is indeterminate and the court must proceed by estimating the factors' relative empirical importance. They also admit that their paper is incomplete, and its empirical methods 'casual and crude'. But they claim that they have identified the correct framework for analysis, setting out a programme for further research, e.g. examining the provisions of actual contracts.

Many critics agree that Posner and Rosenfield's approach is indeterminate. But this has often been seen as a fatal flaw. Only rarely, and through oversimplification, does the 'superior risk bearer' analysis yield firm recommendations for legal doctrine. Michael Trebilcock says the factors involved are 'typically' equivocal or contradictory.[64] Let us first examine the economic analysis of one of the Coronation Cases.

Judge Posner approves the decision in *Krell v Henry*:[65] the parties could not have intended Henry (the hirer) to insure Krell (the owner) against the cancellation of the coronation procession since Krell could re-let the rooms for people to view the later, postponed procession (once King Edward had recovered). Therefore, Krell was the superior risk bearer and the court was right to discharge the contract.[66] But Sir Guenter Treitel criticizes Posner's reasoning.[67] An assumption that Krell was better placed to insure against such loss is questionable when it would not be covered by ordinary household insurance, although insurance was taken out by some of the *commercial* organizations which had erected stands on the coronation route. Secondly, the argument that Krell could recoup his losses in full by re-letting the rooms is less than compelling. The eventual (October) procession was less splendid and followed a different route (although it did in the event traverse Pall Mall, the setting for *Krell*). What if Krell had wasted expenditure in readying the rooms for the original, June procession? And should it really have made a difference if Edward VII had died during his appendectomy – or Britain had become a Republic?

Swan argues that the necessary information was not before the court. Counsel did not present it as a risk allocation case. Renting rooms for coronation processions is an unusual activity for which there is no well-established market and there was no evidence of these parties' expectations. It is this absence of information that makes *Krell* a difficult case.[68] John Wladis argues, to the contrary, that *Krell* was easy to decide. Discharging the contract imposed no loss on Krell – his

---

[64] M.J. Trebilcock, *The Limits of Freedom of Contract* (Harvard University Press, 1993) ch. 5.
[65] [1903] 2 KB 740.
[66] *Northern Indiana,* n.50 above, 277.
[67] Treitel, ch. 7.
[68] Swan, n.54 above.

profits were merely delayed, rather than irretrievably lost – whereas upholding the contract would have meant Henry paying dearly for something of no value (a view of the ordinary London traffic).[69] Given the merits, it is not surprising that the contract was held frustrated.

Wladis admits that the 'peculiar circumstances of the case' means that *Krell* has rarely if ever been applied since. In other words it will be uncommon for loss allocation problems to be so straightforward. But Robert Birmingham doubts this: cases where performance would lead to a straightforward transfer from one party to the other because of unexpected circumstances are 'as plentiful as blackberries'.[70] For example, closure of the Suez Canal would impose losses on ship-owners and corresponding gains on charterers, when they had entered into a fixed price voyage charter. Birmingham argues that discharging the contract would be efficient: there is then no net loss (unlike destruction cases like *Taylor v Caldwell*,[71] where there is an ineradicable loss requiring allocation, rather than just an inter-party transfer). But does Birmingham's proposal not ignore the implicit risk allocation by the parties, when choosing a fixed-price voyage charter in the first place? Also, as Treitel notes, the seller's increased costs of carriage in the Suez Canal cases were more than offset by the rise in price of the goods (that rise also attributable to the interruption of supply on the closure of the canal).[72]

Alan Sykes also considers *Taylor v Caldwell*.[73] The rule that destruction of specific subject matter frustrates the contract is at least clear. But it is much harder to say whether it is efficient. Placing the risk on the owner of the music hall encourages him to take precautions against fire or other loss, and to insure against it. Sykes points to an American case in which it was held (following *Taylor*) that failure of the electricity supply at a theatre, leading to cancellation of a concert, would frustrate the contract between the theatre-owner and concert promoter *unless* it would have been reasonable for the owner to have a back-up generator.[74] Sykes finds that such generators are common in practice, and thus argues that it would cause 'moral hazard' (i.e. deter reasonable precautions) if theatre-owners were discharged from liability on the failure of electricity supply. But on the other hand, discharging the contract and so placing the risk on the concert promoter would prevent 'overreliance' on his part, i.e. investing in the concert on the basis that it was certain to go ahead whereas in fact (like everything in life!) it was not.[75] In the end, Sykes finds that it is no more than conjecture which way these opposing arguments should be balanced. We can have no confidence that the

---

[69] J.D. Wladis, 'Common Law and Uncommon Events: The Development of the Doctrine of Impossibility of Performance in English Contract Law' (1987) 75 *Georgetown LJ* 1575, 1618–21.

[70] R.L. Birmingham, 'Why Is There *Taylor v. Caldwell*? Three Propositions about Impracticability' (1989) 23 *USF L Rev* 379, 393.

[71] (1863) 3 B & S 826.

[72] Treitel, 15–009.

[73] A.O. Sykes, 'The Doctrine of Commercial Impracticability in a Second-Best World' (1990) 19 *JLS* 43.

[74] *Opera Co of Boston v Wolf Trap Foundation* (1987) 817 F.2d 1094.

[75] S.M. Shavell, 'Damages Measures for Breach of Contract' (1980) 11 *Bell Jo Economics* 466.

rule in *Taylor v Caldwell* is efficient (that does not necessarily mean it is inefficient). Nothing in the report of the case gives the information necessary for a full economic assessment.[76]

The doubts whether Posner and Rosenfield's approach is workable in practice go wider than particular cases. John Elofson states that answering the question of which party is better placed to insure is likely to be 'arbitrary and unpredictable' – wholly unclear without minute analysis of each party's risk-pooling ability.[77] Birmingham argues that cases like *Taylor v Caldwell* (where there is a joint net loss, not merely a transfer between the parties) are 'undecidable'. The loss has to be placed on one or other party but without contractual provision to determine this and when neither is at fault, there is no basis on which to do it (or indeed, to divide the loss).[78] As Sykes concludes, 'it is exceptionally difficult to formulate a default rule of contract law that limits discharge to the circumstances in which it is efficient – to administer such a rule, the courts will typically require more information than is reasonably available to them'.[79] Eric Posner has concluded that three decades of economic analysis of contract law generally has been a failure. A prime reason for this is the absence of the empirical data necessary to apply the theoretical economic models in practice.[80]

Richard Posner's theory of risk allocation seems a prime example of a model convincing on the theoretical level only. If people could write the perfect contract, one term in it would be to assign the risk of adverse events to the party best able to cope with them. This would decrease the joint costs of the parties, meaning a larger profit to divide between them. But in the end, we must question whether the courts are really better placed to write such a 'perfect term' than the parties. It seems much easier to 'recognize' that frustration is about risk allocation than to state with precision how the law should go about allocating risks.

One radical deduction from this premise is that there is no need for a doctrine of frustration at all. The law should leave it up to the parties to assign the risks of loss. The default rule is that the loss lies where it falls, unless the parties have contracted out of it. This is the subject of Debate 2.

Debate 2

Do we need the doctrine of frustration?

It is surprising to suggest that a well-established doctrine like frustration might be surplus to requirements. However, as seen above, it is a comparative latecomer in

---

[76] Sykes (1990) 19 *JLS* 43, 85.
[77] J. Elofson, 'The Dilemma of Changed Circumstances in Contract Law: An Economic Analysis of the Foreseeability and Superior Risk Bearer Tests' (1996) 30 *Colum JL & Soc Probs* 1, 13.
[78] Birmingham, n.70 above.
[79] Sykes, n.73 above.
[80] E.A. Posner, 'Economic Analysis of Contract Law after Three Decades: Success Or Failure?' (2003) 112 *Yale LJ* 829. Cf. pp. 117–119 above.

English law, with the rule of 'absolute contracts' persisting into the early twentieth century (excepting the situation of supervening illegality which has always been recognized as discharging a contract, for good but distinctive reasons). So the doctrine's absence is not wholly inconceivable.

That something is possible does not mean that it is a good idea. What is so wrong with frustration that might justify abolition? As seen above, both explanations for the basis of frustration are problematic. The explanation of justice and fairness is extremely ill-defined: more emotional than intellectual, and inconsistent with the rest of contract law. The loss allocation approach seems more consistent with the function of contracts. However, applying it in practice seems as uncertain as the 'justice' approach, even when fleshed out by economic analysis. It is not surprising that with such an uncertain basis, the doctrine has been criticized. Andrew Rogers, formerly chief judge in the commercial court of New South Wales, complains that frustration is 'one of the least successful of the efforts of lawyers to meet the needs of commerce', being both uncertain and inadequate.[81] Elofson dismisses frustration as a legal morass with a needless proliferation of categories and theories.[82]

This is the negative limb of the critique. The positive claim is that allocating the risk of interrupted performance ought in principle to be left up to the parties. This has the appeal of straightforward freedom of contract: it is not for the courts to make the contract. Accordingly, some commentators like Sir John Smith argue that there is simply no room for a distinct doctrine of frustration additional to the court's omnipresent task of determining the meaning of the contract by construction and implication.[83] But if the contract has not allocated the risk then, according to Andrew Kull, a 'principle of inertia' applies – there is nothing to justify the shifting of losses. Accordingly, they must lie where they fall.[84]

Therefore, the nub of the Debate is whether to leave risk allocation to the parties. There are arguments against this. Is it not self-contradictory to relegate to drafters what are by definition *unforeseeable* events? Does this not demand of them 'the foresight of a prophet', as Denning LJ once put it?[85] If Rogers is correct that it would be 'offensive' to commercial parties to hold them bound by contracts whose basis is falsified by subsequent events, should the law not reflect this view?[86] One essential question, then, is how much foresight may reasonably be attributed to the parties. How realistic is it to leave risk allocation purely to them? Should the default rule, in the absence of any discernible intention either way by the parties, be absolute liability or include discharge for interrupted performance?

---

[81] A. Rogers, 'Frustration and Estoppel' in McKendrick (ed.), n.48 above, p. 245.
[82] Elofson, n.77 above.
[83] J.C. Smith, 'Contracts – Mistake, Frustration and Implied Terms' (1994) 110 *LQR* 400.
[84] A. Kull, 'Mistake, Frustration and the Windfall Principle of Contract Remedies' (1991) 43 *Hastings LJ* 1, 6.
[85] *British Movietonews v London and District Cinemas* [1951] 1 KB 190.
[86] Rogers, n.81 above, p. 246.

FORESEEABILITY

Many would object that there cannot be a tacit agreement to let losses lie where they fall when the risk in question was a wholly unforeseeable one. Some go further, and argue that even when risks are foreseeable, even foreseen, this does not mean that the parties necessarily agree to run them.[87] Therefore, the first two questions are: what is reasonably foreseeable, and how contractual silence on a given risk is to be interpreted.

Lord Sands once satirized the view that such astonishing foresight should be attributed to the parties that the frustration of a contract by an extraordinary event could be attributed to their implicit intentions. If a tiger escaped from a 'travelling menagerie', frightening away a person delivering milk, then the dairy might be exonerated from breach of contract, but 'it would seem hardly reasonable to base that exoneration on the ground that "tiger days excepted" must be held as if written into the milk contract'.[88] Two linked points about frustration are made by the judge. First, frustration has to be an extraordinary, unforeseeable event. But secondly, the more extraordinary and unforeseeable the event, the more likely the contract is to be frustrated, but the less plausible it is to attribute this to the parties' intentions.

It really would be expecting 'the foresight of a prophet' if parties were expected to insert specific clauses for the unlikeliest of interruptions, like Lord Sands's tiger. It would also require extremely lengthy contracts! But need the event be foreseen and described so specifically? McKendrick remarks that 'the one thing which we do know about the future is that it is uncertain'.[89] Parties can, and do, include clauses about interruptions in performance in general terms (such as price increases, wars, strikes, Acts of God). Special *force majeure clauses* will be considered in the next section. More generally, the choice of contract and pricing mechanism is an important way of allocating risks (voyage charter or time charter? fixed price, or payment on a 'costs plus' or index-linked basis?). There is always a risk of interrupted performance, even if the precise form that this takes may not be foreseeable – it is a 'known unknown', one of the things that we know that we don't know. This can be guarded against through forward planning. A homely example is budgeting an additional sum for unforeseen 'contingencies' when going on holiday. In the shipping trade, delays of wholly uncertain duration are readily foreseeable.[90] Strikes and wars are allegedly 'unforeseeable' but have been common throughout human history.[91] Interrupted performance is *not* one of the really dangerous 'unknown unknowns', i.e. one of the things that we don't know that we don't know![92]

---

[87] See e.g. C.G. Hall, 'Frustration and the Question of Foresight' [1984] *Legal Stud* 300.
[88] *Scott & Sons v Del Sel* 1922 SC 592, 597.
[89] McKendrick, n.48 above, p. 43.
[90] *Bank Line v Arthur Capel* [1919] AC 435 (Lord Sumner).
[91] L.E. Trakman, 'Frustrated Contracts and Legal Fictions' (1983) 46 *MLR* 39.
[92] Cf. Donald H. Rumsfeld, Defense Department briefing, 12 February 2002.

On this view, all risks are foreseeable to the degree necessary for contractual allocation. Trianitis is the leading advocate.[93] The risk allocation explanation for frustration requires it to fill the gaps left by unforeseeable risks. But Trianitis denies the premise: risks that might be unforeseeable at a very specific level can nevertheless be allocated as part of more broadly framed risk (as Trebilcock puts it, the dichotomy between 'foreseeable' and 'unforeseeable' is simply too crude).[94] It is a myth that risks are ever contractually unallocated, argues Trianitis. The question is the level at which they are dealt with. So, a nuclear accident in a specific Middle Eastern location might be unforeseeable but an increase in the cost of oil (to which the accident will contribute) surely is a foreseeable risk; a *coup d'état* in Panama may not be readily foreseeable, but closure of the Panama Canal is. Since parties can and do make provision for these broadly defined risks there is no justification for court intervention, since it is most unlikely that the party who is the superior bearer of the broadly defined risk will cease to be superior when the risk is specifically defined. Trianitis also argues that courts lack the information to carry out better risk allocation than the parties, echoing other critiques of Posner and Rosenfield's approach. His defence of the foreseeability of interruptions, however (specifically) unusual, makes it much more plausible to leave risk allocation to the contracting parties than Posner and Rosenfield assume.

Some judges deny that foreseeable or even foreseen risks are to lie where they fall, in the absence of provisions to the contrary in the contract. Robert Goff LJ once said in the context of formation of contracts that 'it is difficult to imagine how silence and inaction can be anything but equivocal'.[95] Lord Denning MR suggests that silence over a highly foreseeable risk might show that the parties could not agree, hoping that the problem would not arise but trusting the lawyers to sort it out if it did.[96] Pearson J observes that it might be practically impossible to provide for every foreseen contingency.[97] Both of these comments suggest, in effect, that the cost of negotiating the allocation of the risk is prohibitive.

Lord Denning's comments are open to the objection that if the parties could not agree what was to happen during their negotiations, it would be improper for the court to take sides *ex post facto* once the risk had ripened into loss. Pearson J's dicta are answered in part by Trianitis's point that risks can be allocated in broad categories. Secondly, even if a judicially imposed frustration 'solution' might avoid costs at the negotiation stage, it has costs of its own. Quite apart from the terrifying cost of litigation, the uncertainty of the doctrine has been discussed above. Ironically (given the criticism of their arguments) Posner and Rosenfield argue that parties will be poorly served by a default rule so vague

---

[93] Triantis, n.44 above.
[94] Trebilcock, n.64 above, p. 128.
[95] *The Leonidas D* [1985] 1 WLR 925.
[96] *The Eugenia* [1964] 2 QB 226.
[97] *Sidemar* [1961] 2 QB 278.

and general that the judicial allocation of risks cannot be predicted. The main point of a long-term supply contract is to give certainty of prices, but this would be lost were the court to intervene years later with its view of the superior risk avoider.[98]

The problem here is the unpredictability of the law's response to interruptions in performance (the frustration doctrine), rather than the interruptions themselves. Judge Frank Easterbrook says that: 'To determine whether a rule is beneficial [i.e. economically efficient] a court must examine how that rule influences future behavior'.[99] The allocation of the loss, *ex post facto*, to the superior risk avoider will produce efficient results *only* if future parties know which of them should, according to law, be guarding and insuring against the risk of such loss. If this is wholly unpredictable, it cannot have any effect on contracting behaviour. Pietro Trimarchi argues that frustration is too uncertain to guide behaviour along efficient paths.[100] Elofson remarks that a reasonable failure to predict the law on frustration proposed by Posner and Rosenfield would be all too easy to make; the endemic unpredictability of their analysis undermines its claims.[101]

Elofson does not, however, share the view that because of this failure the doctrine of frustration should be discarded altogether. He agrees that assigning foreseeable risks to the promisor makes sense – the promisor assumes at least the basic risks of performance, and promisors will learn to price in the risk (or insert exculpatory clauses) when there is a rule to that effect. It is also desirable, in cases about rising/falling prices, that foreseeable losses/gains should lie where they fall. This rewards the skill of the parties when making predictions about future price movements.[102] But when there is a loss that could never have been predicted, such as hyperinflation, the parties cannot be accused of making poor use of the available information. There is then no point in saddling the promisor with a windfall loss, and the contract should be discharged.

Elofson argues that this draws the line in the correct way between earned (albeit speculative) gains, and unearned windfalls. One wonders, however, whether the limits of the 'foreseeable', necessary for Elofson's argument to work in practice, are any clearer than the location of the superior risk bearer in Posner and Rosenfield's work. Elofson accuses the latter of 'inescapable subtleties' but he admits that the foreseeability approach requires 'several complicated factual inquiries'.[103] This is undoubtedly true: Alan Schwartz notes that an 'unforeseeable' risk is one of which the party is unaware *and* research to correct that impression would not

---

[98] n.59 above, p. 96.

[99] *Premier Electricial Construction Co v National Electrical Contractors Association* 814 F.2d 358, 366 (7th Cir 1987).

[100] P. Trimarchi, 'Commercial Impracticability in Contract Law: An Economic Analysis' (1991) 11 *Int Rev L&E* 63, 72–73.

[101] J. Elofson, 'The Dilemma of Changed Circumstances in Contract Law: An Economic Analysis of the Foreseeability and Superior Risk Bearer Tests' (1996) 30 *Colum JL & Soc Probs* 1.

[102] Cf. A.T. Kronman, 'Mistake, Disclosure, Information, and the Law of Contracts' (1978) 7 *JLS* 1.

[103] n.101 above, p. 39.

be cost-justified.[104] This means a cost–benefit analysis into the optimal level of foreseeing.[105] This is arguably just as intractable as Posner and Rosenfield.

Clifford Hall argues that foreseeability of a risk does not mean that the parties intend it to lie where it falls, unless they say otherwise.[106] Hall points to the other explanations of contractual silence, as given by Lord Denning and Pearson J. Hall argues instead that one who recklessly runs a known risk will be guilty of self-induced frustration. Of course they probably will not create the event itself (e.g. a war, the closure of the Suez Canal), but they do knowingly create the circumstances whereby those conditions are likely to affect the contract in a material way. This is an interesting argument, and in a leading case since Hall's article, *The Super Servant II*, the Court of Appeal used a notably wide interpretation of 'self-inducement' to preclude frustration.[107] But even on Hall's own analysis, it is the running of a risk which is crucial, and this resembles risk allocation rather than the classic cases turning on causation of the frustrating event. It is not entirely clear how Hall's shift in analysis would help solve the basic problem of where the risk should lie.

In conclusion, there is a clear (albeit rebuttable) presumption in English law that a foreseeable risk, if not otherwise allocated by the contract, is to lie where it falls.[108] There are problems with this, however. Foreseeability is inevitably relative. Was the ill-health of a sixty-year-old monarch not foreseeable in the Coronation Cases? *Everything* is more or less foreseeable. There is bound to be uncertainty where a sharp legal distinction depends upon a quantity like foreseeability which is a continuous variable, a point on a sliding scale.

The only way of avoiding this doctrinal uncertainty would be to ignore foreseeability altogether. But that would mean the courts reversing the allocation of risks by the parties in at least some cases where the risk had been foreseen and the parties had been content to leave it on the promisor – or where it should have been foreseen. A completely different solution is Trianitis's claim that since all risks are foreseeable in broad terms (if not in their specifics), the court can and should leave their allocation to the parties. This might be conceived as a 'penalty default rule', that is to say that if the parties do not want the loss to lie where it falls they had better insert a term to deal with the situation.[109] In practice, this happens very commonly through 'force majeure' clauses, and other contractual devices. Catherine Macmillan points out that before *Taylor v Caldwell*,[110] under the apparently absolute regime of *Paradine v Jane*,[111] sale of goods contracts would often make payment contingent on delivery of goods, so that if a ship was wrecked

---

[104] A. Schwartz, 'Product Liability, Corporate Structure and Bankruptcy' (1985) 14 *JLS* 689, 719.

[105] Cf. Birmingham n.70 above, p. 387.

[106] Hall, n.87 above.

[107] [1990] 1 Lloyd's Rep 1.

[108] Treitel, ch. 13. But N.B. foreseeability 'must not be exaggerated into something critical, excluding, preclusive': *The Sea Angel* [2007] 2 Lloyd's Rep 517, [128] (Rix LJ).

[109] Cf. pp. 116–117 above.

[110] (1863) 3 B & S 826.

[111] (1648) Aleyn 26.

and the goods perished the seller would not be liable for non-delivery.[112] As Lord Alvanley CJ said in 1803, 'the parties know what they are about' in contracting under such a regime (or contracting out of it).[113]

FORCE MAJEURE CLAUSES

Support for the view that the loss should lie where it falls (and frustration abolished) comes from the express provision for interruptions in performance commonly found in commercial contracts. These are usually known as 'force majeure' clauses (after the French doctrine), although that phrase has not become a term of art in English law. Other functionally similar terms are 'hardship clauses' and the like. McKendrick notes that they have virtually taken over from the law of frustration – it is force majeure clauses rather than the legal doctrine that deals with interruptions in performance in 'the vast majority of cases'.[114]

The clauses have various advantages which explain their prevalence. On the practical level, they offer both certainty and flexibility. It is more certain when an express term of the contract will apply (provided it is well drafted and predictably interpreted by the court). Also, the 'triggering events' can be wider than the narrow common law doctrine. Furthermore, the clause may stipulate a range of possible responses to such an event (such as suspension of obligations, duty to renegotiate, re-pricing in accordance with some formula). These may be much more appealing than the drastic effect of frustration – automatic discharge of the contract. McKendrick comments that the 'remedial rigidity of the general law contrasts unfavourably with the flexibility' of force majeure clauses.[115] Sir Guenter Treitel suggests how the clauses could have been used to provide better answers to the Coronation Cases than the common law.[116]

On the theoretical level, too, force majeure clauses are appealing. As Treitel says, the great difficulty with frustration is to find a satisfactory way of allocating losses caused by supervening events without undermining the sanctity of contract.[117] But there is no need to worry about undermining the contract when the parties have expressly said what is to happen![118] These clauses therefore seem to offer many advantages over the common law doctrine. What are the drawbacks?

As with any other contract term, it is difficult to draft the perfect clause, i.e. one which applies in all of the situations where it is intended to apply, but none in which it was not. Moreover, its application must be predictable, otherwise disputes will be generated. Force majeure clauses typically include a list of specific

---

[112] C. MacMillan, '*Taylor v. Caldwell* (1863)' in C. Mitchell & P. Mitchell (eds), *Landmark Cases in the Law of Contract* (Hart Publishing, 2008).

[113] *Beale v Thompson* (1803) 3 B & P 405, 433.

[114] E. McKendrick, 'Force Majeure Clauses: The Gap between Doctrine and Practice' in A. Burrows and E. Peel (eds), *Contract Terms* (Oxford University Press, 2007) p. 233.

[115] McKendrick, n.48 above, p. 44.

[116] Treitel, 12–004.

[117] Treitel, 12–001.

[118] McKendrick, n.114 above, p. 239.

events ('piracy, storms, acts of god, perils of the sea') coupled with a 'wrap-up' clause that should extend the list, *ejusdem generis*, to other similar events ('and any other event outside the parties' control').[119] McKendrick notes a debate over whether to give more priority to the list or the general clause, and concerns that the specific approach brings prolixity without the hoped-for certainty; but in the end he concludes this is matter of style rather than substance.[120]

Of greater concern is the judicial construction of force majeure clauses. They tend to be construed narrowly, *contra proforentem*. For example in *The Playa Larga*, the force majeure clause allowed an extension of 30 days for the shipment of goods in the event of (*inter alia*) 'government action'. The court held that the clause was intended to cover temporary interruptions at the port of loading and not (as had actually happened) a fundamental change of government policy making performance of the contract permanently impossible. Therefore, the common law doctrine of frustration applied instead of the force majeure clause.[121] In other cases, the courts have gone further still and deemed force majeure clauses akin to exclusion clauses, accordingly requiring particularly narrow construction. A good example is *The Super Servant II* in which the Court of Appeal held that a force majeure clause did not extend to a 'peril of the sea' (shipwreck) caused by the promisor's negligence. Bingham LJ held that while the clause was not strictly an exclusion clause it conferred on the promisor a 'right exercisable in a very wide range of circumstances to nullify the contractual bargain made between the parties at no cost to itself and regardless of the loss which the other party may sustain'.[122] Accordingly, the *Canada Steamships* rules were applied to find that the force majeure clause did not apply to the promisor's negligence.

These rules have been criticized elsewhere, and we have seen that their rigidity has been relaxed in recent years.[123] Michael Furmston condemns the narrow approach to force majeure clauses, as 'fundamentally misconceived'. The justification for a narrow doctrine of frustration is that it is for the parties to allocate risks of the adventure. In which case, why should explicit risk allocation through a force majeure clause be limited by 'pre-conceived notions of where the risk should lie derived from a blind application of the doctrine of frustration'?[124] There does seem to be some circularity of reasoning. McKendrick also calls for a more natural interpretation of such clauses,[125] although he notes that s.3 of UCTA 1977 and the UTCCR 1999 may apply.[126] The construction of force majeure clauses seems

[119] Cf. M. Furmston, 'Drafting of Force Majeure Clauses – Some General Guidelines' in McKendrick (ed.), n.48 above.
[120] McKendrick, n.114 above.
[121] [1983] 2 Lloyd's Rep. 171, 188–89.
[122] [1990] 1 Lloyd's Rep 1, 7.
[123] Cf. pp. 102–103 above; *HIH Casualty Insurance v Chase Manhattan Bank* [2003] UKHL 6.
[124] Furmston, n.119 above, p. 58.
[125] McKendrick, n.48 above.
[126] McKendrick, n.114 above.

uncertain and unpredictable, and requires urgent clarification if their benefits are not to be diminished.[127]

If the courts can work with rather than against the draftsmen of such clauses the case for doing without the doctrine of frustration altogether, save in supervening illegality cases, would be strengthened. McKendrick, although he does not go quite this far, has concluded that future elaboration of the law on interrupted performance should focus on force majeure clauses. Widening or reforming the law on frustration is bound to produce great uncertainty; it is better to encourage self-reliance by the parties instead.[128] Taken to its logical conclusion, does this not argue for complete abrogation of frustration?

CONCLUSION

Some modern commentators such as Andrew Kull still subscribe to the *Paradine v Jane*[129] approach.[130] The court should not intervene when the contract does not allocate the risk, since the parties might have done so in the contract. As they have not, the loss lies where it falls. There is nothing in the contract to justify shifting the loss. Thus, there is no need for a doctrine of frustration (apart from the public policy-based rules on supervening illegality). Alan Sykes, as seen above, argues that it is impossible to discover what the optimal rule is.[131] But the tendency, Sykes argues, is for the various factors to count against the frustration doctrine and in favour of holding the promisor strictly liable for non-performance. He is usually in a better place to insure the risk and to take precautions against it (for example hedging against price fluctuations, installing fire alarms or having a back-up generator), whereas frustration decreases the incentives for the promisor to take such precautions (described as 'moral hazard') unless the court can accurately monitor whether efficient precautionary investment has taken place before holding contract frustrated, which Sykes rather doubts. Finally, the rules on frustration tend to be highly uncertain, whereas the strict liability approach is at least simple and predictable in application and 'signals clearly to parties who prefer an alternative allocation of risk that they must bargain for it'.[132] In this 'second-best' world when the theoretical perfection of Posner and Rosenfield is unobtainable, Sykes would abolish frustration.

Most commentators have not gone this far and English law certainly has not. But the case for such radical surgery on a beloved doctrine is strengthened by the finding that in practice, force majeure clauses now do most of the work in this area. Frustration cases are fairly unusual. Those that do arise are notable for

---

[127] See further A. Rogers, 'Foreword' and W. Swadling, 'The Judicial Construction of Force Majeure Clauses' in McKendrick (ed.), n.48 above.
[128] McKendrick, n.48 above.
[129] (1648) Aleyn 26.
[130] Kull, n.84 above
[131] Sykes, n.73 above.
[132] Ibid, p. 76.

the courts ruling the doctrine out.[133] A prominent example is, again, *The Super Servant II*.[134] When one of the promisor's two barges sank they could no longer perform all of their contracts, because each barge had been fully committed. The Court of Appeal held that the promisor's choice to perform another contract with the surviving barge meant that the contract in dispute had not been frustrated. The impossibility of performance stemmed from the promisor's choice, not the sinking. The very broad notion of 'self-induced frustration' here has been much criticized.[135] Treitel asks why the law in effect takes a more stringent approach to frustration when there are several contracts than where there is just one, if frustration has any merit as a doctrine for risk allocation.[136] Treitel also criticizes Dillon LJ's reasoning that as frustration takes place automatically any degree of choice on the part of the promisor must be fatal. This rule is one of the least attractive aspects of frustration and should not be extended, argues Treitel.[137]

Could it be that the courts are approaching frustration so narrowly (and exceptions like self-inducement so broadly) precisely because they *do not* see any merit in it for risk allocation? As Lord Hailsham LC said specifically about leases, echoing the Captain of *HMS Pinafore*, frustration will take place if not never then 'hardly ever'.[138] McKendrick argues that frustration is mostly now raised to address problems for which it is not suited,[139] such as the absence of a power to dismiss 'stale' arbitrations for want of prosecution,[140] or to circumvent employment rules on unfair dismissal.[141] Trebilcock concludes his survey of frustration by concluding that neither fairness nor efficiency-based approaches yield the 'determinate' or 'robust' rules necessary for deciding concrete disputes.[142] Given the sophistication of force majeure clauses and the contrasting difficulties of the legal doctrine, might it not be time to administer the *coup de grace*?[143]

Debate 3

Are the consequences of frustration too inflexible?

Under the current law, 'frustration brings the contract to an end forthwith, without more and automatically'.[144] This drastic result has been much criticized for its

---

[133] E.g. *The Mary Nour* [2008] 2 Lloyd's Rep. 526; *Gold Group Properties v BDW Trading* [2010] EWHC 323 (TCC).

[134] [1990] 1 Lloyd's Rep 1.

[135] E. McKendrick, 'The Construction of Force Majeure Clauses and Self-Induced Frustration' [1990] *LMCLQ* 153.

[136] Treitel, 14–023.

[137] Ibid, 14–024.

[138] *National Carriers Ltd v Panalpina (Northern) Ltd* [1981] AC 675.

[139] McKendrick, n.48 above.

[140] Cf. *The Hannah Blumenthal* [1983] 1 AC 854.

[141] Cf. *Shepherd & Co Ltd v Jerrom* [1987] 1 QB 301.

[142] Trebilcock, n.64 above, p. 144.

[143] Trebilcock, ibid, supports a 'very austere rule' of literal contract enforcement.

[144] *Hirji Mulji v Cheong Yue Steamship Co Ltd* [1926] AC 497.

inflexibility. A more difficult, but equally controversial, question is what happens where performance has commenced when frustration discharges the contract. It is necessary to discuss these questions even if the argument in Debate 2 is accepted and the law abstains from any attempts to allocate risks through the doctrine of frustration. There will still be cases of supervening *illegality* where the contracting parties will have to be disentangled.

Sir Guenter Treitel notes that there has been surprisingly little discussion of the doctrine that the contract is discharged absolutely and automatically.[145] Apparently, it is thought to flow logically from the nature of frustration. The main policy argument is that for the courts to adjust the contract rather than discharge it completely on frustration would be, in effect, to make a contract for the parties. While there are obvious objections to judicial activism some put the matter differently, notably Lords Denning and Wright. Their Lordships pointed out that if the parties had been asked at the time of contracting what they would have wanted on meeting an unexpected interruption, the answer is unlikely to have been to bring the contract to an end automatically.[146] But would the parties have answered 'leave it to the judges to adjust the contract' any more enthusiastically?

Once the contract has been brought to an end, what should be done about losses suffered and/or benefits conferred by the parties? The issue of benefits is more straightforward (although only relatively speaking!). It is now accepted that there is a general legal requirement to make restitution to reverse unjust enrichment. However, English law was slow to recognize the general principle of unjust enrichment (its full recognition came as recently as the 1990s). It was therefore necessary to enact a specific statute in 1943 to deal with the restitutionary consequences of frustrated contracts. We examine the precise meaning of the Law Reform (Frustrated Contracts) Act 1943 in the first section below. Does it need amendment, re-interpretation, or repeal?

An even more difficult question is what to do about losses consequent on a frustrated contract. The starting point has to be 'do nothing' – let the losses lie where they chance to fall. As Holmes said, the law's 'cumbrous and expensive machinery ought not to be set in motion unless some clear benefit is to be derived from disturbing the *status quo*. State interference is an evil, where it cannot be shown to be a good.'[147] There is no general principle of loss shifting, or loss sharing, equivalent to restitution for unjust enrichment. In the absence of a wrong (tort), how then can it be argued that parties to a frustrated contract should share losses between them? The most popular explanation is simple fairness, but economic justifications are possible too. A subsidiary question is how loss allocation would take place (once the principle is accepted). This links back to concerns about judicial discretion.

---

[145] Treitel, ch. 15.
[146] See n.43 above.
[147] O.W. Holmes, 'The Common Law' (1881), Lecture III.

UNJUST ENRICHMENT AND THE ACT OF 1943

The Law Reform (Frustrated Contracts) Act 1943 has been described as 'an elaborate code by which the rights of the parties [can] be re-adjusted in an equitable manner'.[148] The wording is undeniably 'elaborate', yet there is a dearth of judicial authority on how to interpret it – a mere trickle of cases in almost 70 years. The leading analysis remains that by Robert Goff J in *BP v Hunt*.[149] He said the 'fundamental principle' of the Act was the reversal of unjust enrichment. In this section, we assess this view of the Act. Is Goff J's view of its purpose correct? Has it been interpreted correctly, and does it need reform?

For Goff J it was just as important to emphasize what the 1943 Act was *not* designed to do. It was not designed to put the parties back where they were before the contract. It was not designed to apportion losses between the parties (with some exceptions to be discussed below). It was not concerned to place the parties where they would have been had the contract been performed. Some parties might escape from unprofitable bargains, e.g. recovering prepayment for performance that would in fact have been worth less than the contract price.

In the usual terminology then, Goff J denies that the reliance or expectation interests are protected by the Act. Its sole concern is to reverse unjust enrichment, protecting the restitution interest. Of the two operative sections, s.1(2) deals with pre-payments made for performance which, because of frustration, never materialized. Originally, at common law, these had been unrecoverable.[150] The resulting law was described by a Scottish judge as working 'well enough among tricksters, gamblers, and thieves'.[151] Not surprisingly in the face of such criticism, the House of Lords *Fibrosa* case allowed restitution.[152] But the recovery of pre-payments in full (as in *Fibrosa*) could be harsh for the *payee*, who might have begun work for fulfilment of the contract but would not now be compensated for it. Criticism of this by the Law Lords in *Fibrosa* were clearly influential upon the 1943 Act – indeed some took an active part in steering the Bill through Parliament!

S.1(2) duly changed the common law, qualifying the right to recover pre-payments. The court 'may, if it considers it just to do so having regard to all the circumstances of the case' allow retention of pre-payments (wholly or partially) by the person to whom the payment was made, where he has incurred expenses, before the time of discharge, for the performance of the contract. According to Goff J, this allowance for expenses is 'probably best rationalised as a statutory recognition of the defence of change of position'. That is, as Lord Goff later put it himself, 'where an innocent defendant's position is so changed that he will suffer an injustice if called upon to repay or to repay in full, the injustice of requiring him so to

148 *Bank of Boston v European Grain and Shipping* [1989] AC 1056, 1108 (Lord Brandon).
149 *BP Exploration Co (Libya) Ltd v Hunt (No 2)* [1979] 1 WLR 783.
150 *Chandler v Webster* [1904] 1 KB 493.
151 *Cantiare San Rocco SA v Clyde Shipbuilding & Engineering Co Ltd* [1924] AC 226 (Lord Shaw of Dunfermline).
152 *Fibrosa Spolka Akcyjna v Fairbairn Lawson Combe Barbour Ltd* [1943] AC 32.

repay outweighs the injustice of denying the plaintiff restitution'.[153] This would apparently mean that the payee should be able to set off his expenses in full in the situation discussed in s.1(2). Indeed, that was the conclusion of the Law Revision Committee whose report led to the 1943 Act, which had argued that the reason for requiring prepayment was for protection from loss under the contract.[154]

However in the only case directly on point,[155] Garland J described the Committee's reasoning as 'questionable', approving the statement in *Chitty on Contracts* that a more plausible reason for requiring pre-payment was to guard against the payor's insolvency.[156] Garland J also rejected the argument that there should be equal division of the loss between the parties. This might lead to injustice when they were in very unequal positions. Garland J found 'no specific assistance' from *BP v Hunt*, merely remarking that there had been no question of change of position in that case (i.e. Goff J's views were obiter). Thus, eschewing 'rigid rules', Garland J held that the words of the s.1(2) proviso 'clearly confer a very broad discretion' and proceeded to 'do justice' as he saw it, on the facts of the case.

This decision fully lives down to McKendrick's criticism of the courts' approach to the 1943 Act as 'sloppy, unstructured [and] discretionary'.[157] Garland J gives no reason for rejecting Goff J's central claim that the Act's goal is to reverse unjust enrichment, which would logically incorporate defences such as change of position. It is notable that that defence is said to be based on principle rather than 'discretion for the court' in the leading case.[158] The Court of Appeal in *BP v Hunt* displayed equal suspicion of unjust enrichment, simply commenting: 'We get no help from the use of words which are not in the statute'.[159] However, this was at a time when restitution was still not generally recognized in English law,[160] whereas Goff J had long been a campaigner for its recognition.[161] That campaign has now been successful. Does this not strengthen the case for interpreting s.1(2) and its proviso as an early statutory recognition of restitution? However, if that is the case, is there any reason to have the statute at all? It would seem that s.1(2) could be repealed without changing the results of any cases.

If s.1(2) has caused some interesting differences of opinion, s.1(3) bristles with difficulties. It deals with the situation of 'valuable benefits' conferred under the contract, prior to frustration. This is always a more contentious area since as Goff J says in *BP v Hunt*, 'By their nature, services cannot be restored... Furthermore the identity and value of the resulting benefit to the recipient may be debatable.'

---

[153] *Lipkin Gorman v Karpnale* [1991] 2 AC 548, 579.
[154] Cmd. 6009 (1939).
[155] *Gamerco SA v I.C.M./Fair Warning (Agency) Ltd* [1995] 1 WLR 1226.
[156] *Chitty on Contracts*, 27th edn. (1994), vol. 1, p. 1141, para. 23–060, note 51.
[157] E. McKendrick, 'Frustration, Restitution and Loss Apportionment' in A. Burrows (ed.), *Essays on Restitution* (Oxford University Press, 1991) 164.
[158] *Lipkin Gorman v Karpnale* [1991] 2 AC 548, 578.
[159] [1981] 1 WLR 232.
[160] Cf. *Orakpo v Manson Investments* [1978] AC 95, 104 (Lord Diplock).
[161] Cf. R. Goff, 'Reform of the Law of Restitution' (1961) 24 *MLR* 85.

(By contrast, as 'a universal medium of exchange' payment of money confers an undeniable benefit with an objective value.) Where benefits have been conferred under a frustrated contract, the court is empowered by s.1(3) to award 'such sum (if any), not exceeding the value of the said benefit to the party obtaining it, as [it] considers just'. The court must examine all of the circumstances, including (b) 'the effect, in relation to the said benefit, of the circumstances giving rise to the frustration of the contract'.

The impact of this provision on the valuation of the benefit (which provides a ceiling for the 'just sum') has proved controversial. Again, Goff J's is the leading judicial analysis. He explained that there was a choice between valuing the services themselves (e.g. by the claimant's cost of producing them), or valuing the end product of those services. Goff J held that it was the end product of the services that was 'the benefit' for the purposes of s.1(3). He stated that this was 'quite plain' in the light of the proviso (b) quoted above. In Goff J's view this indicated that it was the final state of affairs at the time of frustration that was relevant. But as he noted, this meant that in situation where frustration was (e.g.) the destruction of a partially constructed building, the value of the services would be zero because their end product (the building) was wholly destroyed by the frustrating event. Goff J reached this conclusion with reluctance. He described s.1(3) as 'contrary to principle and capable of producing injustice'; the subsection's division between valuing the benefit and ascertaining the just sum was 'controversial' and created 'considerable problems'. In the building example, the difficulties could have been avoided if Parliament had defined the services themselves as the benefit. But it was for the court to construe the Act as it stood.

It seems, therefore, that Goff J would amend s.1(3) in this respect if given the chance. His interpretation of the subsection has, however, been criticized. Treitel suggests that on textual grounds, the subsection could be construed in a different way.[162] It refers to a benefit obtained 'before the time of discharge'; the reference to the event frustrating the contract in proviso (b) more naturally refers to the 'just sum' than the benefit (which places a cap on the amount recoverable). Thus the court could value the services themselves rather than their end product, as Goff J apparently wished to do. Treitel approves a construction of the section that would maximize the court's discretion.

Haycroft and Waksman point out that if Goff J is right, the Act would not alter the outcome of one of the most criticized of the pre-1943 authorities, *Appleby v Myers* (where the plaintiff had installed machinery in the defendant's factory; the contract was frustrated when the factory burnt down, but the plaintiff's claim for restitution was dismissed).[163] But Stewart and Carter commend Goff J's decision on this point (and indeed *Appleby v Myers*).[164] Where the 'recipient' never in fact

---

[162] Treitel, 15–064.

[163] A.M. Haycroft & D.M. Waksman, 'Frustration and Restitution' [1984] JBL 207; *Appleby v Myers* (1867) LR 2 CP 651.

[164] A. Stewart & J.W. Carter, 'Frustrated Contracts and Statutory Adjustment: The Case for a Reappraisal' [1992] *CLJ* 66.

receives any of the performance he has not been enriched. Therefore, the value of the benefit truly is zero and he should not be required to make restitution. Stewart and Carter are critical of the legislation in New South Wales which expressly requires the event frustrating the contract to be ignored. The rationale is that no service provider would agree not to be paid because of events outside his control. But as Stewart and Carter say, this seems very one-sided: would the employer agree to pay the price of work which was of no value to him?

The concern is, they argue, not really restitution at all but a disguised plea for loss apportionment (the builder of the machinery in *Appleby* obviously suffered a *loss*). But that should be done openly, not by twisting the concepts of unjust enrichment. McKendrick has also noted that the difficult concept of 'benefit' is complicated even further by attempts to work expenditure/loss into it.[165] Whether the law should re-allocate losses at all will be considered below. But for clarity of analysis, this ought to be done explicitly if it is done at all. There are several things that the Act of 1943 does *not* do, as seen above. In particular, it provides no protection for a contractor who begins work under the contract without conferring a benefit on the other side, unless he has stipulated for pre-payment. To compensate such a party (or divide the losses where the performance is rendered worthless by the frustrating event) would require an entirely different statutory scheme. We consider the merits of this in the next section.

The apparent philosophy of the Act is to prevent unjust enrichment when valuable services have been conferred on the other party, or money paid. But it is questionable whether a special statute is still necessary to give effect to a general principle of the common law. That general principle might not have been recognized in 1943 but it is today, so Stewart and Carter make a strong case that if the only concern is to prevent unjust enrichment, the common law can now do so adequately.[166] Thus, the 1943 Act could be repealed.

LOSS SHARING

By contrast with unjust enrichment, there is no general common law principle of loss sharing or loss apportionment. In *Taylor v Caldwell*,[167] the plaintiff hirers claimed their wasted expenditure in preparing for the concerts which would not now take place (i.e. their reliance loss – they did not claim for lost profits). That claim failed because the contract was frustrated – it was a contractual action, or nothing. It has been said that this means there was a rough loss-splitting (the plaintiffs lost their expenses, the defendants lost the music hall itself). But this is purely fortuitous, depending on the accident of the timing of the fire – in other similar cases, the loss could be all on one side.[168] (It is worth noting that the defendant owners had insured the music hall against fire damage, although

---

[165] McKendrick, n.157 above.
[166] Stewart & Carter, n.164 above.
[167] (1863) 3 B & S 826.
[168] Treitel, 15–069.

it is not clear whether that would have covered third-party liabilities.[169]) There is currently no statutory power to apportion losses in England (in contrast with a number of Commonwealth countries and the USA).[170] Should such a statutory power be introduced?

The arguments in favour of loss apportionment fall under two basic headings. First, and most commonly, basic ideas of fairness. Secondly, an argument can be made for the economic efficiency of dividing unexpected windfall losses (and gains). Each position will be examined. They compete with the simple philosophy of the common law under which, absenting allocation by the contract, the loss lies where it falls. The parties are not each other's insurers. On discharge of the contract in circumstances for which they have not made provision their mutual obligations come to an end and they are left to their respective fates. 'Why then should the misfortune of frustration trigger an obligation to cover half or any of the other's loss?'[171]

The most common answer is that fairness requires it. Lord Shaw's scorn for the immoral arbitrariness of the English position (the loss lies where it falls) has been quoted already.[172] McKendrick notes that if the entire doctrine of frustration is based on notions of fairness[173] then 'Justice and reasonableness surely demand that such expenditure be brought into account'.[174] Loss sharing is asserted to be natural and just.[175] But this is open to the same objection as the 'justice' explanation for frustration itself, namely that it is entirely undefined.[176] Charles Fried claims that sharing would be adopted as the rule if a group of people landed on a strange planet; he limits this obligation to 'concrete relations' such as family ties, friendship and contract.[177] Jeffrey Harrison similarly argues that the common law approach misconceives the relationship between contracting parties.[178] Rather than being adversaries at arm's length, Harrison maintains, contractors are engaged in a joint endeavour, more akin to business partners. Accordingly, contract law should take its cue from the law of partnership which requires both profits and losses to be shared. The common law approach is thus said to be 'in stark contrast with the essence of the contract. A loss sharing arrangement is more consistent with the express provisions of the joint undertaking'.[179]

Although it is increasingly accepted that trust and co-operation are important factors in contractual relationships, there is resistance to the idea that those norms

---

[169] MacMillan, n.5 above.

[170] On which see Stewart & Carter, n.164 above.

[171] Ibid, pp. 87–88.

[172] Cf. n.151 above.

[173] Cf. *The Super Servant Two* [1990] 1 Lloyd's Rep 1, 8 (Bingham LJ).

[174] McKendrick, n.157 above.

[175] Cf. Haycroft & Waksman, n.163 above, 215–216; L.E. Trakman, 'Winner Take Some: Loss Sharing and Commercial Impracticability' (1985) 69 *Minn L Rev* 471.

[176] Cf. pp. 124–126 above.

[177] C. Fried, *Contract as Promise* (Harvard University Press, 1981) pp. 70–73.

[178] J.L. Harrison, 'A Case for Loss Sharing' (1983) 56 *S CalLRev* 573.

[179] Ibid, p. 592.

can or should be translated into binding legal obligations. The fear is that law might then 'crowd out' the very co-operation that it wishes to be encouraged.[180] Others would deny even the premise. Goff and Jones once noted that apportionment would treat contracts as a joint venture; for this reason, they preferred the common law approach of leaving post-frustration losses to lie where they fall as 'being more in accordance with business ethics and commercial expectations'.[181] Stewart and Carter agree, arguing that 'Contracting parties do not generally engage in relations out of a spirit of mutual welfare, but rather to serve their own interests'.[182] Also, this is an attitude that is, notoriously, encouraged by the common law in its absence to recognize duties of good faith.[183] Harrison's argument for apportionment is a highly controversial one, therefore.

Glanville Williams accepts that 'natural justice' is silent on the question of apportioning losses for which neither party was responsible.[184] But Williams supports apportionment because it is 'economically sounder': sharing the loss means it is spread more thinly, whereas it might lead to bankruptcy if left to lie on one party alone.[185] Although supported by McKendrick,[186] this argument is dismissed as 'nonsense' by Stewart and Carter.[187] It is just as likely, they point out, that one (wealthy) party could bear the whole loss without difficulty, whereas dividing it would bankrupt the other (impecunious) party. An economically efficient regime, they suggest, is one where the rules are highly predictable. This raises the question of whether loss apportionment (if accepted in principle) should take place according to a fixed formula (such as equal division) or a broad discretion. This will be considered in the next section.

Parchomovsky, Siegelman and Thel have advanced a more sophisticated economic argument for loss-splitting in 'windfall' situations[188] (that is, where a loss is so unlikely to occur that the cost of bargaining over it would be unjustifiable). They point to the fact that people are risk-averse: they prefer the *certainty* of 50 per cent of a given sum to a 50 per cent chance of getting all of it but a 50 per cent chance of getting nothing.[189] Therefore, people will be more satisfied by a 50–50 loss-splitting regime. They point to other benefits. The reason why frustration (and common mistake) cases are amongst the most notoriously difficult in all of contract law, they suggest, is because the courts are required to adjudicate in an all-or-nothing way which will inevitably appear unfair. The loss-splitting proposal would let courts follow their instincts of fairness. They would therefore be less

---

[180] Cf. pp. 71–72 above.

[181] R. Goff & G. Jones, *Law of Restitution* (Sweet & Maxwell, 1st edn, 1966) p. 333.

[182] Stewart & Carter, n.164 above, p. 87.

[183] *Walford v Miles* [1992] 2 AC 128.

[184] G.L. Williams, *The Law Reform (Frustrated Contracts) Act 1943* (London 1944) pp. 35–36.

[185] Ibid, p. 36.

[186] Cf. n.157 above.

[187] Cf. n.164 above, p. 88.

[188] G. Parchomovsky, P. Siegelman & S. Thel, 'Of Equals Wrongs and Half Rights' (2007) 82 *NYU L Rev* 738.

[189] Although these are mathematically identical: $1 \times 0.5 = (0.5 \times 1) + (0.5 \times 0)$.

likely to rely on elusive distinctions such as the 'essential difference' between the contract performance and the change of circumstances. Finally, there would be fewer disputes if the parties knew that the courts would divide windfall losses equally; less incentive to 'gamble' on litigation than under the all-or-nothing regime (either the contract is frustrated or not – with very different consequences for the parties). As Leon Trakman says, 'Parties faced with an all-or-nothing judicial allocation of loss have every incentive to embellish their claims in the hope of being the winner who takes all'.[190]

All of these are sound arguments. But in one respect, the certainty of equal division of losses would be economically inferior to the status quo. When it comes to purchasing insurance against loss, it is much more efficient for a given risk to be entirely upon one of the parties, so that she alone needs to insure. Placing some of the risk on both of the parties requires both of them to insure the relevant proportion, which is always more expensive (in terms of administrative costs) than having the risk entirely on one party. Parchomovsky et al. give recognition to this point in the special situation of goods destroyed after a contract of sale where, as they say, 'the rules allocating the risk to one party or the other provide certainty for the parties and allow them to more economically insure against loss'. But is this a point of general application? All-or-nothing rules provide clearer attribution of risk, at least when those rules are themselves clear. There seems little call from parties themselves for a rigid rule of equal division of losses. Commercial contracts allocate risks to one party or the other, rather than calling for them to be shared. This also throws some doubt on the argument of Parchomovsky et al.

In conclusion, there seems to be a strong sentiment on the part of many commentators that sharing losses is in some way fairer than letting them lie where they fall. Indeed, it is often presented as if it were self-evident. Many of the Commonwealth law reform bodies that have recommended loss-splitting have simply assumed its superior justice.[191] Actually justifying it proves to be more difficult. The 'partnership' explanation is highly controversial, as is the economic argument based on loss-aversion and certainty of outcomes. The basic economic viewpoint is that loss-splitting is a 'zero sum game' – it redistributes the loss between the parties without creating any new wealth (i.e. without diminishing the loss).[192] It does that at considerable administrative expense. Hence the strong presumption that the loss should simply lie where it falls.

REBALANCING THE CONTRACT

Most controversially of all, the law could confer a broad discretion on the courts to 'rebalance' the contract so as to prevent unjust enrichment and apportion losses,

---

[190] Trakman (1985), n.63 above.
[191] Cf. Stewart & Carter, n.164 above.
[192] R.E. Speidel, 'Court-Imposed Price Adjustments under Long-Term Supply Contracts' (1981) 76 *NWULR* 369, 393–94.

in a way maximizing the justice to both parties. This could be seen as the logical culmination of the fairness-based approach to loss apportionment discussed above. An example is the South Australian Frustrated Contracts Act 1988. Its overall aim is 'an adjustment between the parties so that no party is unfairly advantaged or disadvantaged in consequence of the frustration' (s.7(1)). To this end, the Act directs that all of the costs incurred and benefits conferred under the contract be totalled up, and the net gain or loss be divided equally between the parties (s.7(2)). But it goes on to state:

> Where, in the opinion of a court, there is, in the circumstances of a particular case, a *more equitable basis* for making the adjustment referred to in subsection (1) than the one set out in subsection (2), the court may make an adjustment on that basis rather than on the basis of subsection (2).[193]

This statute shows two things. First that, as John Coons points out, moving away from the all-or-nothing approach of the common law need not mean a totally unstructured discretion. The law could instead have a loss-splitting *rule*, the obvious example being equal division between the parties.[194] Trebilcock comments that this is just as predictable as the windfall principle, but with added 'egalitarian appeal'.[195] The South Australia Act cleverly totals both losses and gains before (prima facie) dividing the net result between the parties. However, the power for the court to discard this in favour of some (undefined) 'equitable basis' supports the thesis of Stewart and Carter. They conclude, having compared this statute with the Act of 1943 and equivalent legislation in New South Wales and British Columbia, that it is impossible to reach a workable formula for loss apportionment, i.e. one that is not 'unduly cumbersome'. Particular difficulties are deciding which losses are to be attributed to the frustrated contract (and which referable to the parties' general business activities) and finding an acceptable method for respecting the original bargain. Stewart and Carter therefore conclude that discretion is inevitable – so we might just as well allow the court simply to 'grant relief on such terms as justice requires'.[196] The alternative is complex statutes with uncertain meanings, which well-advised contracting parties would expressly exclude from governing the contract.[197]

As noted above, Lord Wright and Lord Denning MR both argued that had the parties considered the frustrating event at the time of contracting, they would certainly not have said 'it will all be over between us'. Rather, they would have sought to adjust the contract in some way, if possible.[198] This might be thought a serious indictment of the principle that frustration discharges contracts absolutely

---

[193] Section 7(4) (emphasis added).
[194] J.E. Coons 'Approaches to Court Imposed Compromise: The Uses of Doubt and. Reason' (1964) 58 *NWULR* 750.
[195] Trebilcock, n.64 above, p. 145.
[196] US Restatement (Second) of Contracts (1981) § 272(2).
[197] Cf. s.2(3) 1943 Act.
[198] Cf. n.43 above.

and automatically. However, as Treitel observes, judicial reformation of the obligations would be a much more striking interference with the sanctity of contracts than merely to hold both parties discharged.[199] Even in Germany where the courts have this power (*Anpassung*),[200] there is criticism of the discretion that this gives to them. Treitel argues that such matters should in all ordinary circumstances be left to the parties. Should there be general economic dislocation, special legislative intervention can extend and modify the doctrine of frustration: only in war time has such a power been granted in England (the Liabilities (War Time Adjustment) Acts 1941–1944).[201] Treitel notes, however, that where parties both continue performing after the contract is frustrated, a new contract may be held to have arisen with an implicit obligation to pay a reasonable sum (*quantum meruit*) for the services rendered. This resembles what Civilian lawyers would describe as a reformation of the contract, by a juridically separate route.[202]

Kull concurs with Treitel's point about leaving it to the parties.[203] Just as force majeure clauses can be broader and more flexible than the common law when defining 'triggering events', they may also provide a greater range of solutions when such an event occurs. Whether by defining the *effect* of force majeure (e.g. an extension of time periods rather than automatic discharge), or by requiring pre-payments, or staged payments, the flexibility is 'limited only by the energies of the draftsman'.[204] So contracting parties can and do insert terms to deal flexibly with unexpected events. It is true that this may lead to 'ever more detailed and sophisticated drafting,' with consequent expense.[205] However, this cannot be a conclusive point in favour of broad judicial powers of reformation, since these too have very considerable costs. In practice, commercial contracts do not call for courts to exercise broad powers such as those in the US Restatement or the Bürgerliches Gesetzbuch.

CONCLUSION

English law does not currently grant courts discretion to apportion losses and reform contracts. The 1943 Act is statutory reversal of unjust enrichment, with diversions from the common law principles that are now of questionable value. That Act has few defenders, since it adds little to the common law restitutionary remedies. At the same time, it does little to allow loss apportionment (except when benefits have also been conferred). What to do about losses is the important battleground since in the absence of a new statutory jurisdiction, losses will continue to lie where they fall.

---

[199] Treitel, 15–038.
[200] § 313 Bürgerliches Gesetzbuch.
[201] Treitel, 15–040.
[202] Treitel, 15–041.
[203] Kull, n.84 above, pp. 50–51.
[204] Ibid.
[205] *ALCOA v Essex Group* 499 F. Supp. 43 (W.D. Pa. 1980) at 89.

It is tempting to dismiss this harsh and arbitrary position – suitable only for 'tricksters, gamblers, and thieves'.[206] But it is difficult to explain why (former) parties to a frustrated contract ought to share losses, and act as each other's insurers. Moreover, finding a satisfactory basis for the division has proved extremely difficult, as Stewart and Carter's survey of the Commonwealth legislation indicates. The common law rule is very simple by comparison. This simplicity means both that its impact is easy to predict and that the parties can contract out of it with relative ease. If the rule on post-frustration losses is 'harsh' then this provides a good incentive for them to do so. And in practice, through force majeure and hardship clauses and the like, parties commonly do make provision for interruptions in performance.

All of this suggests that simply upholding the contract and otherwise (subject to restitutionary claims) allowing the losses to lie where they fall may be the best policy. Undoubtedly, however, hard cases will occasionally arise. English law will probably retain the frustration doctrine as what A.J. Morris calls a 'gloss' on the usual rules for cases of 'most extreme egregiousness'.[207] But so long as the doctrine exists, it may well be *raised* in considerably less extreme cases. Even if such pleas are unsuccessful, the enforceability of contracts will be weakened, practically speaking.

Further reading

Frustration in general

E. McKendrick, 'Force Majeure and Frustration – Their Relationship and a Comparative Assessment' In E. McKendrick (ed.), *Force Majeure and Frustration of Contract* (2nd edn, Lloyd's of London Press, 1994).

G.H. Treitel, *Frustration and Force Majeure* (2nd edn, Sweet & Maxwell, 2004).

E. McKendrick, 'Force Majeure Clauses: The Gap between Doctrine and Practice' In A. Burrows and E. Peel (eds), *Contract Terms* (Oxford University Press, 2007).

Risk analysis

R.A. Posner & A.M. Rosenfield, 'Impossibility and Related Doctrines in Contract Law: An Economic Analysis' (1977) 6 *JLS* 83.

J. Swan, 'The Allocation of Risk in the Analysis of Mistake and Frustration' In B.J. Reiter and J. Swan (eds), *Studies in Contract Law* (Butterworths, 1980).

A.O. Sykes, 'The Doctrine of Commercial Impracticability in a Second-Best World' (1990) 19 *JLS* 43.

G.G. Triantis 'Contractual Allocations of Unknown Risks: A Critique of the Doctrine of Commercial Impracticability' (1992) 42 *Univ Toronto LJ* 450.

---

[206] Lord Shaw, n.151 above.

[207] A.J. Morris, 'Practical Reasoning and Contract as Promise: Extending Contract-Based Criteria to Decide Excuse Cases' [1997] *CLJ* 147.

Remedies

J.L. Harrison, 'A Case for Loss Sharing' (1983) 56 *S Cal LR* 573.

A. Kull, 'Mistake, Frustration and the Windfall Principle of Contract Remedies' (1991) 43 *Hastings LJ* 1.

E. McKendrick, 'Frustration, Restitution and Loss Apportionment' in A. Burrows (ed.), *Essays on Restitution* (Oxford University Press, 1991).

A. Stewart & J.W. Carter, 'Frustrated Contracts and Statutory Adjustment: The Case for a Reappraisal' [1992] *CLJ* 66.

6

MISREPRESENTATION AND MISTAKE

INTRODUCTION

The theme of this chapter is whether the law should relieve from mistakes due to inaccurate or incomplete information. The basic position in English law combines a wide doctrine of misrepresentation (i.e. misleading positive statements) with a very narrow doctrine of mistake otherwise. Misrepresentation is not itself controversial. Many detailed aspects of the doctrine are, however, questionable. No-one thinks that the highly complex situation regarding damages for misrepresentation is very satisfactory, for example, but since that is a matter of general consensus rather than debate, we will not examine it further here![1] A more fundamental question is why there is no general duty to disclose relevant information during contractual negotiations in English law. This is examined in Debate 1. We then move to the wider question of mistake. Although most accounts of the law of contract include a 'doctrine of mistake', its very existence is in fact debateable. Catherine Macmillan's historical account uncovers the questionable doctrinal basis for mistake at common law.[2] The question for debate therefore becomes the controversial proposition that there should be no doctrine of mistake, as such, and that the problems can be addressed using other doctrines.

Debate 1

Should there be a general duty to disclose relevant information?

The absence of a duty to disclose relevant information to the other side during contractual negotiations is a characteristic feature of the common law. It is also ethically questionable. However, it receives at least a partial defence once wider

---

[1] Cf. J. Poole & J. Devenney, 'Reforming Damages for Misrepresentation: The Case for Coherent Aims and Principles' [2007] *JBL* 269.

[2] C. MacMillan, *Mistakes in Contract Law* (Hart Publishing, 2010).

policy concerns are considered – in particular, the need to give incentives to acquire and use valuable information.

COMPARISONS

Friedrich Kessler and Edith Fine argue that investigating the scope of the duty to disclose is a rewarding exercise for the comparative lawyer, since it leads 'straight to the heart of the philosophy underlying the law of contracts'.[3] And they find a 'profound cleavage' between the common law and Civilian philosophies. Bluntly, the starting point in the common law is that there is no such duty: each party has to look after his own interests. The German and French laws of contract, on the other hand, require disclosure under the pre-contractual duty of good faith.[4] As we shall see, the contrast may be overplayed. English law does not deny a duty to disclose in all situations, any more than the European systems always require it. But the starting points are wide enough apart to throw into doubt the assumption sometimes made that the common law and civilian approaches to good faith are fundamentally the same, save that English law is 'piecemeal' and continental systems recognize a more abstract 'overriding principle'.[5] There are real substantive differences, quite apart from the presentational question of whether a general doctrine can (or should) be 'discerned in the common law dust'.[6]

The English position is not absolute. Certain contracts are classified as being 'of the utmost good faith' (*uberrimae fidei*) and require disclosure of all material facts. This is vitally important in the law of insurance. It is evident that insurers could not price risks without full information about the person seeking insurance. Ironically perhaps, insurance companies have been criticized for over-vigorous use of their right to rescind contracts for non-disclosure; the Association of British Insurers has published a code of practice which aims to curb such behaviour (i.e. bad faith use of the duty of good faith!).[7] There are also various statutory duties to provide information in particular situations.[8] Apart from these true duties of disclosure, omissions to speak may constitute actionable misrepresentation when this renders what has been said positively misleading.[9]

---

[3] F. Kessler & E. Fine, '*Culpa in contrahendo*, bargaining in good faith and freedom of contract: A comparative study' (1964) 77 *Harvard LR* 401.

[4] Cf. P. Legrand, 'Pre-Contractual Disclosure and Information: English and French Law Compared' (1986) 6 *OJLS* 322.

[5] *Interfoto Picture Library v Stiletto* [1989] QB 433 (Bingham LJ).

[6] Cf. M. Clarke, 'The Common Law of Contract in 1993: Is There a General Doctrine of Good Faith?' (1993) 23 *Hong Kong LJ* 318, 319.

[7] Cf. H. Collins, *The Law of Contract* (4th edn, Cambridge University Press, 2003) 209–10.

[8] Cf. Consumer Credit Act 1974, s.60. Cf. Consumer Protection from Unfair Trading Regulations 2008, Reg 6 (but NB.: 'An agreement shall not be void or unenforceable by reason only of a breach of these Regulations' Reg 29).

[9] Collins, n.7 above, pp. 204–205.

'The most important regulation of disclosure of information under the common law [today] derives from the use of implied terms in contracts.'[10] The classical position at the time of *Smith v Hughes* was *caveat emptor* (let the buyer beware).[11] Buyers were deemed capable of demanding (and paying for) a 'warranty' (viz. contractual guarantee of quality) if they wished to have it. But otherwise, they would have no redress if the goods failed to meet expectations of quality, in the absence of a positive misrepresentation by the seller.[12] The 'passive acquiescence of the seller in the self-deception of the buyer' over the value of the goods was not enough to avoid the contract.[13] 'The question [was] not what a man of scrupulous morality or nice honour would do under such circumstances.'[14] According to Blackburn J:

> a mere abstinence from disabusing the purchaser of that impression is not fraud or deceit; for, whatever may be the case in a court of morals, there is no legal obligation on the vendor to inform the purchaser that he is under a mistake, not induced by the act of the vendor.[15]

While this continues accurately to state the law's attitude towards non-disclosure per se, the Sale of Goods Act 1979 now imposes various duties on the seller. The goods must correspond with any description,[16] be of satisfactory quality,[17] and be reasonably fit for any purpose disclosed by the buyer.[18] A sample of goods must correspond with the bulk.[19] These duties give sellers the incentive to draw defects to the buyer's attention.[20] Considering the provisions more generally, there is little room for sellers to palm off goods with undisclosed defects, since they will generally not comply with these implied terms. The seller may have to flag up the unguaranteed nature of the sale, for example second-hand goods sold 'as is'. The doctrine of *caveat emptor*, with its intimate relation to the non-disclosure rule and the narrow doctrine of unilateral mistake, has in these cases largely been reversed.[21] The Sale of Goods Act would not affect the outcome of *Smith v Hughes* itself however, unless the buyer had made his purpose known to the seller (racehorse training, necessitating old oats), or the sample of oats inspected did not correspond to the bulk. There are no implied terms about quality except those contained in the Act.[22] Moreover, as Lord Atkin observed,

---

[10] Ibid, p. 205.
[11] (1871) LR 6 QB 597.
[12] For unilateral mistake cf. pp. 7–9 above.
[13] Ibid, p. 603 (Cockburn CJ).
[14] Ibid.
[15] Ibid, p. 607.
[16] S.13.
[17] S.14(2).
[18] S.14(3).
[19] S.15(2).
[20] S.14(2C)(a).
[21] Cf. P.S. Atiyah & F.A.R. Bennion, 'Mistake in the Construction of Contracts' (1961) 24 *MLR* 421, 430.
[22] S.14(1).

caveat emptor otherwise remains the general rule outside contracts of the utmost good faith.[23]

> *Example 1*: Arnold buys a house from Brackenbury for £1m. It later tran-spires that the house has serious structural defects (of which Brackenbury had been aware) which render it worth much less than £1m. Arnold will have no legal redress against Brackenbury. *Caveat emptor*: 'fraud apart, there is no law against letting [or selling] a tumble-down house'.[24] This remains the law for real property sales. It is well understood, and prudent buyers commission structural surveys before committing to purchase.
>
> *Example 2*: Roderick, a passionate collector of silver, sees a silver cow creamer on sale in Tom's antiques shop for £300. Roderick realises that it is a very rare item worth considerably more. He buys the silver cow without saying anything to Tom. It is eventually sold for £20,000 to pay Roderick's gambling debts. Tom will have no legal redress against Roderick: *caveat venditor* (let the seller beware!).

The latter example reflects the leading American case *Laidlaw v Organ*.[25] The defendant purchased a large quantity of tobacco from the plaintiff merchant, because he had advance knowledge that would (and soon did) make the price of tobacco increase sharply (that the Royal Navy would cease to blockade the port of New Orleans!). The Supreme Court held that the buyer did not have to disclose this information. According to Marshall CJ, 'It would be difficult to circumscribe the contrary doctrine within proper limits, where the means of intelligence are equally accessible to both parties'. This seems quite a weak argument today, since the modern law on insurance has a sophisticated doctrine of 'material' non-disclosure. It may be that a defence on other grounds is possible for *Laidlaw v Organ*. But first we should consider criticisms of the common law.

CRITIQUE

English law's hostility to disclosure has been criticized on both moral and instrumen-tal grounds. As already noted, French and German law derive a duty to disclose from the general duty of good faith. It is the absence of such an ethically inspired doctrine that leaves space for the English approach. Writing in the natural law (i.e. moralist) tradition, Pothier influentially held that sellers are under a legal duty to disclose all information touching the subject matter of the contract. Otherwise the seller would by 'setting a snare' gain an unjust advantage over the buyer, contrary to the good faith that governs the contract.[26] Michael Trebilcock suggests that the common law

---

[23] *Bell v Lever Bros* [1932] AC 161, 227.
[24] *Robbins v Jones* (1863) 15 CB (NS) 221 per Erle CJ.
[25] (1817) 15 US 178.
[26] R.-J. Pothier, *Treatise on the Contract of Sale* (trans. L.S. Cushing) (Little, Brown, 1839) [1762] § 234–38.

here violates the Kantian precept of 'equal respect'.[27] Or as it is sometimes put, the 'golden rule' that you should treat others as you would be treated yourself. Would a non-disclosing seller wish to be treated that way, were the roles reversed?

It is difficult to assess how much traction moral criticisms have in this situation, however. The courts accept that the law is not, in this area, enforcing morality. As seen above, the judges in *Smith v Hughes* explicitly distinguished the (acknowledged) *moral* duty of disclosure from the law of contract.[28] It is said that the common law's historical commitment to free market, individualist ideology explains the rule.[29] This seems a clear case of English law's amorality.

Daniel Friedmann argues that the sharp distinction between the effect of non-disclosure and positive misrepresentation is unjustifiable.[30] As he points out, there is a 'broad avenue' of rescission for misrepresentation. Even when made wholly innocently (i.e. non-negligently) it would be 'moral delinquency [since] no man ought to seek to take advantage of his own false statements'.[31] As Friedmann says, in misrepresentation it is enough to have been responsible for the other party's mistake. But is there not a stronger case for rescission when one is well aware of the other's mistake, but decides to say nothing and deliberately take advantage of it? Friedmann draws a parallel with undue influence: rescission is available when one party is on notice that the other was unduly influenced by a third party, although he is in no way responsible for that behaviour and merely aware of it.[32] From this, Friedmann concludes that equitable rescission should be much broader than the (exceedingly narrow) rule in *Smith v Hughes* that a known-about mistake will avoid the contract only if it relates to the contract's *terms*.[33]

Friedmann seems to think that all known-about ('fundamental') mistakes should lead to this conclusion, because it would be unconscionable for advantage to be taken of them. His analogy with undue influence seems powerful, since it clearly shows that knowledge may be enough for rescission. But perhaps a pragmatic line can be drawn between the situations. The notice doctrine in undue influence was an innovation 'designed to reconcile two powerful interests': protecting wives (in the stereotypical situation) forced to sign over the family home as security for their husbands' businesses, and on the other hand protecting the banks' interest in enforcing the security.[34] The courts have here performed a quasi-regulatory function, even laying down a detailed code of practice for on-notice banks.[35] So this is arguably an example of specialized regulation rather than an exemplification of equitable principles. As for *Smith v Hughes*, this too may be defended pragmatically. It must be

---

[27] M.J. Trebilcock, *The Limits of Freedom of Contract* (Harvard University Press, 1993) p.117.

[28] (1871) LR 6 QB 597.

[29] P.S. Atiyah, *The Rise and Fall of Freedom of Contract* (Oxford University Press, 1979) pp. 402–404.

[30] D. Friedmann, 'The Objective Principle and Mistake and Involuntariness in Contract and Restitution' (2003) 119 LQR 68.

[31] *Redgrave v Hurd* (1881) 20 Ch D 1, 13 (Jessel MR).

[32] Cf. *Barclays Bank plc v O'Brien* [1994] AC 180.

[33] Cf. pp. 7–9 above.

[34] Collins, n.7 above, pp. 150–51.

[35] *Royal Bank of Scotland v Etridge (No 2)* [2002] 2 AC 773.

common in practice for mistakes to be made about value, to the knowledge of the other party. In the absence of some bright-line rule about when a mistake of value is serious enough to be 'fundamental' (Friedmann's condition), relief for unilateral mistakes would potentially undo every bad bargain.[36] The security of contract law would be shaken to its roots. Finally, Friedmann's contention that taking advantage of a (self-induced) mistake is of itself 'unconscionable' rather assumes a high standard of moral behaviour, which the judges have consistently disclaimed.[37]

In the next section we consider whether the non-disclosure rule can be defended from the instrumental perspective by providing incentives for the production of useful information. But it should be noted that the starting point, for economists as for natural lawyers, is in favour of disclosure. Enforcing agreements is presumed to be good for society, because it moves resources into the hands of those who value them more highly. But that presumption crucially depends upon the parties making a free and *well-informed* choice. As Anthony Kronman puts it, 'Information is the antidote to mistake'.[38] In situations where it is impossible for buyers to distinguish the quality of goods on sale, bad goods will inevitably drive out the good.[39] Therefore, the presumption is in favour of disclosure of all relevant information, in order to lead to better-informed, more economically efficient contracting. This stands as an indictment of the *laissez-faire* approach of the common law. Kull notes that 'law and economics' often recommends aggressive intervention in the contracting process, since parties frequently make sub-optimal contracts![40] But again, some line needs to be drawn for practical reasons. As Trebilcock observes, contracting with incomplete information is endemic – it must be rare to make a contract with absolutely *complete* knowledge of all relevant facts, and if this were the requirement of the law few contracts would be enforceable.[41] But economic analysts generally go beyond practicality in defending the non-disclosure rule.

ENCOURAGING THE PRODUCTION AND USE OF VALUABLE INFORMATION

Although a legal duty to disclose relevant information may seem to make obvious economic (as well as moral) good sense, it would act as a disincentive for such information to be gathered in the first place. This would harm society since information is necessary for well-informed trading decisions to be made. The problem was pointed out in a seminal article by Kronman.[42] As he observes, intellectual property rights (e.g. patents or copyright) are commonly justified as providing incentives for creativity – the law grants a (time-limited) monopoly for

---

[36] A. Kull, 'Unilateral Mistake: the Baseball Card Case' (1992) 70 *Washington Univ LQ* 57, 66.
[37] Cf. *Riverlate Properties v Paul* [1975] 1 Ch 133, 140–145 (requiring fraud, sharp practice or unfair dealing).
[38] A.T. Kronman, 'Mistake, Disclosure, Information, and the Law of Contracts' (1978) 7 *JLS* 1, 4.
[39] G.A. Akerlof, 'The Market for "Lemons": Quality Uncertainty and the Market Mechanism' (1970) 84 *Quarterly Jo Ecs* 488.
[40] Kull, n.36 above, p. 77.
[41] Trebilcock, n.27 above, p. 103.
[42] A.T. Kronman, 'Mistake, Disclosure, Information, and the Law of Contracts' (1978) 7 *JLS* 1.

the inventor or artist to exploit her creation.[43] This rewards inventiveness: it is generally accepted that fewer new drugs would be developed if pharmaceutical companies were unable to use their patents to recover the high costs of research. But as Kronman observes, it has been less noticed that allowing parties not to disclose information during contractual negotiations has a similar rewarding effect. Roderick's behaviour in Example 2 above might therefore be justified. Richard Posner says this is 'an example of the traditional economic paradox that private vice can be public virtue'.[44]

However, Kronman does not advocate a non-disclosure rule in all cases but distinguishes between deliberately and casually acquired information. Logically, only the former is susceptible to incentives. Kronman defines 'deliberate acquisition' as that involving costs that would not otherwise be incurred. These include not only the immediate costs of search or analysis but also acquiring the necessary expertise. He distinguishes a stockbroker who appreciates that a share price is likely to fall because of careful analysis of the relevant economic data and someone who overhears information on a bus. Only in the former case is the reward of non-disclosure appropriate, for such costs will not be incurred in the first place if people are compelled to share the fruits of their information gathering. Therefore, the production of such information would decrease rapidly, whereas the casual acquisition of information is unlikely to suffer from a disclosure rule.

Kronman admits that drawing the distinction on a case-by-case basis will be very difficult, and recommends that in practice the courts should use broad categories. For example, information about changing market prices is *usually* acquired deliberately as the large industry of journalists and analysts concerned with the production of such information shows. Therefore, the classic case of *Laidlaw v Organ*[45] was correctly decided.[46] Moreover, Kronman claims that his theory explains the general pattern of liability. Cases where, exceptionally, contracts are avoided for known unilateral mistake (which is exactly the same as requiring the non-mistaken party to reveal the mistake) tend to be situations of clerical errors, such as the wrong price being typed in an offer letter.[47] The knowledge allowing such mistakes to be identified is not 'deliberately acquired' in Kronman's sense. In fact, it is likely to be no more than the common sense precept that if it's too good to be true, it probably isn't. Hence the courts have no sympathy with parties that 'snap up' such astonishing offers.[48] Kronman also suggests why positive misrepresentation always justifies rescission. Such mis-statements lead to false information circulating in the market, which needs to be firmly discouraged, just as production of valuable information is encouraged.

---

[43] Cf. E.C. Hettinger, 'Justifying Intellectual Property' (1989) *18 Philosophy & Public Affairs* 31.
[44] R.A. Posner, 'Let Us Never Blame a Contract Breaker' in O. Ben-Shahar & A. Porat (eds), *Fault in American Contract Law* (Cambridge University Press, 2010) p. 13.
[45] (1817) 15 US 178.
[46] Cf. p. 156 above.
[47] Cf. *Centrovincial Estates*, pp. 4–5 above; *Hartog v Colin & Shields*, pp. 3, 75 above.
[48] *Chwee Kin Keong v Digilandmall.com* [2004] 2 SLR 594.

Kronman's article has been hugely influential.[49] Later commentators, sympathetic to economic analysis of law, have sought to refine Kronman's argument. Others have been critical of his entire philosophy. We examine these contributions to the debate.

Robert Birmingham argues that if we accept the premise of Kronman's argument, even casually acquired information should be non-disclosable.[50] Contract law should encourage the *use* of valuable information, as well as its initial acquisition. So even if the seller's information about the end of the naval blockade in *Laidlaw v Organ* was obtained wholly through luck, it is important that it be acted upon as soon as possible. By buying large quantities of tobacco (at the current price) he raised the market price – a signal for merchants to buy more tobacco and farmers to plant it (what if a farmer was about to plough over a tobacco crop that he wrongly thought was too worthless to bother harvesting?). Or if someone realized, purely by chance, that a book at a car boot sale was a rare first edition, it would be better for him to buy and use it in accordance with its true worth than for it to be used as a door-stop by another buyer ignorant of its rarity.[51] Of course, the point again is that there would be little incentive for people to use this valuable information if the law required prior disclosure. Therefore, the goods might not move to their highest value use.

Cooter and Ulen propose a different distinction from Kronman's. They distinguish 'productive' facts which increase society's wealth overall, and 'redistributive' facts which only serve to alter the wealth distribution between the contracting parties. The latter does not increase overall economic efficiency, and therefore should not demand the rewards of non-disclosure, even when deliberately acquired.[52] Muriel Fabre-Magnan points out that this may be a very difficult distinction to draw – does the 'rediscovery' of a lost old master picture (by re-attribution of the artist) create new value, or simply redistribute value that was always latently 'there'?[53] Cooter and Ulen's view is that 'mixed' productive/ redistributive facts should be treated as the former, meaning a very wide rule of non-disclosure. Fabre-Magnan argues that the same is true of Kronman's original category of deliberately acquired information: because this includes the initial acquisition of the relative expertise, few cases fall outside this category.[54] Even someone who stumbles across a valuable book at the church fête has earlier acquired the expertise to spot the significance of the chance encounter.

If Fabre-Magnan is correct that the economic analyses tend towards a general rule of non-disclosure, this goes some way to answering a criticism put by Kull. He

---

[49] E.g. *United States v Dial* (1985) 757 F.2d 163, 168 (Posner J).

[50] R.L. Birmingham, 'The Duty to Disclose and the Prisoner's Dilemma: *Laidlaw v Organ*' (1988) 29 Wm. & Mary LR 249, 263. Cf. Birmingham's criticisms, pp. 160–161 below.

[51] Trebilcock, n.27 above, pp. 112–13.

[52] R. Cooter and T. Ulen, *Law and Economics* (1st edn, Scott, Foresman & Co, 1988) pp. 259–61.

[53] M. Fabre-Magnan, 'Duties of Disclosure and French Contract Law: Contribution to an Economic Analysis' in J. Beatson and D. Friedmann (eds), *Good Faith and Fault in Contract Law* (Oxford University Press, 1995) pp. 110–11.

[54] Ibid, p. 109.

argues that for courts to draw the fine distinctions required between deliberately and casually acquired information, or productive and redistributive information, would be 'administratively inconceivable'.[55] Therefore, he claims, the traditional blanket non-disclosure doctrine is likely to encourage information production in a socially optimal way, once administrative cost is taken into account.[56] This is not entirely convincing. First, as Trebilcock comments, minimizing administrative costs cannot be the primary goal of the law – this would ultimately require abolition of the entire law of contract![57] Secondly, if a blanket rule is to be preferred, why not use a rule of disclosure? Kull asserts that being free to use information, even that casually acquired, is a fundamental requirement of personal autonomy and that 'Life in a society that could enforce the perfectly efficient disclosure of information would be a totalitarian nightmare'.[58] But this seems a hyperbolic description of a doctrine well established in the Civilian tradition!

Birmingham makes a more fundamental attack.[59] Kronman's argument may lead to *over*-production of information, which is not, of course, costless. Both parties are given incentives to search (the buyer to take advantage of his knowledge, the seller to avoid disadvantage). But *inter se*, they would rationally prefer equal ignorance to equal knowledge, saving the (double) costs of acquiring the information. Furthermore, a (unilaterally) mistaken transaction is not necessarily optimal – hence the general presumption of information disclosure. Thus Kronman would permit non-disclosure only when the social gain from eliciting information outweighs the gain from eliminating mistakes. But, Birmingham comments, the point at which this happens is impossible to determine in practice – it 'eludes like a unicorn'.[60] Birmingham seems, therefore, to favour a blanket disclosure rule. It would avoid over-production, and any fine-gauged rule is unworkable in practice. Pierre Legrand suggests that there will be incentives to acquire valuable information even in a disclosure regime: buyers will still wish to maintain their competitive advantage over other buyers (to whom they would not be required to reveal information).[61] Does a passionate amateur collector, like Roderick, need any incentive to collect information about antique silverware?

CONCLUSION

It is very tempting to prefer moral clarity to an economic analysis which seems riddled with uncertainties. If it is impossible to say how much information should be produced, and of what type, and how best to encourage it, the clarity of a full disclosure regime looks preferable. Of course that is what the ethical perspective

---

[55] Kull, n.36 above, p. 80.

[56] Ibid, p. 61.

[57] Trebilcock, n.27 above, p. 115.

[58] Kull, n.36 above, p. 79.

[59] Cf. n.50 above.

[60] Ibid, 262. NB similar difficulties in IP law in determining the 'efficient' period for patent protection.

[61] Legrand, n.4 above, p. 345.

requires. Legrand criticizes the details of the information–reward argument and, in the end, dismisses it entirely because it permits an 'ascertainable detriment' to the mistaken party which must in the end undermine the 'moral acceptability' of contract law.[62] Kronman once suggested that a farmer whose field was bought by an oil company, without being told of its true value, should rationally permit such advantage to be taken of him: it would 'arguably' work to the farmer's own benefit by decreasing the price that the he has to pay for oil.[63] Trebilcock dismisses this as 'totally speculative and on its face, quite unpersuasive'.[64] Fabre-Magnan suggests that the wide French doctrine of disclosure is 'due to the French obsession with the morality of the law' or, at least, of the alien nature of economic analysis for French lawyers.[65] Her conclusion is that since economic analysis is 'so subjective and diverse' it is right to give priority to ethics.[66]

But Fabre-Magnan allows that even ethically, there may be a case for rewarding those who laboriously uncover valuable information. She criticizes a French case in which a painting, sold at auction as a copy and bought by the French state museums, was ultimately attributed to Poussin by art historians at the Louvre. The original owners successfully had the auction set aside for unilateral mistake and re-sold the painting for a much higher sum. The Louvre recovered only the amount paid in the original sale. It was, Fabre-Magnan remarks, 'unjust' for the museum's expenditure on expert fees, scientific tests and restoration to go unrewarded.[67] Anthony Kronman would say it was 'inefficient'. Perhaps the positions are not so far apart after all.

Even Pothier placed limits on disclosure to reward expeditious sellers.[68] He discussed an ancient case in which a corn vessel arrived at Rhodes in a time of scarcity and sold its corn for a high price without revealing that other vessels were on the verge of arrival. Cicero seems to have thought that good faith required the merchant to reveal this information because of the love that men should bear towards each other. But Pothier held that this went too far. It would compel 'gratuitous beneficence' to compel disclosure of information about circumstances extrinsic to the goods. The merchant had not profited unjustly but received a fair reward for the diligence that allowed him to arrive at the market first. Pothier even argued, for good measure, that Joseph's advice to Pharaoh about the coming famine illustrated the principle.[69] Pothier's opinion shows that even the natural law tradition recognized incentives. Perhaps Kronman's proposal can be defended as an 'equitable' recognition of 'just deserts' for those who have invested in the acquisition of information.

---

[62] Ibid, p. 346.
[63] A.T. Kronman, 'Contract Law and Distributive Justice' (1980) 89 *Yale LJ* 472, 489.
[64] Trebilcock, n.27 above, p. 109.
[65] Fabre-Magnan, n.53 above, p. 109.
[66] Ibid at 120.
[67] Ibid at 116.
[68] Pothier, n.26 above, §242.
[69] Cf. Genesis 41 vv. 29–36.

Debate 2

Do we need 'The Doctrine of Mistake'?

It is controversial to suggest that there is no need for a doctrine of mistake in contract law.[70] Most textbook accounts include a chapter on mistake. The unifying feature of the doctrine is that it leads to contracts being void *ab initio*. This is said to be a logical implication of the absence of the consent necessary for contractual obligation – it is 'negatived' or 'nullified' as Lord Atkin famously, if enigmatically, put it.[71] However, it may be argued that 'mistake' is an ultimately unsuccessful synthesis. A number of separate problems are being addressed using just one category, quite unnecessarily. If these problems were disaggregated they could be understood better. So, many cases see one party's mistake being taken advantage of by the other. Such cases seem akin to misrepresentation and, more generally, unconscionable conduct. In those areas, the courts use flexible concepts and discretionary remedies to fashion appropriate relief. This produces considerable tension with automatic voidness in the 'mistake' category – all misrepresentation cases are by definition mistake cases too, after all. Need the distinction be drawn at all?

A second category considers problems in the formation of contracts. This has been discussed already.[72] There is little scope for 'unilateral' mistakes. The logic of objectivity means that only when the non-mistaken party *knows* that the other is mistaken about the *terms* of the contract will the mistake prevent formation. Non-formation is accurately said to result in a void contract, the mere 'simulacrum' of a contract (as it is sometimes more elegantly put). The elusive distinction between mistakes about 'terms' and about ('mere') quality is of central importance. It coheres with the rules of non-disclosure and *caveat emptor*, discussed above, which still govern much of the law of contract.[73] The distinction is vital to keep unilateral mistakes in their place.[74] The only situations where a mistake is likely to satisfy the stringent test are where there is a clerical error about price (or some other fundamental term) which is so obvious that the offeree must have noticed it.[75] There is more than a trace of sharp practice in such 'snapping up' cases – indeed in Australia, they have been classified as unconscionable conduct rendering the contract voidable and the 'subjective' *Smith v Hughes* mistake doctrine rejected.[76] Finally, if the parties are at cross purposes and the situation is so inherently ambiguous that it is impossible to say on what terms the contract was concluded – indefinite to the point of futility[77] – it will be void

---

[70] Cf. C.J. Slade, 'The Myth of Mistake in the English Law of Contract' (1954) 70 *LQR* 385.

[71] *Bell v Lever Bros* [1932] AC 161, 217.

[72] Cf. pp. 7–9 above.

[73] Cf. Friedmann, n.30 above.

[74] Cf. Kull, n.36 above.

[75] E.g. *Hartog v Colin & Shields*; cf. *Webster v Cecil* (1861) 30 Beavan 62 (refusal of specific performance).

[76] *Taylor v Johnson* (1983) 151 CLR 422, 428–33.

[77] Cf. p. 25 n.161 above.

for uncertainty.[78] It is arguably unnecessary to discuss 'mistake' per se in any of these cases. They are merely applications of the rules on formation (including certainty).

A third category sees both parties sharing a ('common') mistake about some important fact. Here there is no doubt that agreement was reached – the category is quite distinct. (As David Ibbetson suggests, Pothier was able to produce an 'apparently unified theory' of mistake only by exploiting 'terminological ambiguity'.[79]) Justifying legal intervention in these cases poses similar problems to the doctrine of frustration.[80] A particular controversy is whether common mistake must lead automatically to voidness, or whether there is room for a discretionary, flexible approach to rescission. This is dramatized as a jurisdictional squabble, between law and equity. The current English position is that Denning LJ fought the common law – and the law won![81] However, the equitable remedy of *rectification* remains available to ensure that written contracts accurately record the agreement of the parties; it may even correct unilateral mistakes when 'sharp practice' is established.[82]

VOIDNESS AND VOIDABILITY

The debate over mistake is not simply abstract-doctrinal, of academic interest only. It has very real practical significance. Automatic voidness is obviously a drastic remedy. Applied to a contract of sale, it means that no property passes. This entails harsh consequences for any subsequent buyers of the property, for they gain no title from the original buyer, under the rule *nemo dat quod non habet* (no-one can give what he does not have). Yet these extreme consequences necessarily follow from the Will Theory position that mistake is 'the greatest defect that can occur in the contract'.[83] It nullifies consent. But as seen in Chapter 1, English law has decisively repudiated the will theory in favour of an objective approach to contract formation. Why then does a Pothier-derived doctrine of mistake hold sway (however uneasily) in English law? Catharine MacMillan blames the formative treatise writers in England, and particularly Sir Frederick Pollock, for the anomaly. Macmillan's important historical critique will be examined fully below.

The alternative approach to mistake would locate it firmly within equity's concern with unconscionable behaviour, rather than having a fundamental effect on consent. Therefore, by analogy with situations like undue influence, the contract would be voidable – liable to rescission, where appropriate, rather than automatically void. It seems that this was the approach of English law until well into the nineteenth century. Even today, mistakes that are induced by fraud or misrepresentation lead to rescission under those doctrines. (But third party rights

---

[78] *Raffles v Wichelhaus* (1864) 2 H&C 906; *Falck v Williams* [1900] AC 176.
[79] D.J. Ibbetson, *A Historical Introduction to the Law of Obligations* (Oxford University Press, 1999) p. 226.
[80] Cf. Ch. 5 above.
[81] *Solle v Butcher* [1950] 1 KB 671; cf. *The Great Peace* [2003] QB 679.
[82] Cf. p. 8, n.54 above.
[83] R.-J. Pothier, *Traité des obligations* (1761) (trans. Sir W. Jones) 1.1.3 §1.

form an important bar to rescission, so a bona fide purchaser of property that has been fraudulently obtained will gain good title: the initial contract will not be rescinded.[84]) Moreover, sharp practice may justify refusal of specific performance;[85] it is a crucial element of rectification for *unilateral* mistake;[86] it arguably explains the 'snapping up' cases. Therefore, mistake lives on in equity, although disconnected rather than forming 'a doctrine'. Indeed, 'the doctrine of common mistake in equity' has recently been repudiated in England.[87]

Perhaps it is the low profile and enfeebled state of the equitable jurisdiction which leaves room for the subjective doctrine of mistake at law to continue. MacMillan comments that there are few guiding principles on when to apply the equitable rules (flexible; voidability) and when those at law (inflexible; voidness). Indeed, Macmillan argues that the modern law of mistake itself came about 'by mistake'.[88] Equitable mistake was neglected and ultimately forgotten. Meanwhile, an unsatisfactory subjective theory of mistake was incorporated unthinkingly by the House of Lords in *Bell v Lever Bros*.[89] The result is a doctrine that is 'dangerously unreliable'.[90]

View of an expert

Catherine MacMillan

MacMillan's fascinating historical study shows that the modern doctrine of mistake has shallow doctrinal roots. Mistake seems to be the one area of English law where the Will Theory expounded by Pothier has taken hold. But this was possible only by inventing a doctrine which had simply never existed at common law, and sidelining the equitable doctrine of mistake. The result is an inflexible doctrine which is highly anomalous in its subjective basis. Not surprisingly, the courts have attempted to confine it as much as possible.

MacMillan shows that before the fusion of the courts of common law and chancery in 1875 equitable relief was not based on failure of consent, but the effect of mistake upon conscience.[91] Equity was concerned more with the conduct of the parties than the 'metaphysics of formation'.[92] The courts of common law, pre-fusion, knew no separate doctrine of mistake. The first time such arguments were made at law was when a statute of 1854

---

[84] E.g. *Phillips v Brooks* [1919] 2 KB 243.
[85] Cf. *Webster v Cecil*, n.75 above.
[86] *Commission for the New Towns v Cooper* [1995] Ch 259.
[87] *The Great Peace* [2003] QB 679.
[88] C. MacMillan, *Mistakes in Contract Law* (Hart Publishing, 2010) 318 (hereafter 'Macmillan').
[89] [1932] AC 161.
[90] Macmillan, p. 1.
[91] Macmillan, pp. 38–41, 44–49.
[92] Macmillan, p. 159.

allowed equitable defences to be raised in common law proceedings.[93] The reaction of the common law judges was not enthusiastic: they interpreted the statute as permitting only the characteristic total (all-or-nothing) defences at law; conditional relief (such as rectification or rescission on terms) was still available only in equity. This is an antecedent for the all-or-nothing effect of the modern common law doctrine of mistake (voidness). But the pre-fusion common lawyers were well aware of the separate equitable jurisdiction over mistakes and saw no reason to develop their own.[94]

The intellectual shift came with treatise writers such as Judah Benjamin and especially Frederick Pollock, who were keen to restructure the law of contract using the Will Theory (from Pothier and the German authority, von Savigny).[95] This was a monumental task, poorly executed. Macmillan focuses on Pollock's account, given his influence on twentieth-century legal development.[96] Pollock found equity peculiar and anomalous, and the equitable rules were 'sometimes overlooked, sometimes misunderstood and sometime marginalised' before disappearing altogether from later editions of the treatise. Instead, Pollock was clear that the effect of mistake was to render the contract a nullity from the beginning. This followed from the Will Theory. However, 'the invidious results which could occur in commercial practice do not seem to have occurred to him'.[97] Moreover, Pollock offered no guidance on how to distinguish such mistakes (rendering contracts void) from fraud or breach of warranty (which did not).

The greatest problem for Pollock was to reconcile his subjectivist theory with the generally objective approach of English law. In early editions he simply ignored the problem; in the fifth edition of 1889, Pollock endorsed the positivist, objective view of contract promoted by O.W. Holmes, although without wholly discarding the earlier Will Theory. A disjointed account of the law resulted – nowhere more clearly than with mistake. This chapter of Pollock's *Treatise* remained virtually unchanged, thus becoming 'a sort of intellectual orphan'.[98] Macmillan comments that this residuum of the Will Theory 'made little sense, both within itself and in relation to other areas of contract law'.[99] The treatise of Sir William Anson, the chief rival to Pollock's, came close to eliminating mistake as a separate category by its sixth edition (1891). But Anson's failure to complete the narrowing process

---

[93] Macmillan, pp. 84–86.
[94] Macmillan, p. 197.
[95] J. Benjamin, *A Treatise on the Law of Sale* (1868); F. Pollock, *Principles of Contract at Law and in Equity: Being a Treatise on the General Principles Concerning the Validity of Agreements* (1876).
[96] Macmillan, pp. 143–69.
[97] Macmillan, p. 151.
[98] Macmillan, p. 167.
[99] Macmillan, p. 136.

left the same inconsistencies that marred Pollock's treatise.[100] The seminal accounts of mistake were therefore 'confusing and unworkable', the distinction with fraud and the other vitiating factors 'very poorly drawn'.[101]

This unfortunate doctrine, an isolated relic of the Will Theory, was cemented in place as late as 1932 by *Bell v Lever Bros*.[102] *Bell* marked the 'birth of a doctrine of contractual mistake based on a failure of consent. Lord Atkin made the theories of the treatise writers law.'[103] Lord Atkin remarked on the paucity of authority which had also puzzled Wright J and the Court of Appeal in *Bell*'s earlier stages. Macmillan argues that the supposed 'classic mistake' cases from the nineteenth century, such as *Raffles v Wichelhaus* and *Kennedy v Panama Mail Co*, never supported the theory of Pollock and others.[104] But it did not occur to the judges that English law might not have recognized the doctrine of mistake advanced by the treatise writers.[105] Pollock's influence pervaded Lord Atkin's leading speech: no distinction was made between law and equity; mistake destroyed consent, leading to voidness (Lord Atkin uses Pollock's term, 'nullity'). This was a radical, but unnoticed, departure from the equitable doctrines. Macmillan's conclusion is that 'uncritical reliance upon treatise writers, notably Pollock, had produced an unworkable doctrine based upon unsatisfactory precedents'.[106]

Catherine Macmillan's important thesis shows the muddle and forgetfulness that led to the current state of the law on mistake. The twenty-first century began with two leading cases on mistake which were decided in a very conservative way: *Shogun Finance v Hudson*, which reaffirmed *Cundy v Lindsay* on identity mistakes,[107] and *The Great Peace* which departed from *Solle v Butcher* (on the authority of *Bell*) on common mistake.[108] If one thing is clear, it is that rational debate in this area should in future take place on policy grounds. Falling back onto a rigid doctrine of precedent is unconvincing when the reasoning of the leading cases is so flawed.[109]

IDENTITY MISTAKES

This has long been a difficult and controversial area. By a narrow margin the House of Lords refused the opportunity to reform the law in *Shogun Finance v Hudson*.[110]

---

[100] Macmillan, pp. 176–78.
[101] Macmillan, pp. 179–80.
[102] [1932] AC 161; Macmillan, pp. 259–78.
[103] Macmillan, p. 272.
[104] Macmillan, ch. 7.
[105] Macmillan, p. 270.
[106] Macmillan, p. 291.
[107] *Shogun Finance* [2003] UKHL 62; *Cundy v Lindsay* (1878) LR 3 App Cas 459.
[108] Cf. n.81 above.
[109] Macmillan, p. 316.
[110] [2003] UKHL 62.

Every reported case follows a broadly similar fact pattern. A fraudster (the 'rogue') purchases goods on credit by impersonating another (more creditworthy) person or organization. The rogue rapidly sells those goods to an unsuspecting third party, and disappears with his money. The original seller, discovering the fraud, seeks to recover the goods from the innocent third party. Recovery depends on whether the claimant's contract with the rogue is void or voidable. If void, the rogue never gained title to the goods and neither did the third party: the *nemo dat* principle. But if the contract is merely *voidable* the third party is safe since his right to the goods will prevent rescission of the claimant–rogue contract. In all of these cases, remedies for fraud are obviously available (subject to the third-party rights bar). The question is whether the claimant's mistake should additionally render his contract with the rogue void.

This has usually been answered using the principles of formation and construction of contracts – although there has been disagreement over what they are. But Devlin LJ suggested that this was entirely the wrong way of approaching the problem – English law in this area, 'contrary to its habit ... instead of looking for a principle that is simple and just, rests on theoretical distinctions'. The common law's 'true spirit' was to override such very fine distinctions 'when they stand in the way of doing practical justice'.[111] We will return to the 'pragmatic' approach, and Devlin LJ's proposed solution, once we have examined the theoretical controversy.

The contract between the plaintiffs and the rogue in the leading case of *Cundy* is said to have been void because:

> Of him they knew nothing, and of him they never thought. With him they never intended to deal. Their minds never, even for an instant of time rested upon him, and as between him and them there was no consensus of minds which could lead to any agreement or any contract whatever.[112]

Dissenting in *Shogun Finance*, Lord Millett found this reasoning 'unconvincing'. Lord Cairns 'dwelt on the plaintiffs' subjective state of mind, which was of course affected by the fraud, and gave no attention to the question whether, approaching the case objectively, the plaintiffs had accepted [the rogue] Blenkarn's offer'.[113] Lord Millett argues that on an *objective* approach to the facts of *Cundy* the plaintiffs' conduct shows that there was indeed a contract, albeit voidable for fraud. Would the plaintiffs not have been able to sue the rogue for the price of the goods, had they opted to affirm the contract?[114] Lord Denning MR made similar criticisms in *Lewis v Averay*, attributing the voidness rule to 'the French jurist Pothier'. But this was 'no part of English law' and it had 'given rise to such refinements that it

---

[111] *Ingram v Little* [1961] 1 QB 31 at 73–74.
[112] 3 App Cas 459, 465–66 (Lord Cairns LC).
[113] [2003] UKHL 62, [91].
[114] [92]-[93]. Cf. *Lindsay v Cundy* (1876) L.R. 1 QBD 348. Cf Stevens, n.118 below at 117: claimant could 'ratify' the *void* contract.

is time it was dead and buried together'.[115] Lord Denning repudiated the ghostly influence of Pothier's Will Theory, a subjective anomaly in the objective English approach to formation.

On the other hand, we have seen in Chapter 1 that the great authority of *Smith v Hughes*[116] allows one exception to its sternly objective approach, when one party knows the other is mistaken as to the terms of the contract.[117] Therefore, Robert Stevens argues, the 'identity mistake' cases are not a discrete class at all. They are resolved by applying the general approach – was the rogue's identity (about which the mistake was made) a term of the contract or not?[118] Stevens admits that there is 'no litmus test' for this, any more than sometimes the age of the oats will be a term of the contract, and sometimes not. But arguably this understates the problem.

While claimants in many of the cases went to some lengths to identify the (supposed) identity of the rogue,[119] what they were really interested in was his creditworthiness. The rogue invariably impersonates a financially solid citizen for precisely this reason. A unilateral mistake about creditworthiness is more like a mistake as to quality and does not nullify the contract, on the authority of *Smith v Hughes*. Identity is certainly important but as a means to an end or an end in itself? Is the claimant really mistaken about the rogue's identity, or his attributes (i.e. creditworthiness)? Lord Denning MR said this was 'a distinction without a difference,'[120] and Lord Millett comments that the question, did the claimant intend to contract with the rogue believing him to be *X*, or with *X* believing him the rogue, is 'meaningless'.[121] Arguably, only if the other party's identity is intrinsically important should it be a term – as when a famous painter is engaged to paint a portrait.[122]

The majority in *Shogun Finance* held that whether the rogue's identity was a term of the contract must be decided objectively. But they took a wide approach: if his alias was unequivocally identified it forms a term of the contract. With written contracts as in *Cundy* or *Shogun* itself, this process is said to be fairly straightforward. Written negotiations, by describing as one of the parties to the putative agreement an individual who is unequivocally identifiable from that description, preclude any finding that the party to the putative agreement is other than the person so described. The process of construction will lead inexorably to the conclusion that the person with whom the other party intended to contract was the person thus described.[123]

---

[115] [1972] 1 QB 198.

[116] (1871) LR 6 QB 597.

[117] Cf. pp. 7–9 above.

[118] R. Stevens, 'Objectivity, Mistake and the Parol Evidence Rule' in A. Burrows and E. Peel (eds), *Contract Terms* (Oxford University Press, 2007) p.112.

[119] Cf. *Ingram v Little* [1961] 1 QB 31.

[120] *Lewis v Averay* [1972] 1 QB 198.

[121] *Shogun Finance* [2003] UKHL 62, [65].

[122] Cf. *Boulton v Jones* (1857) 6 Weekly Reporter at 108 (Bramwell B).

[123] [2003] UKHL 62, [161] (Lord Phillips MR).

Cundy 'exemplifies' this objective approach.[124] To overrule it would mandate 'a factual inquiry into extraneous facts not known to both of the parties thus depriving documentary contracts of their certainty'.[125] The parties simply are those named in the document: but of course as one of them does not exist (or has had his signature forged), the apparent contract is nullified. In face-to-face negotiations, there is a strong presumption that the claimant intended to deal with the rogue (and not the person the rogue claimed to be), but this could not be an absolute rule.[126] Stevens says, approving *Shogun Finance*, that reduced-to-writing cases are easy to decide and face-to-face dealings an indication the other way, but ultimately whether identity is a term depends on the facts of each case.[127]

This argument seems powerful. But it is not entirely clear why the fact that the rogue's alias has been written down should elevate it to 'term' status, if it is correct (as suggested above) that in most cases it is a means to an end rather than intrinsically important. The House of Lords' concern seemed to be with protecting the integrity of written instruments rather than explaining why identity is fundamental in these cases, but not others – a dichotomy that has frequently led to 'illogical and sometimes barely perceptible distinctions' being drawn, according to Sedley LJ.[128] So, Lord Hobhouse praised the parol evidence rule as being 'fundamental' to and 'one of the great strengths' of English commercial law.[129] While this may be true generally speaking,[130] does it provide the key to identity mistakes?

The argument seems self-contradictory in such cases. The contract signed in *Shogun Finance* was purportedly between the claimant and (the blameless) Mr Patel and not the rogue, because that is what the documentation said. It would, it is said, undermine that contract's certainty to admit evidence to show that it was truly between the claimant and the rogue (and voidable); therefore this evidence was inadmissible. But what was *not* inadmissible, of course, was evidence to show that the supposedly inviolable contract with Mr Patel was no contract at all, because it was a forgery.[131] If part of the rationale for excluding parol evidence is that it would prejudice third parties who rely on documents in necessary ignorance of 'contextual' circumstances,[132] it is perverse to exclude one type of extrinsic evidence which would make the contract voidable (so protecting innocent third parties like the defendant, Mr Hudson), but to *admit* evidence which renders the contract *void* – disastrous for the third party. Lord Millett, dissenting, denied that written document cases were simple questions of construction, admitting of only

---

124 Ibid, [170] (Lord Phillips MR).
125 Ibid, [55] (Lord Hobhouse).
126 Ibid, [187] (Lord Walker).
127 Stevens, n.118 above.
128 *Shogun Finance v Hudson* [2002] QB 834, [11].
129 [2003] UKHL 62, [49].
130 Cf. pp. 78–80 above.
131 Cf. [2003] UKHL 62, [53] (Lord Hobhouse).
132 Cf. pp. 100–101 above.

one answer.[133] He could see no difference in principle in identifying the counter-party in the written and face-to-face cases.[134]

Other powerful criticisms may be made of the *Cundy v Lindsay* approach. The dissenters in *Shogun* sought to equiparate all cases of fraud. Why should it make a difference if fraud takes the form of impersonation or 'identity theft'? Claiming to be creditworthy and claiming to be someone else who is creditworthy 'are merely two ways a crook may assert a spurious creditworthiness' and one would assume there was no difference in substance.[135] For the innocent third party's position to depend on such refined distinctions was 'indefensible'.[136] 'It is little short of absurd that a subsequent purchaser's rights depend on … the precise form the crook's misrepresentation takes.'[137] The law as it stood was a 'quagmire', 'neither fair nor principled'.[138] The Court of Appeal had expressed their disquiet at the state of the law, and the House of Lords should not shirk the opportunity to provide order by overruling *Cundy*.[139] As between the innocent parties, it was fairer to protect the third party defendant than the claimant who had sold the goods on credit – always inherently risky.[140]

In response, Stevens argues that fraud is simply irrelevant if there is no contract in the first place.[141] The logic of this is impeccable; it also misses the point. A more telling point is that 'harshness' for third parties results from the rule *nemo dat quod non habet*. Here, fault is irrelevant – if I leave my keys in the ignition of the car, someone who steals it still cannot pass good title to a third party. If *nemo dat* is thought to produce unacceptable results it should be reformed directly, rather than subverting the rules of contract law.[142] Lord Walker points out that the parties may be equally innocent (or culpable), and so the law cannot lay down a presumption about which party is more often to blame.[143]

Devlin LJ thought that the 'plain answer' was that the loss should be divided between the two innocent parties 'in such proportion as is just in all the circum-stances', including their relative fault. He recognized that legislation would be needed for such a jurisdiction.[144] There are obvious antecedents – Devlin LJ referred to the statutes on joint tortfeasors, contributory negligence and frustration. However, although Devlin LJ's suggestion was referred to the Law Revision Committee, they recommended against apportionment.[145] It would mean 'virtually unrestrained judicial discretion' in an area where certainty was

---

[133] [2003] UKHL 62, [103].
[134] Ibid, [68].
[135] Ibid, [2] (Lord Nicholls).
[136] Ibid, [60] (Lord Millett).
[137] Ibid, [35] (Lord Nicholls). Cf. [33].
[138] Ibid, [84] (Lord Millett).
[139] Ibid, [83] (Lord Millett).
[140] Ibid, [35] (Lord Nicholls); [82] (Lord Millett).
[141] Stevens, n.118 above, p. 115.
[142] Ibid, 115–17.
[143] [2003] UKHL 62, [181]–[182].
[144] Cf. n.111 above.
[145] *Twelfth Report on the Transfer of Title to Chattels* (Cmnd 2958) (1966).

especially important: property ownership. Interestingly, lawyers responding to the Committee's consultation had broadly favoured apportionment but business representatives opposed the discretion since it would add to the cost of legal proceedings. The Committee did recommend, however, that identity mistake should make contracts voidable and not void. This has not been implemented by Parliament, to the regret of Brooke LJ.[146]

The most devastating critique of the current state of the law is Catherine Macmillan's.[147] *Cundy* was not decided on the basis of a subjective doctrine of mistake at all: at first instance, Blackburn J thought so little of the mistake point that he did not call on the defendant's counsel to respond to it.[148] Rather, two doctrines of contemporary (Victorian) criminal law allowed the plaintiffs to recover (the value of) the handkerchiefs. First, it was established that property did not pass when goods were obtained by false pretences;[149] the rogue Blenkarn had been convicted of this offence. Secondly, under the Larceny Act 1861 a victim could recover goods from an innocent third party (to whom a thief had sold them) by a writ of restitution. Consistency between criminal and civil law therefore compelled a decision for the plaintiffs. Contemporary reaction to *Cundy* in the legal press viewed it as a case on criminal fraud and the statutory provisions. As with the speeches in the House of Lords, no mention was made of mistake.

But the elevation of *Cundy* as a 'leading mistake case' came soon thereafter when it was used in Pollock's treatise to support his theory that mistake vitiates consent. However, Pollock ignored the concerns about the criminal law that gave the 'crucial underpinning' for *Cundy*. In our own time, that case is still treated as authoritative for a proposition that it does not support because it is based on considerations that have long since vanished. Macmillan persuasively argues that the repeal of the provisions allowing recovery of stolen property explains the pattern of the subsequent case-law. *King's Norton Metal Co v Edridge, Merrett & Co* is often criticized for drawing an inexplicably fine distinction with *Cundy*, holding the contract voidable because the person impersonated by the rogue was fictitious.[150] *Phillips v Brooks* is also criticized for holding the contract voidable when the parties dealt face to face.[151] But the Sale of Goods Act 1893 had repealed the provisions of the 1861 Act which revested goods obtained by false pretences and was felt to be commercially inconvenient. The process was completed with the Larceny Act 1916. As the criminal law changed, so did the contract cases. A.L. Smith LJ in *King's Norton Metal* ridiculed the suggestion that the fraud should render the contract void.[152]

---

[146] *Shogun Finance* [2002] QB 834, [51].
[147] C. Macmillan, 'Rogues, Swindlers and Cheats: The Development of Mistake of Identity in English Contract Law' [2005] *CLJ* 711; Macmillan, n.2 above, ch. 8.
[148] Cf. (1876) LR 1 QBD 348, 352.
[149] *Kingsford v Merry* (1856) 11 Exch 577.
[150] (1897) 14 TLR 98.
[151] [1919] 2 KB 243.
[152] (1897) 14 TLR 98, 99.

Macmillan's argument, then, is that there is no reason of precedent to follow *Cundy* today. Its true basis has long since vanished. It never supported the subjective mistake theory of Pollock as the decisions following the criminal law reforms demonstrate. It would be preferable to treat impersonation cases consistently with other cases on fraud and hold the resulting contracts voidable. Or in other words, Lord Denning was right.[153]

Cundy has been the obstacle to such consistency – as recognized in *Shogun Finance*. We will never know whether a majority of the House of Lords could have been convinced to depart from it had Catherine Macmillan's historical explanation been available to them. The decision may be different when it next reaches the Supreme Court – but such cases seem to be heard by the highest tribunal about once per century.

NON EST FACTUM

Another situation in which fraud may lead to a contract being void rather than voidable, with the same impact on third parties, is the defence of *non est factum suum* ('it is not my deed'). The extent and indeed the very existence of the defence in its modern form are questionable. Sir John Baker traces the historical development.[154] It was a plea denying the validity of deeds, the core cases being a deed that was invalidly executed or delivered, or an outright forgery. These were necessarily void. By 1582 the defence had been extended to the situation of an illiterate person who had (of necessity) had to rely on someone reading the deed to him before executing it, but an inaccurate account of the contents was given.[155] At this point it seems that the rationale for the plea was deception. By the late nineteenth century, the defence had been extended from deeds in the narrow sense to contracts generally.[156] Then came the 'turning point' at which the defence was rationalized as a lack of consensus – if someone is materially misled 'then his mind does not go with his pen. In that case it is not his deed.'[157] Baker comments that 'the learned judges were wrong to introduce this novel view, which is demonstrably too subjective'.[158] After all, in every case of fraud it may be said that the mind does not go with the pen. Yet such a broad defence would prevent 'any consideration of the plight of innocent third parties'.[159]

Lord Denning MR came close to calling for outright abolition of the defence in *Gallie v Lee* – at least where a person 'of full age and understanding, who can read and write, signs a legal document which is put before him for signature'.[160] The House of Lords did not go so far, although they did attempt to place limits on the

---

[153] *Lewis v Averay,* n.115 above.
[154] J.H. Baker, 'Non est factum' [1970] CLP 53 (hereafter 'Baker').
[155] *Thoroughgood's Case* (1582) Co Rep 9b.
[156] *Foster v Mackinnon* (1869) LR 4 CP 704.
[157] *Carlisle & Cumberland Banking Co v Bragg* [1911] 1 KB 489, 496 (Buckley LJ).
[158] Baker, p. 63.
[159] Ibid, p. 66.
[160] [1969] 2 Ch. 17.

plea.[161] Lord Reid thought that the defence 'must' extend from cases of blindness and illiteracy to 'defective education, illness or innate incapacity', and thought that even persons of full capacity might raise the plea in 'very exceptional circumstances'. Anybody raising the defence must, however, have taken precautions against being deceived. Thus the statement that the mind does not go with the pen was 'far too wide' because it included people who had taken no precautions at all. The defence 'must be kept within narrow limits if it is not to shake the confidence of those who habitually and rightly rely on signatures when there is no obvious reason to doubt their validity'.

Lord Wilberforce held that although in many cases *non est factum* was inappropriate (failure to take precautions) and sometimes unnecessary (outright forgery), to eliminate it altogether would in rare cases deprive the courts of an instrument for doing justice. The hallmark of a void contract was 'when the element of consent to it is totally lacking, that is, more concretely, when the transaction which the document purports to effect is essentially different in substance or in kind from the transaction intended' – or 'basically', 'radically' or 'fundamentally' different. It was this lack of consent rather than any fraud or deception that was crucial. Requiring prudent precautions to be taken by those who were 'illiterate, or blind, or lacking in understanding' would go some way to protecting innocent third parties. But no defined solution could be provided for all cases.

Thus, *non est factum's* basis in subjective consent was reaffirmed. Consistent with the Will Theory's attitude to mistake, its absence necessarily nullifies the transaction. But this is questionable. It is not clear why one tricked into signing a document should be in a better position than one defrauded in another way when the subject matter of that transaction ends up in the hands of a third party. As with identity mistakes, it would be more consistent to treat all fraudulently obtained contracts as *voidable*. Baker comments that the extension of *non est factum* has been 'a farrago of errors'.[162] Again, this shows that a subjective theory of mistake leads to theoretical and practical problems in the law. It is true that the House of Lords attempted to limit the doctrine. But requiring a fundamental error 'of substance or kind' was criticized by Baker: justice should not be achieved 'by subverting the basic principles of law with a gloss of subtle but unfounded distinctions'.[163] It may well be that the distinction, although unworkable and admittedly 'illogical', at least limits the 'dangerous anachronism' of *non est factum*.[164] Would it not be better to discard the special defence altogether?

COMMON MISTAKE

We now consider the most difficult question. What happens when both parties share a mistaken belief about an important fact on which their agreement is based?

---

[161] [1971] AC 1004 (sub nom. *Saunders v Anglia BS*).
[162] Baker, p. 69.
[163] Ibid.
[164] *Gallie v Lee* [1969] 2 Ch. 17, 44 (Salmon LJ).

(for example, when both rely on incorrect data provided by a third party, as in *The Great Peace*).[165] According to *Bell v Lever Bros*, such 'common' mistakes may render the contract a 'nullity'.[166] However, some argue that the problem of the shared mistake requires construction of the contract, not a formal 'doctrine of mistake'. The second controversy, if it be accepted that there *is* such a doctrine, is what the *effect* of mistake should be. The Court of Appeal in *The Great Peace* has reaffirmed the rule that mistake renders a contract void and dismissed Lord Denning's campaign for a discretionary equitable remedy.[167] But the court's reasoning has been questioned on historical grounds. Quite apart from this, strong arguments exist for a flexible solution.

It is universally accepted that construction of the contract has an important role to play in this field. Does the contract expressly or impliedly allocate the risk of the mistake to one of the parties? The debate is over whether anything further is needed. In a well-known judgment, Steyn J commented that most pleas of mistake would fail at the construction 'hurdle', i.e. because most contracts allocate the risk. But he went on to hold that if the contract was 'silent on the point' the court should apply the doctrine of mistake.[168] Some argue that this second stage is simply unnecessary. The point is left highly debateable by *Bell*, where 'their Lordships were inclined to pull together concepts such as risk, intention, implied terms and mistake, without offering suitable guidance on the analytical structure that might disentangle this web of interrelated considerations'.[169] The controversy continues, even after Steyn J's stage-by-stage rationalization.

For Slade, only if a condition can be implied avoiding the contract in the event of the relevant mistake will the contract be void.[170] In formal terms, was the matter over which the parties are mistaken a 'condition precedent' to the obligations, so that if it does not exist the contract falls? Atiyah and Bennion identify 'a palpable *non sequitur*' in saying that because the parties have contracted on some shared fundamental basis its non-existence necessarily renders the contract void 'because it may well be – indeed it usually is – the responsibility of one or other of the parties to see that that basis does exist'.[171] If there is no condition precedent, has not the court 'established that the parties did *not* intend that the contract should be invalidated if it turned out that the [fact] did not exist'?[172] There is simply no room for Steyn J's contractual 'silence' on this analysis. Unless the court infers a conditional precedent (which it usually will not), the parties must be taken to wish the risk of mistake to lie where it falls. This is so even if the mistake renders performance impossible. Non-performance will be treated as breach of contract

---

[165] [2003] QB 679.

[166] [1932] AC 161.

[167] *Solle v Butcher* [1950]1 KB 671.

[168] *Associated Japanese Bank (International) Ltd v Credit du Nord SA* [1989] 1 WLR 255, 268.

[169] A. Chandler, J. Devenney & J. Poole, 'Common Mistake: Theoretical Justification and Remedial Inflexibility' [2004] *JBL* 34.

[170] Slade, n.70 above, p. 399.

[171] P.S. Atiyah & F.A.R. Bennion, 'Mistake in the Construction of Contracts' (1961) 24 *MLR* 421, 426.

[172] J.C. Smith, 'Contracts – Mistake, Frustration and Implied Terms' (1994) 110 *LQR* 400, 407.

in the normal way. For 'the risk of initial impossibility is generally accepted by each party in relation to his own promises'.[173] He is in a better position to know whether his promises are performable – it is not too much to expect that he makes sure there is no impediment to performance.

Atiyah and Bennion argue that the 'principal weakness' of the 'mistake theory' is that it inflates the importance of this factor, crowding out others that are more relevant. So even when there has been a mistake, there is usually another factor such as express or implied terms, or misrepresentation 'which plainly show that the obligations of the parties are *not* inoperative'.[174] It surely cannot be the law that a seller can assert that a contract is 'void' for a (genuine) mistake over some quality that the seller has warranted. Yet in one case the court made exactly this mistake, as a result of considering mistake in isolation from the question of the seller's obligations.[175] By contrast, in *McRae v Commonwealth Disposals Commission* the Australian High Court scathingly dismissed the seller's plea of mistake when it turned out (strangely) that the wrecked ship which had been sold did not exist.[176] This was plainly the seller's responsibility. It was inconceivable that the buyer would have reasoned: 'Of course, if there is no tanker, there is no contract'. In *McRae* the court had to circumvent the codified rule of '*res extincta*' (contract of sale void when the goods have perished),[177] on the rather dubious ground that rather than 'perishing' the tanker never existed in the first place. Atiyah and Bennion suggest that the rule should be repealed – it is an anachronism dating from times of much slower communications, and the risk should be borne by the seller.[178]

There is considerable evidence that the courts are, usually, aware of the importance of respecting the contractual allocation of risk when faced with a plea of mistake. Lord Sumner made the point generally: 'Contracts are made for the purpose of fixing the incidence of risks in advance, and their occurrence only makes it the more necessary to uphold a contract and not make them the ground for discharging it.'[179] This is a point that has been discussed extensively in relation to frustration, in the last chapter. The same analysis applies in both areas, generally speaking.[180] Trebilcock remarks that the issues facing a court keen to intervene to reallocate the risk of mistake are equally intractable.[181] The courts are, if anything, even less likely to intervene over mistakes of existing fact, which are in principle knowable, unlike future events. The general attitude is that the loss lies where it falls. Lord Atkin's speech in *Bell* is, perhaps surprisingly, an excellent example. His Lordship ridiculed the idea that a disappointed buyer could rely on his mistake,

---

[173] Atiyah & Bennion, n.171 above, p. 437.

[174] Ibid, p. 425.

[175] Ibid, p. 433, criticizing *Nicholson & Venn v Smith Marriott* (1947) 177 LT 189.

[176] (1951) 84 CLR 377.

[177] See now Sale of Goods Act 1979, s.6.

[178] Atiyah & Bennion, n.171 above, p. 437.

[179] *Larrinaga & Co Ltd v Société Franco-Américaine* (1923) 29 Com Cas 1 at 19.

[180] Cf. pp. 126–128, 131–140 above and Smith, n.172 above.

[181] M.J. Trebilcock, *The Limits of Freedom of Contract* (Harvard University Press, 1993) p.140.

shared with the seller, about the quality of the goods. No doubt buyers make such mistakes in every bad bargain. But they must extract a warranty of quality or else take and pay for the goods: *caveat emptor*.[182] Similarly, Hoffmann LJ found 'startling' the argument that reliance could be placed on a shared mistake (about the location of a sewer) to avoid a contract for sale of land. This would subvert the allocation of risk – in land sales *caveat emptor*.[183]

In *The Great Peace*, the contract was not 'void for mistake' despite the serious shared mistake. The Court of Appeal purported to equate the tests for 'mistake' and 'frustration': only when performance is rendered *impossible* by the mistake will it render the contract void. If the argument in Chapter 5 is correct, then ironically, the analogy with frustration would serve to kill off the 'doctrine of mistake' altogether.[184] Applying the test, however, the court found that it was not wholly impossible to perform the contract – the Great Peace, although more distant than the parties thought, could still have arrived in time to provide several days' service. Moreover, only when a closer vessel was found did the defendants attempt to cancel their contract with the owners of the Great Peace.[185] The case was decided in a more straightforward way by Toulson J at first instance. He noted that commercial parties often base their decisions on information provided by third parties and take the risk that that information may turn out to be wrong.[186] Moreover: 'If the defendants had wished for a contractual stipulation from the claimants as to the position of the Great Peace, they could have asked for it.'[187] The court was not willing to imply what the parties could, if they had wanted it, expressly stipulated. In other words, the risk lay where it fell. It is not at all clear why this decision should be different if the Great Peace had been so far away that it could not have reached the stricken ship at all. Impossibility seems to be the wrong test.

Andrew Tettenborn has recently proposed a variation on the risk allocation approach.[188] He argues that contracts only deal with *particular* contingencies or uncertainties. Mistake is therefore precluded only *selectively*. For example, in the sale of a painting the buyer is precluded from relying on the fact that she does not after all like the painting or has found another more cheaply elsewhere; the seller cannot rely on her inability to supply it (at all, or as cheaply as she thought she could). And so forth, for most ordinary mistakes. There would be no point in making the pre-arrangement if such factors could be raised as a defence. But according to Tettenborn, it is wrong to conclude that *all* mistakes are thereby precluded, however 'esoteric or uncontemplated'. What if the painting turns out

---

[182] Cf. discussion of Sale of Goods Act implied terms, p. 155 above.

[183] *William Sindall plc v Cambridgeshire County Council* [1994] 1 WLR 1016, 1035.

[184] It is suggested at pp. 121–122 above that a doctrine of supervening *illegality* will always be necessary. But contracts illegal at the outset have never been treated as 'mistake' cases (even when the parties were mistaken about the legality of the agreement).

[185] [2003] QB 679 [165].

[186] (Unreported, 2001) [125].

[187] Ibid, [61].

[188] A. Tettenborn, 'Agreements, Common Mistake and the Purpose of Contract' (2011) 27 *JCL* 91.

to be an undiscovered Picasso? Raising mistake here should not be precluded: 'there is no reason to think that the object of the agreement was to shut out argument that the picture itself was not what it seemed'. Continental legal systems all grant relief in such a case; it is only English law which doggedly refuses. But this is 'misguided and distorted'. It is unconvincing 'to regard a contract as even presumptively imposing a duty to perform its terms come hell or high water'. And if the duty is limited in the way that Tettenborn contends, then allowing relief would not undermine the 'sanctity of contract' – requiring performance 'come what may' would actually go beyond the duty.

This is a controversial argument. Tettenborn advocates a wide doctrine of mistake – whenever the parties are mistaken about a matter which the contract was not intended to 'pre-empt'. The obvious objection is that this would unsettle many transactions and cause great uncertainty. But as explored in greater detail below, Tettenborn would severely limit the *effect* of a successfully raised mistake. In particular, his defence would apply only to executory contracts. This still leaves the question of application: 'In light of the circumstances of the contract, should the promisee be regarded as having bought protection against the risk in issue?' If not, the losses causes by the error lie where they fall. Although claiming that it is less 'vacuous' than ordinary risk analysis, Tettenborn admits that this question will not necessarily be easy to answer. This may understate the difficulties. A much crisper rule is for the losses to lie where they fall in all cases, i.e. if protection is wanted against the risk in issue, it should be stipulated expressly as Toulson J held in *The Great Peace*.[189] The alternative is for the court to take an active role in deciding where the risk ought to lie. When implying a condition precedent in the *Associated Japanese Bank* case, Steyn J observed merely: 'The point is not capable of elaborate analysis. It is a matter of first impression.'[190] If correct, this gives *carte blanche* to the judge.

Why does orthodoxy insist that there is a 'doctrine of mistake' above and beyond the construction approach? The answer is not entirely clear. At a formal doctrinal level we could answer, 'because the House of Lords in *Bell v Lever Bros* said so'. That is how the Court of Appeal, reaffirming orthodoxy in *The Great Peace*, approached the matter. The problem with this, however, is that *Bell* itself rests on shaky foundations. As pointed out above, Lord Atkin's leading speech is concerned largely with placing limits on the mistake doctrine: it was 'of paramount importance that contracts should be observed'.[191] The actual decision in *Bell* has often been criticized for its narrowness. Yet Lord Atkin accepted that a sufficiently fundamental mistake as to quality might nullify consent, avoiding the contract. The result is a confusing judgment. 'It is difficult to establish what the House of Lords decided'.[192] As seen above, Macmillan argues that *Bell* was unhappily influenced by the subjectivist conception of mistake in the leading treatises,

---

[189] Cf. *Paradine v Jane* (1647) Aleyn 26.
[190] n.168 above at 263.
[191] [1932] AC 161, 224.
[192] Macmillan, p. 275.

especially Pollock's – although this had never accurately described English law and did not even fit the generally objective approach of Pollock himself. Lord Atkin unconsciously created an entirely new doctrine under the impression that it was well established at common law.[193]

REMEDIES FOR COMMON MISTAKE

The debate over the effect of common mistake is linked to that over the basis of the doctrine. Under the subjectivist approach in *Bell v Lever Bros*,[194] mistake is held to destroy consensus with the result that the contract is necessarily void.[195] The same result follows from the implication that the existence of the relevant fact was a condition precedent for the contract to come into force.[196] This explains why both these theories plausibly fit the case-law. However, voidness is a drastic outcome. It is problematic to 'unscramble' a contract (especially when the mistake may come to light much later). The effect on third parties has already been discussed.[197] The courts are well aware of these difficulties, which are surely a powerful reason why common mistake is rarely invoked successfully. Because the effect of mistake is draconian, its ambit is necessarily narrow.

Tettenborn therefore accompanies his proposal for a liberalization of the ambit of mistake, discussed above, with a severe limitation on its effect.[198] Tettenborn would only allow mistake to avoid purely *executory* contracts. Avoidance of an unperformed contract means that the promisee loses the prospect of the profit (if any) that would be gained from performance. But this expectation is a 'relatively weak' interest. On balance it is better for it to be sacrificed than for performance to remain due 'come hell or high water'. But things change dramatically once performance begins. Two additional factors come into play. First reliance: one who performs is *ex hypothesi* relying on the contract's existence. Secondly, the interest in not disturbing settled transactions. Both interests are 'much stronger than the pure performance interest'. It would be wrong to leave someone who had started to perform actually out of pocket or require them to give up something they had actually received under the contract. Accordingly, once performance begins, Tettenborn argues that mistake cannot be raised.

This produces a clear-cut rule. A mistaken seller might seem no less deserving of relief a minute after than a minute before delivery. But this is not, Tettenborn claims, an arbitrary distinction: 'a person's moral claim to keep what they already have ought to be regarded as a great deal stronger than one's claim to get what one might be entitled to'. Moreover, the practicalities of avoiding an executory contract

---

[193] Ibid. Cf. Australia: 'theorizing of the Civilians about "mistake"' irrelevant for common law: *McRae* n.176 above.

[194] [1932] AC 161.

[195] Cf. *Norwich Union Fire Insurance Society v Price* [1934] AC 455, 463: 'proof of mistake affirmatively excludes intention' (Lord Wright).

[196] Cf. *Associated Japanese Bank*, n.168 above.

[197] Cf. pp. 164–165 above.

[198] Tettenborn, n.188 above.

are simple – no-one can sue anyone and 'sleeping dogs are left to lie'. Unwinding (part)-executed transactions is much trickier. Tettenborn does allow one further qualification: if a party has reasonably relied on an executory transaction in some way without actually beginning performance, he should be able to claim those expenses when the contract is avoided: 'it is one thing to be generous to a mistaken promisor where the effect is only to deprive a blameless promisee of an unexpected windfall, but quite another where the result is actually to impoverish the latter'.

Tettenborn's proposal is in some ways attractive. Perhaps its most objectionable features (the great width of the ambit of mistake, the narrowness of its effect) cancel each other out? Note that Tettenborn's proposal is very different from ordinary rescission (e.g. for misrepresentation), which can be used retrospectively to avoid a fully executed contract.[199] This equitable jurisdiction will be discussed in the next section.

At the other extreme from Tettenborn are broad statutory jurisdictions such as the New Zealand Contractual Mistakes Act 1977, the purpose of which is 'to mitigate the arbitrary effects of mistakes on contracts' (s.4(2)). To this end, s.7 empowers courts to grant such remedy 'as it thinks just', including cancellation, variation, compensation and restitution, on such conditions as the court thinks fit. This might seem dangerously vague. However, the New Zealand courts say they have 'little desire to allow the Act to become, or to be perceived to be, a regular mode of escape from contractual obligations'.[200] To underline this, the 1977 Act was amended in 2002 to require that the remedial powers 'are not to be exercised in such a way as to prejudice the general security of contractual relationships' (s.4(2)). Chandler, Devenney and Poole report that the courts have identified a number of guiding factors and conclude that 'flexibility in terms of relief has not resulted in an unmanageable discretion'.[201]

It may therefore be possible to have the best of both worlds without the drastic all-or-nothing choice of the existing common law, or the sharp difference between performed and executory contracts in Andrew Tettenborn's account. Indeed, if the bold argument that *Bell* is wrong about mistake at common law becomes accepted, more space opens up for a discretionary approach. Denning LJ's attempt to introduce a flexible doctrine of *equitable* mistake, however, was repudiated in *The Great Peace*.

MISTAKE IN EQUITY

Mistake has clear relevance to the equitable remedies of specific performance and rectification; the concern is not, however, mistake per se but unconscionable behaviour. Rescission is of course available for induced mistakes, i.e. misrepresentation. But whether it is available for unilateral and common mistakes seems doubtful. This is arguably inconsistent, at least when 'unconscionability' is present.

---

[199] Misrepresentation Act 1967, s. 1. Discussed by Tettenborn, n.188 above, at n.114.
[200] *Chatfield v Jones* [1990] 3 NZLR 285, 288 (Cooke P).
[201] Cf. n.169 above.

It is important to stress that equity's rationale for a distinctive approach to mistake (here as elsewhere) is the effect on conscience. Macmillan shows that unconscionability was the historical basis for the Court of Chancery's interventions – consensus per se was irrelevant.[202] But this conscience-focused rationale must be carefully defined if equitable mistake is not to be ridiculed as a 'hovering angel', swooping down to rescue 'the poet or the philosopher, the artist or the moron, who [has] unwittingly wandered into the grim marts of trade and been caught in its toils'.[203] Of course, the judges have long insisted that 'Chancery mends no man's bargain'.[204] It is bad behaviour rather than imprudence that justifies intervention.[205]

The second distinctive feature of equity is flexibility, the 'quintessence' of equitable relief.[206] Rescission, for example, is unavailable where this would affect the rights of innocent third parties, or when it is impossible to return the parties to their original position, although a flexible attitude is taken to *restitutio in integrum* too.[207] Rescission may even be granted 'on terms', e.g. only if the parties undertake to enter into another contract on fairer terms.[208] Whether to grant an equitable remedy is always within the discretion of the court. This is clearly visible in specific performance cases, where the remedy may be declined on the basis of mistake. A classic example is the clerical mistake case *Webster v Cecil*,[209] later explained as one in which the buyer snapped up an offer that he must have realized was mistaken.[210]

Rectification is 'classically' to reform documents that incorrectly record the prior agreement reached by the parties, objectively ascertained.[211] But the courts have recognized (or revived) a jurisdiction to rectify when only one party was mistaken about the contents of the document. Crucially, there must be 'a degree of sharp practice' by the non-mistaken party.[212] This requires knowledge of the other party's mistake, or at least strong suspicion thereof.[213] Combining this with active steps to distract the mistaken party from discovering the truth has been held 'sharp and unconscionable practice', 'quite inequitable' and 'beyond the boundaries of fair dealing even in an arm's length commercial negotiation'.[214]

---

202 Cf. nn.91–92 above.

203 E.W. Patterson, 'Equitable Relief for Unilateral Mistake' (1928) 28 *Columbia LR* 859, 883, 885.

204 *Maynard v Moseley* (1676) Swanst 651, 655 (Lord Nottingham LC).

205 Cf. *Multiservice Bookbinding Ltd v Marden* [1979] Ch 84.

206 Lee Pey Woan, 'Unilateral Mistake in Law and Equity – *Solle v Butcher* Reinstated' (2006) 22 JCL 81.

207 *Erlanger v New Sombrero Phosphate Co* (1878) 3 App Cas 1218.

208 Cf. *Solle v Butcher* n.81 above.

209 (1861) 30 Beavan 62.

210 *Tamplin v James* (1880) LR 15 Ch D 215, 221 (James LJ).

211 Cf. pp. 99–101 above.

212 *Riverlate Properties v Paul* [1975] Ch 133.

213 *Commission for the New Towns v Cooper* [1995] Ch 259. Woan, n.206 above, points out that if the defendant knows about a mistake as to the terms of the contract, and it is amenable to rectification, it cannot be void or there will be nothing to rectify. This casts further doubt on the *consensus ad idem* 'exception' in *Smith v Hughes*, cf. pp. 7–9 above.

214 *Cooper, Commission for the New Towns v Cooper* [1995] Ch 259, 277, 292.

Rescission for common mistake was proposed by Denning LJ in *Solle v Butcher*.[215] This received its quietus in *The Great Peace* on the ground that there was no conceptual room for a separate equitable doctrine of mistake.[216] Accordingly, *Solle* was inconsistent with *Bell v Lever Bros* and should not be followed.[217] This may be criticized on a number of grounds. Most fundamentally, that *The Great Peace* pays *Bell* unwarranted respect. Lord Phillips MR said it was not 'conceivable' that the House of Lords would have overlooked a separate equitable mistake doctrine if one existed.[218] But Macmillan argues that, on the contrary, this is precisely what occurred.[219] The nineteenth-century doctrine of equitable mistake was misunderstood by Pollock, and entirely sidelined in his treatise. The House of Lords cemented his errors in place unawares.[220]

Denning LJ simply attempted to revive the older jurisdiction; he was credited with more innovation than was due by commentators familiar with modern contract treatises rather than old equity jurisprudence.[221] His controversial dismissal of the rule that mistake renders a contract void from *Bell* has much to commend it.[222] But this bold revolt against precedent was always likely to be dismissed as Denningesque insubordination. Moreover, as Macmillan points out, Denning LJ failed to draw on the rectification and specific performance cases to bolster equitable mistake.[223] Yet here, the continuity of equity jurisprudence had never been lost, because these remedies had been assigned exclusively to the Chancery Division in 1875 and the different branches of the High Court maintained considerable independence.[224] John Swan comments that the other equitable remedies are better authority for a distinct equitable doctrine of mistake than *Solle*.[225]

Today, therefore, we see a curious situation in which mistake (accompanied by 'sharp practice') is relevant for specific performance and rectification but not rescission. This is 'curiouser and curiouser' because rectification is actually a more intrusive remedy:

> in rescission the court simply undoes the bargain, provided the parties can be restored to their original position; in rectification for unilateral mistake the original bargain is undone and a different one imposed.[226]

---

[215] [1950] 1 KB 671.

[216] [2003] QB 679. Cf. A.B.L. Phang, 'Common mistake in English law: The proposed merger of common law and equity' [1989] *Legal Studies* 291.

[217] [1932] AC 161.

[218] [2003] QB 679 [118].

[219] Macmillan, p. 315.

[220] Ibid.

[221] Macmillan, p. 285.

[222] [1950] 1 KB 671, 691.

[223] Macmillan, p. 286.

[224] Macmillan, p. 303. Cf. P. Polden, 'Mingling the Waters: Personalities, Politics and the Making of the Supreme Court of Judicature' [2002] *CLJ* 575.

[225] J. Swan, 'The Allocation of Risk in the Analysis of Mistake and Frustration' in B.J. Reiter & J. Swan (eds), *Studies in Contract Law* (Butterworths, 1980).

[226] *Commission for New Towns v Cooper*, n.213 above (Stuart-Smith LJ).

As rectification is available, for example, where one party sets out to ensure that the other does not realize his mistake, should not rescission be available *a fortiori*?[227] The analogy is particularly strong given the remedy of rescission 'on terms' in *Solle* itself – the landlord obtained relief, but on condition that he lease back to the tenant on demand at the full permitted rent.[228] This is similar in outcome to rectification of the contract (if, perhaps, jurisprudentially distinct).

The charge against *The Great Peace*, then, is that it perpetuates the historical misunderstandings of equitable mistake in *Bell*. The court makes no attempt to justify the distinction implicitly drawn between rectification and rescission. The argument that there was 'no room' for equitable mistake also seems very weak. The doctrine is readily distinguishable from the supposed doctrine at law (assuming this exists). First, as argued above, the focus throughout equity is on unconscionable behaviour – the Court of Appeal even quoted a classic authority requiring 'some fraud or surprise upon the ignorant party'.[229] Secondly, the *effect* of equitable mistake is obviously different. Equity is quintessentially flexible, and making contracts voidable offers clear advantages over automatic voidness. Highly experienced commercial judges had commended the flexibility of *Solle* for this reason.[230] In one of the odder features of *The Great Peace*, Lord Phillips MR himself admitted that there was 'scope for legislation to give greater flexibility to our law of mistake,' as rescission on terms had done.[231] That scope for reform exists, of course, only because of his Lordship's own decision to depart from *Solle*! Lord Denning divided judges into 'bold spirits' and 'timorous souls' and so one can imagine his reaction to *The Great Peace*.[232]

Probably legislation will now be required if flexible remedies for mistake are to return to English law. But a bold Supreme Court could, perhaps, revive the historical unconscionability jurisdiction over mistakes,[233] while rejecting the historically dubious view that mistake vitiates consent at law, if the radical arguments ventilated in this Debate were to be accepted.

Further Reading

Pre-contractual disclosure

F. Kessler & E. Fine, '*Culpa in Contrahendo*, Bargaining in Good Faith and Freedom of Contract: A Comparative Study' (1964) 77 *Harvard LR* 401.

---

[227] Cf. Australia: *Taylor v Johnson* (1983) 151 CLR 422. Cf. Woan, n.206 (at n.41): 'no satisfactory attempt has been made to distinguish between the conditions required for the different reliefs of rectification and rescission'.

[228] Cf. *Grist v Bailey* [1967] Ch 532.

[229] *Earl Beauchamp v Winn* (1873) LR 6 HL 223, 233 (Lord Chelmsford) quoted *The Great Peace* n.216 above [110].

[230] Cf. *Associated Japanese Bank*, n.168 above; *West Sussex Properties Ltd v Chichester DC* [2000] NPC 74: 'it can on occasion be the passport to a just result' (Staughton LJ).

[231] [161].

[232] *Candler v Crane, Christmas & Co* [1951] 2 KB 164, 178.

[233] Cf. *Huyton v DIPASA* [2003] 2 Lloyd's Rep 780, [455] (Andrew Smith J).

A.T. Kronman, 'Mistake, Disclosure, Information, and the Law of Contracts' (1978) 7 *JLS* 1.

M. Fabre-Magnan, 'Duties of Disclosure and French Contract Law: Contribution to An Economic Analysis' In J. Beatson and D. Friedmann (eds), *Good Faith and Fault in Contract Law* (Oxford, 1995).

Mistake

P.S. Atiyah & F.A.R. Bennion, 'Mistake in the Construction of Contracts' (1961) 24 *MLR* 421.

J.H. Baker, 'Non est factum' [1970] *CLP* 53.

A. Chandler, J. Devenney & J. Poole, 'Common Mistake: Theoretical Justification and Remedial Inflexibility' [2004] JBL 34.

C. Macmillan, *Mistakes in Contract Law* (Hart Publishing, 2010).

A. Tettenborn, 'Agreements, Common Mistake and the Purpose of Contract' (2011) 27 *JCL* 91.

7

INEQUALITY OF BARGAINING POWER

Debate 1

What is economic duress?

The defence of economic duress is a relative newcomer in English law. At common law, duress was traditionally limited to threats of personal violence or imprisonment.[1] In recent decades the courts have recognized 'duress of goods' (i.e. threats to damage or detain property) and 'economic duress' (wider forms of economic pressure).[2] This expansion has an obvious appeal, since such threats may be equally coercive for the recipient. But defining exactly what economic duress means and placing limits upon it proves extremely difficult. However we must do it since, as Choke J recognized as early as 1467, a wide duress defence would upset 'most obligations in England'.[3] We consider, first, the general question of whether the defence is based on the claimant's vitiated consent or the defendant's wrongdoing. We next examine the elements of the modern defence, namely the extent to which the claimant was coerced by the threat, then what kinds of threats should constitute duress. A particular controversy here is whether threatening breach of contract is economic duress.

THE BASIS OF THE DOCTRINE: 'VITIATED CONSENT' OR 'WRONGFUL THREATS'?

The basic theoretical question about duress is whether it is founded on the claimant's impaired consent or the defendant's wrongful threats. Each of these has a strong intuitive appeal. We do not wish wrongdoers to profit from their wrong, as they presumably would if contracts secured by coercive means were routinely upheld. Equally, as the basis of contract law is *agreement*, the lack of true consent by the promisor would seem fatal.

---

[1] 2 Co Inst 483. *Skeate v Beale* (1841) 11 Ad & El 983.
[2] *The Siboen and The Sibotre* [1976] 1 Lloyd's Rep 293; *The Atlantic Baron* [1979] QB 705.
[3] *Anon* YB M. 7 Edw.IV f.21 pl.24.

Early emphasis was on the latter approach. The first case to give appellate approval to the economic duress was *Pao On v Lau Yiu Long* where Lord Scarman said there must be 'a coercion of will, which vitiates consent': it had to be shown that 'the contract entered into was not a voluntary act'.[4] However, there are difficulties with this. First, it seems inaccurate to say that one faced with a highly unpalatable choice acts 'involuntarily' when she opts for the lesser of two evils. If a highwayman demands: 'your money or your life!', then 'you will doubtless be very eager to accept the first branch of this offer by tendering your money'.[5] Baroness Hale accepts that 'even the person with a knife at her back has a choice whether or not to do as the knifeman says. The question is whether she should have resisted the threat'.[6] Secondly, the criminal law has long accepted that duress does not take away the intentional quality of the act.[7] Duress *excuses* rather than negating criminal intention (*mens rea*); for policy reasons it is not a defence to murder.[8] P.S. Atiyah said that for contract lawyers to adopt the 'overborne will' theory of duress when it had been decisively rejected in contemporary criminal decisions was 'an oversight of monumental proportions'.[9] Peter Birks complained that coercion of the will was a 'plausible-sounding but inscrutable expression [that] serves only to conceal a discretion'.[10]

By 1983 Lord Scarman had repented. He accepted that:

> The classic case of duress is, however, not the lack of will to submit but the victim's intentional submission arising from the realisation that there is no other practical choice open to him.[11]

Lord Goff similarly doubts whether it is 'helpful' to talk of coerced will and vitiated consent.[12] The notion that duress renders the contract involuntary has fallen out of judicial favour. Sir Jack Beatson notes that it remains typical for new ideas to be introduced using the will theory of contract and wonders whether the subsequent change of heart reflects the influence of scholarship.[13] David Ibbetson similarly points out the nineteenth-century treatise writers' determination to conceptualize old-fashioned duress as the vitiation of contractual intent. But this never fitted the common law rules very well (e.g. if the contract were truly formed without consent, should it not be void rather than only voidable?).[14]

If we therefore reject the idea that duress requires involuntariness, what degree of pressure (constraint of choice) is necessary to raise the defence? We could

---

[4] [1980] AC 614, 636.

[5] R.A. Posner, 'Blackmail, Privacy and Freedom of Contract' (1993) 141 *Univ Pennsylvania L Rev* 1817.

[6] *Regina v Hasan* [2005] 2 AC 467, [73].

[7] Ibid, [18] (Lord Bingham); *Lynch v DPP of Northern Ireland* [1975] AC 653.

[8] *Regina v Howe* [1987] AC 417.

[9] P.S. Atiyah, 'Economic Duress and the Overborne Will' (1982) 98 *LQR* 197.

[10] P.B.H. Birks, 'The Travails of Duress' [1990] *LMCLQ* 342.

[11] *The Universe Sentinel* [1983] 1 AC 366, 400.

[12] *The Evia Luck* [1992] 2 AC 152, 166.

[13] J. Beatson, *The Use and Abuse of Unjust Enrichment* (Clarendon Press, 1991) p. 117.

[14] D.J. Ibbetson, *A Historical Introduction to the Law of Obligations* (Oxford University Press, 1999) pp. 234–36.

insist upon complete freedom of decision-making power, on the premise that only under such conditions will parties make the mutually beneficial agreements that form the moral and economic case for the enforcement of contracts. But such freedom is impossible. Economic pressure is endemic in a market economy, as Robert Hale recognized long ago.[15] If we want things, even the necessities of life, we have *no choice but to pay for them*. The free market allows and requires the exercise of, and submission to, economic pressure: whenever 'constraints are imposed by reason of time, money or any other factor, then an element of pressure will be present in the dealings'.[16] So mere constraint of choice cannot constitute economic duress, or Choke J's prophecy about undoing virtually every contract would come to pass. The laws of supply and demand are inexorable. Thus, as Lord Templeman once pointedly said, 'an employer has never been guilty of economic duress if at a time when unemployment is high and workers are weak wages are low'.[17]

Therefore, the pure positions of complete freedom or complete involuntariness are mirages. There is no alternative but to seek a middle course. Given that 'in life, including the life of commerce and finance, many acts are done under pressure' the real question is *which* of 'the various means of obtaining consent' the law regards as (un)acceptable.[18] Emphasis has accordingly moved from the claimant's consent to the threats placing pressure upon her. Commercial pressure exists 'wherever one party to a commercial transaction is in a stronger bargaining position than the other'; the true question is whether it is 'illegitimate' pressure.[19] This central question compels the courts 'to take a stand on that central issue of modern politics, the control of economic power';[20] it will be addressed below.

Donal Nolan comments that it would be an overreaction to the failure of the 'overborne will' theory to focus exclusively on the defendant's illegitimate threats. The court should *also* examine whether they coerced the victim.[21] Thus, a synthesis of the 'claimant-sided' and 'defendant sided' rationales emerges. This is endorsed by Lord Hoffmann.[22] There must be 'pressure amounting to compulsion of the will of the victim and … illegitimacy of the pressure'. The latter requires the court to examine 'first, the nature of the pressure and secondly, the nature of the demand which the pressure is applied to support'.

---

[15] R.L. Hale, 'Coercion and Distribution in a Supposedly Non-Coercive State' (1923) 38 *Political Science Quarterly* 470.

[16] A. Stewart, 'Economic Duress – Legal Regulation of Commercial Pressure' (1984) 14 *Melb Univ L Rev* 410, 422.

[17] *The Evia Luck,* n.12 above at 160 (contrasting treatment of *strikes* as economic duress of *employers*).

[18] *Barton v Armstrong* [1976] AC 104, 121 (Lords Wilberforce and Simon).

[19] *The Universe Sentinel,* n.11 above, 384 (Lord Diplock).

[20] J.P. Dawson, 'Economic Duress – An Essay in Perspective' (1947) 45 *Michigan LR* 253.

[21] D. Nolan, 'Economic Duress and the Availability of a Reasonable Alternative' [2000] RLR 105, 113.

[22] *A-G v R* [2003] UKPC 22, [15]–[16].

WAS THE CLAIMANT COERCED?

There are two issues here. First, the factual question whether the threats did *in fact* cause the claimant to enter into the contract. Secondly, if so, there is the normative question: should the threats have been resisted?[23]

The causation question was posed in a very claimant-friendly way in *Barton v Armstrong*, a case of threats of violence to the person. Provided it could be shown that the threat affected the claimant's decision to enter into the contract in some way, it did not matter that there were 'other more weighty causes which contributed to his decision'.[24] On the facts, as the threats had been 'a' reason for the execution of the deed it was set aside. As noted, this was the same rule applicable to deception, where the law also refuses to examine the relative contributions of different causes.[25] However, Lords Simon and Wilberforce expressly reserved their opinion as to cases not involving violence.[26] Regarding economic duress, Lord Goff subsequently referred to a 'significant cause' for entry into the contract[27] and Mance J distinguished *Barton v Armstrong* to re-impose an explicit but-for test.[28] Ewan McKendrick says that this 'patchwork' approach is unnecessarily complex. In particular, Lord Goff's 'significant' cause is hard to define, sparking Birks's fears of an 'inarticulate discretion'.[29] McKendrick argues that all duress cases should indeed be assimilated with the test in misrepresentation – was the pressure 'a' cause of the contract (even if it cannot be shown a but-for cause)?[30]

If the threat was in fact a cause of the claimant's agreement, was he right to submit to it? The courts usually ask whether the claimant had 'any reasonable alternative' but to submit.[31] As Atiyah says, the real question is the extent to which society can legitimately expect people to stand up to threats rather than (initially) submitting and pleading duress afterwards.[32] In the criminal law the 'steadfastness reasonably to be expected of the ordinary citizen' in the face of threats is a controversial matter.[33] In denying the defence in murder, English law subscribes to the position that one should rather die before taking the life of another under duress – but this is attacked for demanding 'heroism'.[34] In contract law too, Rick

---

[23] Cf. n.6 above (Baroness Hale).

[24] [1976] AC 104, 118.

[25] *Reynell v Sprye* (1852) 1 De G.M. & G. 660, 708.

[26] [1976] AC 104, 121.

[27] *The Evia Luck,* n.12 above, 165.

[28] *Huyton v Cremer* [1999] 1 Lloyd's Rep 620.

[29] Cf. n.10 above.

[30] E. McKendrick, 'The Further Travails of Duress' in A. Burrows and Lord Rodger (eds), *Mapping the Law: Essays in Memory of Peter Birks* (Oxford, 2006); *Edgington v Fitzmaurice* (1885) 24 Ch D 495.

[31] *Victor Green v B&S; Huyton v Cremer,* n.28 above.

[32] P.S. Atiyah, 'Concepts of Duress' (1983) 99 *LQR* 188.

[33] *Regina v Graham* [1982] 1 All ER 801. Cf. K.J.M. Smith, 'Duress and Steadfastness: in Pursuit of the Unintelligible' [1999] *Crim LR* 363.

[34] Blackstone, *Commentaries, IV,* 30; Howe, n.8 above; cf. D. Ormerod, *Smith & Hogan's Criminal Law* (13th edn, 2011) pp. 360–61.

Bigwood says that requiring steadfastness is a 'thoroughly moralized' criterion.[35] But what precisely does it require?

The key is to examine the alternatives: the remedies for a claimant who stands up to the threats, both legal (e.g. damages for breach of contract) and extra-legal (e.g. finding substitute performance). According to Bigwood the alternative must be 'at least as effective, practicable and efficient'.[36] In contrast, Stewart proposes the test of 'no practicable choice at all' but to give in, as a 'reasonably intelligible' limitation on duress. He argues that this would help minimize disruption of commercial bargaining, even though it may be harsh to deny a remedy because there was a feasible (albeit less palatable) alternative.[37]

Bigwood notes an analogy (a fairly loose one?) with the mitigation doctrine, in that both duress and mitigation require someone faced with 'wrongdoing' (threats or breach) to take some responsibility for their actions,[38] hence victims of threats being required to make use of reasonable alternative remedies. However as Beatson comments, the courts tend not to impose exacting requirements through duress any more than mitigation does on promisees claiming damages.[39] They are sympathetic to the practical limitations of legal remedies: injunctions are in the discretion of the court, damages depend on the solvency of the defendant, and the law is always expensive and slow. Bar-Gill and Ben-Shahar claim that the focus on reasonable alternatives and adequate remedies is actually 'redundant', since if they existed the claimant would surely not have surrendered to the threat.[40] Dawson argues that the 'man of firmness' who had stalked the common law of duress since the time of Bracton has been exorcised by the influence of Equity, where 'it was abundantly clear that the weak, the timid, the anxious and submissive were precisely the ones who should and did receive the greatest legal protection'.[41]

Bigwood says that 'no reasonable choice' must be assessed objectively but with regard to the claimant's particular circumstances (such as a father's affection for his son, or a company's cash flow crisis).[42] This 'subjectivized objectivity' has proved a fertile source of dispute in criminal law.[43] More generally, Bigwood accepts that it is 'not easy to state in advance what will amount to an adequate or reasonable alternative'.[44] Ogilvie puts forward the standard of 'commercial morality and prac-

---

[35] R. Bigwood, *Exploitative Contracts* (Oxford University Press, 2003) p. 355.

[36] Ibid, p. 359.

[37] n.16 above, p. 439.

[38] Cf. *British Westinghouse v London Underground* [1912] AC 673.

[39] Beatson, n.13 above.

[40] O. Bar-Gill and O. Ben-Shahar, 'The Law of Duress and the Economics of Credible Threats' (2004) 33 *JLS* 391.

[41] Dawson, n.20 above.

[42] Bigwood, n.35 above, p. 361; cf. *Williams v Bayly* (1866) LR 1 HL 200 and *D&C Builders v Rees* [1965] 2 QB 617.

[43] Cf. J. Horder, 'Occupying the Moral High Ground? the Law Commission on Duress' [1994] *Crim LR* 334.

[44] Bigwood, n.35 above, p. 357.

tice' against which to measure these issues.[45] All of this seems exceedingly, and perhaps excessively, vague. Uncertainty is the greatest challenge for the defence of economic duress.

WERE THE THREATS 'ILLEGITIMATE'?

The big question here is whether to focus on the *illegality* of the threats, or to take the broader view that *lawful but illegitimate* pressure may also constitute duress. A preliminary question is: what is a threat? Rick Bigwood draws a distinction between *offers* to make someone better off, and *threats* to make someone worse off. The distinction hinges on the claimant's notional starting point or 'baseline' of rights and expectations. An easy case is the highwayman's demand, 'stand and deliver!' But in many cases the baseline must be fixed according to 'the standard canons of propriety in dealing prevailing in a relevant community'.[46] This normative question will receive different answers across (and even within) societies, but the judges must decide as best they can. Bigwood denies that this is 'insidious' or 'evasive' behaviour in the absence of a full-blown theory of rights: it is merely 'realistic' for the courts to proceed on a case-by-case basis.[47] Once the courts have determined that a given 'proposal' is a threat rather than an offer, however, they will not be deflected by its presentation as a mere 'warning', for example, *The Alev*, where it was clear that what was presented as inevitable and unfortunate was in substance a threat to extract extra payment.[48] It therefore seems that an incapable or unwilling promisor must be treated as implicitly threatening the promisee with breach.[49] Whether breach of contract should, however, be treated as 'illegitimate pressure' is important and difficult, and is discussed separately below.

It is generally accepted that threats to commit crimes or torts should be 'illegitimate' per se. This is consistent with the rationale denying wrongdoers the fruits of their malefactions. But should this exhaust the category of illegitimacy, i.e. should *only* illegality suffice? In favour of this is the relative certainty of an approach parasitic on the definition of crimes and torts. As will be seen below, lawful act duress poses enormous definitional challenges. It is notable that a foundational principle of tort itself is that intentional infliction of economic harm is actionable only when inflicted through (otherwise) unlawful means.[50] This is to keep the boundaries of liability under control. Moreover, in the criminal law only threats of death or serious violence are sufficient for the defence of duress. Lord Simon accepts that this is an 'arbitrary' distinction, but necessary because the law has to

---

[45] M.H. Ogilvie, 'Economic Duress, Inequality of Bargaining. Power and Threatened Breach of Contract' (1981) 26 *McGill LJ* 289.
[46] Bigwood, n.35 above, p. 283.
[47] Ibid, pp. 321–23.
[48] [1989] 1 Lloyd's Rep 138, 142.
[49] Cf. *Williams v Roffey Bros* [1991] QB 1.
[50] *Allen v Flood* [1898] AC 1.

drawn the line somewhere to place limits on the 'vague and amorphous' concept of duress.[51] So there are close precedents for a limited and parasitic definition.

The main objection to using illegality as the test is its artificial and limited nature. Birks points out that 'those who devise outrageous but technically lawful means of compulsion must always escape [unless] the legislature declares the abuse unlawful'.[52] Obviously, such threats can be equally coercive. Stewart denounces the 'artificial distinctions and judicial contortions' brought about in the economic torts by *Allen v Flood*.[53] When, though, is it 'illegitimate' for a defendant to threaten what he is at perfect liberty to do (e.g. not to trade with the claimant)?[54] As Dyson J says, the courts must separate illegitimate pressure from 'the rough and tumble of the pressures of normal commercial bargaining'.[55] But that is easier said than done!

Bigwood is a prominent defender of lawful act duress. He considers a threat by a wheat board with monopoly power not to supply wheat unless a prospective customer pays more for it. In a well-known decision the High Court of Australia held that since the board had no legal duty to supply the wheat it was within its rights to demand the additional payment and there had been no duress.[56] But Bigwood argues that the case would probably be decided differently today – modern duress has gone beyond technical illegality to enforce the moral sense of the community.[57] This seems a vague yardstick for legal liability, however. Bigwood argues that on a proper analysis of the case the board was abusing its right (not to sell) for a purpose unconnected with that for conferring the power in the first place.[58] But how do we know what the 'purpose' of a right is?[59] English law does not usually proceed on that basis, which is why no general doctrine of 'abuse of rights' exists, in contrast with Civilian countries.[60]

Stewart asks how we are to discern 'commercial morality'. He argues, tentatively, that there is some evidence that it is commercially acceptable to (threaten to) breach a contract to deal with anticipated losses.[61] But Stewart concludes that, abuse of monopoly aside, 'there is little material from which to construct well-defined guidelines of what is commercially "moral"'.[62] Birks warns that:

> discriminating between acceptable and unacceptable pressures is not positive law but social morality... That makes the judges, not the law or the legislature, the arbiters of social evaluation.[63]

---

[51] Lynch, n.7 above, 686–87.

[52] P.B.H. Birks, *An Introduction to the Law of Restitution* (Oxford University Press, 1985) p. 177.

[53] Cf. n.50 above; Stewart, n.16 above, p. 427, n.9.

[54] Cf. *CTN Cash & Carry v Gallagher* [1994] 4 All ER 714 and *Smith v William Charlick* (1924) 34 CLR 38.

[55] *DSND Subsea Ltd v Petroleum Geo-services ASA* (28 July 2000, unreported).

[56] *Smith*, n.54 above.

[57] Bigwood, n.35 above, p. 325.

[58] Ibid, p. 328.

[59] Properly in this case, a 'liberty' – absence of duty.

[60] Cf. H.C. Gutteridge, 'Abuse of Rights' (1933) 3 *CLJ* 22; M. Taggart, *Private Property and Abuse of Rights in Victorian England* (Oxford University Press, 2002).

[61] Cf. *The Siboen and The Sibotre*, n.2 above, where such problems were *falsely* relied upon.

[62] Stewart, n.16 above, p. 431.

[63] Birks, n.52 above, p. 177.

Having cited this passage, Steyn LJ in *CTN Cash & Carry v Gallagher* expressed the need for caution in developing the law on 'lawful act duress'.[64] Although refusing to say this could never be a good defence, and acknowledging contract law's role in promoting 'fair dealing', Steyn LJ argued that a 'radical' extension would cause 'substantial and undesirable' uncertainty in commercial cases because it would involve the courts ruling on what was 'morally or socially unacceptable'. In Australia, Kirby P has also expressed serious misgivings.[65] He refers to the 'unsatisfactory and open-ended formulae' by which economic duress has supposedly been circumscribed, noting that leading cases provide only 'enigmatic' guidance on what amounts to illegitimate pressure. He argued that most cases involved parties with 'seriously unequal economic bargaining positions' and warned that courts should be slow to substitute their judgment for that of sophisticated commercial parties who have 'a better appreciation of the economic forces which are at work'.

There seems to be judicial reluctance to extend 'lawful act duress' to commercial law. Yet (by contrast with undue influence, considered in Debate 2) economic duress has largely developed in commercial cases. When the context is non-commercial, the question of what is 'legitimate' may be even more vexed. In the '*R*' case, the claimant soldier was threatened with removal from a Special Forces unit (the SAS) and return to his regiment, unless he signed a confidentiality agreement about his SAS service. What the army had threatened was undoubtedly lawful (viz. the 'return to unit').[66] But that was not the end of the matter. The court also had to examine the legitimacy of *what was demanded*. Lord Hoffmann simply agreed with the trial judge that the demand for confidentiality was a reasonable one as unauthorized disclosures through memoirs were undermining the effectiveness of the SAS.[67] Maybe so – but what about the soldier's freedom of speech? None of the elaborate balancing between free speech and the public interest familiar from Article 10, European Convention on Human Rights was evident. Should the court not examine human rights norms when considering the legitimacy of demands (at least those by public authorities)?

As Birks says, the extension of duress to lawful acts really is a difficult question.[68] Limiting duress to unlawful threats is highly formalistic and purchases certainty at the price of stultifying rigidity. But the more flexible approach unleashes a doctrine that defies definition. It is all very well to call for identification of the meaning of illegitimate pressure 'with greater precision',[69] but how are we to do it? McKendrick does not say. Ultimately, those who support the wider doctrine must accept this indeterminacy as a price worth paying. Mance J notes that the courts face similar problems when defining unconscionability or the duty of care in

[64] n.54 above, pp. 718–19.
[65] *Equiticorp Finance Ltd (In Liq) v Bank of New Zealand* (1993) 32 NSWLR 50.
[66] n.22 above [17].
[67] Ibid, [17]–[18].
[68] Cf. n.63 above.
[69] McKendrick, n.30 above.

negligence,[70] but invoking such notoriously uncertain areas of law hardly inspires confidence! Bigwood accepts that whereas the boundaries of unlawful threats are 'stable', 'no single test is ever likely to emerge' for lawful act duress.[71] However, he dismisses the 'usual objections [that] have of course flowed from the pens of academics' about the notorious uncertainty of that wider approach.[72] How much certainty can reasonably be expected, Bigwood asks, when 'instance-specific, all-things-considered judgments are virtually inevitable'? Economic duress cases are bound to be complex, controversial and contestable. They are about setting the limits of market power.

This is true. But it might raise questions about the wisdom of assessing lawful pressure against a vague standard of commercial morality in the first place. Bigwood seems to assume that lawful act duress must be part of contract law. But if it were not, the uncertainty that he identifies would not be 'inevitable'. So Andrew Phang argues that faced with a 'lack of viable criteria' for defining illegitimate pressure and *ad hoc* decision making inimical to commercial certainty, the courts may decide to roll back economic duress.[73] Phang suggests this 'emacia-tion' of the doctrine in commercial cases (their heartland!) is already evident in *CTN Cash & Carry*.[74]

ARE THREATS TO BREACH A CONTRACT 'ILLEGITIMATE'?

This is a particularly controversial question. Some argue that breach of contract is 'illegal' in the same way as crime and tort and accordingly to threaten it is economic duress per se. Others argue that a more nuanced view is necessary if contract modification is not to become impossible, or even that such threats should never invalidate modifications.[75] There are two strands underlying the debate. First, a deep theoretical question about whether breach of contract should be treated as 'a wrong'. Secondly, the more pragmatic issue about the desirability of contract modifications.

We start with the latter issue, already examined in Chapter 2. As seen in the previous section, when a promisor is in a position where he cannot (or will not) perform this must be treated as an implicit threat of breach. Therefore, if every breach of contract were illegal and therefore illegitimate pressure for the purposes of economic duress, it would seem that no contract modification (made against the backdrop of unwilling or impossible performance) could ever be enforce-able. Thus as Mindy Chen-Wishart notes, what the relaxation of consideration in *Williams v Roffey Bros* has given with one hand, duress would take away with

---

[70] *Huyton v Cremer,* n.28 above.
[71] Bigwood, n.35 above, p. 301.
[72] Ibid, p. 308.
[73] A. Phang, 'Whither Economic Duress?' (1990) 53 *MLR* 107.
[74] Cf. n.54 above; A. Phang, 'Economic Duress: Recent Difficulties and Possible Alternatives' [1997] *RLR* 53.
[75] Cf. Bar-Gill & Ben-Shahar, n.40 above.

the other.[76] That is not necessarily to be condemned. We saw in Chapter 2 that allowing modifications often subverts the original contractual allocation of risk and undermines incentives to perform for future parties in the same situation.[77] Thus, general invalidation of modifications by duress might be no bad thing. But duress has usually been welcomed as a less blunt instrument for policing modifications than the consideration doctrine. If it is going to invalidate modifications across the board we might as well stick with *Stilk v Myrick* – Chen's Wishart's point.[78]

Is a more differentiated approach possible? Yes, if we accept that a threat to breach is only *sometimes* 'illegitimate' pressure. Bigwood notes a consensus among commentators that the promisor should not take unfair strategic advantage of the promisee, exploiting her vulnerability.[79] But unpacking this raises the policy and desirability of contract modification.[80] The most important factor, according to Bigwood, would be the nature of the circumstances giving rise to the breach.[81] Were they risks allocated by the contract? If so, the promisor should not be allowed to (seek to) shift them to the promisee through renegotiation. This may explain some of the leading cases. Attempting to re-open a contract because of fluctuations in charter market rates was a classic attempt at zero-sum buck-passing.[82] Where currency exchange rates had moved against a party who could have included a price variation clause but had failed to do so, his threat to breach (unless the price in devalued currency was increased) was illegitimate.[83] Bigwood contrasts the 'extremely rare' cases in which the supervening circumstances were 'neither created through any excusable default of [the promisor], nor caused by the materialization of a risk foreseen by the parties and assigned'.[84] Bigwood accepts that assessment of the substantive fairness of the modification cannot be avoided – has the party threatening breach acquired 'more than was fair, reasonable, or necessary … in the light of the changed circumstances'?[85] However, if the argument noted in Chapter 5 is correct, this category is not just rare but non-existent, since all risks have been assigned, implicitly, to the party on whom they fall.[86]

An inevitable problem with this modification-policing role is uncertainty. Bigwood accepts that it raises endemic value choices (discipline and certainty against flexible relief from hardship). Therefore no universal measure for the

---

[76] M. Chen-Wishart, 'Consideration, Practical Benefit and the Emperor's New Clothes' in J. Beatson and D. Friedmann (eds), *Good Faith and Fault in Contract Law* (Oxford University Press, 1995) p.146; *Roffey* [1991] 1 QB 1.

[77] Cf. pp. 48–53 above.

[78] Cf. p. 50 n.70 above.

[79] Bigwood, n.35 above, p. 334.

[80] Cf. V.A. Aivazian, M.J. Trebilcock & M. Penny, 'The Law of Contract Modifications: the Uncertain Quest for a Bench Mark of Enforceability' (1984) 22 *Osgoode Hall LJ* 173.

[81] Ibid, pp. 335–39.

[82] Cf. *The Siboen and The Sibotre*, n.2 above.

[83] Cf. *The Atlantic Baron*, n.2 above.

[84] Bigwood, n.35 above, p. 338.

[85] Ibid, p. 339.

[86] Cf. pp. 126–128, 131–140 above.

propriety of threatened breach is likely to emerge.[87] Again, the question is whether that uncertainty is a price worth paying for the regulatory goals that the differentiated approach will (imperfectly) implement.

Bar-Gill and Ben-Shahar, by contrast, take a clear-cut approach.[88] They argue that prima facie all modifications should be enforceable when induced by a 'credible' threat of breach, meaning a breach that will happen for good independent reasons (e.g. cost increases) if the modification is not made.[89] The argument is simple, perhaps deceptively so. If the modification is not made, the contract will by definition be breached. But the fact that the promisee was willing to make the modification (to pay more, etc.) shows that she would rather have the modification than breach. Thus, refusing to enforce modifications will actually make promisees (the supposed beneficiaries of economic duress) worse off.

The fallacy in this argument is that while it may hold true once 'credible breach' is in prospect, enforcing the modifications may make such breaches *more likely in the first place*. As Posner observes, we prefer our lives to our money when held up by a highwayman but we really want a system which prevents such threats being made.[90] Bar-Gill and Ben-Shahar do admit that the concept of 'credible' threats may be manipulated by the promisor, for example by strategically increasing costs to make performance uneconomic or failing to take precautions against breach.[91] They argue that courts may be able to detect such manipulation. But surely this will be difficult. Also, that the parties may guard against manipulation by contract design; but this too increases the costs of doing business. If such opportunistic behaviour is an ever-present danger rather than (as the authors seems to treat it) a marginal issue, might not a presumption *against* enforcing modifications be preferable?[92] Bar-Gill and Ben-Shahar seem to accept that the first-best solution to the problem would be to improve the remedies for breach of contract. If losses from breach of contract were compensated in full, every rational promisee would hold the breach-threatening promisor to the contract rather than promising to pay more for the same performance.

Having set out the nuanced approach to duress and modification, Bigwood ultimately rejects it. He argues that if contractual rights are to be 'taken seriously' as true legal rights, a threat to breach must be treated as an unlawful threat, and so economic duress per se.[93] Otherwise it suggests that contractual rights are unilaterally destructible. Bigwood notes O.W. Holmes's famous argument that a contract does not impose a true duty to perform (or therefore correlative right to performance) but allows promisors to choose between performance and paying damages.[94]

---

[87] Bigwood, n.35 above, p. 332.
[88] Cf. n.40 above.
[89] For purely opportunistic modifications, cf. pp. 48–53 above.
[90] Cf. n.5 above.
[91] Cf. *Roffey* – negligent failure to control costs.
[92] Cf. Aivazian et al., n.80 above.
[93] Bigwood, n.35 above, pp. 340–44.
[94] O.W. Holmes, 'The Path of the Law' (1897) 10 *Harvard LR* 457.

This position enjoys some support from the exceptional nature of specific performance and punitive damages in the common law. However, Bigwood claims that
Holmes's view has been dismissed by Commonwealth courts and moreover, that
it is unacceptable in principle. It would, he claims, result in contract law's 'demise'
(he does not specify precisely how). Also, he says, parties want performance. In
a very general sense that is no doubt correct, but whether rational parties would
demand performance-oriented remedies is a more difficult question. The answer
cannot be asserted by vague reflections on the 'foundations' of contract law.[95]

Bigwood therefore argues that threats to break contracts should constitute duress
unless they were threats which the recipient should have resisted. Shifting the
modification problem sideways (from 'threat' to 'choice') does not make it easier to
answer, although Bigwood claims it does less damage to contract law as a whole.[96]
But this way of 'controlling' duress in such cases is unlikely to succeed. Given the
courts' indulgent view of both factual causation and the normative test (should
the pressure have been resisted?) it is unlikely to rule out the defence in many
cases. As seen, Bar-Gill and Ben-Shahar argue that the test will always be satisfied,[97]
and Bigwood himself seems to concede that this will 'virtually always' be the case
in practice.[98] In which case, Bigwood's argument reduces to the 'no modification'
position on duress which is functionally equivalent to *Stilk v Myrick*. There are, as
seen, arguments in favour of that. But should we be more convinced by analysis of
the (economic) incentives, or by reflections on the 'rights' generated by contracts?

Debate **2**

The nature of undue influence and unconscionability

In addition to the wrongs of force (duress) and fraud (misrepresentation), the law
protects vulnerable contracting parties from more 'subtle' and 'insidious' abuse by
those who exert influence over them,[99] and against manipulation and exploitation generally. These doctrines are conventionally divided between 'undue influence' and 'unconscionable dealing'. Here we will examine their theoretical basis
(in particular as claimant-sided or defendant-sided doctrines), before considering
whether they should be merged.

THE BASIS OF UNDUE INFLUENCE

Undue influence is often said to be indefinable,[100] sometimes (regrettably) with
'apparent pride'.[101] The outlines, however, are clear enough. When one party to

---

[95] Cf. Ch. 9 below.
[96] Bigwood, n.35 above, p. 344.
[97] Cf. n.40 above.
[98] Bigwood, n.35 above, p. 356.
[99] *Allcard v Skinner* (Lindley LJ).
[100] Ibid.
[101] R. Bigwood, *Exploitative Contracts* (Oxford University Press, 2003) p. 378.

a contract is in a position to influence the other, and the influenced party enters into a transaction that is not readily explicable by the relationship between the parties, equity presumes that 'undue influence' has been exercised to procure it. This renders the transaction voidable. The presumption is not raised where the (presumed) 'victim' had the transaction explained to her (full and meaningful advice). It is said that such advice 'emancipates' her from the other's influence.[102] Equity also intervenes, of course, when it is positively proved that undue influence was exercised. Historically at least, the equitable jurisdiction regulated wider forms of pressure than common law duress.

This appears to be a doctrine based on the powerful party's (actual or presumed) wrongdoing. But against the admitted weight of opinion, Birks and Chin argue that undue influence is a 'claimant-sided' doctrine.[103] It is true that many cases (they suggest 95 per cent) *do* involve some kind of wrongdoing. But it is a mistake to conclude that 'wicked exploitation' is an *essential condition* when undue influence can succeed without it. Birks and Chin point to the classic case of *Allcard v Skinner* where a nun donated all her worldly goods to the convent.[104] The Court of Appeal stressed that the Mother Superior had behaved impeccably, but undue influence was made out. Or in *Simpson v Simpson* a dying man who was absolutely dependent on his (third) wife transferred much of his property to her in the last months of his life.[105] The gifts were voidable for undue influence (in addition to his lack of mental capacity). But it would be 'not merely superfluous but embarrassing' to cast aspersions on the wife's behaviour (when the judge pointedly had not).[106]

Birks and Chin argue that the basis of relief, and the meaning of the 'awesomely ambiguous' term 'undue', is simply *excessive dependence* by the victim on the defendant. There is too much influence on one side (the defendant's) and too little autonomy on the other (the victim's). The presumption is rebutted when the victim has been cured of her excessive dependence through independent advice. The 'closest congeners' of undue influence are cases of lack of capacity, e.g. through mental impairment.[107] The sole vice in cases like *Simpson* and *Allcard* is 'serious and exceptional' impairment of autonomy. Cases of 'actual undue influence' (when misconduct is proven) should be 'decanted back into duress' in the interests of 'intellectual order' (i.e. they have a quite different juridical basis). Since the recognition of economic duress such cases, although traditionally dealt with in Equity,[108] are better accommodated there.

As noted, however, this is not the mainstream view. Bigwood puts forward a sophisticated wrong-based account of undue influence. Not, however, a

---

[102] Ibid, pp. 265–66.
[103] P.B.H. Birks & N.Y. Chin, 'On the Nature of Undue Influence' in J. Beatson & D. Friedmann (eds), *Good Faith and Fault in Contract Law* (Oxford University Press, 1995).
[104] Cf. n.99 above.
[105] [1992] 1 FLR 601.
[106] Birks & Chin, p. 72.
[107] Cf. *Hart v O'Connor* [1985] 1 AC 1004.
[108] E.g. *Williams v Bayley* (1866) LR 1 HL 200.

generalized concept of 'victimization'[109] but one specifically aimed at protecting fiduciary relationships.[110] Bigwood admits that there can be no exhaustive definition of when relationships are (in this context) 'fiduciary'.[111] Indeed, the vagueness of fiduciary duties generally is notorious – Sir Anthony Mason comments that they are 'a concept in search of a principle'.[112] Here, Bigwood argues, equity looks for a capacity to influence which is so great that the victim may be said to display 'deferential trust'. Once this 'fiduciary' situation is established then in accordance with the general rules on fiduciary duties, the defendant is no longer entitled to deal in a self-interested and competitive way. Equity presumes (from cynical generalization about human nature!) that the position of influence may be abused.[113] Hence the defendant is required to practise self-denial, unless he takes positive steps to emancipate the victim from his influence, for example, by ensuring that independent advice is given. This is a 'prophylactic' approach. There is no inference that the defendant *has* positively acted wrongfully, but he must practise self-denial to *prevent* the possibility of abuse, as a matter of 'public policy'.[114]

On Bigwood's account, the defendants in cases like *Allcard* and *Simpson* are indeed wrongdoers in the sense of breaching their fiduciary duties. Provided that they were aware of the dependency by the other party, the strict duty not to deal self-interestedly with her comes into play. If fiduciaries knowingly breach that duty then *ipso facto* there has been exploitation of the victim – albeit through a 'decidedly *passive* process'.[115] This does not necessarily involve actively 'wicked exploitation', given the presumptive and prophylactic form of the fiduciary duty. The *non sequitur* in Birks and Chin's argument is to assume that because the defendants in *Simpson* and *Allcard* were not 'wicked', the relief must be 'claimant-sided'. This ignores the possibility of a strict, prophylactic approach. The virtue of those defendants is not to the point. To be a 'passive exploiter' carries less stigma.[116]

Bigwood points to other problems with Birks and Chin's account. It seems 'most irregular', linguistically, to refer to the *victim's mental state* as 'undue'.[117] The more obvious connotation is impropriety of some kind. More importantly, Bigwood argues that according to the driving principle of 'corrective justice' we must advert to the justice for *both* parties before setting a contract aside. If the defendant is wholly innocent of any kind of wrongdoing there is nothing to connect him to the claimant's plight; it would be wrong to inflict the loss of the contract on a defendant who bears no responsibility for the claimant's bad bargain.[118]

---

[109] Cf. *Natwest Bank v Morgan* [1985] AC 686.
[110] Bigwood, n.101 above, ch. 8.
[111] Ibid, p. 407
[112] A. Mason, 'Themes and Prospects' in P. Finn (ed.), *Essays in Equity* (1985), p. 242 at p. 246.
[113] Bigwood, n.101 above, p. 446.
[114] Cf. *Allcard v Skinner*, n.99 above, 171 (Cotton LJ).
[115] Bigwood, n.101 above, p. 466 (original emphasis) (and cf. ch. 4 passim).
[116] Ibid, p. 475.
[117] Ibid, p. 474.
[118] Ibid, pp. 467, 475–76.

If accepted, this last argument is the fatal blow against any kind of claimant-sided rationale. But the remainder of the debate between Bigwood and Birks and Chin seems almost semantic – whether passive breach of a prophylactic fiduciary duty is properly 'wrongdoing'. Bigwood admits that his argument faces formidable difficulties in England as a matter of precedent.[119] In *Natwest Bank v Morgan* Lord Scarman explicitly rejected the 'public policy' view of undue influence.[120] Although Lord Browne-Wilkinson was to note the difficulty of reconciling these dicta with the traditional approach in which fiduciaries *as a class* bore the onus of demonstrating the righteousness of transactions with beneficiaries,[121] to Bigwood's great chagrin the House of Lords in *Royal Bank of Scotland v Etridge* did not consider, let alone restore, the fiduciary approach.[122] Thus, he concedes, the 'prophylactic content and function of the traditional presumption are gone', along with the higher regulatory goal of protecting fiduciary relationships from abuse.[123] Bigwood is sharply critical of *Etridge* for ignoring the fiduciary approach which (he argues) would provide the 'touchstone' for liability that Lord Nicholls disavowed.[124] Indeed, Bigwood argues it is 'elemental to [the] very illumination and proper administration' of undue influence.[125]

Mindy Chen-Wishart rejects the 'bipolar' opposition between purely claimant-sided and defendant-sided explanations.[126] In her view, which seems intuitively plausible, *both* impaired consent *and* wrongdoing are required. Chen-Wishart deplores Birks and Chin's characterization of trusting relationships. These, she points out, are entirely ordinary, occurring every day between family members, lovers, friends, colleagues and others. Trust might sometimes be romantic or naïve, but it is wrong to see it as subnormal, impairing judgment by 'morbid dependency'.[127] Is it not insulting to claimants to view them as mentally impaired? Of the nun in *Allcard*, Lindley LJ famously said that 'although [she] was a religious enthusiast, no one could treat her as in point of law *non compos mentis*'.

Moreover, Chen-Wishart argues that such trusting relationships are healthy (and probably inevitable). First, as Kekewich J said in *Allcard*, it is a rare person who has the strength of mind and character to act wholly independently of others' influence, and such influence can often be exercised for good.[128] Moreover, Chen-Wishart satirizes the law's vision of the 'Super-Detached Man' whose cold independence in personal relationships would be mechanical, disrespectful and

---

[119] R. Bigwood, 'From *Morgan* to *Etridge*: Tracing the (dis)integration of undue influence in the United Kingdom' in J. Neyers et al. (eds.), *Exploring Contract Law* (Hart Publishing, 2009).

[120] Cf. n.109 above.

[121] *CIBC Mortgages v Pitt* [1994] AC 200.

[122] [2002] 1 AC 773.

[123] Bigwood, n.119 above, p. 389.

[124] Ibid, p. 416.

[125] Ibid, p. 483.

[126] M. Chen-Wishart, 'Undue Influence: *Beyond* Impaired Consent and Wrongdoing towards a Relational Analysis' in A. Burrows and Lord Rodger (eds), *Mapping the Law: Essays in Memory of Peter Birks* (Oxford University Press, 2006).

[127] Cf. Birks & Chin. n.103 above, p. 82.

[128] Cf. n.99 above.

odd.[129] But this is a 'simplistic paradigm'. The more realistic 'Relational Hero' rightly throws himself into those relationships. The law should in no way seek to discourage that. But at the same time, such openness leaves him open to exploitation by significant others, and pathological abuse of relationships should be policed. This should be done by identifying and applying the norms governing such relationships – how friends, family or lovers ought to treat each other.

Chen-Wishart argues that this 'relational' analysis explains the pivotal role of independent advice. The question is whether the defendant has shifted his obligation to protect the claimant onto a third party, the adviser. If he has successfully done so 'the paradigm will have changed; from a relational to an arm's length one, leaving the defendant free to deal self-interestedly with the claimant'.[130] Chen-Wishart also emphasizes the role of substantive fairness. Requiring that the transaction 'calls for explanation' is disingenuous. The explanation for the gift in *Allcard* was obvious: the nun had taken strict vows of poverty! There was nothing to 'explain'. But the transaction was 'objectively inappropriate' as it seriously compromised the nun's future autonomy.[131] She would have had no money on which to live if she decided to leave the convent (as in fact had happened). Another formulation is to ask whether the transaction was 'explicable by the parties' relationship'. Thus, an 'unreasonably large gift that is disproportionate to the gratitude, love, or affection evinced by the evolution of the party's relationship' would be dubious.[132] Since influence within close relationships is not bad ('undue') in itself, only by considering the fairness of the resulting transaction can the line be draw. There is a world of difference between a mother encouraging children to do their homework and to hand over their savings!

Chen-Wishart does not directly respond to Bigwood's fiduciary argument. Their approaches are similar to the extent that they emphasize the law's concern to protect exploitation *within relationships*. Like Bigwood, Chen-Wishart expressly accepts that undue influence can be entirely 'passive' (an omission to obtain independent advice or otherwise deal fairly). On the other hand, Bigwood's 'prophylactic' doctrine is stricter by design, and seems to require the universally 'detached' approach to close relationships that Chen-Wishart dismisses. She argues for a more nuanced doctrine, focused on the relationship in each case, the norms governing it and the fairness of the resulting transaction. Of course this will be more difficult to apply and lack the salutary effect of the fiduciary's stern self-denial. Each has its costs and benefits.

UNCONSCIONABILITY

Rick Bigwood states that the law prevents 'exploitation of special advantage' when two basic conditions are met: serious vulnerability on the part of the claimant

---

[129] M. Chen-Wishart, 'Undue Influence: Vindicating Relationships of Influence' [2006] *CLP* 231.
[130] Ibid, p. 260.
[131] Cf. *Cheese v Thomas* [1994] 1 All ER 35.
[132] [2006] CLP 231, 256. Cf. *Hammond v Osborne* [2002] EWCA Civ 885.

and (at least) awareness of this by the defendant. The normal rules of competitive bargaining are then suspended – the defendant cannot pursue his interests at the expense of the other party's.[133] But as Bigwood accepts, there is 'startling diversity' among courts and commentators who attempt to explain and apply these principles.[134] In England, a leading statement is by Peter Millett QC (as he then was):

> First, one party has been at a serious disadvantage to the other, whether through poverty, or ignorance, or lack of advice, or otherwise … [S]econd, this weakness of the one party has been exploited by the other in some morally culpable manner … And third, the resulting transaction has been, not merely hard or improvident, but overreaching and oppressive.[135]

In short, Millett concluded, there must be 'some impropriety, both in the conduct of the stronger party and in the terms of the transaction itself (though the former may often be inferred from the latter in the absence of an innocent explanation)'.

The first element (disadvantage) is unproblematic in theory but difficult in practice. One classic example of the necessary vulnerability is 'poor and ignorant persons'[136] (which Megarry J rendered as 'a less highly educated member of a lower income group' to comply with 'the euphemisms of the 20th century').[137] But taking this 'cornerstone' requirement of 'special disadvantage', Devenney and Chandler find it 'vague', 'elusive' and 'shrouded in mystery,' suggesting that disadvantage becomes 'special' simply when the law recognizes it as grounds for relief.[138] Obviously, this is unhelpful. As Fullagar J once said, the grounds are 'of great antiquity and can hardly be satisfactorily classified'.[139] Capper believes this limb of unconscionability so broad that cases of undue influence could easily fit within it.[140]

The requirement of 'unconscionable conduct' by the defendant also bears strong parallels to undue influence.[141] Lord Brightman states that 'unconscientious use of power' includes 'the passive acceptance of a benefit in unconscionable circumstances'.[142] Devenney and Chandler stress that the defendant's knowledge is the key criterion. Beyond this there is no need for 'wicked exploitation'. The defendant's actual conduct is, they argue, 'irrelevant', given only his 'passive acceptance' of the contract. These are the arguments used by Bigwood to support a defendant-sided conception of undue influence.[143] Devenney and Chandler join Capper in calling for an assimilation of unconscionability and undue influence.

---

133 Bigwood, n.101 above, ch. 6.
134 Ibid, p. 237.
135 *Alec Lobb (Garages) v Total Oil* [1983] 1 WLR 87, 94–95.
136 *Fry v Lane* (1888) 40 Ch 312.
137 *Creswell v Potter* [1978] 1 WLR 255 (note).
138 J. Devenney & A. Chandler, 'Unconscionability and the Taxonomy of Undue Influence' [2007] *JBL* 541.
139 *Blomley v Ryan* (1956) 99 CLR 362 at 403.
140 D. Capper, 'Undue Influence and Unconscionability: A Rationalisation' (1998) 114 *LQR* 479.
141 The need for 'harsh terms' will be considered in the next debate, below.
142 *Hart v O'Connor*, n.107 above.
143 Cf. pp. 197–199 above.

Capper suggests that retaining needless doctrinal divisions may confuse litigants and courts alike, and endorses Waddams' argument that a merged doctrine may expose policy questions and thus improve legal development.[144] Plus, Capper remarks, undue influence is so imprecise that its absorption would not 'obviously rid the law of useful analytical tools'.

Bigwood agrees that, like undue influence, unconscionability involves exploitation of weaker parties. He argues that the defendant must be guilty of some blameworthy conduct – corrective justice requires a causal and culpable linkage with the claimant.[145] But again, Bigwood accepts that passive exploitation (i.e. accepting benefits in the knowledge of the claimant's weakness) is enough. Exploitation can vary from 'the depths of depravity to the misplaced kindly intention';[146] the question is whether there was a 'sufficient divergence from … commercial morality'.

However, despite the similarities Bigwood would maintain undue influence as a separate category. Claimants here are protected by a rebuttable presumption, whereas in unconscionability they bear a 'fairly substantial persuasive burden' of proof.[147] This reflects public policy. In unconscionability the parties are 'at arm's length' whereas the starting point for fiduciaries requires subordination of their interests to protect the weaker party. In short, the misconduct in undue influence is simply worse. We are (typically) vigilant with strangers but expose ourselves by reposing trust in fiduciaries. For the fiduciary to betray that trust involves 'hypocrisy, infidelity … an "attack *from within*"'.[148] Bigwood says that such 'treachery' is a 'higher order of wrongdoing altogether'. In this he has Dante's support: in the *Divine Comedy*, Treachery merits the Ninth and lowest (i.e. worst) Circle of Hell; Avarice (greed) only the Fourth.[149]

Mindy Chen-Wishart's 'relational' thesis of undue influence is consistent with its status as a distinct wrong. Indeed, she also opposes the merger of 'actual undue influence' with economic duress as proposed by Birks and Chin (and supported by Devenney and Chandler as ending the jurisdictional, law-equity duality). Chen-Wishart argues that the 'pressure' necessary to trigger actual undue influence is typically lower than that seen in economic duress ('relatively innocuous').[150] The reason why this may nevertheless coerce the claimant is precisely because of the relationship of influence between the parties. That relationship makes the defendant's 'otherwise low level coercion legally relevant'. Accordingly, the parties' intimate relationship is of the essence to such a claim, which is 'undue influence' and not 'economic duress' (usually arm's length cases, as seen above). Together, Bigwood and Chen-Wishart present interesting arguments of principle

---

[144] Capper, n.140 above; S.M. Waddams, 'Unconscionability in Contracts' (1976) 39 *MLR* 369.
[145] Bigwood, n.101 above, p. 247.
[146] Cf. L.A. Sheridan, *Fraud in Equity: A Study in English and Irish Law* (Pitman Press, 1957) p. 214.
[147] n.101 above, p. 400.
[148] Ibid, (original emphasis).
[149] Fraud, however, is condemned to the Eighth Circle.
[150] [2006] CLP 231.

(beyond the more familiar, but timid, arguments from precedent) for retaining undue influence as a separate category.

SUBSTANTIVE FAIRNESS?

Contract orthodoxy holds that courts are limited to policing the contracting process, but are not concerned with the fairness of the resulting contract. Duress, unconscionability and undue influence are thus usually conceived as 'procedural' wrongdoing. But Atiyah doubts whether such a sharp line can be drawn, suggesting that a 'fair' procedure cannot exist in the abstract any more than a 'fair' price.[151] Once the law takes an interest in bargaining processes it is 'of necessity compelled to take an interest in the substantive justice of contracts', he concludes.[152] Is this correct?

It does seem plausible to argue that something beyond 'fair procedures' is needed to apply the doctrines discussed in this chapter. As seen, economic duress ('illegitimate pressure') defies definition once the parasitic doctrine of 'independent unlawfulness' is given up. If anything, unconscionability and undue influence are even harder to define. Is it not sensible to use a grossly unbalanced contract as, at least, *evidence* of this elusive illegitimate pressure or exploitation? Indeed, it seems to be built into the standard definitions of undue influence (an 'inexplicable' transaction) and unconscionability (an 'oppressive' bargain).

Greene has argued that the 'undisclosed major premise' in cases of alleged mental incapacity – assimilated with unconscionability in England[153] – is the fairness of the resulting contract.[154] While in some (unusual) cases evidence of mental abnormality might be overwhelming, most cases are not obvious ones and the courts then fall back instinctively upon the fairness of the contract in evaluating mental capacity. An abnormal transaction is an *unfair* one. Mindy Chen-Wishart similarly argues, after an exhaustive study of New Zealand cases, that ostensibly procedural tests (unconscionability, undue influence or economic duress) are indeterminate and are given meaningful content only by consideration of the fairness of the contract terms themselves.[155] Indeed, Chen-Wishart concludes, the substantive test is to the fore. The merest procedural improprieties are seized upon when the resulting contract was grossly unbalanced. Conversely, even egregious misconduct is not 'unconscionable' when the contract seems to the court fair and reasonable.[156]

Chen-Wishart argues that a similar approach was taken in *Credit Lyonnais v Burch*.[157] The central factor of the case was the 'astonishing' and 'extreme substan-

---

[151] P.S. Atiyah, 'Contract and Fair Exchange' in *Essays on Contract* (Oxford University Press, 1990).

[152] Ibid, p. 354.

[153] *Hart v O'Connor*, n.107 above. Cf. Bigwood, n.101 above, p. 229, n.15.

[154] M.D. Green, 'Proof of Mental Incompetency and the Unexpressed Major Premise' (1944) 53 *Yale LJ* 271.

[155] M. Chen-Wishart, *Unconscionable Bargains* (Butterworths, 1989).

[156] See also J. Gordley, 'Equality in Exchange' (1981) 69 *Calif LR* 1587.

[157] [1997] 1 All ER 144. M. Chen-Wishart, 'The *O'Brien* Principle and Substantive Fairness' [1997] *CLJ* 60.

tive unfairness' of the agreement by the claimant to guarantee her employer's debts, pledging her home as security. This meant that 'otherwise commonplace' facts were treated by the Court of Appeal as giving rise to a presumption of undue influence, one that was extremely difficult for the bank (put on notice by the unfairness of the transaction) to rebut. But what appears to be a massive, arguably 'aberrant' extension of the three-party-notice variant of undue influence is readily explicable if the court, in the end, found the 'shocking' imbalance of the transaction decisive of itself.

This is a controversial claim. The courts routinely insist that there must be procedural misconduct but Chen-Wishart says these 'judicial articulations do not accurately reflect judicial actions'.[158] Such allegations of mass deception by the court – even if in promotion of a Noble Lie – are bound to meet stern resistance. After all, the rule that the courts will not inquire into the substantive fairness of a transaction is deeply rooted. It is famously embodied in the doctrine that 'consideration need not be adequate'. Moreover, its theoretical underpinnings go to freedom of contract itself, since the 'just value [of a contract] is that which [the Appetite of the Contractors] be contented to give'.[159]

Against this, Gordley advocates that contract law should embrace 'justice in exchange'.[160] He argues that this is necessitated by the true and original purpose of Aristotle's 'corrective justice', which is to ensure that the just distribution of society's resources is maintained. Unfair contracts unsettle that distribution. However, this is a controversial role for corrective justice in itself.[161] Bigwood argues that to accept rules based on ancient markets or outmoded conceptions of values would reject modern contract law that is, for better or worse, premised on a subjective theory of value. Gordley's 'substantive fairness' would disturb the allocation of tolerable risks in the contracting 'game'. Corrective justice in the liberal theory of contract is satisfied by voluntariness alone.[162] Bigwood also emphasizes the practical difficulties in the courts trying to regulate fair terms. It is not simply a matter of applying some readily available 'market price'. In the modern economy, price is a complex function of risk, opportunity, investment, hidden costs, marginal and average costs, etc.[163] Even proponents of substantive regulation retreat to a procedural fairness, faced with these insuperable administrative difficulties in deciding the 'fair price'.[164]

Nevertheless, Bigwood has to accept that the substantive imbalance of a contract may furnish vital *evidence* of procedural unfairness – especially in 'passive' exploitation cases where there will be no outward sign of misconduct.[165] This is,

---

[158] Ibid, p. 64.

[159] Hobbes, *Leviathan* (1651), Ch. XV.

[160] J. Gordley, *The Philosophical Origins of Modern Contract Doctrine* (Clarendon, 1991).

[161] S.A. Smith, 'Troubled Foundations for Private Law' (2008) 21 *Can Jo L & Juris* 459.

[162] Bigwood, n.101 above, p. 223.

[163] Ibid, p. 185.

[164] Ibid, p. 186, citing A. Wertheimer, *Exploitation* (Princeton, 1996) p. 225.

[165] Bigwood, n.101 above, p. 269. Similarly, R. Epstein, 'Unconscionability: A Critical Reappraisal' (1975) 18 *J L&E* 293.

of course, the standard position in undue influence and unconscionability. It is accepted that improper conduct can be inferred from the harsh terms of the resulting transaction.[166] Chen-Wishart argues that this is what happened in *Burch* – an otherwise weak case of undue influence was transformed by the extremely unbalanced underlying transaction. How much difference is there, in the end, between accepting that unfairness may supply decisive 'evidence' and the unorthodox claim that it may ground intervention 'in itself'? In practice, it seems, very little. But as a theoretical matter, this is much more important. It may be that Chen-Wishart is right that if we examine what the judges actually decide, they do police substantive fairness. If so, transparency would require that they should admit that they are doing it. But perhaps honesty, in this instance, would be dangerous if it led towards a general judicial power to regulate the terms of contracts – for how could this be resisted? So if the courts do display polite hypocrisy in these matters, it may be for good reason.

Debate 3

How should contract law protect consumers?

Drawing together the threads of this chapter and the earlier discussion of standard form contracts,[167] we now examine the proper role for the regulation of consumer transactions. Particular attention will be paid to the Unfair Terms in Consumer Contracts Regulations 1999.

CONSUMERS: UNEQUAL BARGAINING POWER?

It is a trite observation that most consumers are at a disadvantage when dealing with a business. This is particularly so with standard form contracts, when a raft of detailed terms is presented to the consumer on a 'take it or leave it' basis. When the terms of the resulting contract are adjudged harsh in substance, does this not satisfy the basic requirements of unconscionable dealing – the business taking advantage of its stronger position to extract an advantageous contract? Rick Bigwood argues that use of standard forms should not in itself give rise to an inference of unconscionability.[168] The cost of such a presumption would be too high, given the widespread use of such forms. It is therefore generally accepted that there is no procedural misconduct per se in using standard forms.[169] (Again, this ultimately seems to be an argument from the cost-saving convenience of the 'mass produced contract'.[170]) Unconscionability aims to prevent the exploitation of unusually vulnerable people;[171] but '*All* members of modern Western society

---

[166] Cf. n.135 above (Peter Millett QC).
[167] Cf. pp. 84–87 above.
[168] R. Bigwood, *Exploitative Contracts* (Oxford University Press, 2003) p. 274.
[169] Ibid, p. 275.
[170] Cf. pp. 68, 78, 84–87 above.
[171] Bigwood, pp. 200–201.

are vulnerable ... to the standardized contract'.[172] The 'random and *ad hoc*' law of unconscionability is quite unsuited for the regulation of such endemic problems. Instead, Bigwood argues, dedicated laws addressing the substance of standard forms are necessary. He notes that legislative schemes and administrative agencies have played a larger role than the common law in this respect.[173]

Some go further and question whether the common law should play any role. As seen in the previous section, there are practical and theoretical objections to assessing 'fair pricing'. A wider form of the same debate asks whether contract law should promote 'distributive justice' (i.e. of resources across society) as advocated by Anthony Kronman.[174] Kaplow and Shavell argue that private law is ill-suited to such a role. The tax and benefit system is a more powerful tool because it can redistribute 'from all the rich to all the poor'.[175] It is '*ad hoc* and inefficient' only to redistribute from those who end up in court (rather than everyone who pays tax). It does seem questionable to tax (in effect) only those who make contracts with poorer individuals. Trebilcock also rejects Kronman's thesis.[176] He suggests that the political temptation to redistribute through contract is strong since 'the social costs involved are largely off-budget, do not require the raising of tax revenues, and appear to impose costs on relatively small and often somewhat unromantic sub-sets of the population' (such as loan sharks and slum landlords).[177] Mill noted that regulating the fairness of transactions one by one was 'to nibble at the consequence of unjust power, instead of redressing the injustice itself'.[178] But Trebilcock argues that when market pressure results from *structural economic phenomena* (e.g. cartels, monopolies, unionized labour), the complexity and sheer volume of information requires a specialized agency to act as regulator, not the ordinary courts.

Similarly, Schwartz argues that all regulation of contracts boils down to price control, to which the courts are not suited.[179] As will be seen in the next section, the 1999 Regulations aim to regulate the fairness of consumer contracts except for the 'core' terms – the price and the definition of the subject matter. This apparently accepts the warnings against judicial price regulation, but by drawing a distinction between 'price' and 'non-price' terms that Schwartz thinks untenable.

THE UNFAIR TERMS IN CONSUMER CONTRACTS REGULATIONS 1999

This legislation renders unenforceable terms which 'have not been individually negotiated' when they cause 'a significant imbalance in the parties' rights and obligations ... to the detriment of the consumer' (Reg 5(1)). However, the court

---

[172] Ibid, p. 276 (emphasis added).
[173] Ibid, pp. 275–77.
[174] A. Kronman, 'Contract Law and Distributive Justice' (1980) 89 *Yale LJ* 472.
[175] L. Kaplow & S. Shavell, 'Why the Legal System Is Less Efficient than the Income Tax in Redistributing Income' (1994) 23 JLS 667, 674.
[176] M.J. Trebilcock, *The Limits of Freedom of Contract* (Harvard University Press, 1993), ch. 4.
[177] Ibid, p. 260.
[178] J.S. Mill, *Principles of Political Economy* (1848).
[179] A. Schwartz, 'Seller Unequal Bargaining Power and the Judicial Process' (1974) 49 *Indiana LJ* 367.

is not to assess the fairness of a term defining 'the main subject matter of the contract' or 'the adequacy of the price or remuneration' given in exchange for it (Reg 6(2)). This exception seems to preserve room for freedom of contract. As Collins describes, it was inserted into the draft Directive late in the (EU) legislative process, and despite its 'obscure' wording may be seen as a victory for free competition over substantive fairness.[180] But is the distinction it draws stable?

Lord Mustill notes that declining to enforce *any* term of a contract distorts the shape of the bargain: 'one party ... no longer receives the full consideration for his own promise'.[181] The rights and obligations on each side are a package, and all of them feed into the 'headline' monetary price. This is easily illustrated by considering the business model of 'no frills' airlines. In theory, they offer the same basic service (flying passengers from A to B) at lower prices precisely because they do not offer the same level of subsidiary services (in-flight meals, customer support, etc). Were the law to insist that the 'frills' be re-instated, it seems clear that the headline price would go up. The distinction between 'price' and 'other' terms looks decidedly unstable.

A possible defence of the distinction draws on consumer psychology. At least to some extent it seems that consumers look only at headline prices, and not at the fine print of what is being provided. Behavioural economists refer to the greater 'salience' of price in decision making.[182] This may lead to a 'race to the bottom' as sellers maximize profits by disclaiming peripheral obligations (to which consumers are relatively insensitive) rather than raising prices (which consumers would certainly notice).[183] The usual discipline of competition does not apply to the peripheral terms to the extent that they are ignored in consumer decision making. If this is correct then Reg 6(2) can be defended as leaving consumers to decide for themselves things that are salient in their decision making (what they pay and what they primarily get), while subjecting the 'small print' to judicial regulation.

This approach was adopted by the Court of Appeal in the notorious bank charges litigation,[184] but not by the Supreme Court.[185] The Office of Fair Trading began legal proceedings against the high street banks about their practice of charging customers who exceed their agreed overdrafts, write 'bouncing' cheques and so forth. A preliminary question was whether the charges were reviewable at all. The Court of Appeal reasoned as follows:

> The object of Reg 6(2) is to exclude from assessment for fairness that part of the bargain that will be the focus of a customer's attention when entering into a contract, that is to say the goods or services that he wishes to acquire and the price he will have to pay for doing so. Market forces [can] and should be relied upon to control the fairness of this part of the bargain.

---

[180] H. Collins, 'Good Faith in European Contract Law' (1994) 14 *OJLS* 229.
[181] Mustill, 'Decision-Making in Maritime Law' [1985] *LMCLQ* 314, 323.
[182] E.g. O. Bar-Gill, 'Bundling and Consumer Misperception' (2006) 73 *Univ Chicago LR* 33.
[183] M.A. Eisenberg, 'The Limits of Cognition and the Limits of Contract' (1995) 47 *Stanford LR* 211.
[184] *Office of Fair Trading v Abbey National plc* [2009] EWCA 116.
[185] [2009] UKSC 6.

> Contingencies that the customer does not expect to involve him will not
> be of concern to him. He will not focus on these when entering into the
> bargain. The [charges] fall into this category.[186]

However this was rejected by the Supreme Court as overly complex. The Court
of Appeal had departed from the text of the Regulations to promote 'the notion
that freedom of contract should prevail [only] where there has been meaningful
negotiation between supplier and consumer'.[187]

In the end, Lord Walker found it 'quite a short point'.[188] The provision by the
bank of, for example, an unauthorized overdraft is a service, part of the package
of services provided under its contract with the customer. The charge levied for
the service is, similarly, (part of) the price that the customer pays for that package
of services. There was no principled basis on which to single out one part of the
services provided (or payments required) for special treatment, or to distinguish
'core' and 'ancillary' payments or services.[189] Accordingly, the disputed charges fell
squarely within Reg 6(2) and could not be reviewed.[190] It was irrelevant that they
were 'contingent, uneconomic, unadvertised and imperfectly understood'.[191]

Lord Walker noted the *reductio ad absurdum* argument as expressed by Lord
Steyn (and canvassed above) – 'in a broad sense all terms of the contract are in
some way related to the price or remuneration'.[192] For Lord Walker, the limiting factor is that only *monetary* payments can properly be seen as the 'price or
remuneration'[193] – a narrow construction not mandated by the interpretive provisions in Reg 3. But as Mindy Chen-Wishart notes, this leaves little room for the
application of the fairness test – only the consumer's non-monetary obligations
and any terms indicated as unfair under the Regulations' 'greylist' (Schedule 2).[194]
The exception has largely swallowed the rule. This was always likely, given its
instability, once the argument from consumer perceptions was rejected.

Chen-Wishart hails the decision as a 'bitter blow' to consumers and the authority of the Office of Fair Trading. Lord Walker accepted that the decision would
cause 'great disappointment and indeed dismay to a very large number of bank
customers who feel that they have been subjected to unfairly high charges', but
said that their remedy was for Ministers and Parliament to reconsider the narrow
ambit of the 1999 Regulations.[195] But one suspects that while 'feeling our pain' the
Supreme Court judges simultaneously sighed with relief, for by nipping the bank
charges case in the bud they avoided the horribly difficult question which would
have come next: were the charges actually unfair? The banks had publicly stated

---

[186] Ibid, [79] (Lord Phillips's summary).
[187] Ibid, [45].
[188] Ibid, [38].
[189] Ibid, [39]–[40].
[190] Ibid, [47].
[191] Ibid, [36].
[192] *Director General of Fair Trading v First National Bank plc* [2001] UKHL 52, [34].
[193] [2009] UKSC 6, [42]–[43].
[194] M. Chen-Wishart, 'Transparency and Fairness in Bank Charges' (2010) 126 *LQR* 157.
[195] [2009] UKSC 6, [52].

that if levying such charges were to be outlawed, it would spell the end of free banking for in-credit customers. The stance is understandable since they would have lost 30 per cent of their revenue at a stroke and banks, notoriously, are not charities. In-credit customers might well have thought this change 'unfair'.

At bottom the issue was whether the cross-subsidy of 42 million in-credit bank customers by those 12 million customers who regular incur charges was fair or not. As Lord Walker observed (although not answering the question), this 'imponderable' matter depends whether the latter group is perceived as 'spendthrift and improvident' or 'disadvantaged and finding it hard to make ends meet'.[196] Fairly obviously, this would require a judgment of social policy. Even if the court were to decide that the regularly charged 12 million were a vulnerable group requiring protection, striking the charges down as unfair might not have the intended effect. If a bank decided that the perpetually overdrawn habits of such customers (which would presumably increase) were costing it too much revenue (that it could no longer recoup), it might decide to terminate their contracts altogether. A bank is not legally obliged to accept someone as its customer, after all. Thus, the 'disadvantaged' might, *in extremis*, find it difficult to access commercial banking services at all.

Similar arguments have been made about 'regulatory backfiring' with such policies as rent restriction and minimum wage laws. Keeping rents artificially low is said to discourage provision of private rental accommodation (as it becomes unprofitable), meaning housing shortages, homelessness and (ironically) driving up market rents. Now, the effect of the (former) Rent Acts and the National Minimum Wage Act 1998 are much debated. Collins argues that the impact of regulation is highly unpredictable, and only empirical study can reveal its actual consequences.[197] It is obvious that such exercises are way beyond the capacity of the courts, however.[198] It is not surprising if the Supreme Court wished to avoid confronting such choices in such an economically far-reaching case as the bank charges litigation.

Further Reading

P.S. Atiyah, 'Economic Duress and the Overborne Will' (1982) 98 *LQR* 197.

M.A. Eisenberg, 'The Limits of Cognition and the Limits of Contract' (1995) 47 *Stanford LR* 211.

P.B.H. Birks & N.Y. Chin, 'On the Nature of Undue Influence' in J. Beatson & D. Friedmann (eds), *Good Faith and Fault in Contract Law* (Oxford University Press, 1995).

M. Chen-Wishart, 'The *O'Brien* Principle and Substantive Fairness' [1997] *CLJ* 60.

R. Bigwood, *Exploitative Contracts* (Oxford University Press, 2003).

O. Bar-Gill and O. Ben-Shahar, 'The Law of Duress and the Economics of Credible Threats' (2004) 33 *JLS* 391.

---

[196] Ibid, [1]–[2].

[197] H. Collins, *Regulating Contracts* (Oxford University Press, 1999) pp. 276–78.

[198] Cf. J. Gava & J. Greene, 'Do We Need a Hybrid Law of Contract? Why Hugh Collins Is Wrong and Why It Matters' [2004] *CLJ* 605.

M. Chen-Wishart, 'Undue Influence: *Beyond* Impaired Consent and Wrongdoing towards a Relational Analysis' in A. Burrows and Lord Rodger (eds), *Mapping the Law: Essays in Memory of Peter Birks* (Oxford University Press, 2006).

M. Chen-Wishart, 'Undue Influence: Vindicating Relationships of Influence' [2006] *CLP* 231.

8

PARTY-AGREED REMEDIES

INTRODUCTION

It is claimed that:

> No aspect of a system of contract law is more revealing of its underlying
> assumptions than is the law that prescribes the relief available for breach.[1]

We have seen in Chapter 2 that estoppel's relationship to the law of contract
depends on the remedial response to estoppels.[2] Nevertheless, there are grounds
for caution. As Lord Diplock pointed out in an important opinion, remedies are
just as much within the competence of the parties as the primary obligations of
the contract itself.[3] freedom of contract implies that just as contractors may decide
what duties they assume to each other, they may also determine the consequences
of breaching those duties. (The consequences are an important aspect of the duty
itself, after all.) In this chapter, we examine two remedies that may be stipulated by
the parties under the terms of the contract: termination and liquidated damages.
According to Hugh Collins, most written contracts pay 'considerable attention'
to remedies and so the remedy for breach is usually to be found in the contract
terms.[4]

There are, however, limits on this 'remedial' freedom of contract – it would be
as misleading to say that the parties' intentions are the *sole* factor as to deny that
they have any role to play. First, if there is no express provision for remedies in
the contract they arise *as a matter of law*. In other words, the law supplies certain
remedies as 'default terms' (viz. if the parties fail to do so). So, the courts also
decide the availability of termination at common law. Moreover, if the parties
have made no provision for liquidated damages, the law of course imposes liability to pay judicially assessed compensation. This 'default' damages remedy is so
important and complex that it will be considered in the next chapter.

---

[1] E.A. Farnsworth, 'Damages and Specific Relief' (1979) 27 *Am Jo Comparative Law* 247.
[2] Cf. pp. 58–61 above.
[3] *Photo Production v Securicor* [1980] AC 827.
[4] H. Collins, *The Law of Contract* (Cambridge University Press, 4th edn, 2003) p. 365.

Secondly, even where the parties have included express remedial provisions in the contract it is necessary to examine how the courts give effect to them. Sometimes there seems to be judicial resistance to a party-determined remedy of termination for breach, which is given effect by the court's 'interpretation' of the relevant term. There is clearly an implicit policy at work. With liquidated damages, policy has hardened into the rule that 'penal' clauses are unenforceable. A common factor here seems to be judicial dislike of penal remedies.

Debate ❶

When should termination be allowed in response to breach of contract?

Termination is a powerful remedy. The promisee is afforded means of 'escape' from an undesirable contract by exercising his option to bring it to an end. Obviously, it may be undesirable to remain in a continuing contractual relationship with someone who has been in serious breach of the contract. The promisee may also wish to escape from a contract which has turned out to be a bad bargain for reasons quite separate from the breach. In turn, this may inflict heavy losses on the promisor, for example where he has wasted money in preparing for performance (thereby providing a powerful incentive for him to perform). In the archetypal case, A orders goods from B at say £100 per ton; B delivers goods that do not comply with the description in the contract, although this does not affect their value. However, by the time the goods are tendered, the market price has collapsed to £70 per ton. Thus A rejects the goods and terminates the contract. This is legally unimpeachable. The motive of a promisee when terminating is 'irrelevant' for there is 'no doctrine of good faith in the English law of contract'.[5]

In England, termination is a self-help remedy: the promisee does not need to apply to the court, but simply makes his election between terminating and affirming the contract. Common lawyers take this for granted but the situation in French law is very different – termination can only be ordered by the courts, which take the view that the fate of a contract is performance and so termination is absolutely the last resort, for the most serious cases.[6] Self-help remedies offer numerous advantages for the party to whom they are granted.[7] The expense and delay of court proceedings necessary for a remedy in damages (or specific relief) are avoided. More importantly, the limits on availability of other remedies, such as mitigation of damages, and the penalty rule on agreed damages, are inapplicable. Whether such a sharp difference of approach is justified may be questioned. Some argue that the behaviour of the buyer in the archetypal case mentioned above

---

[5] *James Spencer v Tame Valley Padding* (CA 1998, unreported) (Potter LJ).

[6] Y.-M. Lathier, 'Comparative Reflections on the French Law of Remedies for Breach of Contract' in N. Cohen & E. McKendrick (eds), *Comparative Remedies for Breach of Contract* (Hart Publishing, 2005).

[7] Cf. D. Harris, D. Campbell & R. Halson, *Remedies in Contract and Tort* (2nd edn, Cambridge University Press, 2002), ch. 3.

should be unlawful. The question then arises whether this should be curbed by some concept of abuse of rights. However, English law's (indirect) response has been the rise of the innominate term.

The terminology in this area is notoriously unstable and confusing – in despair, Lord Wilberforce said that 'To plead for complete uniformity may be to cry for the moon'.[8] Probably the most confusing usage is to talk about 'rescission' (prospectively, from the point of breach) since this sounds the same as rescission *ab initio* (from the outset) as the remedy for misrepresentation, duress and undue influence. In fact the effect and theoretical basis of those remedies is entirely distinct. Therefore we will here refer to *termination* as the remedy for breach.

WHEN IS TERMINATION AVAILABLE AS A MATTER OF LAW?

There is no question that parties can (in principle) freely choose termination as a remedy for breach. Even a matter 'apparently of very little importance' can be rendered 'essential' by the parties, provided they 'sufficiently express an intention' to that effect.[9] But as Diplock LJ observed in leading case *Hongkong Fir Shipping v Kawasaki Kisen Kaisha (The Hong Kong Fir)*, 'human prescience being limited' the contract seldom makes exhaustive provision about termination, and often fails to discuss it at all. In the absence of contractual (or Parliamentary) provision, it is for the court to decide whether breach should entitle the innocent party to terminate.[10]

There are two basic approaches. The first, '*ex ante*' strategy seeks to classify terms of the contract according to their abstract importance, asking whether a term is important enough to justify termination in the event that it is breached. If so, it is a 'condition' (and if not, a 'warranty'), according to the dichotomous taxonomy hallowed by the Sale of Goods Act. Second, there is the case-by-case '*ex post*' approach which looks at a given breach and asks whether its consequences are serious enough to justify termination. The two approaches can be brought into synthesis, formally at least. One could say that classification as a condition means that every breach of that term is deemed sufficiently serious to justify termination (so that the factual *ex post* inquiry is unnecessary). Or one could say that the *ex post* approach represents a new kind of term, between the condition and the warranty – the unimaginatively titled 'innominate' or 'intermediate' term. Thus, the 'classification' inquiry determines whether the *ex post* inquiry has to be undertaken, or whether the 'always' or 'never' approach of the condition/ warranty is in play.

This standard classification approach still raises the crucial question of when the court should prefer the condition (or warranty) and when the innominate term. Each has its intrinsic virtues (and vices). By making it clear that every (or no) breach permits termination, the condition/warranty brings great clarity.

---

[8] *Photo Production v Securicor* [1980] AC 827, 844.
[9] *Bettini v Gye* (1876) LR 1 QBD 183, 187 (Blackburn J).
[10] [1962] 2 QB 261.

Everybody knows where they stand. Long ago Lord Mansfield CJ said that certainty was 'the great object' of mercantile law.[11] But this clarity comes at a price. Breach of a condition enables termination even when, with the benefit of hindsight, the consequences of breach were insufficiently serious to justify that remedy. The converse is true with warranties.

The 'innominate term' approach is much more finely calibrated and thereby avoids these problems. Its central insight is that many terms may be breached in different ways with different consequences, some extremely serious and some trivial. A classic example is a ship-owner's duty to a charterer to maintain the ship in a 'seaworthy' state. A breach of that term encompasses anything from a sinking vessel to the lack of a medicine chest, or a second anchor, or even a nail.[12] Because of this inherent variability, it is 'unthinkable' that seaworthiness is a condition.[13]

The difficulty with tailoring the remedy to the seriousness of the breach is unpredictability. How serious, precisely, must the consequences of breach be? In *The Hong Kong Fir* itself, Diplock LJ asked whether breach would deprive the innocent party of 'substantially the whole benefit' that he was intended to gain under the contract. Salmon J and the Court of Appeal expressly drew a parallel with the test for frustration. This would indicate a very narrow role for termination (bordering on 'the warranty') given how rarely the courts hold contracts frustrated.[14] In *The Hong Kong Fir* itself the charterers were not entitled to terminate the contract despite the 'conspicuous incompetence' of the crew (including a drunken first engineer), the ship's 'halting progress' from Liverpool to Osaka and then 15 weeks of repairs on arrival. While this 'frustration' approach has occasionally been applied,[15] for the most part it has (rather puzzlingly) been ignored. Donal Nolan wonders whether it has been thought simply too strict.[16]

Instead, the courts have generally taken a looser and even more unpredictable approach. 'Will the consequences of the breach be such that it would be unfair to the injured party to hold him to the contract and leave him to his remedy in damages?'[17] Of course, all cases are different and no exhaustive definition of 'sufficiently serious' is possible. This is well demonstrated by *Aerial Advertising Co v Batchelor's Peas* in which the plaintiffs had towed a banner (EAT BACHELOR'S PEAS) over the main square of Salford during the two-minute silence on Armistice Day, causing public outrage.[18] The defendants purported to terminate the contract and Atkinson J accepted their argument: further performance would not just be pointless but actually counterproductive since people seeing the advertising banner would be reminded of the Salford *faux pas*. So Bachelor's Peas were entitled

---

[11] *Vallejo v Wheeler* (1774) 1 Cowp 143, 153.

[12] *Hongkong Fir*, n.10 above (Upjohn LJ).

[13] Ibid, (Sellers LJ).

[14] Cf. pp. 139–140 above.

[15] Cf. *The Angelia* [1973] 1 WLR 210, 223 (Kerr J).

[16] D. Nolan, '*Hongkong Fir Shipping Co Ltd v Kawasaki Kisen Kaisha Ltd* (1961)' in C. Mitchell & P. Mitchell, *Landmark Cases in the Law of Contract* (Hart Publishing, 2008).

[17] *Decro-Wall v Practitioners in Marketing* [1971] 1 WLR 361 (Buckley LJ).

[18] [1938] 2 All ER 788.

to refuse further performance that was 'commercially wholly unreasonable'. Few would disagree with the outcome of the case, but it shows the infinitely various circumstances of 'sufficiently serious breach'.

How then should the courts proceed? The Sale of Goods Act, as noted, classifies implied terms into conditions and (more rarely) warranties. Lord Diplock deplored this dichotomy. It is clear that, as in *The Hong Kong Fir*, terms other than those classified by statute *may* be held 'innominate' and subject to the seriousness test. In the typical case, the court is faced with a purported termination and the question is whether the term breached was a condition or not. In theory this depends on the intentions of the parties but, where they are silent, the ultimate test is to consider 'the nature, purpose and circumstances of the contract' to arrive at what 'must inevitably involve a value judgment about the commercial significance of the term in question'.[19] However, different courts have approached that 'value judgment' in very different ways.

In *The Mihalos Angelos* the Court of Appeal held that an 'expected readiness for loading' clause in a charterparty was a condition.[20] Megaw LJ observed that in commercial law, 'Where justice does not require greater flexibility, there is everything to be said for, and nothing against, a degree of rigidity in legal principle'. Conditions provide a 'firm and definite rule', allowing the parties (and their legal advisers) to state categorically what their position is, instead of pondering whether the court will find the consequences of breach sufficiently serious. But Slynn J leant in favour of innominate terms in a case of first impression,[21] and in *The Hansa Nord* it was held that an express term about the quality of goods was 'innominate'.[22] On the facts, the court was clearly concerned that the defect in the goods was being seized upon as an escape route from a bad bargain. Roskill LJ said:

> In principle contracts are made to be performed and not to be avoided according to the whims of market fluctuation and where there is a free choice between two possible constructions I think the court should tend to prefer that construction which will ensure performance and not encourage avoidance of contractual obligations.[23]

A 'notice of readiness' clause was again considered, by the House of Lords, in *Bunge v Tradax*.[24] It was classified as a condition. The serious breach test would 'fatally remove from a vital provision in the contract that certainty which is the most indispensable quality of mercantile contracts' (Lord Wilberforce). It was necessary in international trade to take decisions quickly and in confidence; but if the term were innominate, 'litigation would be rife and years might elapse before

---

[19] *State Trading Corp of India v Golodetz* [1989] 2 Lloyd's Rep 277 (Kerr LJ).
[20] [1971] 1 QB 164.
[21] *Tradax International SA v Goldschmidt SA* [1977] 2 Lloyd's Rep 604.
[22] [1976] QB 44.
[23] Cf. (similarly) *The Gregos* [1994] 1 WLR 1465, 1475 (Lord Mustill).
[24] [1981] 1 WLR 711.

the results were known' (Lord Lowry). But although Lord Wilberforce said that time clauses would 'usually' be conditions in commercial contracts, this is by no means always the case.[25] Sir Guenter Treitel remarks that there has been a flood of cases on this issue since *Bunge* but no entirely coherent pattern emerges; decisions seem to depend on commercial convenience in each case.[26] It is easy to establish whether someone has been punctual or late (contrast 'seaworthiness'), but delays can be trivial or serious. There seem to be strong competing objectives: clear-cut certainty on one side, judicial control (especially over opportunistic behaviour) on the other.

CONTROLLING TERMINATION: RULES OF LAW

One way for the court to control termination is by holding an unclassified term to be 'innominate' (or indeed, a warranty). But what if the term is expressly classified as a condition by the parties, by precedent, or by statute? The Sale of Goods Act implies a condition that goods must comply with any description in the contract. The courts have construed this very strictly. Leading examples include *Re Moore and Landauer* (fruit packed in cases of 24 tins instead of 30 tins as specified in contract)[27] and *Arcos v Ronaasen* (contract required timber ½ inch thick, but most was fractionally wider).[28] Lord Wilberforce described these decisions as 'excessively technical and due for fresh examination' but as yet, this has not occurred.[29] Why are these decisions so criticized? In *Arcos*, Lord Atkin said that aside from 'microscopic deviations' ignored by the maxim *de minimis non curat lex*,

> A ton does not mean about a ton, or a yard about a yard. Still less when you descend to minute measurements does ½ inch mean about ½ inch. If the seller wants a margin he must and in my experience does stipulate for it.

However, the concern is that this stringent approach (one conducive to certainty) means that buyers frequently obtain an excuse, without any real reason, for rejecting contracts when prices have dropped.[30] Some would call this behaviour 'opportunistic'. It is a problem that Lord Atkin himself acknowledged – buyers are particularly keen to stand on their strict legal rights in a falling market. But, his Lordship claimed, these rights were not 'in excess of business needs'.

Brownsword is highly critical of this unconcern with the motives of the terminating party.[31] Surely, he asks, if we were designing the law afresh, the relevant question for termination would be whether the innocent party had good reason to withdraw from the contract. This could be met by showing, for example, the

---

[25] Cf. *Golodetz*, n.19 above.

[26] G.H. Treitel, *Some Landmarks of 20th Century Contract Law* (Clarendon Press, 2002).

[27] [1921] 2 KB 519.

[28] [1933] AC 470.

[29] *Reardon Smith Line Ltd v Hansen-Tangen* [1976] 1 WLR 989.

[30] *Shand v Bowes* (1877) LR 2 QBD 112 (Mellish LJ). But cf. (1877) LR 2 App Cas 455.

[31] R. Brownsword, 'Bad Faith, Good Reasons and Termination of Contracts' in J. Birds et al. (eds), *Termination of Contracts* (Wiley Chancery, 1995).

breaching party's lack of commitment to the contract, or inability to perform it, or doubtful solvency (so as to pay damages). Brownsword therefore argues that the traditional definition of conditions conferring 'peremptory' rights of withdrawal is mistaken – they should be treated only as *presumptive* rights to terminate, conditional on good reason being shown (unless the parties explicitly stipulate such a peremptory right). The current approach, by allowing withdrawal for collateral economic reasons, makes performance a matter of convenience only. A restrictive approach to termination would return contracts to an affair of *obligation*.

In 1994 the Sale of Goods Act was amended so that, under s.15A, a buyer may not reject goods for breach of one of the implied conditions where it is 'so slight that it would be unreasonable for him to reject them'. The Law Commission argued that it was an 'abuse' of the right to reject when breach was insignificant.[32] However, the Commission declined to define or list examples of 'abusive' behaviour by buyers, since cases are 'infinitely variable'.[33] This gives rise to the obvious criticism (really the same one as for innominate terms): how is the buyer faced with a breach of condition to know whether it is 'too slight' for him to reject? Apart from uncertainty, the legislation inadequately addresses the 'mischief'. S.15A does not expressly mandate an examination of the buyer's reasons for rejecting. No doubt courts might take motives into account, openly or otherwise. The same may indeed be true at common law where, according to Treitel, the innominate term has been used to curb 'what may, without being too tendentious, be called abuses of the right to reject'.[34] (It is noteworthy that in *The Hong Kong Fir*,[35] there had been a drastic fall in charter rates making the charterer keen to escape.) But the innominate term inquiry is also, in theory at least, about the seriousness of breach rather than the promisee's motives and good/bad faith. If Parliament or the courts are to create a novel jurisdiction of this kind, it should at least be done explicitly. Even applying the mechanical question of 'slightness' will not be easy – as Treitel observes, the difference between ½ and 9/16 inch in *Arcos* (one of the *bête noir* decisions) is by no means obviously 'slight', at least as a proportion.

Moreover, legal regulation of opportunistic behaviour sometimes creates as many problems as it solves. Where it is vaguely defined it provides fresh occasions for opportunism.[36] As seen, such vagueness is probably unavoidable, given the 'manifold' grounds of 'human errancy'.[37] How does vague regulation of opportunism mean more opportunism? Let us imagine that a seller realizes that goods are substandard but delivers them anyway. The buyer objects and threatens to reject the goods. The seller in turn warns the buyer that if he rejects, the seller will allege that the buyer has acted unreasonably under s.15A and therefore has no right to reject. This will place the buyer in a difficult position because if the seller

---

[32] Law Com No 160 'Sale and Supply of Goods' (1987), paras 4.18–4.19.
[33] Ibid, para 4.17.
[34] Treitel, n.26 above, p. 119.
[35] [1962] 2 QB 261.
[36] C.J. Goetz and R.E. Scott 'Principles of Relational Contract' (1981) 67 *Virginia LR* 1089.
[37] *Donoghue v Stevenson* [1932] AC 562, 619 (Lord Macmillan).

does ultimately convince the court that s.15A applies, the buyer (in wrongfully rejecting the goods) will *himself* be in breach of contract. Therefore the prudent buyer might well accept the goods in such a situation (unless perhaps the defects were so gross as to make the seller's s.15A argument untenable).

In other words, the vagueness of s.15A *may be used opportunistically by the seller*, to undermine the buyer's statutory right of rejection. This shows the 'reflexive' nature of opportunism.[38] Arguably, s.15A moves the implied terms a lot closer to warranties (where termination is never possible) than the conditions that they purport to be. (The same argument may be made for innominate terms.) It is notable that s.15A does not apply to *consumer* buyers – the Law Commission argued that this would undermine their rights (if sellers could threaten them with a counterclaim when the consumer purported to reject). Of course commercial buyers face absolutely the same problem. It is not at all clear why the law (as reformed) seems more concerned about buyer opportunism than seller opportunism. When similar reforms were discussed in the US, merchants argued that they could enforce 'commercial morality' against unreasonably rejecting buyers much more effectively than the law; the sanction would be damage to the buyer's reputation and unwillingness to do business with him in future.[39] The saving grace of s.15A is that it does not apply when 'a contrary intention appears in, or is to be implied from, the contract'. Nevertheless, it remains as a trap for the unwary.

It is worth noting that the courts, despite initial attraction,[40] rejected an extension of equity's 'relief against forfeiture' doctrine from its familiar property sphere (e.g. mortgages and leases) to charterparties. The problem occurs when the shipowner terminates the charter and withdraws it from service for non-payment of hire. Of course, this will be very advantageous to the owner, and damaging to the charterer, in a rising freight market. Nevertheless, Lord Diplock dismissed the relief as a 'beguiling heresy',[41] expressly approving the judgment of Robert Goff LJ. Goff LJ said that the 'policy which favours certainty in commercial transactions is so antipathetic to the form of equitable intervention invoked by the charterers' that it must be rejected.[42] Even if it were to be successfully invoked only in rare cases, it might be *raised* by charterers in many more and 'the mere possibility that it may be exercised can produce uncertainty, disputes and litigation, and so prevent parties from knowing where they stand'. In any event, large commercial parties could protect themselves by inserting a suitable clause in the contract, for example, the common 'anti-technicality' clause which requires notice to be given before termination.[43]

---

[38] D. Campbell, 'The Incompleteness of Our Understanding of the Law and Economics of Relational Contract' [2004] *Wisconsin L Rev* 645, 664–65.
[39] Z.B. Wiseman, 'The Limits of Vision: Karl Llewellyn and the Merchant Rules' (1987) 100 *Harvard LR* 465.
[40] *The Laconia* [1977] AC 850, 874 (Lord Simon of Glaisdale).
[41] *The Scaptrade* [1983] 2 AC 694.
[42] [1983] 1 QB 529.
[43] Construed strictly against ship-owners in *The Afovos* [1983] 1 WLR 195.

The Privy Council has subsequently held that the seller in a large commercial land transaction lawfully terminated the contract (and forfeited the buyer's deposit) when the buyer was ten minutes late in tendering the purchase price.[44] Absolute punctuality was imperative in the volatile Hong Kong property market. Following *The Scaptrade* Lord Hoffmann recognized that:

> Even if it is most unlikely that a discretion to grant relief will be exercised, its mere existence enables litigation to be employed as a negotiating tactic. The realities of commercial life are that this may cause injustice which cannot be fully compensated [1997] AC 514, 519.

It seems that the courts have, in cases involving large commercial parties, preferred the crisp rules in *Arcos* – leaving it for them to stipulate for leeway (such as a margin of error, or notice period) if protection is desired. Even Lord Denning MR accepted the need for clear rules that can be applied with speed, precision and certainty.[45] In this setting the insertion of a quasi abuse-of-rights doctrine into commercial sales in s.15A looks anomalous. But the courts are not consistent in their preference for clear-cut certainty, as shown by the innominate terms jurisprudence and some courts' construction of express termination clauses.

CONTROLLING TERMINATION: CONTRACT INTERPRETATION

Even where the parties expressly classify a term as a condition, the courts sometimes refuse to take this at face value. This reveals hostility to 'peremptory termination'. But the policy is given effect indirectly and not through the explicit rules, as discussed in the previous section. Atiyah observes that 'too little attention has hitherto been paid to what is involved in the technique of construction, a technique which has absorbed almost as much of the law of contract, as negligence has absorbed of the law of torts'.[46] This area is a good example.

The classic case is *Schuler v Wickman*.[47] It was stated to be 'a condition of this contract' that Wickman, Schuler's sales representatives, visit the six largest UK motor manufacturers at least once a week to solicit orders. There were 'considerable failures' in this regard (Lord Reid), and Schuler purported to terminate the contract. The question, according to Lord Reid, was whether any failure, however small, entitled Schuler to terminate. Given the number of visits that were required in total during the contract, his Lordship thought this was:

> so unreasonable that it must make me search for some other possible meaning of the contract. If none can be found then Wickman must suffer the consequences. But only if that is the only possible interpretation.

---

[44] *Union Eagle v Golden Achievement* [1997] AC 514.
[45] *The Laconia* [1976] QB 835, 849.
[46] P.S. Atiyah, 'Judicial Techniques and Contract Law' in *Essays on Contract* (Oxford University Press, 1990).
[47] [1974] AC 235.

Not surprisingly, faced with such a stiff test, Schuler lost. Another 'possible' interpretation was that the parties had not intended to use condition in its technical sense as justifying termination for any breach.

Lord Reid did not disguise his view that the condition approach was unreasonable, and that he would only be driven to hold that the parties intended it if they made their intention 'abundantly clear'. Lord Wilberforce dissented. Referring to the different nationalities of the companies in the litigation he said:

> to call the clause arbitrary, capricious or fantastic, or to introduce as a test of its validity the ubiquitous reasonable man (I do not know whether he is English or German) is to assume, contrary to the evidence, that both parties to this contract adopted a standard of easygoing tolerance rather than one of aggressive, insistent punctuality and efficiency. This is not an assumption I am prepared to make, nor do I think myself entitled to impose the former standard upon the parties if their words indicate, as they plainly do, the latter.

In other words, Lord Wilberforce saw no necessary objection to the 'condition' interpretation, and absolutely no justification for giving the contract its apparent plain meaning. *Schuler v Wickman* purports to be a disagreement about the meaning of words, but clearly this is a proxy for deeper disagreements about termination.

The moral of *Schuler* seems to be that using the word 'condition' is not enough to oblige the courts to treat a term as a condition. But in *Rice v Great Yarmouth BC* even a clause entitling the council to terminate with immediate effect for 'a breach of any of [the contractor's] obligations' failed to have this effect.[48] Hale LJ refused to accept that the 'draconian consequences' of termination could be visited upon the contractor for any breach, however small. His obligations (gardening services for the council) were 'multi-faceted' and could be breached in a number of ways, like seaworthiness in *The Hong Kong Fir*.[49] Accordingly, it was not any breach of contract which justified termination, but only if breaches were cumulatively serious enough.

Simon Whittaker is highly critical of this decision.[50] Does it not make a nonsense of the express words of the contract, by reintroducing the common law test of innominate terms? He suggests that the Court of Appeal might have been concerned by public law unlawfulness on the part of council officials (animus towards the contractor). But if so, this should have been tackled through judicial review, not by approaching contractual construction in a way inappropriate to the commercial sphere.[51] At best, *Rice* will serve to encourage ever more elaborate

---

[48] (2001) 3 LGLR 4.
[49] [1962] 2 QB 261.
[50] S. Whittaker, 'Termination Clauses' in A. Burrows & E. Peel (eds), *Contract Terms* (Oxford University Press, 2007).
[51] Where *Rice* has since been applied, cf. *Peregrine Systems v Steria* [2004] EWHC 275 (TCC).

and detailed termination clauses. At worst, it represents a judge-assumed power to review clauses' reasonableness without the sanction of legislation.

Whittaker criticizes this regulation-through-interpretation as an 'opaque' and 'uncertain' technique.[52] *Pace* Atiyah, the criticism has eminent judicial supporters. When relief against forfeiture of charterparties was rejected, the courts made it clear that it must not creep back indirectly. According to Lord Salmon, still less would it be acceptable for the courts to intervene by 'torturing the language of the charter in an effort to extract from it a meaning which it does not bear, but might, if it did, lead to a less harsh result'.[53] Goff LJ said that direct equitable relief was 'a far more attractive proposition than the distortion of contractual terms by an over-benevolent construction'.[54] Such warnings were ignored in *Schuler* and *Rice*.

As seen in Chapter 4, the starting point for contractual interpretation remains '*contra proferentem*', but the stringency of that rule has been relaxed in recent years.[55] In part this is due to the Unfair Contract Terms Act 1977, but also to the emphasis on 'natural interpretation' championed by Lord Hoffmann. Of course, this would also require the courts to enforce the plain meaning of conditions or termination clauses. UCTA probably has no direct relevance here,[56] but *consumers* can plausibly argue that peremptory termination is an unfair term contrary to the 1999 Regulations.[57] It is arguable that there is no need for strained construction of conditions in either consumer or commercial contracts. However, if courts persist in 'regulation-through-interpretation' draftsman will try to judge-proof termination clauses, as Whittaker says. The result may be a vicious circle of complex, prolix drafting.[58]

Debate 2

Should penalty clauses be allowed?

English law distinguishes between the agreement of liquidated damages (a genuine pre-estimate of loss) and unenforceable penalties (an amount 'extravagant and unconscionable ... in comparison with the greatest loss that could conceivably be proved').[59] The penalty doctrine is a major limit on the freedom to stipulate remedies for breach. Yet its basis is controversial and elusive. Diplock LJ once refused to attempt rationalization of the rule 'where so many others have failed', commenting only that it was *sui generis*.[60] This is damning politeness! The usual explanations are that penalties are assumed (or deemed) to be 'unconscionable',

---

[52] Whittaker, n.50 above, p. 283.
[53] *The Laconia* [1977] AC 850.
[54] *The Scaptrade* [1983] 1 QB 529.
[55] Cf. pp. 101–105 above.
[56] Whittaker, n.50 above, notes a debate about s.3(2)(b).
[57] N.B. Schedule 2, para (g), in particular.
[58] Cf. Lord Hoffmann in *Ali v BCCI* [2002] 1 AC 251 (pp. 103–104 above).
[59] *Dunlop Pneumatic Tyre Co Ltd v New Garage and Motor Co Ltd* [1915] AC 79.
[60] *Robophone Facilities v Blank* [1966] 1 WLR 1428.

or that there is a rule of 'policy' that only *compensatory* measures of damages (as favoured by the common law) may be stipulated. Neither of these is entirely convincing. Some economic explanations for the penalty rule have been offered, but these too have their weaknesses. Ultimately, the rule may have to be treated as a mere artefact of legal history.

LIQUIDATED DAMAGES

There are many advantages to the inclusion of a liquidated damages clause. As Andrew Burrows points out, it creates a debt rather than true 'damages'.[61] The stipulated sum is simply claimed as something to which the promisee is entitled (upon breach), and none of the quantification difficulties and limitations associated with damages for breach is applicable. This saves expenditure on enforcement for the parties and the public purse. Also, the exact liability is known from the outset, and both parties may insure accordingly. ('Limitation of damage' clauses may be seen as a species of liquidated damages.[62]) Against the cost savings, and increased certainty, must be set the cost of negotiating the clause in the first place.

A further advantage may be to ensure full compensation of the promisee. As noted, common law damages are limited by principles such as remoteness and mitigation. Moreover, through the (presumptive) bar on non-pecuniary damages, subjective or idiosyncratic values (i.e. in excess of the objective market value) are not protected. Goetz and Scott argue that an important role of the liquidated damages clause is to protect these interests.[63] The parties can go beyond the limits of common law damages when stipulating the agreed sum.

However, is this not in danger of being an unenforceable penalty, since (by definition) the sum will be higher than that awarded at common law? Probably not, since the classic formulation requires a pre-estimate of 'loss' rather than 'common law damages'. If damages will be difficult to prove after the event, that is a good reason to agree a sum in advance. Although it may well exceed what could be (proven and) recovered at law, the uncertainty gives the parties considerable freedom in their 'estimating' – the results (within outer limits of plausibility) are unlikely to be deemed penal. A study of holiday cancellations shows the difficulty of pre-estimating loss in practice.[64]

What of a sum which is higher because it includes losses not recoverable at law (even when proven)? In an old penalty case Lord Eldon recognized that someone might set an 'extraordinary value' on some item of property, that there was nothing irrational in this, and that it would thus be 'extremely difficult to apply with propriety the word "excessive" to the terms in which parties choose to contract'.[65]

---

[61] A. Burrows, *Remedies for Torts and Breach of Contract* (Oxford University Press, 3rd edn, 2004) p. 440.

[62] Cf. Harris, Campbell & Halson, n.7 above.

[63] C.J. Goetz & R.E. Scott, 'Liquidated Damages, Penalties and the Just Compensation Principle: Some Notes on An Enforcement Model and a Theory of Efficient Breach' (1977) 77 *Columbia LR* 554.

[64] A. Milner, 'Liquidated Damages: An Empirical Study in the Travel Industry' (1979) 42 *MLR* 508.

[65] *Astley v Weldon* (1801) 2 B & P 346

Diplock LJ held that including losses that would be too remote as damages did not render a clause penal.[66] Burrows accepts, more generally, that parties can contract out of common law rules such as mitigation (or the absence of contributory negligence).[67] Halson suggests (enigmatically) that this should depend on the policy of the rule in question.[68] Another way of putting the same point, perhaps, is to ask whether it is a default term (out of which parties may contract) or a mandatory rule that may not be altered. The better view seems to be that an estimate of actual losses rather than those legally recoverable is required. After all, limitations on damages are in principle enforceable (subject to UCTA).[69] If the parties can agree to under-compensatory remedies, why not to over-compensatory?

PENALTY CLAUSES

The utility of liquidated damages clauses is undermined by the penalty clause rule. It is difficult to draw the line between them – Collins remarks that there can be no clear distinction[70] – and the threat of litigation compromises the certainty that agreed damages are supposed to bring. What justifies this costly intrusion on freedom of contract?

Certain 'moralistic' explanations need not detain us long. It is sometimes suggested that the state must have a monopoly over coercion. But while there is good reason to regulate private use of force and imprisonment, it is not obvious that the financial incentives (or disincentives) provided in contracts raise the same concerns. Collins doubts that these are properly to be thought coercive.[71] Secondly, it is objected that people should not be able to bargain away their freedom (e.g. sell themselves into slavery). But all contracts limit the parties' future freedom of action to some extent. It seems melodramatic to suggest that commercial parties agreeing a penalty clause are enslaving themselves. The traditional description of a penalty clause may be one '*in terrorem*' but as Lord Radcliffe observed, 'penalties may quite readily be undertaken by parties who are not in the least terrorised by the prospect of having to pay them'.[72] Few penalties have the grotesque quality of Shylock's 'pound of flesh '.[73]

The historical explanation for the rule seems to be unconscionability. Equity intervened against penal bonds from the sixteenth century. However, as David Ibbetson points out, the jurisdiction was narrowly conceived by the courts in the eighteenth and nineteenth centuries.[74] But this 'emasculated' penalty doctrine

---

[66] *Robophone Facilities*, n.60 above.

[67] Burrows, n.61 above.

[68] Harris, Campbell & Halson, n.7 above at p.137.

[69] *Ailsa Craig Fishing v Malvern Fishing* [1983] 1 WLR 964.

[70] Collins, n.4 above, p. 374.

[71] Ibid, p. 377.

[72] *Campbell Discount v Bridge* [1962] AC 600.

[73] *The Merchant of Venice*, Act IV, Scene 1. This condition would anyway be unenforceable on public policy grounds.

[74] D.J. Ibbetson, *A Historical Introduction to the Law of Obligations* (Oxford University Press, 1999) pp. 213–14. Cf. n.65 above.

was then expanded in the leading *Dunlop Pneumatic Tyre Co Ltd v New Garage and Motor Co Ltd*[75] case under the influence of Scots law which treated the stipulation of sums to compel performance as 'unconscionable'.[76] But the unconscionability explanation seems both too broad and too narrow. It is over-broad because it applies to freely agreed contracts between sophisticated, well advised parties of equal bargaining power. There seems little room to infer advantage-taking in such cases.[77] Secondly, the penalty doctrine's limits mean it can be circumvented by clever drafting. It does not apply to sums payable other than on breach.[78] It does not apply to deposits even though it is recognized that a deposit 'creates by the fear of its forfeiture a motive in the payer to perform the rest of the contract'.[79] Since such clauses can, presumably, be unconscionable too, this rationale for the penalty doctrine would entail its extension to them.[80] But arguably there is no sensible stopping point. As Goetz and Scott suggest, 'There is no reason to presume that liquidated damages provisions are more susceptible to duress or other bargaining aberrations than other contractual allocations of risk'.[81] If so, there is no obvious need for any special regulation beyond the ordinary unconscionability doctrine.

The test for a penalty is 'firmly based on the loss concept' that prevails in the law of contract damages.[82] Burrows says that the most 'straightforward' and 'powerful' argument against penalty clauses is that they contradict the usual compensatory principle.[83] But this is not self-evident. Burrows, as seen, accepts that the parties may contract out of certain limits in the law on damages. Why does this not extend to the 'compensatory principle' itself? Why should it be treated as a mandatory rule whereas, for example, mitigation and remoteness are only default rules? Burrows offers no explanation.

Burrows notes that hostility to penal remedies for breach of contract has been weakening. The account of profits ordered in *A-G v Blake* is a prime example.[84] However, that case is probably to be confined to its extreme facts – extensions to mainstream commercial cases have been criticized.[85] Burrows argues that penalty clauses should now be enforceable, but only where the law itself awards penal remedies. So a clause requiring disgorgement of profits should be allowed in *Blake*-like situations, but not in ordinary commercial contracts.[86] Burrows sees the penalty doctrine as standing (or falling) with the 'compensation principle'.

---

[75] [1915] AC 79.

[76] Ibbetson, n.74 above, pp. 255–56.

[77] Cf. pp. 204–205 above.

[78] *Export Credits Guarantee Dept v Universal Oil Products* [1983] 2 All ER 205.

[79] *Howe v Smith* (1884) 27 Ch D 89.

[80] Cf. Law Com Consultation Paper 61 (1974).

[81] Cf. n.63 above.

[82] Harris, Campbell & Halson, n.7 above, p. 138.

[83] Burrows, n.61 above, p. 451.

[84] [2001] 1 AC 268. Cf. D. Fox, 'Restitutionary Damages to Deter Breach of Contract' [2001] *CLJ* 33 and pp. 254–257 below.

[85] E.g. *Esso Petroleum Co Ltd v Niad Ltd* [2001] EWHC Ch 458; J Beatson, (2002) 118 LQR 377.

[86] Burrows, n.61 above, p. 445.

We discuss in Chapter 9 the common law's preference for compensating loss rather than compelling performance (or penalizing breach). Campbell and Harris criticize *Blake*.[87] They lament that the only justification offered for the radical outcome was 'abstract restitutionary reasoning'.[88] What would have been more convincing, they argue, is evidence that promisees are dissatisfied with the current rate of breach and wish for legal remedies to curb it. They think it 'extremely likely' that parties are, on the contrary, content with the traditional position which allows 'efficient breaches' of contract.[89] But this could be disproved by citing contract clauses requiring the disgorgement of profits from breach. For Campbell and Harris, it is axiomatic that such supra-compensatory clauses should be enforced. For these authors, it is the parties' intentions that should lead the law of damages and not – as for Burrows – vice versa. Burrows tacitly assumes that the compensatory principle is a mandatory rule, from which no escape is permissible. Is there any reason of policy for such an approach? Economic analysis has suggested some possible justifications.

ECONOMIC ANALYSIS OF PENALTY CLAUSES

Aristides Hatzis notes that this is one of the few issues in contract law and economics where commentators disagree widely.[90] However, a number of cogent arguments in defence of the penalty rule have been made. The most prominent relies on the concept of 'efficient breach'.[91] The basic idea is that breach of contract can sometimes be an economically good thing that (therefore) lowers the parties' costs. Economically rational contractors therefore do not wish to obstruct such breaches (compare the comments of Campbell and Harris in the previous section). Penalty clauses, being designed to discourage breach, are inconsistent with the economically optimal outcome. Therefore, according to the 'efficient breach' theory, they should be invalid.

This is a clear defence of the penalty rule but there are difficulties with it. First it assumes the validity of the 'efficient breach' analysis, but this is by no means clear. Secondly, as Goetz and Scott point out, a penalty clause does not necessarily rule out 'efficient breaches'.[92] The stipulated sum may exceed the promisee's loss, but if it requires only *partial* disgorgement of the breaching party's profits, he will still have economic reason for 'efficient' (i.e. profitable, or loss-saving) breach.[93] Thirdly, and most fundamentally, the argument is a paternalistic one. It tells the parties that they cannot have a penalty clause because, as economically rational

---

[87] D. Campbell & D. Harris, 'In Defence of Breach' [2002] *Legal Studies* 208.

[88] Ibid, p. 233.

[89] Cf. pp. 238–243 below.

[90] A.N. Hatzis, 'Having the Cake and Eating It Too: Efficient Penalty Clauses in Common and Civil Contract Law' (2003) 22 *Int Rev Law & Economics* 381.

[91] Cf. pp. 238–243 below.

[92] Cf. n.63 above. Cf. T. Wilkinson-Ryan, 'Do Liquidated Damages Encourage Breach? A Psychological Experiment' (2010) 108 *Michigan LR* 633.

[93] There is also the possibility of parties 'bargaining round' the penalty, after breach. Cf. pp. 241–243 below.

parties, they ought to favour efficient breach. But as Posner J argues, the parties have presumably weighed the costs (that efficient breaches might be deterred) against the benefits of the penalty clause; why should the court impose its own view? It also seems 'odd that courts should display parental solicitude for large corporations' (as were the parties in that case).[94] Even if the efficient default rule compensates loss (rather than compelling performance) the parties should be free to contract out of it.

Another problem is that the paternalistic intervention of the penalty doctrine, which is supposed to prevent the conferral of a supposed windfall on the promisee, results in an actual windfall for the promisor.[95] He will have been paid a premium price to agree to a supra-compensatory clause. If it is declared unenforceable by the court, the promisor keeps this premium without bearing the burden. Accordingly, Halson argues that if the penalty doctrine is retained the court should revise the contract to adjust downward the price paid by the promisee.[96]

An alternative defence of the penalty rule is proposed by Clarkson, Miller and Muris.[97] They correctly note that if the clause is truly supra-compensatory, the promisee will be better off in the event of breach than if the contract is performed. Therefore, the promisee will have an incentive to bring about breach of the contract. This might be possible to do (but hard to detect) in situations where the promisor needs the promisee's co-operation for performance. Such behaviour is wasteful – the promisee expends resources trying to induce breach and the promisor in trying to defend himself. But this game makes neither party better off – no valuable goods or services are produced. Accordingly, the courts should discourage it by not enforcing clauses which are supra-compensatory when the promisee has the opportunity to engage in hard-to-detect obstruction of performance.

Hatzis argues that the promisor can defend himself against such opportunism by the inclusion of suitable terms in the contract.[98] However as Clarkson, Miller and Muris pointed out, such defensive measures are themselves expensive. Hatzis also underrates the difficulty not only of detecting the obstructionism but *proving* it to the court. Knoeber suggests a different way to curb promisee opportunism.[99] If the penalty is paid to a third party rather than to the promisee himself, the promisor has incentive to perform while the promisee (who no longer benefits directly) has no reason to engineer breach. This mechanism is apparently common in agriculture, where vegetable growers pay a fine to their trade association (in addition to damages to the buyer) if they break forward supply contracts, e.g. to take advantage of a rising market. In the end, however, freedom of contract is the

---

[94] *Lake River v Carborundum Co* (1985) 769 F.2d 1284.

[95] Hatzis, n.90 above.

[96] Harris, Campbell & Halson, n.7 above, 147.

[97] K.W. Clarkson, R.L. Miller & T.J. Muris, 'Liquidated Damages v. Penalties: Sense or Nonsense?' [1978] *Wisconsin LR* 351.

[98] Cf. n.90 above.

[99] C.R. Knoeber, 'An Alternative Mechanism to Assure Contractual Reliability' (1983) 12 *JLS* 333.

main response to Clarkson et al. As Hatzis says, the parties must be taken to have weighed the benefits of the penalty against the costs of possible opportunism. It is paternalism for the court to refuse to enforce it.

Real-world contracting parties do not always act rationally. Psychologists and economists have begun to model the irrational nature of much decision making.[100] Robert Hillman notes that some of those limitations on rationality may justify the penalty rule.[101] For example, people tend to give too little emphasis to remote future possibilities, especially adverse events like breach of contract, given the 'optimism bias'. Therefore they may pay little attention to a penalty clause, perhaps justifying judicial intervention. But there seem to be just as many reasons against intervention: if people feel strongly enough to contract out of the rules on damages this suggests that they have thought it through. Also, where would we stop – should the court be able to re-write the entire contract because of cognitive biases? And what of the cognitive limitations of the judges themselves? Hillman concludes that behavioural law and economics cannot justify the penalty rule.

The economic case in favour of enforcing penalties has largely been covered already. They reflect the parties' deliberate allocation of risk. Also, where one party really desires performance (rather than compensation in lieu), perhaps because of very high subjective value (e.g. photography for a wedding) and is willing to pay the premium necessary to secure the promisor's agreement, why should the penalty not be enforceable? One further point is that agreeing to performance on pain of penalty can be used to signal reliability.[102] Dnes suggests that new firms are deterred from bidding for government contracts in the UK because they cannot signal their credibility through penalty clauses.[103] This makes public tendering less competitive than it otherwise might be. This is a public cost of the penalty rule.

CONCLUSIONS

The penalty doctrine can be explained as a mere historical artefact of the common law. As seen above, its contemporary form is only a century old, and derives from Scottish influence. *Dunlop Pneumatic Tyre Co Ltd v New Garage and Motor Co Ltd*[104] was also influenced by the South African view that the promisee would be 'unjustly enriched' by the penal sum.[105] This is ironic since it seems that the Civilian tradition has long welcomed penalty clauses, from classical Roman law

---

[100] E.g. D. Kahneman, P. Slovic & A. Tversky, *Judgment Under Uncertainty: Heuristics and Biases* (New York: Cambridge University Press, 1982); C.R. Sunstein (ed.), *Behavioral Law & Economics* (Cambridge University Press, 2000).

[101] R.A. Hillman, 'The Limits of Behavioural Decision Theory in Legal Analysis: The Case of Liquidated Damages' (2000) 85 *Cornell LR* 717.

[102] *Lake River*, n.94 above, 1289 (Posner J).

[103] A.N. Dnes, *The Economics of Law* (Thomson, 1996) p.99.

[104] [1915] AC 79.

[105] Cf. Ibbetson, n.74 above, p. 255; *Hills v Colonial Government* (1904) 21 SCC 59, 78–79.

onward.[106] Even if this is now in decline,[107] Hatzis contends that Civil law shows its clear economic superiority to the common law in this matter.[108]

English law is now softening its stance to penalties. Colman J held it would be 'highly regrettable' if the enhanced rates of interest on international loans were unenforceable in London when they were enforceable in rival financial centres such as New York.[109] In *Murray v Leisureplay*, the court similarly took account of commercial practice and expectations, as well as the parties' reasons for stipulating a sum which exceeded common law damages.[110] In *Phillips Hong Kong v A-G of Hong Kong* Lord Woolf warned that

> the court has to be careful not to set too stringent a standard and bear in mind that what the parties have agreed should normally be upheld. Any other approach will lead to undesirable uncertainty especially in commercial contracts.[111]

Thus in commercial cases there is a strong presumption in favour of enforceability. After all, there can be little danger of 'unconscionability'. On the other hand, Diplock LJ said that the penalty rule had not 'outlived its usefulness' 'in these days when so often one party cannot satisfy his contractual hunger *a la carte* but only at the *table d'hote* of a standard printed contract'.[112] There is a case for protecting consumers faced with such 'contracts of adhesion'.[113] But this is surely not a problem limited to penalty clauses. Consumers now enjoy the general protection of the Unfair Terms in Consumer Contracts Regulations 1999, where paragraph (e) in Schedule 2 specifically recognizes a term requiring payment of 'disproportionately high … compensation' as presumptively unfair. This seems quite adequate to protect those most vulnerable to 'unfair' penalties (in addition to equitable doctrines such as unconscionability). Accordingly, Louise Gullifer has suggested that there is no reason to retain the common law penalty doctrine.[114] Abolition may be the way ahead although it is not currently on the law reform agenda.[115]

Further Reading

K.W. Clarkson, R.L. Miller & T.J. Muris, 'Liquidated Damages v. Penalties: Sense Or Nonsense?' [1978] *Wisconsin LR* 351.

---

[106] R. Zimmermann, *The Law of Obligations: Roman Foundations of the Civilian Tradition* (Oxford, 1990) pp. 95–113.
[107] Cf. U. Mattei, 'The Comparative Law and Economics of Penalty Clauses in Contracts' (1995) 43 *American Journal of Comparative Law* 427.
[108] Hatzis, n.90 above.
[109] *Lordsdale Finance v Bank of Zambia* [1996] QB 752.
[110] [2005] EWCA Civ 963.
[111] (1993) 61 BLR 41.
[112] *Robophone Facilities*, n.60 above.
[113] Cf. pp. 85–87 above.
[114] L. Gullifer, 'Agreed Remedies' in A. Burrows & E. Peel (eds) *Commercial Remedies: Current Issues and Problems* (Oxford University Press, 2003).
[115] Cf. Scottish Law Commission Report 171, Penalty Clauses (1999).

C.R. Knoeber, 'An Alternative Mechanism to Assure Contractual Reliability' (1983) 12 *JLS* 333.

R. Brownsword, 'Bad Faith, Good Reasons and Termination of Contracts' in J. Birds et al. (eds), *Termination of Contracts* (Wiley Chancery, 1995).

L. Gullifer, 'Agreed Remedies' in A. Burrows & E. Peel (eds) *Commercial Remedies: Current Issues and Problems* (Oxford University Press, 2003).

A.N. Hatzis, 'Having the Cake and Eating It Too: Efficient Penalty Clauses in Common and Civil Contract Law' (2003) 22 *Int Rev Law & Economics* 381.

S. Whittaker, 'Termination Clauses' in A. Burrows & E. Peel (eds), *Contract Terms* (Oxford University Press, 2007).

9

JUDICIAL REMEDIES: PERFORMANCE OR COMPENSATION?

INTRODUCTION

Every breach of contract gives rise to remedies as a matter of law, even when the contract is silent on the question. These judicial remedies (damages and specific performance) are ultimately default rules out of which the parties may contract.[1] As Epstein puts it, 'The operative rules should be chosen by the parties for their own purposes, not by the law for its purposes'.[2] Nevertheless, the rules applying in default of party agreement illuminate the basis of obligation as perceived by contract lawyers. In particular, remedies point up the contrast between 'moral' and 'instrumental' approaches to law. This is the most hotly contested area of contract theory.

It might seem obvious that remedies should enforce the promisee's *right* to performance of the contract, and redress the *wrong* of the promisor's breach. This corresponds to the remedies of specific performance (enforcing the contract) and damages (compensating losses caused by breach). But some would challenge the basic assumptions. Is there really a 'right' to performance? Is breach meaningfully a 'wrong' that should be condemned and even punished? Waddams comments that while there is a public interest in discouraging, for example, torts, a breach of contract is by contrast not 'inherently objectionable'. Breaches are wrongful 'only in the sense that a private agreement has made them so'.[3] Lawyer-economists have argued that breach can be economically beneficial ('efficient') and that such breach should be tolerated, even encouraged, by the law. If that is correct then speaking of a 'right' to performance in all cases is a distraction from efficient contracting.

Exploring the various 'interests' that might be protected through contract remedies can be traced to a seminal 1936 article by Fuller and Purdue.[4] Daniel

---

[1] In practice written contracts commonly make explicit provision for remedies: cf. Collins, p. 211 above.
[2] R.A. Epstein, 'Beyond Foreseeability: Consequential Damages in the Law of Contract' (1989) 18 *JLS* 105, 108.
[3] S.M. Waddams, 'Gains Derived from Breach of Contract' in D. Saidov & R. Cunnington (eds) *Contract Damages: Domestic and International Perspectives* (Hart Publishing, 2008) p. 196.
[4] L.L. Fuller & W.R. Purdue, 'The Reliance Interest in Contract Damages' (1936) 46 *Yale LJ* 52 and 373.

Friedmann argues that the substance of their analysis is mistaken – the 'reliance interest' should not take precedence over the 'expectation' (or 'performance') interest.[5] But Kreitner argues that any theory, like Friedmann's, which aims at a single unified explanation oversimplifies the matter; such reductionism attempts too much and explains too little.[6] Kreitner advocates a richer account. The leading cases involve a range of competing considerations.[7] Lon Fuller himself did not simply argue for the priority of reliance damages – he believed there was a spectrum of enforceability (although Fuller realized that this would offend lawyers who desire simplicity – '*elegantia juris*').[8] Fuller began with the range of remedies and asked what social purposes they might further, whereas Friedmann (for example) starts from the position that a 'contractually binding promise' must be enforced by law.

Richard Craswell argues that Fuller and Purdue's taxonomy (the expectation, reliance and restitution interests) is no longer useful in analysing the modern law.[9] Whichever purpose we might identify for contract law (whether efficiency, morality, redistribution etc), it does not correspond to their tripartite classification. Craswell finds that the principles underlying judicial decisions about remedies cut across Fuller and Purdue's categories. So not all cases awarding 'reliance' damages have the same rationale. Sometimes they are a proxy for hard-to-assess 'expectations'.[10] In other cases awarding reliance (e.g. contracts which are unenforceable for formalities reasons) the quantum is quite deliberately below the 'expectation' level. Referring to a single 'reliance' interest obscures these differences (and the link between the former cases and 'expectation' damages).

Craswell therefore proposes a different classification. His starting point is the expectation interest as the standard remedy. Secondly, there are remedies that *exceed* the expectation interest (e.g. punitive damages or account of profits). Thirdly, there are cases where the remedy is *below* the expectation interest (some reliance and restitution awards; most cases where damages are limited by doctrines such as mitigation or remoteness). It might appear that, cut it as you like, the law of remedies (like Caesar's Gaul) is divided into three parts!

Arguably, however, both Fuller's and Craswell's taxonomies underplay the most important division of all, between rights and wrongs. Should contract remedies primarily be concerned with the enforcement of the right to contractual performance? Or with redressing the wrong of breach, by compensating the losses flowing from it? It is usually thought that in the common law, contract remedies are concerned with the latter, and that performance is a secondary concern. But this is increasingly questioned. Scholars have argued with some success for the

---

[5] D. Friedmann, 'The Performance Interest in Contract Damages' (1995) 111 *LQR* 628.

[6] R. Kreitner, 'Multiplicity in Contract Remedies' in N. Cohen & E. McKendrick (eds), *Comparative Remedies for Breach of Contract* (Hart Publishing, 2005) p. 28.

[7] Kreitner suggests the 'cost of cure' debate: cf. *Ruxley Electronics v Forsyth* [1996] AC 344.

[8] Cf. letter from Fuller to Karl Llewellyn, quoted Kreitner ibid at pp. 22–33.

[9] R. Craswell, 'Against Fuller and Purdue' (2000) 67 *Univ Chicago LR* 99.

[10] Cf. M.B. Kelly, 'The Phantom Reliance Interest in Contract Damages' [1992] *Wisconsin LR* 1755; *The Mamola Challenger* [2011] 1 Lloyd's Rep 47.

expansion of performance-oriented remedies both old (specific performance) and new (account of profits; 'substitutionary damages'). Much of Craswell's second (supra-expectation) group falls into this category. The calls to shift emphasis onto performance are the subject of this chapter.

The Debate

Should contract remedies enforce performance?

The primary remedy for breach of contract is damages. Their aim is to compensate the promisee's losses from breach. Often there may be no loss, as when substitute performance is readily available in the market at a price no higher than the contract price. Here, damages will be nominal only. The promisee must mitigate his losses by employing the substitute. English law traditionally does not award supra-compensatory damages to deter breach. The court does have discretion to order the promisor to perform, but 'specific performance' is awarded only when damages would be 'inadequate'.

This picture is in many ways puzzling. Why are the law's default remedies not designed to ensure performance? (Furthermore, note the hostility to party-agreed incentives to perform, such as penalty clauses.[11]) Is obtaining performance not the whole point of entering into a contract in the first place? On this view, the law of contract remedies is seriously defective. Specific performance should be the primary remedy where possible, bolstered by remedies tailored to deter breach (punitive damages and disgorgement of the profits of breach). The arguments for this position are clear, powerful and increasingly influential.

The structure of remedies indicates that English law does not take the right to performance (and the wrong of breach) seriously. If we accept the law as it is rather than dismissing it, this suggests that such a right does not, in fact, exist. This seems to pose a jurisprudential dilemma: should lawyers start from 'first principles', or with the legal rules as they are? However, there is also a theoretical defence of the status quo's toleration of breach and failure to enforce performance. Economic analysis of law has attempted to prove that breach of contract may be positively desirable, improving the position of the parties and society generally, and making better use of scarce resources. This theory is offensive to those who believe that contracts are morally binding promises. But any amorality is cheerfully accepted by lawyer-economists, taking their cue from Oliver Wendell Holmes. However the 'efficient breach' theory has also been attacked from within, that is its economic coherence has been questioned.

We examine these main theoretical perspectives on performance-oriented remedies first, focusing on specific performance. Then we turn to the other remedies affected by the debate – 'substitutive' remedies, punitive damages, disgorgement and restitution. At the heart of the matter the same question arises in each

---

[11] Cf. pp. 223–228 above.

case: should the primary concern of contract remedies be to enforce performance or not?

RIGHTS AND REMEDIES

Lionel Smith characteristically argues that for English contract law to 'take contractual rights seriously' it must protect them (ideally) by enforcing the contract.[12] This syllogism between rights and (performance) remedies is common and seems intuitively obvious. Many would accept without further argument that there is a right to performance and that the law should enforce it. In Fried's celebrated 'promissory' account the point is dealt with very briefly; Fried thinks it incontestable that 'to the extent that contract is grounded in promise, it seems natural to measure relief by the expectation'.[13]

A number of responses are, however, possible. Craswell points out that since the court is imposing a default remedy rather than enforcing any explicit promise, 'any remedy the court picks will be equally consistent (or equally inconsistent) with "the will of the parties"'.[14] We have seen above that terms 'implied by law' into contracts across the board have no connection with party intentions (or in Fried's words, their promises).[15] More generally, the method of deduction from an abstract right has been questioned. Corbin suggested that the common law does not have 'any substratum of grand eternal principles' and that any argument from principle 'almost always involves a subtle begging of the question'.[16] Thus Kreitner criticizes the rights-based theories for assuming that contracts must be enforced, when the extent to which they are binding is precisely the question at issue.[17]

A more developed argument builds an analogy with property rights. Lionel Smith argues that the *only* difference between property and contractual rights is the class against whom they may be enforced: property binds the whole world whereas a contract binds only the parties to it.[18] But the distinction does not require that contractual rights are enforceable to a lesser *extent*. Smith argues, following Friedmann,[19] that just as property cannot be taken without the owner's permission, even with payment of damages, so contracts must be performed (rather than breached with payment). This is true even when the 'borrower' might value the property more highly than the owner – as Friedmann observes there is no doctrine of 'efficient theft'.

---

[12] L. Smith, 'Understanding Specific Performance' in N. Cohen & E. McKendrick (eds), *Comparative Remedies for Breach of Contract* (Hart Publishing, 2005).

[13] C. Fried, *Contract as Promise* (Harvard University Press, 1981) p. 18.

[14] Craswell, n.9 above, p. 133.

[15] Cf. pp. 111–119 above.

[16] A.L. Corbin, 'The Restatement of the Common Law by the American Law Institute' (1929) 15 *Iowa LR* 19, 35.

[17] Kreitner, n.6 above, p. 35.

[18] L. Smith, 'Disgorgement of the Profits of Breach of Contract: Property, Contract and "Efficient Breach"' (1994) 24 *Can Bus LJ* 121.

[19] D. Friedmann, 'The Efficient Breach Fallacy' (1989) 18 *JLS* 1.

A number of responses are possible. Friedmann's 'efficient theft' argument gains its powerful rhetorical impact from the crime of stealing, treated as a serious wrong as far back as the Twelve Tables of Rome (449 BC), and the biblical Ten Commandments. Yet breach of contract is, of course, not a criminal offence, and even those who strenuously proclaim its wrongfulness, like Friedmann, have not called for its criminalization. Criminal rhetoric aside, it is misleading to suggest that all property rights receive the same (very high) level of protection in private law. An order for re-delivery of wrongfully detained goods (rather than damages) is available only when the court in its discretion thinks it appropriate, and not as of right.[20] The tort of conversion does not apply at all to intangible 'property'.[21] In the tort of nuisance (protecting the use and enjoyment of land), the court sometimes awards damages in lieu of an injunction to restrain the infringement,[22] similarly with infringement of restrictive covenants,[23] although in both cases an injunction is the primary remedy.[24]

Guido Calabresi and Douglas Melamed influentially analyse the degree to which entitlements *should* be protected.[25] Some rights are protected by criminalization or within private law, by a 'property rule' or 'liability rule'. In the former, interference with the entitlement is prohibited (e.g. by injunction). This means that for it to pass from the holder to another, there must be negotiated agreement on the transfer and its price, whereas under a 'liability rule' the law will not restrain interference with the entitlement. This means that it may be unilaterally appropriated with payment to the holder of damages (as assessed by the law). Under this framework, even real property rights are not automatically entitled to specific relief (Calabresi and Melamed's discussion focuses on nuisance). As seen above, this corresponds to the position in English law. If the protection of property rights is more nuanced than Friedmann's 'efficient theft' assumes, then *a fortiori* we cannot assume that contracts *must* as a matter of doctrinal logic always be enforced. According to Craswell, hardly any scholars since Calabresi and Melamed 'would assert that, by defining the right at issue, we have automatically defined the appropriate remedy'.[26]

Elsewhere, Friedmann has accepted that 'the mere recognition of a specific right does not provide answers to all issues regarding the remedies available for its protection'.[27] However, neither (he claims) does it tell us nothing. The remedy for breach of contract is not 'completely divorced from the nature of the right' as Fuller and Purdue assumed. Just as it 'follows as a matter of course' that a property owner is entitled to return of misappropriated property or the equivalent

---

[20] Torts (Interference with Goods) Act 1977, s.3.

[21] *OBG Ltd v Allan* [2008] 1 AC 1, criticized S. Green, 'The Subject Matter of Conversion' [2010] *JBL* 218.

[22] E.g. *Miller v Jackson* [1977] QB 966; *Dennis v MoD* [2003] EWHC 793 (QB).

[23] E.g. *Wrotham Park Estate v Parkside Homes* [1974] 1 WLR 798.

[24] *Shelfer v City of London Electric Lighting Co* [1895] 1 Ch. 287.

[25] G. Calabresi & A.D. Melamed, 'Property Rules, Liability Rules and Inalienability: One View of the Cathedral' (1972) 85 *Harvard LR* 1089.

[26] Craswell, n.9 above, p. 123.

[27] Friedmann, n.5 above.

in damages, so it is 'obvious' that contract remedies must protect the perform-ance interest. On this simple basis, Fuller and Purdue's championing of 'reliance damages' is wrong.

Friedmann's position seems to be that the existence of a right to contractual performance tells us nearly everything (although not perhaps absolutely every-thing) about the remedy to protect it. Such sweeping reasoning is not, perhaps, entirely convincing as a response to P.S. Atiyah's thoughtful defence of the 'reli-ance' approach.[28] Atiyah suggests it is also obvious that relied-upon promises are worthier of legal protection than purely executory agreements. Atiyah therefore rejects the central place in contract theory given to the protection of execu-tory contracts through performance remedies. Why should people not be able to change their minds before performance has commenced? With the partially carried-out agreement as an alternative paradigm, Atiyah questions whether performance remedies are appropriate, rather than compensating detrimental reli-ance (or reversing benefits conferred). Is there a *right* to contractual performance or not?

HOLMES AND CONTRACTUAL RIGHTS

Oliver Wendell Holmes famously remarked that: 'The duty to keep a contract at common law means a prediction that you must pay damages if you do not keep it – and nothing else'.[29] Therefore, the 'so-called primary rights and duties' in contract have been 'invested with a mystic significance beyond what can be assigned and explained'. Holmes did not ignore specific performance, but approved of its secondary nature: promisors undertake *either* performance *or* the payment of damages *at their election*.[30] This fits with Holmes's insight that contracts are often best understood as devices for the allocation of risk. As a matter of law one can validly 'promise' that it will rain tomorrow, and be liable in damages if it does not, even though the weather is (obviously) outside one's control. The promisor is not really promising to make it rain but is undertaking the risk of it not happening and to pay damages if it does not. Specific performance has no role to play in such financial apportionment of risks. The analysis is equally valid for a contract to deliver a bale of cotton.[31]

Holmes's claim that there is no duty to perform a contract (and thus no right to have it performed) has been much criticized. If it is correct, then how can there be logical room for the doctrine of frustration when it is never impossible to pay damages?[32] Pollock argued that a man 'bespeaking a coat from his tailor will scarcely be persuaded that he is only betting with the tailor that the coat will not

[28] P.S. Atiyah, *Essays on Contract* (Oxford University Press, 1990), ch. 2 and pp. 87–89, 167–78.

[29] O.W. Holmes, 'The Path of the Law' (1897) 10 *Harvard LR* 457.

[30] Ibid, citing *Bromage v Genning* (1617) 1 Rolle 368.

[31] Holmes, *The Common Law* (1881) 299–300. Cf. p. 126 above.

[32] R. Stevens, 'Damages and the Right to Performance: A *Golden Victory* or Not?' in J. Neyers et al. (eds), *Exploring Contract Law* (Hart Publishing, 2009) p. 172.

be made'.[33] As Buckland said, 'One does not buy a right to damages, one buys a horse',[34] and Oliver LJ agrees that 'the purpose of a contract is performance and not the grant of an option to pay damages'.[35] Friedmann avers that 'contracts are made in order to be performed' – 'usually the one and only ground for their formation'.[36] There is empirical corroboration of these intuitive points. Bernstein reports that commercial parties buying cotton for use in weaving desire delivery of the cotton itself (on which their operations depend), not compensation in lieu.[37] Baron and Wilkinson-Ryan find a widespread social attitude that failure to perform a contract is morally wrong, even when full expectation damages are paid.[38]

Holmes accepted that his approach would offend 'those who think it advantageous to get as much ethics into the law as they can'.[39] Holmes's distinctly amoral theory of contract obligation does explain several differences between the common and civil law. In theory at least, specific performance is the primary remedy in Civilian systems.[40] Richard Posner argues that this explains why civilians generally require fault for liability for breach of contract,[41] in contrast with the common law where Lord Edmund-Davies 'axiomatically' says it is, in general, 'immaterial why the defendant failed to fulfil his obligation, and certainly no defence to plead that he had done his best.'[42] On Holmes's theory the promisor is only insuring the promisee against the risk of non-performance, and providing he pays up he has not really done anything wrong. (As seen, he may 'promise' things that are wholly outside his control; fault-based liability would be impossible here.) But, Posner says, where courts routinely order promisors to perform on pain of punishment, this can hardly take place on a no-fault basis.[43] Thus, Holmes described deep-rooted and distinctive institutions of the common law of contract: both the strictness of liability and the primacy of damages.

The finding that Holmes's theory is at odds with commercial expectations would presumably have troubled him more than its immorality. However, Markovits and Schwartz have recently argued that promises in commercial

---

[33] F. Pollock, *Principles of Contract* (Stevens, 3rd edn, 1881) p.xix.

[34] W.W. Buckland, 'The Nature of Contractual Obligation' (1944) 8 *CLJ* 247 (citing Digest 18.4.21).

[35] *George Mitchell v Finney Lock Seeds* [1983] QB 284, 304.

[36] Friedmann, n.5 above.

[37] L. Bernstein, 'Private Commercial Law in the Cotton Industry: Creating Cooperation through Rules, Norms, and Institutions' (2001) 99 *Michigan LR* 1724, 1755–56.

[38] J. Baron and T. Wilkinson-Ryan, 'Moral Judgment and Moral Heuristics in Breach of Contract' (2009) 6 *Jo Empirical Legal Stud* 405.

[39] Holmes, 'The Path of the Law', n.29 above.

[40] Cf. PECL art. 9:102, n.2: 'The basic differences between common law and civil law are of theoretical rather than practical importance.'

[41] For the 'ethical credo' in Germany, cf. S Grundmann, 'The Fault Principle as a Chameleon of Contract Law: A Market Function Approach' in O. Ben-Shahar & A. Porat (eds), *Fault in American Contract Law* (Cambridge University Press, 2010) pp. 43–44.

[42] *Raineri v Miles* [1981] AC 1050, 1086. Cf. G.H. Treitel, 'Fault in the Common Law of Contract' in M. Bos & I. Brownlie (eds) *Liber Amicorum for the Rt Hon Lord Wilberforce* (Clarendon, 1987).

[43] R.A. Posner, 'Let Us Never Blame a Contract Breaker' in O. Ben-Shahar & A. Porat (eds), *Fault in American Contract Law* (Cambridge University Press, 2010).

contracts should after all be interpreted 'disjunctively', either to perform or to pay damages. Thus payment of damages is not a breach of contract.[44] They claim that every rational promisee would prefer this 'liability rule' (in Calabresi and Melamed's terminology) to a 'property rule' (i.e. specific performance). Thus, disjunctive obligations should be seen as a term 'implied in fact' (i.e. by the implicit intentions of the parties). A promisor will charge a higher price for a good or service when he is prevented from breaching. The promisee will prefer the expectation damages regime and the lower price that it brings because this rule has lower costs associated with it.

The 'transaction cost' approach to contract performance will be considered below. Markovits and Schwartz's claim that a promisor who promptly pays damages is not in breach of contract is controversial. It follows logically from their (and Holmes's) view that this is an option that the promisor may freely take. But it does seem at odds with the usual language of 'breach'.[45] To say the least, they would redefine the concept of breach in an unfamiliar way. Moreover, is it not immoral to pay damages instead of performing, as researchers have found? Markovits and Schwartz accept that this is true, but in certain cases only, viz. family and marital relationships (and perhaps certain long-term business ventures based on sharing). It would be a 'category mistake' to offer $50 as compensation for failing to cook a promised dinner for one's family! But this hardly applies to a factory's failure to supply widgets.

Baron and Wilkinson-Ryan similarly argue that societal condemnation of breach of contract (even when damages are paid) is an 'overgeneralized heuristic'.[46] That is to say a rule of thumb ('heuristic') useful in the everyday social context (personal promises) is being read across into commercial situations where it is inappropriate. Paying one's sister a sum of money instead of coming to her birthday party is not *comme il faut*. But damages *are* an appropriate way of redressing commercial failures to deliver goods or services. Wilkinson-Ryan has found that including a liquidated damages clause in a contract may correct this tendency: it is viewed as the accepted price of non-performance.[47]

The common theme here is that moral intuitions about breach properly apply in some but by no means all contract situations. In business in particular, where 'money talks', the payment of damages on non-performance should not be seen as wrongful, especially if this would mean lower costs for the parties – the 'efficient breach' hypothesis. Even such a staunch believer in the moral duty to perform contracts as Ralph Cunnington concedes that where the interest in performance is purely economic, 'the parties understand their obligations as disjunctive,

---

[44] D. Markovits & A. Schwartz, 'The Myth of Efficient Breach: New Defenses of the Expectation Interest' (2011) 97 *Virginia LR* 1939.

[45] Cf. A.S. Gold, 'A Property Theory of Contract' (2009) 103 *NWULR* 1, 54 (cited by Markovits and Schwartz).

[46] Cf. n.38 above.

[47] T. Wilkinson-Ryan, 'Do Liquidated Damages Encourage Breach? A Psychological Experiment' (2010) 108 *Michigan LR* 633.

requiring them either to perform or to pay damages'.[48] Cunnington claims that such scenarios are 'rare' and that more commonly there is a non-pecuniary interest in performance. But this contradicts the traditional obsession of English contract law with commercial contracts. In the leading modern case on specific performance, Lord Hoffmann emphasized (in refusing the remedy) that both parties were sophisticated commercial organizations with purely financial interests in performance.[49] Therefore damages were entirely adequate. Cunnington's point enjoys some validity: it is the increasing recognition of *non-commercial* interests which has led to the questioning of market value expectation damages in recent years. Orthodoxy still treats such cases as exceptional, however.

EFFICIENT BREACH

A staple example of law and economics, perhaps its characteristic theory, is 'efficient breach'. The claim is that breach of contract may increase wealth (or decrease costs) overall, and should accordingly be permitted provided that expectation damages are paid. This provides a ready explanation for the secondary place of specific performance in the common law. The theory overtly defies the moral duty to keep one's promises: Robert Birmingham, its originator, explicitly said that encouragement of profitable breach 'through elimination of moral content from the contract promise' could be socially desirable.[50] Efficient breach is best introduced by way of example.

> *Example*: David agrees to sell a cow, Buttercup, to Eddie for £1,000. Brian then offers to buy Buttercup for £1,500. According to 'efficient breach', David should sell the cow to Brian and pay damages to Eddie. If Eddie's expected profit from this transaction would have been £200 (because he valued Buttercup at £1,200), it may be seen that David and Brian are *both left better off* by David's breach (Brian gets the cow, David keeps £300 of the 'overbid' – £500 less the £200 damages paid to Eddie) and Eddie is *left no worse off*, since he has been fully compensated for his lost profit.

Everyone's a winner in this (im)morality tale of everyday country folk. At least, some are better off and nobody is made worse off. If quaint notions of promise keeping stand in the way of such an 'efficient' outcome, perhaps they should be discarded. The consequence for remedies is that specific performance should not be available – David should be free to sell Buttercup to Brian provided he pays Eddie expectation damages.

---

[48] R.M. Cunnington, 'The Inadequacy of Damages as a Remedy for Breach of Contract' in C.E.F. Rickett (ed.), *Justifying Private Law Remedies* (Hart Publishing, 2008) p. 131.
[49] *Co-operative Insurance Society v Argyll Stores* [1998] AC 1, 18.
[50] R.L. Birmingham, 'Breach of Contract, Damage Measures, and Economic Efficiency' (1970) 24 *Rutgers LR* 273, 292.

This 'overbidder' situation (where someone comes along and makes a higher offer, like Brian) is the 'poster child' (i.e. exemplar) for efficient breach.[51] However, David Campbell states that it occurs rarely in practice.[52] Qi Zhou points out that if the subject matter of the contract is generic then the 'overbid' will simply reflect the increase in market price that the promisor will anyway have to pay the promisee in damages; so there is no incentive to breach. If it is unique, specific performance will be awarded; breach will not be possible.[53] But for Campbell, this does not invalidate 'efficient breach'. Its true importance, he argues, is not breaching to make profit but breaching *to limit losses*.[54] Not infrequently, costs grow in an unanticipated fashion so that a contract can no longer be profitably performed at the agreed price. If the promisor can compensate the promisee's expectation losses more cheaply than continuing with performance, what would be the point of insisting that he perform? This would obviously be wasteful.

> Breach allows flexibility into the system of exchanges, allowing parties relief from unanticipated expensive obligations when further performance would merely be wasteful as the plaintiff can be compensated in damages.[55]

This seems a more realistic and attractive defence of breach.[56] A survey of business people found wide agreement that it would be seriously unethical to breach a contract to make higher profits elsewhere, i.e. the 'overbidder' situation.[57] So efficient breach in its original 'overbidder' presentation is radically at odds with business practice. Moreover, Eisenberg argues that the elimination of morality from contract performance may be inefficient.[58] The contracting system depends not only on legal remedies, but on internalized (self-enforcing) moral norms and social sanctions, i.e. the reputational damage from breaching those norms. (In practice, such informal sanctions are relied upon widely, and formal litigation is extremely rare.[59]) If efficient breach were successful in removing the moral duty to keep contracts by 'washing it in cynical acid',[60] these supports might be gravely weakened. This would mean an increased reliance on formal legal sanctions to ensure performance – at considerably greater expense. Shiffrin raises the concern

---

[51] Cf. M.A. Eisenberg, 'Actual and Virtual Specific Performance' (2005) 93 *California LR* 975, 998.

[52] D. Campbell, 'Breach and Penalty as Contractual Norm and Contractual Anomie' [2001] *Wisconsin LR* 681. Cf. I.R. Macneil, 'Contract Remedies: A Need for Better Efficiency Analysis' (1988) 144 *J Institutional & Theoretical Econ* 6, 15 ('so rare as to be almost nonexistent').

[53] Qi Zhou, 'Is a Seller's Efficient Breach of Contract Possible in English Law?' (2008) 24 *JCL* 268. *Quaere* whether the dichotomy is this clear – is a named cow purchased for a commercial dairy 'unique'? Cf. J. Berryman, 'Specific Performance, Uniqueness and Investment Contracts: A Canadian Perspective' [1984] *Conveyancer* 130.

[54] Campbell, n.52 above, pp. 687–91.

[55] Ibid, 690. Cf. the extremely narrow 'escape' afforded by frustration, pp. 139–140 above.

[56] See further D. Campbell & D. Harris, 'In Defence of Breach' (2002) 22 *Legal Stud* 208.

[57] D. Baumer & P. Marschall, 'Willful Breach of Contract for the Sale of Goods: Can the Bane of Business Be An Economic Bonanza?' (1992) 65 *Temple LR* 159.

[58] Eisenberg, n.51 above, pp. 1012–13.

[59] Cf. Baumer & Marschall, n.57 above (businesses simply refuse to do business again with parties which breach 'wilfully').

[60] Cf. Holmes, n.29 above.

that for the law to permit deliberate breach of contract to make increased profits may contribute to 'a culture ... in tension with the conditions for the maintenance of moral character' generally.[61] According to Dawinder Sidhu, deliberate breach 'degrades' contracting, permits abuse of trust and 'corrupt[s] the integrity and cooperative essence of society'. These damaging 'externalities' (i.e. social costs) must be taken into account by advocates of efficient breach.[62]

But accusations of immorality are harder to maintain when a promisor breaches to cut his losses, i.e. when compensating the promisee's expectation interest will cost less than continuing to perform. Responding to Shiffrin, Shavell argues that rational parties want performance to continue when costs unexpectedly increase if and only if its value exceeds the increased cost. Had they been able to write an exhaustively detailed contract (catering for all contingencies), breach when the cost exceeds the value is exactly what the parties would have allowed.[63] An important reason for refusing specific performance in *Co-operative Insurance v Argyll Stores* was the undesirability of forcing the defendants to keep open a supermarket that was trading at a loss.[64] This would have been unfair as well as wasteful – the plaintiffs would be enriched at the defendants' expense, the latter being 'bound hand and foot, in order to be made subject to any extortionate demand'.[65] As David Howarth remarks, to insist on performance at a loss reflects not the 'sanctity' of contract but 'contractual sadism'![66] Bar-Gill and Ben-Shahar anyway note that for many commercial parties a contract is not a sanctified gospel but a mutually advantageous instrumental arrangement. Why then condemn the search for more profitable opportunities which increase the size of the contractual 'pie' available to both parties? If they thought of it, they would probably include a term permitting such behaviour.[67] But even if the moral objections to efficient breach can be answered, there are other difficulties.

EFFICIENT BREACH: CRITIQUE

Critics point to doctrinal obstacles to efficient breach and the ultimate indeterminacy of the supporting economic analysis. First, the theory requires the promisee in the earlier example, Eddie, to be no worse off after the breach. This means making Eddie whole so that he is indifferent between performance and damages. However as Eisenberg points out, the limits on damages (e.g. mitigation, remoteness, irrecoverable costs of litigation) mean that in practice promisees do

---

[61] S.V. Shiffrin, 'The Divergence of Contract and Promise' (2007) 120 *Harvard LR* 708.

[62] D.S. Sidhu, 'The Immorality and Inefficiency of an Efficient Breach' (2006) 8 *Transactions (Tennessee Journal of Business Law)* 61.

[63] S. Shavell, 'Why Breach of Contract May Not Be Immoral Given the Incompleteness of Contracts' in O. Ben-Shahar & A. Porat (eds), *Fault in American Contract Law* (Cambridge University Press, 2010).

[64] Cf. n.49 above.

[65] *Isenberg v East India House Estate Co Ltd* (1863) 3 De GJ & S 263, 273 (Lord Westbury LC), cited ibid.

[66] D. Howarth, 'Against *Lumley v Gye*' (2005) 68 *MLR* 195.

[67] O. Bar-Gill & O. Ben-Shahar, 'An Information Theory of Willful Breach' in O. Ben-Shahar & A. Porat (eds), *Fault in American Contract Law* (Cambridge University Press, 2010).

not receive full compensation.[68] (Of course this can be viewed as an argument for better compensation rather than a fatal blow for efficient breach.) Qi Zhou argues that efficient breach is unlikely to take place in English law.[69] Eddie may be able to sue Brian for the tort of inducing breach of contract. Also, if the property in Buttercup had passed to Eddie before David sold her, David will be liable to Eddie in the tort of conversion; by 'waiving the tort' Eddie can require David to hand over the profits of Buttercup's sale to Brian. Both these (possible) actions would deter Brian and David (respectively) from engaging in 'efficient breach'. But it must be noted that the tort of inducing breach has been fiercely attacked for having this effect,[70] and disgorgement of profits is only exceptionally required for breach of contract as such (i.e. when it does not involve conversion).[71]

A more fundamental criticism maintains that the 'efficient' outcome does not require a breach of contract. The important thing is for the performance to be transferred to the party who values it the most – Brian in the cow case. But instead of David unilaterally breaching his contract to sell Buttercup to Eddie he could negotiate to be released from this commitment *by agreement*. In a system where specific performance was the normal remedy, parties could 'bargain around' it. By 'bribing' Eddie not to enforce the contract David could still sell Buttercup to Brian at a profit, but with Eddie's consent. The main difference seems to be the distribution of benefits. In the negotiation scenario, the profits from Brian's 'overbid' are shared between David and Eddie, whereas under 'efficient breach' David keeps the lot. But while David's profit would necessarily be smaller in the former case, he would still have an incentive to sell to Brian (producing the efficient outcome) so long as he could keep some of the profit.

Which then is the more 'efficient' – breach, or performance transferred by consent? It might seem *fairer* for the profits to be shared between David and Eddie, and certainly preferable from Eddie's perspective. However, Markovits and Schwartz argue that this benefit is illusory since in a world where sellers cannot realize the full profit (or cost saving) from 'efficient' breach, the price charged for supplying an otherwise identical service will necessarily be higher.[72] That is buyers will always pay more under a property rule (specific performance); they are paying for their share in the profits of efficient breach. Hence there is no distributive difference between the property rule and liability rule (damages). The choice between them ultimately depends on their respective transaction costs.[73] In particular, with a property rule will the parties realistically be able to 'bargain around' the order for specific performance? If (inefficient) performance would often result from a property rule because bargaining around it would be too costly,

---

[68] Cf. Eisenberg, n.51 above.
[69] Cf. n.53 above.
[70] Cf. Howarth, n.66 above, and pp. 289–292 below.
[71] Cf. pp. 252–257 below.
[72] Cf. n.44 above. Eisenberg (2006), n.188 below, makes the same point in reverse – buyers should receive a lower price when the seller is free to breach.
[73] Cf. Calabresi & Melamed, n.25 above.

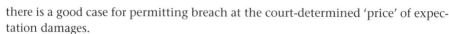

there is a good case for permitting breach at the court-determined 'price' of expectation damages.

Defenders of efficient breach argue that the property rule (viz. specific performance) necessitates an extra step before Buttercup can be transferred to her highest-value owner, Brian – viz. to release David from his obligation to Eddie. These negotiations are likely to be protracted and difficult. They involve a 'bilateral monopoly': Eddie is the only person from whom David can buy the release, and David is the only person to whom Eddie can sell. Moreover, it is a 'zero sum game' – every additional pound gained by Eddie is at David's direct expense. It is argued that such negotiations will be hard-fought and costly, and may fail when the parties cannot agree a price. Accordingly, the property rule would obstruct efficient outcomes. It would be better to allow unilateral breach by David on the payment of damages. This is what rational parties would want.[74]

However, this argument is incomplete and unbalanced. The alternative remedy, 'breach and pay damages', is certainly not cost-free. Eddie will have to sue David for breach of contract; litigation is proverbially expensive. Negotiations to settle such an action are also 'bilateral monopolies' where agreement may be difficult to reach. Thomas Ulen suggests that settlement may be made easier by the pre-existing relationship between the parties who will have 'bargained to provide for many contingencies including, possibly, breach'.[75] But surely the seller's breach will disrupt that relationship. Ian Macneil comments that '"talking after a breach" may be one of the most expensive forms of conversation to be found, involving, as it so often does, engaging high-price lawyers'.[76] Macneil's intuition is, therefore, that the liability rule (permitting efficient breach) will have higher costs than the property rule (specific performance). The very name 'efficient breach' is a misnomer which begs the question (since *breach* is not a necessary requirement of transferred performance). Macneil accuses lawyer-economists of ideological bias towards the self-interested, breach-first-pay-later approach presupposed by efficient breach, rather than the consensual behaviour which would be encouraged if specific performance required negotiated release. Bar-Gill and Ben-Shahar, indeed, propose an economic argument against deliberate breach: it reveals a self-serving and dishonest nature. Such behaviour should be condemned for the other undetected harm that may probably be inferred from it.[77]

Ultimately, however, Macneil does not come to a final view. He is at pains to emphasize that the respective incidence of costs is a question that can only be solved by empirical investigation – data from 'the real world of contracts' rather than the 'deductive sector of academia'. Without detailed empirical data, which would be difficult if not impossible to collect, we cannot make a reliable decision

---

[74] E.g. W. Bishop, 'The Choice of Remedy for Breach of Contract' (1985) 14 *JLS* 299; Markovits and Schwartz, n.44 above.

[75] T. Ulen, 'The Efficiency of Specific Performance: toward a Unified Theory of Contract Remedies' (1984) 83 *Michigan LR* 341, 369.

[76] I.R. Macneil, 'Efficient Breach of Contract: Circles in the Sky' (1982) 68 *Virginia LR* 947.

[77] Cf. n.67 above.

between the property and liability rules. Macneil condemns arguments for efficient breach which implicitly make empirical claims without any supporting evidence. Others such as Anthony Kronman and Alan Schwartz note the difficulty in comparing the costs to court and parties of specific performance (especially monitoring compliance with an order) with the cost of assessment of damages.[78] Lionel Smith comments that the economic analysis is 'voluminous' but 'pretty inconclusive'.[79] Accordingly he dismisses efficient breach. Arguably, indeterminacy seems to be a failing of law and economics generally. As Kreitner and Stephen Smith point out, contract remedies could be designed to provide incentives for a variety of economically desirable behaviour, for example, commitment to performance by promisor, self-protection and level of reliance by promisee, limiting drafting costs and dispute-resolution costs, etc. Since these incentives may conflict and there is no overarching criterion to rank their importance, there can be no unified economic theory of remedies.[80]

Eric Posner concludes that economic analysis of contract fails because of its indeterminacy.[81] However Bishop, in response to Macneil, comments that in the real world we often have to choose rules according to the best available evidence without the luxury of final empirical confirmation.[82] It may be true that this is realistically the best that we can do. But that could be a good reason to eschew (indeterminate) economic analysis altogether. It is fair to point out that some of the criticisms of efficient breach in the previous section (that it will undermine trust, decrease the efficacy of the contracting system and rot the moral fibre of society) are also empirical claims lacking supporting evidence. But avoiding such reasoning seems impossible for economic analysis, whereas doctrinal and rights-based approaches can proceed without the need for empirical data which are usually non-existent.

SPECIFIC PERFORMANCE

Specific performance is a supplementary remedy in English law. This is explicable for historical reasons – it is an equitable remedy, therefore available in the court's discretion rather than as of right, as a gloss on the common law. It is available only when (common law) damages are 'inadequate'. The continued submergence of specific performance beneath damages is, however, criticized by commentators from two schools. First, those who assert the moral priority of a right to performance see enforcement of contracts as the natural remedy. Secondly, and more nuanced, there are arguments that enforcement would be the more efficient

---

[78] A.T. Kronman, 'Specific Performance' (1978) 45 *Univ Chicago LR* 351; A. Schwartz, 'The Case for Specific Performance' (1979) 89 *Yale LJ* 271.

[79] Smith, n.12 above, p. 225.

[80] Kreitner, n.6 above, p. 27; S.A. Smith, *Contract Theory* (Oxford University Press, 2004) p. 412.

[81] E.A. Posner, 'Economic Analysis of Contract Law After Three Decades: Success or Failure?' (2003) 112 *Yale LJ* 829, 834–39 (remedies). Cf. generally pp. 116–119 above.

[82] Bishop, n.74 above.

default remedy for breach, all things considered. In other words, that this is what rational parties want.

Lionel Smith exemplifies the first approach. Specific performance is a 'whole-hearted endorsement of the plaintiff's entitlement to performance'.[83] Damages in the expectation measure may put the promisee where he would have been had the contract been performed, but specific performance goes one better. It *prevents* 'expropriation' of the promisee's entitlement. Smith points out that compelled performance may cost the defendant more than his profits (or savings) from breach, and may benefit the claimant more than damages because limits (in particular mitigation) are circumvented. But this is of no concern. Specific performance is not a compensatory remedy at all. It is concerned with enforce-ment of the primary duty. Its expansion should be welcomed for hastening the assimilation between contract and property that began with *Lumley v Gye*,[84] promoting 'rapprochement' between the common and civil law, and above all 'tak[ing] contractual obligations more seriously'.[85] Smith dismisses the economic analysis of specific performance for its indeterminacy.[86] No doubt any inef-ficiency is to be accepted as 'the price of achieving the moral goal of contract remedies'.[87]

The simplicity and power of this argument cannot be denied. But is it too simple? Do contracting parties actually want to bind the promisor to perform however costly this turns out to be, subject only to the ultimate escape of insolvency? Promisors will surely demand a much higher price for entering into such daunting obligations. Might promisees (at least sometimes) prefer cheaper contracts in which breach will generate only a claim for damages? Why must the logic of corrective justice (relied upon by Smith) obstruct such a preference? It will be seen that these questions get to the very heart of the law of contract. Is it a set of mandatory rules deduced from the requirements of corrective justice, as Smith seems to think? Or is it better viewed as a facilitative department of law where (within the limits of public policy) the parties are free to determine both obligations and the extent of their enforceability? The judicial view in England has been to allow party modification of remedies, apart from the penalty rule.[88] This is more harmonious with a 'default rule' approach. It is possible to defend specific performance from this perspective too. The difference is that it is then only a presumptive remedy, which the parties should be free to change.

Schwartz argues for specific performance as the default contractual remedy.[89] Obviously, individual parties have different remedial preferences but it would be prohibitively costly to uncover these in each case afresh. Replying to Kronman,

---

[83] Smith, n.12 above, p. 230.

[84] (1853) 2 E & B 216. Cf. pp. 287–292 below.

[85] Smith, n.12 above, p. 233.

[86] Cf. pp. 116–119 above.

[87] Schwartz, n.78 above, p. 278.

[88] E.g. *Photo Production v Securicor* [1980] AC 827, 849 (Lord Diplock). Smith, n.12 above, concedes (against his thesis) that common law judges are practically minded.

[89] Schwartz, n.78 above.

Schwartz denies that there are stable category-wide preferences, e.g. specific performance for sale of 'unique' goods only.[90] Someone purchasing a house, for example, may actually prefer damages for fear that the vendor will cause hard-to-prove damage to the property during the action for specific performance. Conversely the buyer of generic goods may prefer specific performance if he fears that a money judgment will not be satisfied. Schwartz concludes that the court should order specific performance whenever the claimant requests it. Damages generally undercompensate promisees. If specific performance is sought it shows that the promisee believes damages would undercompensate him. It also reveals the promisee's view that the benefits of specific performance outweigh its costs, in particular defective performance by a reluctant or hostile promisor. Many promisees will prefer to obtain substitute performance elsewhere and then sue for damages, rather than 'hold their affairs in suspension while awaiting equitable relief'.[91]

While some promisees might prefer specific performance to overcome under-compensation, might they also seek it strategically to gain a *supra*-compensatory pay-off from a promisor seeking to gain profits elsewhere – or cut his losses?[92] Schwartz accepts that this potential for 'exploitation' counts against specific performance, but argues that such 'abuse' is unlikely when, for the reasons mentioned above, there are strong practical reasons against seeking specific performance. But is it convincing to suggest that the promisee's request always means undercompensation and never 'abuse'? Perhaps not – will the practical difficulties of enforcement actually matter if the promisee seeks the order only as a means of extracting payment? This is inconvenient for Schwartz, for it would require the courts to establish the promisee's motive for seeking specific perform-ance in every case. This would be an extremely difficult task.

Schwartz accepts that specific performance would be an infringement of the liberty of individual service providers (and *a fortiori* employees), but not when services are provided by a corporation. Nor would compulsion to convey generic goods, a mere aspect of wealth, infringe liberty. Schwartz finds a stronger case when there is sentimental attachment, as to a home or artwork, but notes these are cases (land and unique chattels) where specific performance is currently available. This might require reconsideration, provided 'a coherent theory of the "personality aspect" of property ownership' can be developed.[93]

Finally Schwartz argues that routine specific performance would save contract drafting costs. At the moment, parties find it difficult to compel performance since the courts strike down penalty clauses.[94] Furthermore, the parties cannot reduce the court's discretion to a mere 'rubber stamp' by inserting a specific perform-

---

[90] Kronman, n.78 above.
[91] Schwartz, n.78 above, p. 277.
[92] Cf. *Co-operative Insurance v Argyll Stores*, n.49 above.
[93] Schwartz, n.78 above, p. 298.
[94] Cf. pp. 223–228 above.

ance clause.[95] Campbell argues that as just parties cannot directly stipulate for the penalty of imprisonment in the event of breach of contract (for obvious reasons), they should not be able to do this indirectly by requiring specific performance (enforced via contempt of court).[96] But these points apply with much less force to financial penalties. A more straightforward way of avoiding the difficulties Schwartz identifies would be to enforce overtly penal clauses between parties of equal bargaining strength. Elsewhere, Schwartz has argued that rational promisees are unlikely to purchase supra-compensatory remedies (whether penalty or 'specific performance' clauses).[97] These will cost more, and yet return nothing in exchange for the higher price when the promisor performs. Therefore, agreed damages clauses are more likely to be genuine pre-estimates of loss than penal by design, and should be enforceable.

SUBSTITUTIONARY DAMAGES

As Andrew Burrows remarks, one symptom of the academic fascination with remedies is a proliferation of labels.[98] 'Substitutionary damages' are prominent among the newcomers. Stephen Smith says there is nothing mysterious about them: substitutionary damages are 'the closest substitute possible for doing what the defendant should have done in the first place', a monetary equivalent of specific relief when specific performance itself is unavailable or inappropriate.[99] It follows that although they do not raise all of the concerns that pertain to specific performance (especially the compulsion of labour), substitutionary damages are susceptible to some of the same criticisms. In particular that they undermine the mitigation principle.[100] Is it convincing to argue that mitigation is relevant only to the compensation of loss, and not to remedies which (directly or indirectly) enforce the primary duty under the contract?

Substitutionary damages do not compensate losses. They eliminate or prevent them.[101] They are due whenever someone is 'hindered of his right' even when 'it does not cost [him] one farthing'.[102] Robert Stevens describes the 'vindication' of the right to contractual performance.[103] Stevens argues that it is in principle always

[95] *Quadrant Visual Communications v Hutchison Telephone* [1993] BCLC 442 (Stocker LJ).

[96] D. Harris, D. Campbell & R. Halson, *Remedies in Contract and Tort* (2nd edn, Cambridge Unversity Press, 2002), p. 195.

[97] A. Schwartz, 'The Myth That Promisees Prefer Supracompensatory Remedies: An Analysis of Contracting for Damages Measures' (1990) 100 *Yale LJ* 369.

[98] A. Burrows, 'Damages and Rights' in D. Nolan & A. Robertson (eds), *Rights and Private Law* (Hart Publishing, 2011).

[99] S.A. Smith, 'Substitutionary Damages' in C.E.F. Rickett (ed.), *Justifying Private Law Remedies* (Hart Publishing, 2008) pp. 102–3.

[100] Burrows, n.98 above. Cf. pp. 249–250 below.

[101] Smith, n.12 above.

[102] *Ashby v White* (1703) 2 Ld Raym 938 (Holt CJ), quoted Stevens, n.32 above.

[103] Stevens, n.32 above. See also D. Pearce & R. Halson, 'Damages for Breach of Contract: Compensation, Restitution and Vindication' (2008) 28 *OJLS* 73.

available (although in most cases there *is* actual loss, for which the promisee is to be compensated, which conceals the vindicatory/substitutionary remedy).[104]

This radical new remedy has been proposed as the solution to the difficult problem of the promisee's remedy in contracts entered into on behalf of a third party.[105] However, it is not limited to three-party contracts. Two further examples will be considered here. First, the market damages rule for sale of goods, and secondly, the 'cost of cure' measure for defective performance.

The Sale of Goods Act 1979, s.53(3) enacts the rule that 'prima facie' damages for defective goods are the difference in value between the goods as delivered and their market value had they been of satisfactory quality. In *Slater v Hoyle & Smith* the seller tendered defective cloth; however, the buyer was able to sell it on to a manufacturer at the full price for cloth of 'merchantable quality'.[106] That is, the sub-buyer (manufacturer) raised no objection to the inferiority of the cloth. The court held that the buyer was nevertheless able to claim from the seller the diminution in market value owing to the inferiority of the goods. The sub-contract with the manufacturer was to be ignored.[107] Stevens says that no satisfactory argument can show that the buyer suffered a *loss* in this situation. Accordingly, the court remedied the diminution in value of the buyer's contractual right even though he suffered no loss. Stevens cites this as a clear example of damages as a substitute for the infringed right (to goods of satisfactory quality).[108]

However, Bridge offers a more practical explanation for the tenacity of the market damages rule.[109] Simply, it is easier to administer. The task of the court is greatly simplified by applying the (publicly available) market price on the date of delivery rather than addressing complex causal questions on the facts of each case. This is important if we are to have clear-cut rules of law and not 'factual discretion'.[110] 'A full commitment to legal certainty favours a clear rule that is not compromised by immediate fact.'[111] English commercial judges combine a commitment to commercial certainty with 'realisation, bordering on resignation, that perfect compensation is simply an impossible ideal'.[112]

One does suspect that a hard-nosed commercial judge like Scrutton LJ in *Slater* would be surprised to be cited by Stevens in support of the abstract rights-based approach! Stevens argues that 'certainty' does not explain cases like *Slater*, for why would courts ever award consequential loss for defective delivery were the simplification of damages their greatest imperative?[113] In a *reductio ad absurdum*

---

[104] Cf. also R. Stevens, *Torts and Rights* (Oxford University Press, 2007) ch. 4.
[105] *Panatown Ltd v Alfred McAlpine Construction Ltd* [2001] 1 AC 518 and pp. 280–286 below.
[106] [1920] 2 KB 11.
[107] *Rodocanachi v Milburn* (1887) 18 QBD 67, 77 (Lord Esher MR); *Williams v Agius* [1914] AC 510, 523 (Lord Dunedin).
[108] Stevens, n.32 above.
[109] M. Bridge, 'The Market Rule of Damages Assessment' in D. Saidov & R. Cunnington (eds), *Contract Damages: Domestic and International Perspectives* (Hart Publishing, 2008).
[110] Ibid, p. 455.
[111] Ibid, p. 426.
[112] Ibid, p. 435.
[113] Stevens, n.32 above.

it would be extremely 'certain' to award £100 (no more, no less) for *every* breach of contract, but nobody argues for that.[114] Thus, Stevens says, certainty is only a second-order principle of justice. That may be true. But there is a tension between perfect justice and efficient administration.[115] The market rule may represent one area in which the latter has prevailed. If so, it is not to be explained by the 'substitutionary' thesis at all.

Let us turn to consider defective performance of a building contract. If the law wishes to enforce the owner-employer's right, specific performance presents difficulties. In particular, monitoring compliance with the order will not be straightforward and if the builder is an individual it will seriously infringe his liberty. Accordingly, Stephen Smith argues that this is a good case for damages in an amount necessary to purchase substitute performance from another source.[116] Of course, other builders are readily available. Substitution is therefore possible. (Smith contrasts an injunction to prevent breach of a restrictive covenant – it is impossible to purchase substitute performance because only the person subject to the covenant can comply with it.)

In *Radford v de Froberville* the defendant failed to build a boundary wall. Even though this had no effect on the value of the plaintiff's land, the court awarded damages sufficient to have the wall built.[117] Lord Goff and Lord Millett explain this as a fuller recognition of the performance interest.[118] Oliver J placed some stress on the plaintiff's genuine desire to build the wall. In *Ruxley Electronics v Forsyth* a swimming pool was supposed to have a 7′6″ deep diving area; the pool as built was only 6′ deep. It was held that this was no less suitable for diving and no less valuable. The owner sued the builders for the cost of digging the pool down to the contractual depth, which would cost £21,560. The Court of Appeal held that the owner could recover that 'cost of cure'; it was irrelevant whether he intended to carry out the work.[119] But the House of Lords reversed this decision, asking if it was *reasonable* to cure the defects? [120] On the facts, it was not. Even a genuine intention to spend the damages on curing defects could not render reasonable what was objectively unreasonable.

Ruxley has been much debated. One controversial issue concerns intention. There is judicial support for the view that the claimant's intention is irrelevant to award of the 'cost of cure'.[121] Some would argue that this reflects the growing concern with substitute performance rather than compensation – examining the content of the contractual right rather than the deterioration in the promisee's factual position. Smith argues, however, that an intention to 'cure' must be proven

---

[114] Ibid, p. 196.
[115] Bridge, n.109 above.
[116] Smith, n.99 above.
[117] [1977] 1 WLR 1262.
[118] *Panatown*: cf. pp. 280–286 below.
[119] [1994] 1 WLR 650.
[120] [1996] AC 344.
[121] *Bellgrove v Eldridge* (1954) 90 CLR 613, 620; *De Beers v Atos Origin IT Services* [2010] EWHC 3276 (TCC), [345].

before such damages are awarded (and indeed they should be clawed back if not spent on 'cure').[122] The whole point of the award is so that substitute performance can be obtained. For Smith, the confusion stems from failing to keep separate the compensation of loss from the substitutionary function (curing defective perform-ance). With ordinary damages (compensation), it is true that what the claimant does with his damages is of no concern to the defendant: if someone's watch is stolen they are not obliged to spend the damages recovered on a new watch.[123] But it is different when the sum awarded is a *substitute* for the right in question.

It is curious that Smith's requirement (intention to carry out the repairs) was supported by the majority judges in *Panatown*,[124] who are generally taken to have *opposed* the 'performance interest' analysis (compare Lords Goff and Millett, dissenting). This seems one area where 'substitutionary damages' may confuse as well as illuminate. Another problem with *Ruxley* is the 'reasonableness' quali-fication. Its precise meaning is hard to discern from the speeches.[125] In several commercial cases the courts have been unwilling to award the 'cost of cure'.[126] In *The Rozel* Phillips J distinguished the (Court of Appeal) decision in *Ruxley* because the obligation breached was not 'an end in itself, reflecting a personal preference' but one 'inserted into a commercial contract because it has financial implications'.[127] In such a case it would be unreasonable to incur the cost of cure when this did not bring a commensurate increase in financial value. It therefore seems that the difference in market value is to be preferred in commercial cases. It is only when performance has intrinsic importance (i.e. irrespective of its market value) that the 'substitutionary' cost of cure measure will be 'reasonable'.

But the most obvious 'reasonableness' concern in *Ruxley* was waste, as in Lord Jauncey's example of demolishing a building to replace a course of yellow bricks with the blue bricks stipulated in the contract.[128] Lord Jauncey does not explain why it would 'clearly' be unreasonable to award damages necessary to effect such a cure, but evidently believes it would be wasteful to expend such sums on a sound structure in the interest of 'aesthetic pleasure'. The same concern probably explains the refusal to award the cost of cure in *Ruxley* itself. In other words, Mr Forsyth was required to mitigate his loss by accepting the non-compliant, but perfectly usable, swimming pool.

Now this point cannot be taken too far. The courts have sometimes awarded 'cost of cure' when carrying out the repairs is more expensive than the economic benefits that it brings.[129] Thus there is no requirement that the promisee must *always* mitigate his loss by declining to 'cure' defects when this would not

---

[122] Smith, n.99 above.

[123] *Ruxley* [1994] 1 WLR 650, 657 (Staughton LJ).

[124] E.g. 574 (Lord Jauncey). Cf. *Force India*, n.137 below [484].

[125] J. O'Sullivan, 'Loss and Gain at Greater Depth: The Implications of the *Ruxley* Decision' in F. Rose (ed.) *Failure of Contracts – Contractual, Restitutionary and Proprietary Consequences* (Hart Publishing, 1997).

[126] E.g. *The Alecos M* [1991] 1 Lloyd's Rep 120.

[127] [1994] 2 Lloyd's Rep 161.

[128] [1996] AC 344, 358.

[129] Cf. *Radford*, n.117 above.

produce a commensurate increase in value. But the mitigation principle is triggered when the cost of cure would be 'wholly disproportionate'.[130] Also as seen, in commercial cases it may be that the promisee is *always* required to mitigate in this fashion.

As noted above, substitutionary damages are incompatible with the mitigation principle. Thus Smith argues that the 'reasonableness' qualification in *Ruxley* should rather be understood as one of the grounds for refusing specific performance – hardship on the defendant.[131] Any qualification to specific performance must logically apply to remedies substituting for it. According to Smith, the qualification fits better with the substitutionary nature of 'cost of cure' damages; it would be highly anomalous to have a 'reasonableness' requirement for ordinary compensatory damages which are available as of right. That may be true, but if 'reasonableness' is a cipher for mitigation the anomaly disappears, since mitigation is an ordinary principle of compensation.

The 'substitutionary' approach may be proposed as the solution to other problematic situations (originally discussed, perhaps inappropriately, in terms of loss). Janet O'Sullivan gives the example of 'a contract for the purchase of vintage champagne, which the seller breaches by supplying sparkling wine' – can it be doubted that the buyer has a remedy 'even if he or his guests consume the sparkling wine happily without noticing the difference'?[132] In *White Arrow Express v Lamey's Distribution* the plaintiffs paid for a 'de luxe' delivery service but the defendants provided only a standard service.[133] The plaintiffs did not allege that this had led to any loss of business, damage to reputation or other loss, simply that they had not got what they paid for. Bingham MR said that the law would be defective if it gave only nominal damages to one who paid a premium but obtained substandard service. (He gave other examples: paying for an expensive meal and being served a cheaper one; purchasing lessons from a world-famous violinist and receiving them from a 'musical non-entity'.) It would 'defy common sense' to hold that there was no loss and no financial disadvantage in such cases. However, it was still necessary to prove what had been lost, the plaintiff had failed to do so on the facts, and the claim failed.

'Substitutionary damages' could be used instead. Clearly the promisee's right is violated in all these examples. Without more, the law could therefore award damages in an amount suitable to purchase what was due to the promisee. Making allowance for what was actually received under the contract, this would be a 'topping up' exercise – the difference between the market value of what was provided and of what was required under the contract. This would resemble the rule in sale of goods cases where the difference in value is awarded even when no loss seems to have occurred.

---

130 [1996] AC 344, 354.
131 Smith, n.99 above. See e.g. *Patel v Ali* [1985] Ch 283.
132 O'Sullivan, n.125 above.
133 [1995] CLC 1251.

Another view is possible. In all these cases the defendant has cut corners or 'skimped' on performance.[134] Yet the promisee has paid the full price. Thus, the defendant has been enriched at the promisee's expense. Might not a restitutionary solution be considered, focusing on the defendant's gain (cost saving) irrespective of the promisee's provable loss? Although Lord Woolf MR has proposed 'restitutionary damages' in such situations,[135] there are difficulties. English law allows restitution of a payment only when there has been a *total failure* of the condition (or traditionally 'consideration') on which it was made. Although much criticized, the rule has been expressly approved by Lord Goff.[136] Bingham MR indeed held that the claim in *White Arrow* was 'no more than an attempt to make good a partial failure of consideration under the guise of a claim for damages' and should accordingly be dismissed. By contrast, in *Van der Garde v Force India Formula One* 'performance damages' were awarded even though they were sought as a fall-back to a restitutionary claim which foundered on the 'total failure of consideration' rule.[137] Stadlen J, distinguishing *White Arrow*, was careful to emphasize that the value of the services which had not been provided had to be established by evidence, and this value was 'conceptually quite distinct' from the contract price.[138] Thus, it was not a disguised claim for partial restitution. However, the contract price might provide *evidence* of the market value.[139]

It follows that the substitutionary claim, while strictly speaking distinct from restitution, was able to perform much the same role. It is notable that Stadlen J expressed 'considerable regret' that the restitutionary claim failed in *Force India* (associating himself with critics of the 'total failure' rule).[140] Schwartz and Scott explicitly argue that 'cost of cure' damages can reverse the unjust enrichment of contract-breakers.[141] They argue that promisees usually pay for the cost of cure as part of the contract price. For example, a landowner granting a mining lease will receive a lower rent when the mining company is obliged to restore the land to its previous state at the end of the lease.[142] If the company fails to perform this reinstatement it is unjustly enriched – it has gained the benefit of the lower rent without performing the service required. Similarly builders will charge more when obliged to cure any defects in construction (as expressly required in some standard construction contracts). This tends to be overlooked because the separate services are provided by one contractor under a 'bundled' price. So Schwartz and Scott argue for disaggregating the contract price to recognize that the 'reinstatement' obligation has in fact been paid for by the promisee. This would allay fears

---

[134] Cf. *City of New Orleans v Firemen's Charitable Association* (1891) 9 So 486.

[135] *A-G v Blake* [1998] Ch. 439, 458. Cf. [2001] 1 AC 268, 286 (Lord Nicholls).

[136] *Stocznia Gdanska SA v Latvian Shipping Co* [1998] 1 WLR 574, 590.

[137] [2010] EWHC 2373 (QB).

[138] Ibid, [487].

[139] Ibid, [433], citing Morritt LJ in *White Arrow*, n.133 above.

[140] Ibid, [367].

[141] A. Schwartz & R.E. Scott, 'Market Damages, Efficient Contracting, and the Economic Waste Fallacy' (2008) 108 *Columbia LR* 1610.

[142] Cf. *Tito v Waddell* [1977] Ch 106; *Peevyhouse v Garland Coal & Mining Co* (1962) 382 P.2d 109.

that the cost of cure represents an 'uncovenanted profit' for claimants who do not genuinely intend to spend the damages on rectifying the defects.[143] Thus, the restitutionary analysis provides another answer to the conundrum about the claimant's intentions.

In addition to the moral force of the restitutionary analysis, Schwartz and Scott claim that cost of cure damages are also more efficient. As seen, they are often criticized for leading to economic waste. But this ignores the point that expensive-to-remedy defects could often have been avoided very cheaply by the contractor taking more care in the first place, for example, had the builder in *Ruxley* measured the depth of the pool during excavation. If builders know they will ultimately be liable for curing such defects they will take care to prevent them in the first place. In other words, the courts have been guilty of looking only at the *ex post facto* 'cost of cure' and ignoring the long-run incentive effect of such liability. Against this, Campbell argues that it is unlikely that builders would take on such onerous, near-absolute obligations to cure in cases like *Ruxley*, or if they did the contract price would be very high to cover 'extraordinarily careful ground surveys or taking out insurance against a potentially huge liability'.[144]

Schwartz and Scott conclude that the routine award of cost of cure (at the market rate) is the efficient default rule. It would be much more predictable than the current approach with its unpredictable qualifications of 'intention' and 'reasonableness' and is what rational contracts would want (both efficient and fair). Of course as a default, parties may contract out of it when hard-to-prevent defects would prove inordinately costly to repair. As with specific performance, therefore, it is possible to construct instrumental arguments in favour of 'substitutionary damages' as a default rule. The methodology is wholly alien to the rights reasoning of, say, Robert Stevens, but the conclusion is similar – as a default position.

DETERRING BREACH: PUNITIVE DAMAGES AND DISGORGEMENT OF PROFITS

For those who believe that breach of contract is a moral wrong, it follows that it should, where appropriate, be punished. Moreover, the contract breaker should not profit from his breach.[145] Also it may be possible to formulate economic arguments for the deterrence of breach: economic analysis of law revolves around the provision of incentives for efficient behaviour. English law has not, however, traditionally sought to punish breach or strip contract breakers of profits.

It is axiomatic that punitive (or 'exemplary') damages are not available for breach of contract in English law.[146] Lord Atkinson said it would lead to 'confusion and uncertainty in commercial affairs' if motive were taken into account. Should

---

[143] Cf. *Radford v De Froberville* [1977] 1 WLR 1262, 1270 (Oliver J).

[144] Harris, Campbell & Halson, n.96 above, p. 275.

[145] E.g. P. Jaffey, 'Efficiency, Disgorgement and Reliance in Contract: A Comment on Campbell and Harris' [2002] *Legal Studies* 570, 574.

[146] *Addis v Gramophone Co* [1909] AC 488.

recovery of a debt depend on whether parties have been 'harsh, grasping, or piti-less, or even insulting' or on the contrary 'suave, gracious, and apologetic'?[147] This rule has not been judicially challenged.[148] Stephen Smith admits that the absence of punitive damages is 'a genuine puzzle' for rights-based theories of contract.[149]

Nicholas McBride accordingly argues for the award of punitive damages.[150] His starting point is that deliberate breach of a common law duty should be punished through private law if it will not receive criminal sanction. This is the basis for punitive damages in tort. McBride finds no sufficient difference between tort and contract; accordingly punitive damages should be available in contract cases too. McBride does not entirely reject Holmes's view that as entering into contractual relations is a voluntary matter, so contractors should be able to specify the conse-quences of their contract.[151] But if this is correct then remedies should be analyzed by asking what contractors may reasonably be taken to want from the law. Is there any appetite for punitive damages? McBride makes no attempt to show that there is, for he does not think it relevant. He actually accepts the basic claims of 'effi-cient breach' as evidence that punitive damages would be inefficient but simply states that the courts have not accepted the theorem. It may be doubted whether this is true – the glaring absence of punitive damages is actually good support for an implicit acceptance of 'efficient breach'.[152] Even if it were true, there is surely room for the theorist to inquire whether the law *should* prefer economic efficiency to the protection of abstract common law 'rights'.

William Dodge argues that punitive damages are in fact efficient.[153] Dodge makes the case on efficiency grounds for 'property rules' prohibiting unilateral interference with the contract right.[154] These have been considered above under specific performance,[155] so the essence of Dodge's claim need not be examined afresh. The only novelty is Dodge's argument that whereas specific performance has various difficulties which limit its scope (e.g. difficulty of supervising compli-ance), punitive damages can be awarded in every case of deliberate breach.[156] So it should always be awarded, at least where specific performance is not available.[157] Significantly, however, Dodge argues for punitive damages as a default rule out of which the parties may contract, in particular if they are happy with 'either performance or damages', as Holmes famously suggested.[158] Dodge observes that whereas parties could contract for ordinary (compensatory) damages under such

---

147 Ibid.
148 Even in tort, punitive damages have been confined: *Rookes v Barnard* [1964] AC 1129.
149 S.A. Smith, *Contract Theory* (Oxford University Press, 2004) p. 418.
150 N.J. McBride, 'A Case for Awarding Punitive Damages in Response to Deliberate Breaches of Contract' (1995) 24 *Anglo-Am LR* 369.
151 O.W. Holmes, *The Common Law* (quoted ibid, 380).
152 McBride, n.150 above, 384–86 relies heavily on the tort in *Lumley v Gye*, on which cf. pp. 287–292 below.
153 W.S. Dodge, 'The Case for Punitive Damages in Contracts' (1999) 48 *Duke LJ* 629.
154 Cf. Calabresi & Melamed. n.25 above.
155 Cf. pp. 243–246 above.
156 Dodge, n.153 above, pp. 683–84.
157 Ibid. p. 685.
158 Ibid. p. 679.

a rule, at present the law does not allow them to stipulate a property rule (i.e. penal payments or specific performance).[159] Dodge's method contrasts with that of McBride – to dismiss Holmes, and thereby 'demonstrate' that there is a duty to perform in all cases and that this 'entails' punitive damages. The similarity of the outcome should not obscure the distinctive reasoning, and how it might be countered.

It also used to be axiomatic that contract damages were assessed according to the promisee's loss, and any gains made by the promisor from the breach were irrelevant.[160] This is equally offensive to rights-based theories. From such a starting point it is natural that a culpable contract breaker should give up, or 'disgorge' or 'account for' the profits of his wrong. Such profit-stripping would put the *promisor* where he would have been had he performed the contract[161] – a neat symmetry with putting the *promisee* in that position via compensatory damages.[162]

Birks notes problems with 'restitution for wrongs'. They give a windfall to the claimant (viz. a remedy in excess of his loss) and tend to 'negative and suppress economic activity without regard to harm done'.[163] But he also praises disgorgement's potential as a deterrent. Its exact correspondence with the 'wrongdoer's' profits is preferable, in Birks's view, to the indeterminate quantum of punitive damages.[164] But will a restitutionary approach be sufficient to teach contract breakers that 'breach does not pay',[165] if that is the objective? Campbell argues that even total disgorgement is 'punishment at zero risk'. The contract breaker is liable to lose his profits (and no more) *if and only if* he is taken to court, as he frequently may not.[166] Thus a punitive award *in excess* of the profits from breach seems necessary if breach is to be deterred.[167] But ultimately, the respective efficacy of the remedies needs to be established empirically.[168]

In contrast with punitive damages per se English law has seen significant development in this area. In *A-G v Blake* Lord Nicholls held that in accordance with a supposed academic consensus an account of profits could be ordered in suitable cases of breach of contract.[169] It was better to recognize this openly than to strain other concepts (such as property rights or fiduciary duties). Lord Nicholls also deplored punitive damages as 'speculative and unusual'.[170] The 'devilishly difficult' thing was identifying the circumstances in which account of profits was appropriate. Lord Nicholls stressed that the remedy would be limited to cases where the

---

[159] Albeit this rule has been criticized: cf. pp. 223–228 above.
[160] *Teacher v Calder* [1899] AC 451.
[161] R. Cooter & T. Ulen, *Law and Economics* (3rd edn, 2000) p. 234.
[162] *Robinson v Harman* (1848) 1 Ex Rep 850.
[163] P.B.H. Birks, 'Civil Wrongs – A New World' In *Butterworths Lectures 1990–1991* (1992).
[164] Cf. Lord Reid's concerns about uncertainty in *Broome v Cassell & Co* [1972] AC 1027. Cf. n.167 below.
[165] Cf. *Rookes v Barnard,* n.148 above, 1227 (Lord Devlin).
[166] Harris, Campbell & Halson, n.96 above, p. 607.
[167] Cf. *Snepp v United States* (1980) 444 US 507, 523 (Brennan, Marshall and Stevens JJ dissenting). The *majority* decision was relied upon in *A-G v Blake,* n.169 below.
[168] Harris, Campbell & Halson, n.96 above, p. 608.
[169] [2001] 1 AC 268.
[170] Commenting ibid, 288, on *Snepp*; cf. n.167 above.

ordinary remedies were inadequate. Otherwise, the only guidance was to look at all the circumstances (e.g. the nature of the term breached, the consequences of breach), a 'useful general guide' being whether the claimant had a legitimate interest in depriving the defendant of his profit.[171] But 'cynical and deliberate' breach to make a profit elsewhere was not sufficient. It would be difficult and indeed 'unwise' to be more specific. Lord Steyn said availability should be 'hammered out on the anvil of concrete cases'. Arguably the only concrete thing to emerge from *Blake* was the account ordered in the case itself from the MI6 traitor, George Blake. Lord Nicholls is right to describe the facts as 'exceptional'. But none of this provides much guidance for the future.

Uncertainty, then, is an obvious problem with *Blake*.[172] Lord Hobhouse in dissent predicted 'very far reaching and disruptive consequences' for commercial law.[173] Prior to *Blake*, claims for disgorgement in such cases had been summarily dismissed.[174] When shortly afterwards such a claim succeeded,[175] the reaction was one of alarm. This was rapidly revealed in the (exceptional) publication of an arbitration award, in suitably anonymous form, arbitration decisions usually being confidential. In *The 'Sine Nomine'* the arbitrators declared their robust opposition to disgorgement for breach of contract, going so far as to say that: 'International commerce on a large scale is red in tooth and claw'. Therefore, commercial law 'should not make moral judgments, or seek to punish contract-breakers'.[176]

A deeper problem is the form of the reasoning and Lord Nicholls's belief that the consensus of opinion favoured a disgorgement remedy in contract. The underlying concept in *Blake* is recognition of the performance interest: 'more fully to make undertaking a contractual obligation *mean* performance'.[177] It hardly needs to be said in the light of earlier sections of this Debate that this is not accepted by every commentator. Campbell has been a prominent critic of *Blake*.[178] The decision 'flatly conflicts with normal contractual principles' and was a 'major exercise of judicial legislation'. Campbell argues that whereas the House of Lords held it 'axiomatic' that every breach of contract is a wrong, 'there is no more sure way of misunderstanding the law of contract remedies'. The category error is to view remedies as normative theory external to the contract, rather than an implied term that applies only in default of agreement by the parties.[179] It is important that we have an efficient default rule, otherwise parties will have to contract around it in every case. But nothing was produced to justify the major change in remedies save for 'abstract restitutionary reasoning'. Social efficiency is 'utterly neglected' in the restitutionary literature on which Lord Nicholls relied.

---

[171] Cf. Harris, Campbell & Halson, n.96 above, 263: 'this merely rephrases the issue'.
[172] Cf. Waddams, n.3 above, 204–206, defending 'multiple cumulative factors' reasoning.
[173] n.169, p. 299.
[174] E.g. *The Siboen and The Sibotre* [1976] 1 Lloyd's Rep 293, 337.
[175] *Esso Petroleum v NIAD* [2001] EWHC 458 (Ch).
[176] [2002] 1 Lloyd's Rep 805.
[177] Harris, Campbell & Halson, n.96 above, p. 264. Cf. Friedmann, n.5 above.
[178] Ibid, pp. 262–85.
[179] Cf. Epstein, n.2 above.

There is no evidence that promisees are dissatisfied with the standard regime of expectation damages. A purely theoretical approach supplanted the necessary debates of public policy. Contract law should 'provide workable remedies in support of commercial exchange' rather than correcting 'abstract "wrongs"'. The extension of disgorgement (and the performance interest) in *Blake*, Campbell concludes, 'simply misunderstands the function of contract remedies'. So much for consensus![180]

The evidence of the *Sine Nomine* arbitration is that at least some practising commercial lawyers share Campbell's concern over *Blake*. A recent attempt to explain when account of profits is an appropriate remedy may allay these fears. In *Vercoe v Rutland Fund Management* Sales J said it is time to go beyond the traditional categories of equity and common law, contract and property, which may be 'accidents of history'.[181] A 'more principled' approach would grant disgorgement where the claimant's rights are of a 'particularly powerful kind'. Traditionally, that has meant property rights.[182] But as his Lordship points out, many kinds of property are 'regularly bought and sold in a market' and therefore it may be appropriate to protect their infringement with a reasonable buy-out fee.[183] Account of profits (full disgorgement) should be reserved for rights 'where it would never be reasonable to expect that [they] could be bought out for some reasonable fee, so that [they are] accordingly deserving of a particularly high level of protection'. Another way of putting this is to distinguish between ordinary commercial situations in which 'a degree of self-seeking and ruthless behaviour is expected and accepted to a degree' where profit-stripping would be inappropriate, and the special duties of trust and confidence assumed by a fiduciary. George Blake, of course, fell into the latter category. But if Sales J's analysis is correct, ordinary contract law will be unaffected by *Blake* since ordinary commercial self-interest should not be punished by ordering an account of profits.

Cunnington criticizes the notion of 'legitimate interest' in *Blake* as 'hopelessly ill-defined'.[184] Instead he argues that account of profits should be ordered whenever the court wishes to award specific performance or an injunction but cannot do so, for example, where the breach is irredeemably past (as in *Blake* itself). Cunnington accepts that as damages are the primary remedy and specific performance secondary, this makes account of profits a *tertiary* remedy. But this does not imply a marginal role, it seems. Cunnington argues that the courts must order account of profits whenever specific relief is impossible to 'vindicate' bargained-for performance, otherwise contract rights will be left 'hopelessly unprotected' and

---

[180] Cf. also Campbell & Harris, n.56 above.
[181] [2010] EWHC 424 (Ch), [337]–[345].
[182] In *Blake* Lord Hobhouse dissented because the account of profits was 'a remedy based on proprietary principles when the necessary proprietary rights are absent' [2001] 1 AC 268, 299.
[183] Cf. *Wrotham Park Estate v Parkside Homes* [1974] 1 WLR 789; pp. 257–263 below.
[184] R. Cunnington, 'The Measure and Availability for Gain-Based Damages for Breach of Contract' in D. Saidov & R. Cunnington (eds) *Contract Damages: Domestic and International Perspectives* (Hart Publishing, 2008) p. 235.

'society's confidence in the institution of contracting ... severely undermined'.[185] Cunnington's commitment to the legal rule that damages are normally adequate and specific relief an exceptional remedy seems to be weak.[186] But his references to 'society's confidence in contracting' are, one suspects, too vague to satisfy Campbell's criticisms of *Blake's* abstract reasoning.

Disgorgement can be defended instrumentally.[187] Eisenberg does so, criticizing much of the existing pro-disgorgement arguments for their intuitive and 'relatively conclusory' moral character.[188] Eisenberg accepts that contract is 'primarily about efficiency'. His argument in favour of disgorgement is closely associated with his criticisms of efficient breach.[189] Obviously, disgorgement removes the incentive to breach when approached by an 'overbidder'. The remedy also bolsters specific performance. Disgorgement is perhaps the only suitable remedy in cases like *Blake* concerning confidential government information. Once it has been published injunctions are no longer available; compensatory damages will be nominal because the information has no financial value as such. Eisenberg also recommends disgorgement in the 'skimping' cases although it has been argued above that these might instead be solved by using the cost of cure or 'substitutionary damages'.[190] Again we see that whereas the 'rights-based' perspective on contract remedies gives a clear and simple answer (which might not fit well with the law as it is!), there is vigorous debate among efficiency theorists over the best default rule.

WROTHAM PARK DAMAGES

Finally, we examine an exceptional species of damages whose basis is so controversial that to avoid begging the question they are best described eponymously. In *Wrotham Park Estate v Parkside Homes* the defendant built more houses than permitted under a restrictive covenant held by the plaintiffs.[191] However, the extra houses had not diminished the value of the plaintiffs' estate 'by one farthing'. Nevertheless, Brightman J rejected the submission that damages must therefore be nominal. 'Common sense' dictated 'compensation' of the plaintiffs. The defendants should not be left 'in undisturbed possession of the fruits of their wrongdoing' when they had 'invaded the plaintiffs' rights in order to reap a financial profit'. Refusing to order that the houses be torn down (an 'unpardonable waste'), Brightman J held that a 'just sum' in lieu of the injunction was what 'might reasonably have been demanded by the plaintiffs from Parkside as a *quid pro quo*

---

[185] Ibid, pp. 240–42.
[186] Cf. also Cunnington, n.48 above.
[187] Acknowledged in Harris, Campbell & Halson, n.96 above, p. 284, citing R. O'Dair, 'Restitutionary Damages for Breach of Contract and Efficient Breach' [1993] *CLP* 113.
[188] M.A. Eisenberg, 'The Disgorgement Interest in Contract Law' (2006) 105 *Michigan LR* 559, 578.
[189] Cf. n.51 above and generally pp. 239–243 above.
[190] Cf. pp. 250–252 above.
[191] [1974] 1 WLR 798.

for relaxing the covenant'. This was assessed as 5 per cent of the defendants' profits from the additional houses.

Such damages have in principle been available in contract since the approval of *Wrotham Park* in *A-G v Blake* as a (hitherto) 'solitary beacon' showing that '[contract] damages are not always narrowly confined to recoupment of financial loss'.[192] Chadwick LJ says that the common feature between *Blake* and *Wrotham Park* is judicial recognition of 'the need to compensate the claimant in circumstances where he cannot demonstrate identifiable financial loss'.[193] Peter Smith J says it is important to award 'genuine relief' for wrongs and not 'something akin to a Pyrrhic result'.[194] Exceptionally *Wrotham Park* damages are necessary, at the court's discretion, to avoid the justified criticism that a wrongdoer had escaped sanction.[195]

But these seem rather strange comments on the face of it. To suggest that 'genuine relief' might require punishment contradicts the longstanding opposition of English law to punitive damages in contract. It is no less surprising to identify a 'need' for compensation when there has been no loss. It is true that ordinary compensatory damages will give no remedy in these cases. But that does not prove that damages are inadequate – they 'adequately' reflect the absence of loss! What is there to compensate?

These puzzles introduce the vexed question of how *Wrotham Park* damages are to be justified. There are three competing explanations, each with formidable support. First, an extended notion of *compensating loss* – the 'lost opportunity to bargain'. Secondly, a straightforwardly *restitutionary* remedy. Thirdly, valuing the *invasion of the right*, irrespective of the claimant's loss or defendant's gain. The difficulties in deciding the basis for and availability of *Wrotham Park* damages shows that reasoning about justice, rights and wrongs is not necessarily clearer than the search for efficient default rules!

Sharpe and Waddams argue that *Wrotham Park* damages are awarded when a right is appropriated without the owner's consent because such conduct deprives him 'of the opportunity to bargain with the defendant, and to set his own price on his consent'.[196] Courts recognize that the power to veto others' use is part of the value of rights-holding which an owner can profitably exploit, hence infringements are prevented by injunction even when no (other) loss would be suffered.[197] But when specific relief is impossible, or inappropriate as in *Wrotham Park* itself, the rights holder loses the opportunity to extract payment for infringement. It is entirely appropriate to compensate this loss through damages in lieu of specific relief. Sharpe and Waddams therefore provide a rationale for *Wrotham Park* and a clear criterion for the availability of such damages in contract, viz. where specific

---

[192] [2001] 1 AC 268, 283. Cf. *Surrey CC v Bredero Homes* [1993] 1 WLR 1361.
[193] *World Wide Fund for Nature v World Wrestling Federation* [2007] EWCA Civ 286, [59].
[194] *WWF* case [2006] EWHC 184 (Ch), [129].
[195] Ibid, [137].
[196] R.J. Sharpe & S.M. Waddams, 'Damages for Lost Opportunity to Bargain' (1982) 2 *OJLS* 290.
[197] *Goodson v Richardson* (1874) LR 9 Ch App 221.

relief (protection via a 'property rule') is in principle available because damages are inadequate but either cannot be awarded on the facts, or the court declines to do so in its discretion.[198]

According to Craig Rotherham, the lost opportunity analysis is 'analytically misconceived' and now has 'very little support from academic commentators'.[199] Most prefer restitutionary explanations, as explored below. The main problem with 'lost opportunity' arguments is that for the loss to be real it must be shown not only that the claimant in theory *could* have bargained for consensual release of the contract but in fact *would* have done so. This was not satisfied in *Wrotham Park* itself – the plaintiff estate would never have obtained the consent of all its tenants (the ultimate beneficiaries of the covenant) to its relaxation.[200] Under such circumstances it is purely fictitious to say that a valuable opportunity has been lost, for it is one that the claimant would never have taken.

This does seem a formidable objection. It has curious implications. It would seem that a claimant who would have allowed breach in return for payment, had her permission been sought, has damages, whereas another who would *never* have allowed breach on any consideration is left without remedy. This would be a sliding scale sliding in the wrong direction. Perhaps, however, it is consistent with the hierarchy of remedies suggested in the *Vercoe* case.[201] One who would have been willing to grant release (presumed in commercial situations) recovers a 'reasonable fee' for the unilateral infringement, i.e. *Wrotham Park* damages.[202] But where the right is so important that paid infringement would not have been contemplated, it receives the higher protection of account of profits. So one response to the widely expressed 'fiction' criticism of Sharpe and Waddams' analysis is to limit 'lost opportunity' damages to cases where the opportunity *would* have been taken, and remedy 'no consent' cases with the disgorgement deterrence of *Blake*.

For Andrew Burrows a subsidiary criticism is the impossibility of showing that the right would have been sold (if at all) at the price fixed by the court.[203] Inevitably that is correct since the courts formulate a 'notional bargain' in which the parties are deemed to act reasonably.[204] The court must set a fair price within the parameters of ordinary commercial negotiations.[205] In truth more precise guidance is impossible. Brightman J's 'great moderation' in *Wrotham Park*[206] has been described as the sole factor making the 'complete arbitrariness' of quantification

[198] Cf. J. Beatson, *The Use and Abuse of Unjust Enrichment* (Oxford University Press, 1991) pp.15–17 (restitution as 'monetized specific performance').

[199] C. Rotherham, '*Wrotham Park* damages and accounts of profits: Compensation or restitution?' [2008] *LMCLQ* 25.

[200] *A-G v Blake* is similar, indeed *a fortiori*.

[201] Cf. p. 256 above.

[202] Cf. *Experience Hendrix v PPX Enterprises* [2003] EWCA Civ 323.

[203] A.S. Burrows, 'Are "damages on the *Wrotham Park* basis" compensatory, restitutionary or neither?' in D. Saidov & R. Cunnington (eds) *Contract Damages: Domestic and International Perspectives* (Hart Publishing, 2008).

[204] *Pell Frischmann Engineering Ltd v Bow Valley Iran Ltd* [2009] UKPC 45, [46]–[54].

[205] *Vercoe v Rutland Fund Management* [2010] EWHC 424 (Ch), [292].

[206] [1974] 1 WLR 798, 815.

acceptable, but even moderation has been cast aside as awards have swelled under the influence of *Blake*.[207] Sharpe and Waddams suggested it would be 'not unfair to assume that the defendant would have paid ... the full amount of his net gain from acquiring the right'.[208] Surely, though, the defendant would never have agreed to this – what could be the point of acquiring the right if it was guaranteed to be unprofitable? Perhaps Sharpe and Waddams' argument is to be understood as simplifying the quantification inquiry. The defendant can hardly complain if the full measure of his profits is used as the 'hypothetical bargain' – he should have asked permission first. In other words, this measure encourages actual negotiation. But this approach would unite *Wrotham Park* with *Blake* (full disgorgement) and make it harder to maintain that the former is actually a compensatory remedy.

Whether the quantification difficulties are a fatal objection depends on commentators' other commitments. Burrows advocates a restitutionary analysis of *Wrotham Park* in which the 'hypothetical bargain' is in fact retained, albeit downgraded to a mere 'assessment mechanism' for settling quantum.[209] For Campbell, however, the entire jurisprudence is misconceived. *Wrotham Park* postulates that there was no bargain but the parties could at the outset have agreed in their contract, through a 'bespoke clause', that any profits made by breach be paid over to the claimant (in whole or in part).[210] Thus the parties themselves would state the remedy for breach – and that would be it. If they have not done so, there is no basis for *Wrotham Park* damages at all.

The alternative restitutionary analysis of *Wrotham Park* has obvious appeal. The damages are assessed according to (a proportion of) the defendant's profits. It might therefore seem clear that some form of gain-based remedy is involved. However Bingham MR denies this, defending the 'hypothetical bargain' analysis and observing there is an 'obvious relationship' between the defendant's profits and how much he would have been willing to pay to obtain the claimant's consent.[211] But those like Rotherham who dismiss the 'fictitious' lost bargain analysis for the reasons just discussed conclude that restitution is the obvious alternative explanation. Rotherham contrasts the 'reality' of the defendant's enrichment with the fiction of the lost opportunity to bargain.[212] Burrows describes restitution as 'the most convincing and satisfying rationale'.[213] By contrast Campbell, although he agrees that the lost bargain theory is 'completely artificial', argues that restitution is an 'even greater' artificiality. Restitutionary reasoning '*must* undermine freedom of contract' because it is not interested in the parties' intentions, only with correcting abstract wrongs.[214]

---

[207] D. Campbell, 'The Extinguishing of Contract' (2004) 67 *MLR* 818, discussing *Lane v O'Brien Homes* [2004] EWHC 303 (QB).

[208] Cf. n.196 above, 296.

[209] Burrows, n.203 above, p. 177.

[210] (2004) 67 MLR 818, 824–26.

[211] *Jaggard v Sawyer* [1995] 1 WLR 269, 282.

[212] Cf. Rotherham, n.199 above.

[213] Burrows, n.203 above, 185.

[214] Campbell, n.207 above, 827 (original emphasis). Cf. pp. 255–256 above.

Why should the court 'exceptionally' employ a restitutionary remedy in these cases? Why should *Wrotham Park* yield only partial restitution as opposed to the total disgorgement in *Blake*? The answers are not wholly clear. Rotherham suggests the enduring judicial popularity of the 'lost opportunity' analysis is because restitution for wrongs is, by contrast, inherently controversial.[215] It 'looks beyond the moral claims of the parties before the court' to provide incentives for efficient action. Apart from noting the complex political concerns that this raises, however, Rotherham does not explain what, when and how such incentives should be provided. He certainly does not engage with those, like Campbell, who argue that restitutionary damages for breach of contract are always presumptively inefficient. Rotherham's conclusion seems to be that the persistent and misguided compensatory view of *Wrotham Park* has obstructed the formulation of the necessary principles. But his preferred solution is distinctly incomplete!

Burrows, too, leaves the analysis of these points somewhat vague. He agrees that *Wrotham Park* is 'exceptional', although less exceptional than the full disgorgement remedy in *Blake*. But he does not say precisely when it should be available.[216] Burrows denies that disgorgement must be an all-or-nothing matter. Removing a 'fair proportion' of the profits is a 'sensible mid-position, whether justified by a policy of reasonable deterrence or corrective justice'.[217] But while sensible compromise is always appealing, is this sufficient justification for *Wrotham Park*? Burrows does not explain what 'reasonable deterrence' is or how the courts are to calculate it. As seen above, his quantification mechanism is the 'hypothetical bargain', which is not ostensibly concerned with deterrence at all (unless it means full disgorgement as Sharpe and Waddams contend, and which Burrows rejects).

Graham Virgo points out that equity frequently allows retention of a proportion by the defendant when ordering an account of profits, to reflect that which derives from the defendant's time and skill in exploiting the opportunity rather than the wrong itself.[218] Virgo uses the same 'causal' analysis to explain why there is only partial restitution in cases like *Wrotham Park*: most of the profits derive from the defendant building the houses.[219] This is certainly one solution to the conundrum of why *Wrotham Park* restitution is partial whereas in *Blake* it is total – the 'equitable allowance' is in the court's discretion and depends (*inter alia*) on the defendant's 'good faith'. Obviously in *Blake* this was lacking. Is Virgo's explanation preferable to that in *Vercoe* which focuses on the claimant's interest and her attitude to invasion of it, rather than the defendant's conduct?[220]

---

215 Rotherham, n.199 above, pp. 52–54.
216 A.S. Burrows, *Remedies for Torts and Breach of Contract* (Oxford University Press, 3rd edn, 2004) p. 407: the courts have a discretion 'although clear principles should, in time, develop'.
217 Burrows, n.203 above, p. 179.
218 G. Virgo, 'Restitutionary Remedies for Wrongs: Causation and Remoteness' in C.E.F. Rickett (ed.), *Justifying Private Law Remedies* (Hart Publishing, 2009) p. 309.
219 Ibid, p. 311.
220 Cf. p. 256 above. Virgo notes that deliberate breach of contract was expressly rejected by Peter Smith J in *WWF*, n.194 above.

The third explanation for *Wrotham Park* focuses on the invasion of the claimant's rights. It expressly does not depend on establishing any loss on the claimant's part – or indeed gain on the defendant's. This offers distinct advantages. Of course the whole *Wrotham Park* 'problem' is that ordinary loss (diminution in value) is absent, and the 'loss of opportunity' measure has been heavily criticized as artificial. But Mitchell McInnes argues that the true focus should not be the bargain itself (which may or may not be artificial) but the claimant's rights – demanding compensation for relaxing those rights is the basis of the bargain.[221] The rights analysis would also explain why *Wrotham Park*-type damages are awarded even where the defendant has not profited from the infringement.[222] Virgo has to treat this as a hybrid compensatory-restitutionary approach, whereas Burrows prefers an 'objective view of compensation'.[223] But neither explanation is wholly satisfactory and both have to depart from the preferred restitutionary analysis.

Robert Stevens, again, is the most prominent advocate of the rights valuation approach.[224] *Wrotham Park* is simply a prominent example of what Stevens argues is the general approach under which vindicating rights is the law's primary purpose (with compensation/restitution of 'consequential' loss/gain only a secondary concern). The idea that invasion of rights in itself requires substantial damages is, however, alien to traditional legal doctrine and hard to grasp.[225] Responding to McInnes, Rotherham argues that breaching a right does not necessarily entail a loss, noting the award of *nominal* damages for breaches where no loss can be proved.[226] For Burrows, the inability of Stevens's theory to account for nominal damages is one reason to reject it.[227] Burrows points out that Stevens would up-end the law of damages by placing vindication of rights at its core (currently an exceptional case, as with *Wrotham Park*) rather than the usual compensation of loss. Further, Stevens cannot explain the 'duty' to mitigate or the courts' increasing tendency to use improvements in the claimant's position to reduce damages.[228] Nor can Stevens explain why any date other than that of breach (the invasion of rights) should be used for assessment of damages.[229] In the end, for Burrows, the flaw is 'in imagining that we sensibly can, or would want to, put a value on the right that has been infringed without considering the consequential impact of that infringement'.[230] That is a fundamental challenge to Stevens's explanation of *Wrotham Park*, and his rights-based approach to contract remedies generally.

Therefore the rival explanations of *Wrotham Park* all face powerful criticisms. None of them fits all the existing case law. Is a 'hybrid' explanation the best

---

[221] M. McInnes, 'Gain, Loss and the User Principle' [2006] RLR 76.
[222] *Inverugie Investments v Hackett* [1995] 1 WLR 713.
[223] Cf. Virgo, n.218 above, 315–16; Burrows, n.203 above, 180 n.50.
[224] R. Stevens, *Torts and Rights* (Oxford University Press, 2007) ch. 4.
[225] Cf. pp. 282–285 below.
[226] Rotherham, n.199 above.
[227] Burrows, n.203 above.
[228] E.g. *Bence Graphics v Fasson* [1998] QB 87; cf. pp. 247–248 above.
[229] Cf. *The Golden Victory* [2007] UKHL 12. But cf. Stevens, n.32 above.
[230] Burrows, n.203 above, p. 185.

compromise or is that really just indecision? The most distinctive approach is that of Campbell who, consistent with his criticisms of *Blake*, argues for the abolition of *Wrotham Park* damages.[231] But the majority position seems to be that the claimant 'deserves' a remedy in such cases, despite the absence of loss (as ordinarily defined). Whether an exceptional remedy (compensatory or restitutionary) or exemplifying the universal concern to protect rights, *Wrotham Park* is a prime example of the shifting concern of English law to protect promisees' 'performance interests'. It also illustrates the difficulty of departing from the well-established approach of compensating loss.

Further Reading

Performance remedies: moral arguments

L. Smith, 'Disgorgement of the Profits of Breach of Contract: Property, Contract and "Efficient Breach"' (1994) 24 *Can Bus LJ* 121.

D. Friedmann, 'The Performance Interest in Contract Damages' (1995) 111 *LQR* 628.

L. Smith, 'Understanding Specific Performance' In N. Cohen & E, McKendrick (eds), *Comparative Remedies for Breach of Contract* (Hart Publishing, 2005).

R. Stevens, 'Damages and the Right to Performance: A *Golden Victory* Or Not?' In J. Neyers et al. (eds), *Exploring Contract Law* (Hart Publishing, 2009).

A. Burrows, 'Damages and Rights' In D. Nolan & A. Robertson (eds), *Rights and Private Law* (Hart Publishing, 2011).

Performance remedies: instrumental arguments

O.W. Holmes, 'The Path of the Law' (1897) 10 *Harvard LR* 457.

G. Calabresi & A.D. Melamed, 'Property Rules, Liability Rules and Inalienability: One View of the Cathedral' (1972) 85 *Harvard LR* 1089.

A. Schwartz, 'The Case for Specific Performance' (1979) 89 *Yale LJ* 271.

I.R. Macneil, 'Efficient Breach of Contract: Circles in the Sky' (1982) 68 *Virginia LR* 947.

D. Campbell & D. Harris, 'In Defence of Breach' (2002) 22 *Legal Stud* 208.

E.A. Posner, 'Economic Analysis of Contract Law After Three Decades: Success or Failure?' (2003) 112 *Yale LJ* 829.

R. Kreitner, 'Multiplicity in Contract Remedies' in N. Cohen & E. McKendrick (eds), *Comparative Remedies for Breach of Contract* (Hart Publishing, 2005).

A. Schwartz & R.E. Scott, 'Market Damages, Efficient Contracting, and the Economic Waste Fallacy' (2008) 108 *Columbia LR* 1610.

S. Shavell, 'Why Breach of Contract May Not Be Immoral Given the Incompleteness of Contracts' in O, Ben-Shahar & A. Porat (eds), *Fault in American Contract Law* (Cambridge University Press, 2010).

D. Markovits & A. Schwartz, 'The Myth of Efficient Breach: New Defenses of the Expectation Interest' (2011) 97 *Virginia LR* 1939.

---

[231] Campbell, n.207 above.

Wrotham Park damages

R.J. Sharpe & S.M. Waddams, 'Damages for Lost Opportunity to Bargain' (1982) 2 *OJLS* 290.

D. Campbell, 'The Extinguishing of Contract' (2004) 67 *MLR* 818.

C. Rotherham, '"*Wrotham Park* Damages" and Accounts of Profits: Compensation Or Restitution?' [2008] *LMCLQ* 25.

A. Burrows, 'Are "Damages on the *Wrotham Park* Basis" Compensatory, Restitutionary Or Neither?' in D. Saidov & R. Cunnington (eds) *Contract Damages: Domestic and International Perspectives* (Hart Publishing, 2008).

10

THIRD PARTIES

THE LAW

> *Example*: Angus and Becca agree that in exchange for payment of £200 by
> Becca to Angus, Angus will mow the lawn of Christopher (an elderly friend
> of Becca's) every week for one year. Becca pays Angus the £200 and Angus
> mows Christopher's lawn for six months. Angus then stops mowing the
> lawn.

The classical common law position in this scenario is that Christopher has no
right to require performance by Angus, for two reasons. First, Christopher is not
a party to, i.e. not 'privy' to, the contract. Angus undertakes an obligation to
Becca; Christopher is simply not a promisee. This is the requirement of 'privity of
contract'. Secondly, the doctrine of consideration requires that a person seeking to
enforce an obligation must have paid for it. Becca and not Christopher has given
consideration. Thus, only Becca has an enforceable right against Angus.

Clearly then, privity poses a great obstacle from Christopher's perspective.
Unless he could show that, for example, Becca had entered into the contract with
Angus as Christopher's agent, or that Becca unequivocally constituted herself a
trustee of Angus's promise to her for Christopher's benefit, Christopher would
traditionally have no right to enforce the promise. But Christopher's position has
been transformed by the Contracts (Rights of Third Parties) Act 1999. Under this
statute, a third party enjoys the right to enforce the contract (subject to defences
that the promisor might have raised against the promisee (s.3)) where the parties
expressly confer such a right (s.1(1)(a)), or where the contract purports to confer a
benefit upon the third party and the right would be consistent with the contract's
'proper construction' (ss.1(1)(b) and 1(2)).

Indeed, the contracting parties are prevented from varying the contract without the third party's consent, once he has relied upon it or signified his assent to
it (s.2(1)). In the scenario above, let us imagine that Angus offers to refund £100
to Becca if she will agree to discharge the outstanding six months of the contract,

and Becca agrees. But Angus and Becca will be unable to vary the contract in this way without Christopher's agreement, once he has expressed his assent to the original contract to Angus (which seems highly likely, at least implicitly, given that Angus is to perform on Christopher's property) or relied upon the contract.

In the original hypothetical example, Becca as promisee will have an action against Angus for breach of contract. What remedies are available? This is a common law question, unaffected by the 1999 Act (s.4).[1] It is often assumed that Becca's damages would be purely nominal. The loss in our scenario seems to be Christopher's (namely his uncut grass). Claimants are not usually allowed to recover damages for another's loss. One way around this problem is for Becca to claim specific performance rather than damages,[2] although it is not entirely clear why the award of nominal damages is 'inadequate' so as to justify the equitable remedy if the basis on which damages are assessed as nominal is correct. Alternatively, an exception to the rule that one cannot claim damages on behalf of another has been recognised in the situation where X owes a contractual duty to Y not to damage property belonging to Z.[3] Lord Denning MR argued for a more wide-ranging exception in the context of the promisee booking a holiday on behalf of a group.[4] Most radical of all, some judges have argued that Becca should be able to recover substantial damages in her own name for the loss of expected performance.[5] These arguments came to a head in the difficult and important decision of the House of Lords in *Panatown Ltd v Alfred McAlpine Construction Ltd*,[6] which will be discussed in detail in Debate 2.

Debate 1

What rights should third parties have?

This might appear a non-debate. For years judges were dismissive of the doctrine of privity, most notably Lord Denning in, for example, his great dissent in the leading case *Scruttons v Midland Silicones*,[7] or later Lord Diplock (deploring 'an anachronistic shortcoming that has for many years been regarded as a reproach to English private law').[8] In an influential judgment,[9] Steyn LJ stated:

> The case for recognising a contract for the benefit of a third party is simple and straightforward. The autonomy of the will of the parties should be respected. The law of contract should give effect to the reasonable expectations of

---

[1] Save to the extent that the promisor is protected against double liability (s.5).
[2] Cf. *Beswick v Beswick* [1968] AC 58.
[3] Cf. *The Albazero* [1977] AC 774.
[4] *Jackson v Horizon Holidays* [1975] 1 WLR 1468.
[5] *Linden Gardens Trust v Linesta Sludge Disposals* [1994] 1 AC 85, 97 (Lord Griffiths).
[6] [2001] 1 AC 518.
[7] [1962] AC 446.
[8] *Swain v The Law Society* [1983] 1 AC 598, 611.
[9] Cited in Law Commission Report 242 (1996), para 1.1, and by Lord Irvine LC introducing the Contracts (Rights of Third Parties) Bill: Lords Hansard, 11 Jan 1999, Col. 20.

contracting parties. Principle certainly requires that a burden should not be imposed on a third party without his consent. But there is no doctrinal, logical or policy reason why the law should deny effectiveness to a contract for the benefit of a third party where that is the expressed intention of the parties. Moreover, often the parties, and particularly third parties, organise their affairs on the faith of the contract. They rely on the contract. It is therefore unjust to deny effectiveness to such a contract. I will not struggle further with the point since nobody seriously asserts the contrary.[10]

This judicial criticism culminated in the Contracts (Rights of Third Parties) Act 1999, based on a report by the Law Commission.[11]

However, contrary to Steyn LJ's view, some commentators did seriously defend the doctrine of privity. Their defence of the common law position stands now as a challenge to the 1999 Act. It is worth considering these views since it is usually assumed that privity was wholly indefensible and that its abrogation by the 1999 Act must be an unqualified Good Thing.

Privity's defenders argue that the rule is required by the notion of contracts as bilateral promises. By contrast, there is no coherent doctrinal basis for granting rights to non-parties. Privity reform has placed pragmatic convenience, the satisfaction of commercial expectations, above theoretical coherence. But sceptics argue that the problems laid at privity's door were usually the result of entirely different rules (such as the definition of loss, or the effect of death on contractual rights). It would be more rational to address such failings directly. Finally, to the extent that privity itself was commercially obstructive, familiar devices such as agency and collateral contracts were available to prevent defeated expectations while deftly avoiding a direct challenge to privity itself.[12] Accordingly, the pragmatic case for reform was considerably weaker than appears at first sight, and whether it outweighs the requirement for coherent principles may be questioned.

THE DOCTRINAL LOGIC OF PRIVITY

It has been argued that privity is a necessary feature of English contract law, being based on the reciprocal 'bargain theory' (requiring consideration for a contract to be enforceable). More fundamentally, it is said to stem from the very nature of contracts as voluntary obligations. Stephen Smith puts this neatly: promissory obligations 'do not exist in the air: they are obligations undertaken to particular persons, extending to and only to those persons'.[13] As contractual obligations are burdensome it is important that we are able to control their scope, i.e. to determine the beneficiaries of the right to performance.

---

[10] *Darlington BC v Wiltshier Northern* [1995] 1 WLR 68.
[11] See n.9 above.
[12] H. Collins, *The Law of Contract* (Cambridge University Press, 4th edn, 2003) p. 309.
[13] S.A. Smith, 'Contracts for the Benefit of Third Parties: in Defence of the Third-Party Rule' (1997) 17 *OJLS* 643, 645.

Peter Kincaid has been the most consistent champion of the privity doctrine. Would-be reformers of the privity doctrine, he complained, routinely state that privity leads to 'unjust' outcomes without specifying precisely what is unjust about them.[14] The allegation of 'injustice' seems to focus upon the promisor – that he would be free to break his promise without sanction, since the third party cannot sue (and arguably the promisee, who can sue, has suffered no loss) – thus allowing the promisor to 'snap his fingers at a bargain deliberately made'.[15] The promisor could also be thought unjustly enriched, if he received payment but then did not perform, as Gaudron J has held.[16] But Kincaid identified two fundamental problems with this line of reasoning.

First, it is incorrect to consider a contractual duty 'in isolation from its corresponding right'. Contractual duties are not owed to the whole word like criminal or tort duties, but only to those with corresponding rights to enforce them. There must be a personal link between the right and duty.[17] Thus privity is 'more of a corollary than a rule'.[18] Focusing upon the promisor's duty in the abstract is inconsistent with the general common law approach to civil liability, where the concern is to give redress to the claimant (promisee), not to punish the defendant. Gaudron J's approach is flawed for the same reason: 'She would give the third party a right to sue if the promisor has been paid, because not to do so would be to allow the promisor to be unjustly enriched. She does not require the plaintiff to show that the enrichment has been at his expense.'[19]

Secondly, Kincaid defends privity using the bargain theory of consideration, entrenched in English law from the early nineteenth century. Since *Eastwood v Kenyon* neither the most serious intention to bound, nor the weightiest moral obligation, has sufficed for a binding contract.[20] Something of economic value must be given in exchange for the promise. This means, again, that focusing on the promisor's undertaking alone is incorrect: as Kincaid says, 'the intent of the promisor, with its moralistic, civil-law flavour, was rejected as the basis of contractual liability'.[21] Thus Lord Denning's emphasis on the sanctity of promise was mistaken.[22] The question of 'who can sue' is also answered by the bargain theory, which 'reflects the common law's ... focus ... upon the plaintiff's cause of action, not the abstract enforceability of the promise. It is the plaintff's role in the bargain as promisee and payer of the price demanded which qualifies him for the right to sue. To remove these elements is to remove the essentially reciprocal nature of contract.' In conclusion, Kincaid's argument was that privity

---

[14] P. Kincaid, 'Third Parties: Rationalising a Right to Sue' [1989] *CLJ* 243.

[15] *Dunlop Pneumatic Tyre Co Ltd v Selfridge & Co* [1915] AC 847, 855 (Lord Dunedin).

[16] *Trident General Insurance Co Ltd v McNiece Bros Pty Ltd* (1988) 165 CLR 107.

[17] The 'purely bilateral *vinculum juris*' [juridical tie] that Steyn LJ dismissed as 'technical' in *Darlington BC v Wiltshier Northern* [1995] 1 WLR 68.

[18] P. Kincaid, 'The UK Law Commission's Privity Proposals and Contract Theory' (1995) 8 *Jo Con Law* 51.

[19] [1989] CLJ 243, 256.

[20] (1840) 11 Ad & E 438.

[21] [1989] CLJ 243, citing *Coulls v Bagot's Executor* (1967) 119 CLR 460, 498 (Windeyer J).

[22] Cf. *Smith and Snipes Hall Farm v River Douglas Catchment Board* [1949] 2 KB 500, 514.

reformers had to explain the basis of the third party's right, and not just the promisor's duty.

Kincaid also attacked the Law Commission's basis for third-party rights: that this would give effect to the intentions of the parties, in accordance with the Will Theory of contract.[23] For Kincaid, this misunderstood the promissory basis of the theory: promises are undertakings made *to* someone, and 'Privity is simply an application of the principle that the promisor defines his right-holder (the person to whom he makes the promise). The will theory thus prescribes the privity rule (you cannot sue on a promise not made to you).'[24] The parties'-intentions justification was anyway 'weak': the promisor could protect the third party simply by performing, and the promisee by suing the promisor (potentially with strengthened remedies – but that was quite different from giving rights to the third party). This leads on to the argument that the real problems in three-party situations were caused by other rules of contract law (such as the definition of loss) rather than privity itself.

WAS PRIVITY THE REAL PROBLEM?

Stephen Smith accepts the fundamental logic of privity: a promise is enforceable only by the person to whom it is made. Smith suggests that dissatisfaction with privity has been caused by its status as a locus of *other* unsatisfactory rules. In respect of none of the under-protected interests in the privity cases 'is the third-party rule the reason why the protection is inadequate. The inadequacies stem from general problems in the law of obligations'.[25] Of course if this argument is accepted, it shows that the decision to give contractual rights to third parties was mistaken. Rational reform would, instead, have tackled the 'inadequacies' directly.

Reverting to our hypothetical example, it might be thought inadequate that, on Angus's breach, Becca cannot recover substantial damages. Accepting that, under the promissory theory, Becca is the proper claimant here (being the promisee), the problem is not privity at all,[26] but rather the traditional assumption that she could recover only nominal damages. This arguably undervalues her performance interest (as will be considered in Debate 2). The rule could be reformed directly: Smith states that it 'undoubtedly stems from the evidential difficulties involved in placing monetary figures on hard-to-quantify losses', commenting that such evidential problems cannot, however, justify routine under-compensation of promisees. But tackling this problem does not justify granting any rights to Christopher, the third party.

---

23 Law Commission CP 121 (1991), Para 5.5(a).

24 Kincaid, n.18 above.

25 S.A. Smith, 'Contracts for the Benefit of Third Parties: In Defence of the Third-Party Rule' (1997) 17 *OJLS* 643, 658.

26 Lord Millett points out in *Panatown* [2001] 1 AC 518 that such questions arise equally in two-party cases such as *Ruxley Electronics v Forsyth* [1996] AC 344.

It is worth raising one slightly specialized issue here because it touches on a case that is often used to justify the 1999 reforms, *Beswick v Beswick*.[27] It is said to be intolerable that in such a case the third party would ordinarily be left without a remedy on the promisee's death since an executor has no duty to enforce a promise for the benefit of a third party, as opposed to benefiting the estate itself (in *Beswick* the plaintiff was coincidentally also the promisee's executrix, bringing an action to benefit herself *qua* third party). Recognising a third-party contractual right, it is argued, prevents death from thwarting the promisee's intentions. Again though, as Smith points out, while the normal outcome might seem unsatisfactory this is an artefact of the general rules for enforcing the rights of the departed. If those rules are too restrictive, the problem should be tackled directly. Robert Stevens argues that the Act's solution to the *Beswick* problem is anyway questionable.[28] The Law Commission decided that the privity 'problem' should not be solved by strengthening the promisee's remedies because the promisee might be dead (or impecunious or otherwise unable to claim). Yet as Stevens says, people are often unable to bring claims, but that does not in itself justify transferring their rights to someone else.

Another unsatisfactory aspect of the hypothetical case would be if Angus could keep all of the £200 payment, despite not completing performance. He would be unjustly enriched. Does this not justify a third-party right against Angus? First, note that the enrichment would be at Becca's expense rather than Christopher's. Secondly, the problem stems from the general requirement in the English law of restitution that to recover a sum of money paid when there is a 'failure of consideration' (i.e. the basis for the payment), that failure must be 'total'.[29] This much-criticized rule stems from the reluctance of English courts to apportion payment in cases of partial performance. Its application is quite general, in two-party cases as well as three. The unjust enrichment 'problem' is not caused by privity.

What if, in the hypothetical case, Christopher had relied upon Angus's promised performance, for example by giving his lawnmower away to charity? There is a case for protecting reasonable reliance by compensating the detriment incurred thereby. But English law does not allow promissory estoppel to be used to found a cause of action.[30] Once again, note that this is a general problem (or debate) that arises *just as readily in two-party situations* (imagine that Angus had directly promised to mow Christopher's lawn free of charge, without Becca being involved at all). Although there may be certain different questions in a three-party situation,[31] the fundamental issue here is not one to do with privity at all.

As these examples show, there are gaps in protection of the promisee's expectation and restitutionary interests and the third party's reliance interest. But none of these is a problem that requires reform of the privity doctrine. The first demands a

---

[27] [1968] AC 58.
[28] Robert Stevens, 'The Contracts (Rights of Third Parties) Act 1999' (2004) 120 *LQR* 292.
[29] *Whincup v Hughes* (1871) LR 6 CP 78. Cf. p. 251 above.
[30] *Combe v Combe* [1951] 2 KB 215. Cf. pp. 62–63 above.
[31] How reasonable is it to rely upon a promise *made to someone else*?

reconceptualization of the promisee's loss; the second a revision of the requirement for total failure of consideration; and the third, a possible extension of estoppel.

THE COHERENCE OF THE 1999 REFORMS

The Law Commission's Report (and therefore the 1999 Act) have been criticized for lacking any coherent theory of the third party's rights. The Commission seemed to view the intentions of the parties as the prime justification for the third party's rights: if such rights were desired by the parties, the law should give effect to their intentions.[32] This is reflected in the test for creation of rights in ss.1(1)–(2) of the 1999 Act. However, as shown above, the third party's rights effectively take precedence over those of the parties when the latter wish to vary the contract but the third party's rights have 'crystallized', through reliance or communicated assent: s.2. At this stage, as Catherine Mitchell puts it, the Law Commission seem to view third parties as the main victims of the privity rule, without acknowledging (let alone justifying) the switch from the earlier justification (thwarting the intentions of the parties).[33] As Mitchell points out, if protecting the expectations of the third party were the main concern, 'recourse to the intentions and will of the contracting parties is unnecessary in justifying reform'.[34] Conversely, if the parties' intentions truly were the driver for reform, the third party's rights would rise and fall with the fluctuations thereof. Presenting both (inconsistent) justifications at once is simply incoherent.

Considering the test for 'crystallization', Smith suggests that the role of reliance is 'obscure' since it does not determine the quantum of the third party's remedy. He dismisses the Law Commission's explanation (protecting reasonable reliance) as question-begging: 'An unreasonable expectation is not turned into a reasonable expectation by reliance.'[35] The other trigger for irrevocability, communicated assent, is more straightforwardly contractual. 'The final result is a sophisticated, but ultimately *ad hoc*, balancing of different interests.'[36] The shape of the third party's *sui generis* rights derives from the Commission's 'desire to get around (without directly addressing) a number of distinct problems in the law of obligations in a single move'. As seen above, Smith argues that they would be more rationally tackled head-on. This would ensure the coherence of contract law.

Having defended the doctrinal necessity of privity both before and after the Law Commission's consultation paper, but seen his arguments dismissed in the final report, Kincaid assessed 'the significance of the fact that no one cares about that thesis'.[37] For Kincaid, this indicated that the Commission 'do not really attach much importance to coherent reasoning'. Their view of contract law seemed more pragmatic than doctrinally logical, with economic efficiency

---

[32] Cf. Law Com 242, para 3.1.
[33] C. Mitchell, 'Privity Reform and the Nature of Contractual Obligations' (1999) 19 *Legal Studies* 229.
[34] Ibid, p. 241.
[35] Smith (1997) 17 *OJLS* 643, 659 n.60.
[36] Ibid, 660.
[37] P. Kincaid, 'Privity and Private Justice in Contract' (1997) 12 *Jo Con Law* 47.

to the fore: '"Intention" and "injustice to the third party" are imprecise, partly formed ideas that are put on the scales along with public ideas like efficiency and convenience to tip the scales in favour of reform.' The proposals (subsequently enacted by Parliament, of course) were 'impressionistic'. Whether this matters depends, as Kincaid says, whether we view contract law as primarily a matter of individual justice, or 'just a pragmatic series of adjustments to make the economy work better'. Kincaid himself clearly takes the former view, but many would take the latter. Beale opines that Kincaid's view that the promisee should enforce the promise on behalf of the third party requires a 'tour around the houses', great commercial inconvenience in the interests of doctrinal purity.[38]

PRAGMATISM

As the previous section suggests, the main reason for the 1999 Act may well be to satisfy 'the reasonable expectations of honest men' by recognising third-party rights to the extent that commercial practice demands them.[39] Steyn LJ castigated privity as a 'technical' doctrinal requirement that had been 'barely tolerable in Victorian England' and had 'no place in our more complex commercial world'.[40] He suggested that the inflexibility of English contract law placed it at a disadvantage within the EU single market, observing that 'it is a historical curiosity that the legal system of a mercantile country such as England, which in other areas of the law of contract (such as, for example, the objective theory of the interpretation of contracts) takes great account of the interests of third parties, has not been able to rid itself of this unjust rule'. Lord Goff describes both the theoretical appeal, but the practical inconvenience, of privity: 'The rule, seen in the abstract, is rational and very understandable in a law of contract which includes the doctrine of consideration; but it has given rise to great problems in practice – because, both in commerce and in the domestic context, parties do enter into contracts which are intended to confer enforceable rights on third parties'.[41] As he went on to say, the common law created various exceptions to privity to ease these practical difficulties, even before the 1999 Act. The debate over exclusion clauses is an excellent example.

> *Example*: E Ltd agrees to transport goods belonging to D Ltd by sea. The contract between them contains a clause in which D Ltd undertakes not to bring an action in negligence against E Ltd, or their servants or agents, including independent contractors. The goods are damaged when being carelessly unloaded by F Ltd, stevedores engaged for that purpose by E Ltd. D Ltd accepts that it has no action against E Ltd, but wishes to claim in tort against F Ltd for the damage to the cargo.

---

[38] H. Beale, 'A Review of the [1999 Act]' in A. Burrows and E. Peel (eds), *Contract Formation and Parties* (Oxford University Press, 2010).

[39] Cf. Steyn, 'Contract Law: Fulfilling the Reasonable Expectations of Honest Men' (1997) 113 *LQR* 433.

[40] *Darlington BC v Wiltshier Northern* [1995] 1 WLR 68.

[41] *Panatown* [2001] 1 AC 518.

The reaction to this scenario has changed over the years; Lord Goff once referred to the swinging 'pendulum of judicial opinion' on the matter.[42] In *Scruttons v Midland Silicones* the House of Lords (Lord Denning dissenting) was emphatic that a third party (like F) could not rely on an exclusion clause in a contract between others (D and E).[43] However, in a later 3–2 decision the Privy Council gave effect to a clause very similar to that in the hypothetical case, in *The Eurymedon*.[44] Lord Wilberforce, for the majority, announced a credo for the commercially pragmatic judge:

> It is only the precise analysis of this complex of relations into the classical offer and acceptance, with identifiable consideration, that seems to present difficulty, but this same difficulty exists in many situations of daily life, e.g., sales at auction; supermarket purchases; boarding an omnibus; purchasing a train ticket; tenders for the supply of goods; offers of rewards; acceptance by post; warranties of authority by agents; manufacturers' guarantees; gratuitous bailments; bankers' commercial credits. These are all examples which show that English law, having committed itself to a rather technical and schematic doctrine of contract, in application takes a practical approach, often at the cost of forcing the facts to fit uneasily into the marked slots of offer, acceptance and consideration.

Observing that the exemption clause was 'designed to cover the whole carriage from loading to discharge, by whomsoever it is performed', Lord Wilberforce held that a new unilateral contract (containing the exclusion clause) arose between the stevedores and cargo owners when the stevedores unloaded the cargo (the carriers acting as agents for the owners). However, this was stretching matters too far for the dissenting judges, Viscount Dilhorne observing that: 'Anxiety to save negligent people from the consequences of their negligence does not lead me to give an unnatural and artificial meaning to the clause and a meaning which the words it contains do not bear'.[45]

Subsequently, however, *The Eurymedon* has been welcomed and followed.[46] The Chief Justice of Australia said that the decision 'was of great moment in the commercial world and, if I may say so, an outstanding example of the ability of the law to render effective the practical expectations of those engaged in the transportation of goods. It is not a decision of its nature to be narrowly or pedantically confined.'[47] Nevertheless, as Lord Goff pointed out, 'so long as the principle continues to be understood to rest upon an enforceable contract as between the cargo owners and the stevedores entered into through the agency

---

[42] *The Mahkutai* [1996] AC 650.

[43] [1962] AC 446; contrast *Elder, Dempster & Co Ltd v Paterson Zochonis & Co Ltd* [1924] AC 522.

[44] *New Zealand Shipping v A M Satterthwaite & Co* [1975] AC 154.

[45] Concerns about exemption clauses could now be addressed directly through the Unfair Contract Terms Act 1977, s.2(2).

[46] Unanimously in *The New York Star* [1981] 1 *WLR* 138.

[47] *The New York Star* [1979] 1 Lloyd's Rep 298 (Barwick CJ).

of the shipowner, it is inevitable that technical points of contract and agency law will continue to be invoked by cargo owners seeking to enforce tortious remedies against stevedores'.[48] It was quite legitimate to raise such points. Therefore it might be preferable to recognize a 'fully-fledged exception to the doctrine of privity of contract, thus escaping from all the technicalities'. Similar criticisms could, no doubt, be made of the other routes by which exclusion clauses have been given effect in three-party situations, such as altering the incidence of tort liability.[49]

The appeal of the 1999 Act, therefore, is that it provides a direct path for enforcement of contract terms by a third party. In the hypothetical case, F Ltd could straightforwardly rely on the exclusion clause agreed between D Ltd and E Ltd to defeat the action in negligence.[50] In a wide variety of other common commercial situations, it might be very useful to create enforceable third-party rights. Insurance policies are often taken out for the benefit of third parties. The large number of parties working on any major construction project will usually necessitate obligations between parties not directly in privity. It may also be desirable to create guarantees of quality that endure for the benefit of future owners of a building, given the absence of tort remedies against a negligent builder.[51]

However, we might ask how much practical difference the 1999 Act's 'fully fledged exception' to privity has made. The desire for third-party rights in the situations just mentioned is not new; prior to 1999 there were other ways to obtain them. We have already seen the story of exclusion clauses. In areas requiring, for example, indemnities or buildings guarantees for third parties, an express contract between the third party and the promisor ('collateral' to the main contract) would bring this about. In certain commercial sectors at least it seems that there was little demand for the 1999 reforms, and sometimes outright hostility: the construction industry lobbied, unsuccessfully, to be exempted from the scope of the 1999 Act.[52] It is hardly then surprising that as Andrew Burrows, the Law Commissioner responsible for the Report and the 1999 Act, lamented, the industry-standard JCT construction contracts expressly excluded the Act as a matter of course when it first came into effect.[53] Beale notes that the JCT has now made use of the 1999 Act to give rights against builders to subsequent purchasers or tenants of a building.[54] But a main construction employer's rights against sub-contractors are still to be determined by separate collateral contracts, Beale laments.[55] There is some inconsistency here, but as Stevens says, 'it may be doubted whether there really is any great inconvenience in drafting and entering into separate contracts', which can

---

[48] *The Mahkutai* [1996] AC 650.
[49] See e.g. *Norwich City Council v Harvey* [1989] 1 WLR 828; *London Drugs v Kuehne & Nagel* [1992] 3 SCR 299.
[50] S.1(6); s.6(5).
[51] *Murphy v Brentwood DC* [1991] 1 AC 398.
[52] Stevens, n.28 above.
[53] A. Burrows, 'The Contracts (Rights of Third Parties Act) 1999 and Its Implications for Commercial Contracts' [2000] *LMCLQ* 540.
[54] Beale, n.38 above.
[55] Ibid.

be tailored to meet the needs of individual sub-contractors, in the light of events subsequent to the original contract.[56]

With third-party liability insurance, there has long been specific legislation conferring rights on third-party victims in the event that the insured becomes insolvent.[57] Where a policy is taken out on someone else's behalf (e.g. an employer purchasing health insurance for its employees), the 1999 Act might seem to plug an important gap in the law. But as Beale says, the strict legal position is academic since the Financial Ombudsman takes a dim view of insurers seeking to deny liability to the employees in such a case.[58] And even without this public regulation, no insurer would stay in business for long if he refused to honour such policies.[59]

CONCLUSION

The debate over privity may be seen as a dispute between doctrinal and pragmatic approaches to contract law. From the doctrinal perspective, privity has a simple and compelling appeal, being the corollary of the bilateral contractual relationship. The theoretical basis of the Contracts (Rights of Third Parties) Act 1999, by contrast, seems equivocal. It is not clear whether third-party rights are justified by the intentions of the contracting parties or by the desire to protect the (reliance or expectation?) interests of the third party. The question is whether this matters. English contract law has always displayed a robust pragmatism, preferring commercial convenience to doctrinal purity, exemplified in *The Eurymedon*.[60] It might seem obvious that privity was a 'pestilential nuisance',[61] and that its abolition should be welcomed for removing unaccustomed rigidity from the law.

On the other hand, privity had certain practical advantages. Under the rigid common law regime, every promisor knew to whom he was potentially liable for non-performance. With the statutory relaxation of privity there is the potential for liability to remote parties in a lengthy chain or complex web of contracts, as commonly found in, for example, the construction industry. This might upset settled commercial expectations. Hopefully the courts will be sensitive to this in applying the test of party intentions and 'the proper construction of the contract' under ss.1(1) and 1(2) of the Act. But those provisions are held to create a rebuttable presumption in favour of third-party rights.[62] It is not surprising that, as seen, the construction industry's attitude has been to take no chances, initially excluding the Act altogether in the standard JCT contract forms. This is commonly seen in many other standard form contracts. While Beale has found some use being

---

[56] Stevens, n.28 above.

[57] Third Parties (Rights Against Insurers) Act 2010 (replacing Act of 1930).

[58] Beale, n.38 above.

[59] Stevens, n.28 above.

[60] *New Zealand Shipping v A M Satterthwaite & Co* [1975] AC 154.

[61] J.N. Adams & R. Brownsword, 'Privity of Contract – That Pestilential Nuisance' (1993) 56 *MLR* 722.

[62] *Nisshin Shipping v Cleaves & Co* [2004] 1 Lloyd's Rep 38, [23] approving Burrows, n.53 above, p. 544.

made of the Act one decade on,[63] this remains cautious. Commercial attitudes view the Act as a potential hazard, a trap for the unwary as much as a beneficial facility. Hugh Collins – certainly no black-letter fetishist – identifies the potential for indeterminate liability as the weightiest argument in favour of privity.[64]

To the extent that privity was an obstacle in the parties' way, it could usually be circumvented by a device such as a collateral contract or (if intended to be irrevocable) by constituting the promisee a trustee of the promise for the third party. But as Collins observes, such stratagems 'all require a degree of legal skill, and it must be questioned whether the law of contract serves its purpose of buttressing market transactions adequately when it requires traders to secure the services of a lawyer before they can give effect to their joint intentions'.[65] The extensive litigation over exclusion clauses, with the associated expense and uncertainty, is certainly a reproach to English commercial law. Privity was evidently a trap for the unsophisticated parties in *Beswick v Beswick*[66], and the perceived unfairness to the third party in *Beswick* has often been at the forefront of the emotional case for reform. On the other hand, as pointed out above, the problem in that case could arguably better be resolved by reforming the promisee's remedies (considered below) or reconsidering the effect of death on legal claims generally. Whether the value of rescuing inadvertent parties like the Beswicks from privity is worth the costs of the 1999 Act – both practical and doctrinal – will continue to be debated by those who question the consensus that privity was undeniably a Bad Thing.

Debate 2

Claims by the promisee

As stated at the start of the chapter, it is often assumed that under the privity regime, while the third party, Christopher, would be unable to sue Angus for his failure to mow Christopher's lawn, Becca (who has employed Angus to do this) would recover only nominal damages. This has been said to create a 'legal black hole' into which the claim for substantial damages falls to its oblivion, allowing 'the wrongdoer [to] escape … scot-free'.[67] The Contracts (Rights of Third Parties) Act 1999 has provided one way of filling the 'black hole', by allowing the third party (Christopher) to sue in his own name. A second solution would be substantial damages for the promisee (Becca). Whether such claims should be allowed, and on what basis, has been much discussed. The position taken on this question will feed back into Debate 1 on the third party's rights and remedies.

---

[63] Beale, n.54 above.
[64] Collins, n.12 above, p. 317.
[65] Ibid, p. 319.
[66] [1968] AC 58.
[67] *G.U.S. Property Management Ltd. v Littlewoods Mail Order Stores Ltd.*, 1982 SLT 533, 538 (Lord Keith).

WHOSE LOSS?

To clarify the debate, the first and most fundamental question is: whose loss is it when Angus fails to mow Christopher's lawn? The assumption is often made that this is Christopher's loss: he suffers an overgrown garden. But this might well be questioned. Brian Coote takes the point discussing the situation that has arisen in many of the cases, where B employs A to do building work on C's land.[68] Here, argues Coote, the third party, C, 'would, so far as the building contract was concerned, have received the improvements as a benefit akin to a gift. It then has to be asked how far one can be said to have suffered loss or damage just because a gift one has received is defective?' That C has not suffered any loss in such cases enjoys support from *Murphy v Brentwood DC*. Lord Oliver, considering an owner-occupier who inherits defective property, said: 'He suffers, in fact, no loss save that the property for which he paid nothing is less valuable to him by the amount which it will cost him to repair it if he wishes to continue to live in it.'[69]

Instead, argues Coote, it is the promisee (Becca) who has suffered substantial loss: simply, that she has not received the performance to which she was entitled. As Lord Templeman once put it, 'A man who pays something for nothing truly incurs a loss'.[70] In the three-party context, Lord Griffiths famously suggested that it would be 'absurd' if the promisee could not recover substantial damages, when he 'did not receive the bargain for which he had contracted' (again considering building work to be done on the land of a third party).[71] It may be that the question 'whose loss?' should be answered differently depending on the precise factual situation at hand. For example when B engages A to carry goods belonging to C, and they are negligently damaged by A, it seems hard to deny that the loss is truly C's.[72]

The answer to the question is extremely important. If the loss is truly the third party's then the promisee's claim for substantial damages must be a 'surrogate' claim – *on behalf of* the third party, whereas if the loss is the promisee's own loss, her claim for substantial damages is not made on behalf of anyone else. Much of the case-law has proceeded on the basis that the loss is the third party's and the promisee is advancing a surrogate claim. But in *Panatown Ltd v Alfred McAlpine Construction Ltd* the House of Lords considered the alternative 'promisee's loss' analysis at some considerable length.[73] We will examine these approaches in turn.

PROMISEE CLAIMING ON BEHALF OF THIRD PARTY

The case-law since the 1970s contains several examples of successful claims of this kind. However, their rationale remains obscure. In *Jackson v Horizon Holidays*

---

[68] B. Coote, 'The Performance Interest, *Panatown*, and the Problem of Loss' (2001) 117 *LQR* 81.
[69] [1991] AC 398, 488.
[70] *Miles v Wakefield Metropolitan District Council* [1987] AC 539, 560.
[71] *Linden Gardens Trust v Linesta Sludge Disposals* [1994] 1 AC 85, 97.
[72] Cf. *The Albazero* [1977] AC 774; *The Aliakmon* [1986] AC 785.
[73] [2001] 1 AC 518.

the plaintiff recovered damages for the disappointment of both himself and his family, when the holiday which he had booked on all their behalf failed to live up to expectations.[74] Builders have been held liable to pay substantial damages to their employers when defects were discovered in buildings that, by the time of breach, had been vested in a third party,[75] or which belonged to a third party from the outset.[76] The promisee, Becca, would be required to account for these damages to the third party, Christopher, at common law.[77] (This is quite different from the promisee holding the promise (and therefore the damages) *on trust* for the third party, for then the contract could be varied only with the third-party beneficiary's consent.[78]) But the doctrinal basis for such liability is controversial. Even after the leading case of *Panatown Ltd v Alfred McAlpine Construction Ltd*,[79] McKendrick laments that English law is unable coherently to explain the rationale either of the general rule (only promisee's loss recoverable) or the exceptions to it.[80]

So Lord Denning MR's judgment in *Jackson* has received only hesitant support from the House of Lords.[81] The building cases were founded on *Dunlop v Lambert*,[82] an early shipping case approved in *The Albazero* despite Lord Diplock describing its reasoning as 'baffling'.[83] Lord Diplock accepted that it was anomalous to allow a contracting party who had not suffered any loss to recover substantial damages on behalf of a third party who had. But such recovery was 'not entirely unfamiliar' to English commercial law.[84] That the rule in *Dunlop v Lambert* would add another exception to the principle that damages compensate the promisee's loss was not, therefore, sufficient reason to 'jettison it', especially when 'there may still be occasional cases in which the rule would provide a remedy where no other would be available to a person sustaining loss which under a rational legal system ought to be compensated by the person who has caused it'.[85]

Thus, the doctrine seemed to be conceived wholly pragmatically, as a way of ensuring that the third party's losses could be compensated through the mechanism of the promisee suing. It followed that where the third party had an action in its own right, *Dunlop v Lambert* was inapplicable, as in *The Albazero* itself and

---

[74] [1975] 1 WLR 1468.

[75] *Linden Gardens Trust v Linesta Sludge Disposals* [1994] 1 AC 85.

[76] *Darlington Borough Council v Wiltshier Northern* [1995] 1 WLR 68.

[77] *Joseph v Knox* (1813) 3 Camp 320; *The Abazero* [1977] AC 774, 846, per Lord Diplock.

[78] *Beswick v Beswick* [1966] Ch. 538, 555 per Lord Denning MR.

[79] [2001] 1 AC 518.

[80] E. McKendrick, 'The Common Law at Work: The Saga of *Alfred McAlpine Construction Ltd v. Panatown Ltd*' (2003) 3 *OUCLJ* 145.

[81] *Woodar Investment Development Ltd. v Wimpey Construction U.K. Ltd.* [1980] 1 WLR 277, 283–84, 293–94, 297, 300–301.

[82] (1839) 6 Cl & F 600.

[83] *The Albazero* [1977] AC 774, 843.

[84] [1977] AC 774, 846. Lord Diplock referred specifically to bailment, subrogation and insurance of goods. See further *Panatown* n.79 above at 582 per Lord Millett: 'In all these cases the common law, following the law merchant, has been able to reconcile the practical needs of commercial men with principle by attributing the loss to the contracting party.'

[85] [1977] AC 774, 847. See similarly p. 824 (Ormrod LJ).

most other cases involving carriage of goods by sea.[86] Coote identifies as many as six competing explanations of 'varying degrees of plausibility' for the *Dunlop v Lambert* rule in the judgments at the various stages in *The Albazero*.[87] Lord Diplock, according to Coote, endorsed 'a rule of law depending on what appears to be a fiction conditioned by the contemplation and intention of the parties'. Nevertheless, for better or worse the rule was cemented in place as a matter of positive law in *The Albazero* and followed in the building cases.

In *Darlington BC v Wiltshier Northern*,[88] the Court of Appeal allowed the promisee to recover substantial damages by applying *Dunlop v Lambert*. But Steyn LJ would have welcomed a direct challenge to privity and deplored the fact that even if the case went to the House of Lords, counsel had indicated that they would still rely on the 'juristic subterfuge' of surrogate damages.[89] Again, it appears that the rationale was simply to circumvent the privity doctrine: the promisee's action was a device to compensate the third party. But if so, it would be more rational and certainly more straightforward to grant rights of action to the third party! That was evidently Steyn LJ's view, which soon came to fruition in the Contracts (Rights of Third Parties) Act 1999. The question then arises whether there is any need, and therefore any room, for actions by the promisee on the third party's behalf since the 1999 Act.

Panatown suggests not.[90] Here, as in the *Darlington* case, the plaintiffs (Panatown) had employed the defendant builders McAlpine to erect buildings on land belonging to another, Panatown's sister company UIPL Ltd. The work was done defectively and the issue was whether Panatown could recover substantial damages. The majority in the House of Lords held that they could not do so, because the third-party owner, UIPL, had a direct right of action against McAlpine for defective work under a 'Duty of Care Deed' (DCD) executed between UIPL and McAlpine at the same time as the contract between Panatown and McAlpine. The finding has been criticized. Burrows argues that the point of the DCD (which was assignable) was to provide a remedy for negligent work by the builders for successors in title to UIPL who would not have an action in tort.[91] The DCD contained rights inferior to those that Panatown enjoyed under the contract and so cannot have been intended to exclude Panatown's claim.[92] However, this argument was directly rejected by the House of Lords. Lord Clyde said that even if the DCD and contract remedies 'do not absolutely coincide, the express provision of the direct remedy for the third party is

---

[86] Because transfer of the Bill of Lading transfers 'all rights of suit under the contract of carriage': Carriage of Goods by Sea Act 1992, s. 2(1). The principle was established soon after *Dunlop v Lambert*: cf. Bills of Lading Act 1855 (which the 1992 Act replaced).

[87] B. Coote, '*Dunlop v. Lambert*: The Search for a Rationale' (1998) 13 *JCL* 91.

[88] [1995] 1 WLR 68.

[89] Ibid 78, quoting Lord Diplock in *Swain v Law Society* [1983] 1 AC 598, 611.

[90] *Panatown Ltd v Alfred McAlpine Construction Ltd* [2001] 1 AC 518.

[91] A. Burrows, 'No Damages for a Third Party's Loss' (2001) 1 *Oxford U Commw LJ* 107; cf. *Murphy*, n.69 above.

[92] Cf. *Panatown* at 559 per Lord Goff: 'It is arguable that, having regard to the evident purpose of the DCD, it was not intended that UIPL should itself enforce its rights under the DCD against McAlpine'.

fatal'.[93] *Dunlop v Lambert* was to be invoked only for filling gaps in the third party's protection; when the third party had a right of action, there was simply no gap to fill. As Lord Millett put it, 'the function of the rule was to escape the undesirable consequences of the privity rule, and it does not apply where it is not needed'.[94]

Since the 1999 Act contracting parties have always had the option of granting to third parties the right to enforce terms directly. Indeed, there is a rebuttable presumption that they intend to do so.[95] Therefore a 'gap' in the third party's protection can now arise *only* when the parties positively intend that he should not have a right of action. Hence it appears there can be no longer be room 'to treat the parties as having entered into the contract on the footing that [the promisee] would be entitled to enforce contractual rights for the benefit of those who suffered from defective performance'.[96] If the parties have such an intention, then the third party will have a direct right pursuant to the 1999 Act.[97] If they do not intend the third party to have a right of action, it is difficult to see how they can intend that the promisee can recover damages on his behalf. Any weakness in the third party's position is now attributable to the parties' intentions, and not the rigidity of the classical privity doctrine. If the surrogate action was born of necessity under the privity regime, its expedient rationale has lapsed with the statutory reforms.[98]

Finally, it is worth noting a classic escape route from the thorny issue of the promisee's damages. In *Beswick v Beswick*, the House of Lords ordered specific performance of the contract.[99] This might be thought to protect the third party while avoiding 'overcompensation' of the promisee. But on the traditional view that specific performance is awarded only when damages are inadequate, we might put the argument back one stage. If the award of nominal damages to the promisee in *Beswick* would have been 'inadequate', why would only nominal damages have been awarded in the first place? *Beswick* avoids rather than addresses the underlying issue. The later cases have at least attempted to grapple with it.

The award of surrogate damages pursuant to *Dunlop v Lambert* seems to have been a pragmatic plugging of the gap created by privity. Rather more far-reaching is the argument that substantial damages should be awarded to protect the promisee's own performance interest. To this we now turn.

THE PROMISEE'S OWN INTEREST

As seen above, some (such as Coote) have argued that breach by Angus causes loss to the promisee, Becca, and that she should be able to recover substantial damages

---

[93] [2001] 1 AC 518, 532.

[94] [2001] 1 AC 518, 583.

[95] Cf. n.62 above.

[96] *Linden Gardens* [1994] 1 AC 85, 115 per Lord Browne-Wilkinson.

[97] Which will of course bar any claim by the promisee on the third party's behalf: Law Commission Report 242 (1996) para.11.17.

[98] Surrogate claims by the promisee are not allowed in Scotland, where direct third party rights have long been recognized: e.g. *Clark Contracts v Burrell Co (No.2)* 2003 SLT 73.

[99] [1968] AC 58.

in her own name. This position is closely aligned with the broader concern with protection of the 'performance interest' in contract.[100] Lord Griffiths's revolutionary espousal of this view in *Linden Gardens* attracted only provisional support from his colleagues.[101] When their Lordships returned to the matter in *Panatown Ltd v Alfred McAlpine Construction Ltd*,[102] however, even the absence of criticism of Lord Griffiths's position in the 'substantial amount of academic discussion'[103] cited did not convince the majority. Only Lord Goff and Lord Millett (in dissent) squarely accepted this 'broad ground' for the recovery of substantial damages by the promisee, Panatown, as opposed to the 'narrow ground' based on *Dunlop v Lambert* discussed in the previous section.[104] Lord Millett explained that these alternative bases for the claim were mutually exclusive: 'The rule in *Dunlop v Lambert* is an (incidental) exception to the general rule that a plaintiff can only recover damages for his own loss. Lord Griffiths's broader principle treats the plaintiff as recovering for his own loss, and is thus is an application of the general rule and not an exception to it.'[105]

Lord Goff made clear that the issue was not about privity of contract, but the damages recoverable by one contracting party from another.[106] The most important authorities relied upon by Lords Goff and Millett are two-party disputes, in particular *Ruxley Electronics v Forsyth*.[107] The basic point is that the promisee has not received the performance to which he is entitled.[108] Lord Millett said that the 'language of defeated expectation' in cases such *Radford v de Froberville* was the key to the *Panatown* dispute.[109] It gave ample authority for awarding substantial damages to the promisee for his defeated interest in having the contract performed. Otherwise, Lord Goff said, the promisor could breach 'with impunity'.[110] The opposite view (that the promisee's damages are nominal) arose out of 'the narrow accountants' balance sheet quantification of loss which measures the loss suffered by the promisee by the diminution in his overall financial position resulting from the breach'.[111]

Because Lords Goff and Millett would have awarded damages to protect the promisee's own interest in performance, it made no difference that the third party might have a right of action also. On the facts, therefore, UIPL's rights against McAlpine under the Duty of Care Deed were irrelevant to Panatown's right to substantial damages.

100 Coote, n.68 above. See pp. 232–238 et seq above.
101 [1994] 1 AC 85, 112 (Lord Browne-Wilkinson).
102 [2001] 1 AC 518.
103 [2001] 1 AC 518, 548 (Lord Goff).
104 (1839) 6 Cl & F 600.
105 [2001] 1 AC 518, 587.
106 [2001] 1 AC 518, 552.
107 [1996] AC 344.
108 [2001] 1 AC 518, 547.
109 [2001] 1 AC 518, 590; cf. *Radford v de Froberville* [1977] 1 WLR 1262.
110 [2001] 1 AC 518, 546.
111 [2001] 1 AC 518, 588 (Lord Millett).

Just as Lord Griffiths's initial suggestion of this 'broad ground' approach in *Linden Gardens* attracted academic support, most commentary on *Panatown* has favoured Lords Goff and Millett, and the performance interest of the promisee.[112] McKendrick argues that contracts are increasingly made not for financial gain, but to promote quality of life (instancing consumers and altruists – the latter no doubt inspired by Lord Goff's recurrent example of a philanthropist who employs builders to repair the roof of the village hall, in *Panatown*).[113] Contract law should therefore reflect the inherent value of performance, rather than requiring the promisee to show that he is financially worse off in every case. This would be to employ an 'impoverished conception ... of all relationships in society ... in purely financial terms'. Stevens also supports the broad ground/performance interest. In his critique of the 1999 Act, Stevens argues that if the law allows the promisee to recover substantial damages for her disappointed expectation, the 'lacuna' that the Act is supposed to fill is shown not to exist.[114] He notes that the 'keenest supporters' of the Act are 'strongly critical' of the performance interest approach to *Panatown*.[115] They could just as easily reply that the keenest supporter of that approach to remedies is the 1999 Act's fiercest opponent (Stevens)! Stevens's point shows the relationship between the Debate about the promisee's interest and that over privity and third-party rights.

THE PERFORMANCE INTEREST

The 'broad ground' in *Panatown Ltd v Alfred McAlpine Construction Ltd*[116] is also supported by the concept of 'substitutionary damages' championed by, amongst others, Robert Stevens.[117] The law should value the right and award damages as a substitute for its infringement. On this analysis it is 'apparent' that the dissenters in *Panatown* were correct to award substantial damages to the promisee.[118]

Pearce and Halson have also called for the recognition of 'vindicatory damages', a 'rights-based' rather than 'loss-based' remedy.[119] They cite three-party cases as an example of where compensatory damages may fail to provide an adequate remedy. Thus, vindication of the promisee's right to performance should be the goal of a damages award. To similar effect, Webb has argued that we must distinguish sharply between the right to performance and the compensation of loss.[120] Lords

---

[112] E.g. Coote, n.68 above.

[113] McKendrick, n.80 above. See further E. McKendrick, 'Breach of Contract and the Meaning of Loss' [1999] *CLP* 37.

[114] Stevens, n.28 above, p. 300.

[115] Ibid., citing N. Andrews, 'Strangers to Justice No Longer: The Reversal of the Privity Rule under the Contracts (Rights of Third Parties) Act 1999' [2001] *CLJ* 353, 377 and Burrows, n.91 above.

[116] [2001] 1 AC 518.

[117] R. Stevens, *Torts and Rights*, Ch. 4; R Stevens, 'Damages and the Right to Performance: A *Golden Victory* Or Not?' in J. Neyers et al. (eds), *Exploring Contract Law* (Hart Publishing, 2009). Cf. pp. 246–252 above.

[118] Stevens 'A *Golden Victory* or Not?' at 188.

[119] D. Pearce and R. Halson, 'Damages for Breach of Contract: Compensation, Restitution and Vindication' (2008) 28 *OJLS* 73.

[120] C. Webb, 'Performance and Compensation: An Analysis of Contract Damages and Contractual Obligation' (2006) 26 *OJLS* 41.

Goff and Millett were striving to protect the performance interest in *Panatown*, rather than to compensate any meaningful loss. Webb argues that talking about 'loss' in an extended sense, when what is really at stake is the right to performance, permits a good performance-interest claim to be rebuffed by an argument that no compensable loss has been suffered (as Lord Clyde correctly argued in *Panatown*). The debate is taking place at cross-purposes, in Webb's view.

All of these positions share the common feature that what is important is the *right* to performance, and not any identifiable *loss* stemming from breaching that right. The question then arises: how is such an intangible thing to be quantified? Webb advocates cost-of-cure damages, 'not because this is the measure of the loss caused by the breach ... [but] simply because it gives effect to [the promisee's] interest in performance'.[121] But Stevens disagrees: the cost-of-cure measure is only *evidence* for quantifying the lost performance.[122] The difference in value between what has been provided and what should have been provided is available as of right. The promisee cannot automatically recover all the losses that flow from breach, as in *Ruxley Electronics v Forsyth*[123] where as a matter of mitigation, it would have been unreasonable for the promisee to incur the cost of extending the swimming pool to the contractual depth.[124] The problem with Stevens's argument is that it does not define how the loss *should* be quantified: what precisely is the cost-of-cure evidence of?[125]

Burrows is the most prominent critic of the 'broad ground' in *Panatown* and, in particular, of Stevens's thesis of 'substitutionary damages'.[126] If it is really the case that breach of contract is, in itself, a substantial loss then would a buyer recover substantial damages when a seller fails to deliver goods that have declined in value from the contract price (i.e. when the breach would enable the buyer to escape from a bad bargain)?[127] Should substantial damages be available when the right-holder has taken no steps to mitigate his loss, or where the loss has, in fact, been erased subsequent to breach?[128] These problems – or arguably, absurdities – stem from the approach of valuing the right rather than the circumstances and consequences of its infringement.[129] Burrows concludes that it is 'simply untrue' that there is 'automatically a pecuniary loss' whenever there is a breach of contract.[130] This was Lord Clyde's view in *Panatown*, which Burrows approves:

---

[121] Ibid. See pp. 246–252 above.

[122] Stevens, 'A *Golden Victory* or Not?' at 190–91.

[123] [1996] AC 344.

[124] See pp. 249–250 above.

[125] Commenting on *White v Jones* [1995] 2 AC 207, Stevens says that the promisee/testator's loss would be much less than the third party/legatees', but does not say what the promisee's loss actually would be.

[126] Cf. pp. 246–252 above.

[127] Burrows, n.91 above.

[128] A. Burrows, 'Damages and Rights' in D. Nolan and A. Robertson (eds), *Rights and Private Law* (Hart Publishing, 2011).

[129] J. Edelman, 'The Meaning of Loss and Enrichment' in *Philosophical Foundations of the Law of Unjust Enrichment,* Chambers, Mitchell and Penner (eds) (Oxford University Press, 2009) 211 at 219.

[130] Burrows, n.91 above, p. 109.

the requirement of proving loss has the merit of being clear and simple.[131] It may be noted that in an entirely different context (false imprisonment by public body) the Supreme Court has explicitly rejected a head of 'vindicatory damages' separate from compensatory and exemplary damages.[132] Where no loss in the ordinary sense can be proved, common law rights are sufficiently vindicated by the award of nominal damages (or a declaration).[133]

In the three-party situation, Burrows argues that the broad ground inevitably leads to double liability for the promisor. If the basis for awarding substantial damages to the promisee is that he has himself suffered loss (or at least, that his 'performance interest' has been violated, sounding in damages), then there can be no basis for requiring him to pay those damages over to the third party. But on what ground could a separate claim for damages by the third party be resisted by the promisor? Each party is conceived of suffering separate losses.

Lords Goff and Millett were alive to this problem and met it on the facts by suggesting that Panatown would be under a duty to account to UIPL for any damages received. Lord Millett argued that this was because of the payment arrangements within the group of companies. Alternatively, payment to UIPL would be an implied condition of its consent to the work being done on its land, according to Lord Goff. But even if these explanations fit *Panatown*, they do not solve the fundamental problem. If the broad ground is to have the courage of its convictions, its supporters should allow that the promisee could simply keep the damages for himself.[134] The philanthropist in Lord Goff's example could decide not to repair the village hall roof after all, even though he was compensated in an amount that would allow him to do so. This might seem harsh on the third party (the village hall committee in Lord Goff's scenario), but since the 1999 Act they could be granted a right to enforce the contract themselves. Assuming that they could also recover substantial damages, the harshness would instead fall on the builder, who would be required to compensate two parties twice over in respect of what would traditionally be viewed as the same loss.

This was the reason that Lord Jauncey gave for awarding Panatown only nominal damages (given that UIPL had a right of action under the DCD): 'McAlpine cannot be mulcted twice over in damages'. Even Lord Browne-Wilkinson, although willing to assume the validity of the broad ground in principle, ultimately ruled it out for similar reasons. He postulated the situation in which Panatown recovered substantial damages, barring a claim for the cost of repairs by a successor in title to UIPL, 'X', to whom the DCD had been assigned. It would be 'another piece of legal nonsense' if 'the party who had suffered real, tangible damage, X, could recover nothing but Panatown which had suffered no real loss could recover damages'.

---

[131] Burrows, ibid, p. 112.

[132] *Regina (Lumba) v Home Secretary* [2011] UKSC 12 (Lord Hope, Lord Walker and Baroness Hale dissenting on this point).

[133] Ibid [101] (Lord Dyson).

[134] As Lord Clyde pointed out, requiring Panatown to hand the damages over to UIPL approximated to the 'narrow ground' (*Dunlop v Lambert*).

Thus, 'the broad ground' poses a problem of double recovery, unless we are happy to deny a claim for substantial damages for the third party. In the building cases like *Panatown*, that means the owner of the land. As seen above, Coote argues that the third party has in effect received a gift worth less than if it was in a perfect state of repair, which is not really a loss. However, such an approach strikes fundamentally at the privity reforms. If Coote's logic be accepted, it would seem that third parties cannot *ever* recover damages, even when they have a right to enforce a contract term under the 1999 Act. Some commentators would be satisfied with that conclusion. As pointed out above, Stevens is well known both as a proponent of the 'substitutionary damages' thesis that underlies the broad ground and as a leading critic of the 1999 Act. Stevens's position is therefore that the promisee should recover substantial damages and the third party should recover nothing – he defends the common law privity doctrine.

Coote adopts a more nuanced position. Considering cases like *Dunlop v Lambert*[135] and *The Albazero* (where goods damaged by breach of contract belong to a third party),[136] he admits that 'it might understandably be questioned how their loss could be accounted a loss to [the promisee] rather than to their actual owner'.[137] The loss claimed was not the failure in performance per se, but the damaging *consequences* of that failure. Thus, Coote endorses the *Dunlop v Lambert* rule rather than the 'broad ground' in such cases, with the promisee to hold the damages on account for the owner of the goods. Commenting on *Panatown*, Coote suggests that the promisee's claim should operate 'at two levels': under the ordinary common law for his own performance interest, and the special *Dunlop v Lambert* rule for 'losses actually suffered by the third party'.[138] Coote admits that this bifurcated solution is 'slightly inelegant'. It is notable that other commentators sympathetic to the broad ground agree that consequential losses suffered by the third party cannot be treated as the promisee's own loss.[139] It therefore seems that few of the commentators – or judges – who have supported the broad ground have been willing to accept that all losses flowing from breach of contract are the promisee's. Instead, a distinction must be drawn between 'inherent' defeated expectation and 'losses consequent upon it'.[140] The distinction may be very difficult to draw in practice. Is the cost of repairing a defective building 'inherent' or 'consequential' loss?

CONCLUSIONS

This second Debate is both difficult and important. It fits into the wider current debates about the nature of contract remedies and, therefore, rights.[141] The

---

[135] (1839) 6 Cl & F 600.
[136] [1977] AC 774.
[137] Coote, n.87 above.
[138] Coote, n.68 above.
[139] McKendrick, n.80 above.
[140] Cf. Stevens, n.117 above.
[141] Cf. Ch. 9 above.

controversial notion of the performance interest – and its protection through such exotic remedies as vindicatory or substitutionary damages – is at the heart of the case for substantial damages for promisees, like Becca, faced with breach in a three-party situation. This approach conceives the claim *as the promisee's own*. The alternative explanation is that the promisee recovers damages *on behalf of the third party's loss*. This seems to have little justification save as a common law expedient to circumvent the privity rule. Accordingly, it has little to recommend it since the 1999 reforms, and might now be seen as an historical curiosity.

Secondly, the debate is important for its close relationship with the debate on third parties' rights. Those who advocate compensation for the promisee's own substantial loss see such compensation, rather than third-party rights, as the correct way to fill the 'black hole' created by privity. The purest statement of this approach would exclude claims by the third party altogether to prevent double liability of the promisor. All loss is the promisee's – and this is not in any way harsh on the third party who is a donee and not privy to the contract. Conversely, those who are opposed to the award of substantial damages for defeated expectations per se, such as Andrew Burrows, who see the loss as properly 'belonging' to the third party, dismiss the broad ground altogether and see the fully-fledged exception to privity in the 1999 Act as preferable to the 'subterfuge' of *Dunlop v Lambert*.

Debate 3

Should contracts bind third parties?

At first sight the obvious answer to this question seems to be 'no, and the law does not allow it'. Take the following example:

> *Example*: Ermintrude and Florence agree that Ermintrude will dig Florence's garden, and be paid for this work by Dougal.

It is clear that Ermintrude and Florence cannot bind Dougal to pay for the work in this way. It would be monstrous if they could, a violation of the very basic notion of contract as a freely undertaken obligation. Dougal has undertaken nothing. This is the uncontroversial limb of privity – parties cannot impose obligations upon strangers to the contract.

However, people are regularly placed under the (negative) duty *not to interfere with the contract of another*. Formally speaking, these duties do not arise 'out of contract' but are imposed by other departments of the law – tort and property. Nevertheless they are relevant here, because they considerably bolster the bindingness of contracts, extending the reach of contractual obligations. The debate therefore mirrors that 'within' contract law about the extent to which breach of contract should be condemned, tolerated or positively welcomed. It is vital not to have an over-compartmentalized view of law. Otherwise we might endorse fundamentally incompatible doctrines simply because they inhabit different chapters of the textbook (or different textbooks). Tony Weir expressed exasperation that a class of Texan university lawyers could accept efficient breach in the morning and liability for inducing breach of contract in the afternoon torts class.[142]

THE TORT OF INDUCING BREACH OF CONTRACT

> *Example:* Famous soprano Johanna Wagner enters into a contract to sing at the opera house belonging to Lumley. A rival impresario, Gye, offers Miss Wagner more money to come and sing at his opera house. Miss Wagner accepts Gye's offer, and tells Lumley that she will not sing for him.

These are, in outline, the facts of the seminal case of 1853 in which the Court of Queen's Bench held, by a majority, that Gye was liable to Lumley in tort for the loss caused by Miss Wagner's breach of contract.[143] While the decision seemed to be based primarily upon the action for 'enticing away a servant' in the Statute of Labourers 1349,[144] the judges made some wider observations. Erle J thought that Gye would be liable as a joint wrongdoer with Miss Wagner for having 'procured' her breach of contract. Erle and Crompton JJ observed that there might be legal limits on what the plaintiff could recover from the promisor (e.g. an action in debt would be limited to principal and interest), and as Crompton J also pointed out, 'The servant or contractor may be utterly unable to pay anything like the amount of the damage sustained entirely from the wrongful act of the defendant'. These judges clearly, then, saw Gye's tort liability as plugging gaps in Lumley's contractual remedies against Wagner. Coleridge J dissented, observing that 'in respect of breach of contract the general rule of our law is to confine its remedies by action to the contracting parties'.

After languishing in obscurity for some decades, *Lumley v Gye* was cemented in place in a spate of industrial relations cases around the turn of the twentieth century.[145] It is now usually accepted that there is a general tort of inducing breach of contract (no longer limited to the Statute of Labourers, or analogous cases).[146] But the width of the tort has long caused consternation.[147] Is it really sensible that if A offers to buy goods from B that B has already promised to sell to C, A commits a tort? This would be startling – the entire competitive structure of the market order

---

[142] J.A. Weir, *Economic Torts* (Clarendon, 1997) p. 4.

[143] *Lumley v Gye* (1853) 2 E & B 216. Lumley's action subsequently failed at trial, since the jury found that Gye '*bona fide* believed that the agreement with the plaintiff had ceased to be binding upon Miss Wagner'; see S.M. Waddams, 'Johanna Wagner and the Rival Opera Houses' (2001) 117 *LQR* 431.

[144] Which makes the 'gendered explanation' of the tort's genesis rather implausible: cf. S.L. Swan, 'A New Tortious Interference with Contractual Relations: Gender and Erotic Triangles in *Lumley v. Gye*' (2012) 35 *Harvard Jo Law & Gender* (forthcoming).

[145] M.R. Macnair, 'Free Association versus Juridification' (2011) 39 *Critique* 53.

[146] *OBG Ltd v Allen* [2008] 1 AC 1 is the most significant recent decision.

[147] Cf. F. Bowes Sayre, 'Inducing Breach of Contract' (1923) 36 *Harvard LR* 663.

would prima facie be rendered illegal.[148] As Coleridge J commented in his *Lumley v Gye* dissent, 'important contracts are more commonly broken with than without persuaders or procurers'. Moreover, the tort renders all strikes illegal *at common law* – the organizing trade union is inevitably inducing breach of its members' contracts of employment – and it is only by statute that (since 1906) unions have enjoyed immunity from suit over industrial action.[149] Furthermore, as Peter Gibson LJ has observed, the tort is 'inconsistent with contractual principles, in particular in breaching the privity rule'.[150] How is such wide-ranging liability to be justified?

According to Rix LJ, the 'philosophical basis' of *Lumley v Gye* 'appears to be that contracts should be kept rather than broken'.[151] G.H.L. Fridman comments operatically that the tort 'gird[s] contracts with a protective shield similar to, but more real than, the magic fire surrounding Brunnhilde'.[152] Thus, *Lumley v Gye* bolsters the sanctity of contract.[153] Daniel Friedman argues that its existence is conspicuous evidence against 'efficient breach' and the argument that there is no such thing as a duty to perform a contract.[154] But this point may be, and has been, reversed – to the extent that we do not wish to compel the performance of wasteful, inefficient contracts, it is the tort of inducing breach of contract that is erroneous, and should be discarded.[155]

This then is the heart of the debate. *Should* the law extend the liability of contract breakers to third parties who 'induce' breaches of contract? Simester and Chan correctly note that the 'instrumental reasons for safeguarding contracts against strangers ... depend, in turn, upon the grounds for protecting contracts more generally'.[156] They rely upon Raz's defence of contract law as the protection of the socially useful practice of promising.[157] As Simester and Chan put it, legal enforcement of contracts gives 'opportunity for personal and social advancement through reliable coordinated economic activity'. Persuading a promisor to breach undermines the very status of his promise as a pre-emptive reason for action. Thus, tort defendants' behaviour in these cases strikes at the heart of contract law and rightly attracts liability. For Simester and Chan, this is an across-the-board point: *all* contracts are to be protected against such interference. But it is not clear why every single breach of contract must be taken to undermine the institution of contract law. David Howarth advocates a more differentiated approach, with the opposite presumption – that breach of contract may be, and often is, justified.

---

[148] H.S. Perlman, 'Interference with Contract and Other Economic Expectancies: A Clash of Tort and Contract Doctrine' (1982) 49 *Univ Chicago LR* 51.

[149] Cf. now Trade Union and Labour Relations (Consolidation) Act 1992.

[150] *Millar v Bassey* [1994] EMLR 44, 63.

[151] *Stocznia Gdanska SA v Latvian Shipping Co & Ors (No. 2)* [2002] EWCA Civ 889, [130].

[152] G.H.L. Fridman, '*Lumley v Gye* and the (Over?)Protection of Contracts' in J. Neyers et al., *Exploring Contract Law* (Hart Publishing, 2008) p. 228. Cf. Richard Wagner, *Die Walküre* (1870).

[153] Fridman, ibid at 229, questions whether we should 'elevate the mundane, though useful, concept of contract into something more sublime'.

[154] D. Friedman, 'The Efficient Breach Fallacy' (1989) 18 *Jo Legal Studies* 1, 20.

[155] D. Howarth, 'Against *Lumley v Gye*' (2005) 68 *MLR* 195.

[156] A.P. Simester & Winnie Chan, 'Inducing Breach of Contract: One Tort Or Two?' [2004] *CLJ* 132.

[157] J. Raz, 'Promises in Morality and Law' (1982) 95 *Harv LR* 916.

View of an expert

David Howarth

Howarth's powerful critique of the tort of inducing breach of contract will be outlined here.[158] The basic case against *Lumley v Gye* is that it assumes that there is something inherently wrong in persuading someone to breach his contract, whereas such breach may in fact be economically or morally justified.[159] The tort's foundation is the 'sanctity' of contract; its congeners are cases like *Attorney-General v Blake*, which seek to deter the 'wrong' of breach of contract.[160] However, 'contract law is largely about commerce, not holiness'. Deterring breach of contract across the board may be 'a menace to much of commercial life'. It is damaging to competition 'to turn into a tort the everyday commercial act of offering someone a better deal'.

The tort undoubtedly provides incentives for the performance of contracts, as, for example, Simester and Chan argue. But their advocacy of the tort is flawed by the assumption that it is always a public good for every contract to be performed. This is clearly not the case, given the presence of contracts which turn out to be incapable of efficient performance, through, for example, unexpected changes in the cost of production. These situations are common enough, indeed inevitable given the limited prescience of contracting parties. Far from being immoral for a promisor to breach in such circumstances, it is *immoral for the promisee to insist upon performance at a loss* (instead of accepting damages to compensate the promisee's expectations). Such behaviour is 'contractual sadism'. Economic efficiency also supports breach in these cases. There is no evidence that parties would seek to re-insert *Lumley v Gye*-style obligations via terms of their contracts, if the tort did not exist.[161] Thus, both efficiency and morality can justify breach – and yet the tort incentivizes performance.

Although *Lumley v Gye* has consequences for commercial contract law generally, its greatest significance is in the sphere of industrial relations. Trade unions organizing strikes inevitably commit the tort, by procuring breach of employment contracts. Such liability is of great use to employers, who wish to preserve their relationships with their employees and will not sue them for losses resulting from their breaches of contract, but who suffer no such compunction about suing unions with whom they have no interest in maintaining relationships! While the unions now enjoy statutory immunity, the rules governing this are technical and employers are still often successful in obtaining injunctions to prevent strikes,

---

[158] Howarth, n.155 above.
[159] (1853) 2 E & B 216.
[160] [2001] 1 AC 268. Cf. pp. 254–257 above.
[161] Cf. D. Campbell & D. Harris, 'In Defence of Breach' (2002) 22 *Leg Stud* 208.

the point being that these remain illegal at common law.[162] The irony here is that even if the tort can be defended as 'upholding the institution of contract law', as Simester and Chan argue following Raz, it is not an institution which the trade unions have traditionally used. Rather like the National Health Service, contract law is a state service into which people are entitled to opt – or not. Unions' collective bargaining agreements with employers are presumed not to be legally enforceable.[163] There can be no hypocrisy in unions seeking to free themselves from the bonds of *Lumley v Gye* when they make no use of the legal institution that it protects. The tort truly imposes contractual liability on 'unwilling participants', in the broadest sense, in its core application.

Howarth admits that the 'nihilistic' course of outright abolition of *Lumley v Gye* is very unlikely, politically speaking, given employers' interests and public memories of strike chaos in the 1970s. This seems to be his favoured option in principle – it would restore the efficient situation in which a promisee could recover expectation damages from a breaching promisor, and nothing further. If such remedies against the promisor are inadequate, the obvious response should be to strengthen them rather than to impose liability on third parties. Of course as Crompton J observed in *Lumley v Gye* itself, the promisor might not be good for the damages, but the insolvency of one's contracting partner is one of the risks taken in choosing to contract with someone. The promisee should not be able to externalize that risk upon the third party.[164]

Nevertheless, in a spirit of realism Howarth recommends a wide general 'justification' defence, as a 'prudent' alternative to outright abolition of the tort. This would require courts to make normative judgements about the moral and economic justification for inducing breach of contract, on a case-by-case basis. The disadvantage of this is that it would require judges to rule on the substantive merits of strikes, a move unlikely to be popular with trade unions. But Howarth suggests that unions would be wise to accept this degree of public accountability for their actions. Moreover, it would be preferable to the status quo in which courts 'rely silently on an assumption that all persuasion to breach a contract is immoral'.

As Howarth's assault on *Lumley v Gye* emphasizes, there is a strong connection between the tort and the wider 'efficient breach' debate.[165] The tort presupposes a strongly enforceable right to contractual performance. Thus, Weir and Friedmann are right to point to the inconsistency between

---

[162] Cf. (e.g.) *Metrobus v UNITE* [2009] EWCA Civ 829; *Network Rail v RMT* [2010] EWHC 1084 (QB).
[163] *Ford v AEU* [1969] 2 QB 303; Trade Union and Labour Relations (Consolidation) Act 1992, s. 179.
[164] Cf. R. Bagshaw, 'Inducing Breach of Contract' in J. Horder (ed.), *Oxford Essays in Jurisprudence* (Fourth Series, Oxford University Press, 2000): contractors may know of the risk of insolvency but why should this entail that they take the risk of others deliberately interfering with their contracts?
[165] See pp. 238–243 above.

the tort and efficient breach.[166] But as Howarth shows, this is not necessarily an argument against efficient breach – conversely, it can be an argument for the abolition of the tort.

Mike Macnair lays even greater stress upon the industrial relations context for *Lumley v Gye*.[167] He argues that it was flawed from the outset, as pointed out in Coleridge J's dissent. Not only would the tort upset the ordinary workings of a competitive economy, it effaced the conceptual distinction between contracts binding on the parties to them and property rights that bind everyone, 'a basic principle of Western legal ideas since the Romans'. Therefore, Macnair shows, the principle was rarely argued and never applied for decades after *Lumley v Gye* (1853). It was treated as an anomalous 'outlier' case by authoritative writers such as Anson and Pollock.

The upsurge of trade union activity in the 1890s provided the opportunity for the tort's elevation to the legal canon. The aim of the courts, Macnair argues, was clear: to 'find a stick to beat unions and strikers' after the earlier judicial weapon of criminal conspiracy had been withdrawn.[168] Weak reasoning and eagerness to sacrifice coherent development of the law characterize the key cases of 1893–1905, all evidence of 'spectacular institutional bias' on the part of the judiciary. In Macnair's decidedly radical view, then, *Lumley v Gye*'s canonical status is a product of naked class bias. He calls for its statutory abolition with a declaration that its creation was a judicial usurpation of legislative power. Macnair's polemic shows the political importance of matters that are regularly presented as neutral outcrops of dry legal concepts, or disguised by the rhetoric of the Rule of Law (which Macnair also sees as 'antithetical to democracy' since it has at its core 'the sanctity of private property').

The judiciary are, perhaps, alive to the sensitivities in this area. Peter Gibson LJ insisted on proof of *intentional* interference with contractual rights for liability in the tort. As he pointed out, such interference is the inevitable result of both industrial action and ordinary trade competition, and the law should not discourage competition by granting an action to unsuccessful competitors.[169] Similarly, Arden LJ held that the mental element in *Lumley v Gye* was infliction of harm as the defendant's purpose. Her Ladyship argued for a restrictive approach to the tort, lest 'competition and entrepreneurialism' be inhibited.[170] On the other hand, Sedley LJ said that 'economic theories are not neutral: they are not infrequently ideologically charged, and they are heavily divergent'. It was not the common law's job, in his view, to take sides on the economic consequences of inducing breach of contract: 'Anything that makes it easier to interfere with other people's

---

[166] nn. 142 and 154 above.
[167] Macnair, n.145 above.
[168] Conspiracy and Protection of Property Act 1875; cf. *R v Bunn* (1872) 12 Cox CC 316.
[169] *Millar v Bassey* [1994] EMLR 44, 63–64.
[170] *Mainstream Properties v Young* [2005] EWCA Civ 861 [76].

contracts might be thought to promote competition but to disrupt commerce'.[171] When the case reached the House of Lords the need for intentional inducement of breach was affirmed, but with no direct reference to the economic policy questions that had been aired in the Court of Appeal.[172] Baroness Hale argued that Parliament was better suited to the resolution of debates about fair and unfair competition or trade union activity, which required a cautious approach to the economic torts.[173] But while such judicial abstentionism pretends to neutrality, it is little more than an endorsement of the status quo which, as seen above, does not lack fierce critics. The controversy surrounding the tort in *Lumley v Gye* is unlikely to die down in the near future – whether for contract lawyers or trade union campaigners.

THE EFFECT OF PROMISES ABOUT THE USE OF PROPERTY UPON SUBSEQUENT OWNERS

There is one further situation where equity has recognized that a contract may bind third parties. Where a property owner makes promises about how he will use the property, later owners of that property may, if they have notice of the promise, be bound by it. This is well established in respect of real property, ever since the leading case of *Tulk v Moxhay* in 1848.[174] The owner of Leicester Square had promised the plaintiff not to build on the square; the defendant, to whom the land had been sold, now wished to develop the land even though he bought it with notice of the non-development covenant. Lord Cottenham LC held the defendant bound. If he were not then such covenants would be virtually meaningless since covenantors could escape by selling the land for its full value to a purchaser taking free of the undertaking: 'nothing could be more inequitable'.[175] Thus by a straightforward notion of binding the purchaser's conscience equity arrived at a result directly contrary to privity of contract.

It is not a sufficient justification of this result to say that these are 'property cases' and that property rights, by definition, bind third parties. The whole issue is whether the obligations should be recognized as having this proprietary effect or not, so to start by assuming that they are property rights is to reason in a circle, begging the question. Nevertheless, *Tulk v Moxhay*, like Leicester Square, stands to this day as a pillar of the land law.

However, the doctrine has had a much more hesitant reception in cases about chattels. In *De Mattos v Gibson*,[176] Knight Bruce LJ enunciated a principle similar to that in *Tulk v Moxhay* in the case of a ship subject to a charterparty – the defendant mortgagee of the vessel could be bound to perform the charterparty entered into

---

[171] Ibid [92]–[93].
[172] Sub nom. *OBG Ltd v Allen* [2008] 1 AC 1.
[173] Ibid, [306].
[174] 2 Phillips 774.
[175] Ibid, 778.
[176] (1858) 4 De G & J 276.

by the mortgagor. But *De Mattos* was disapproved by, for example, Scrutton LJ,[177] before being relied upon by the Privy Council in the *Strathcona* case.[178] The latter decision was then boldly declared to be mistaken and not followed by Diplock J sitting at first instance in *Port Line v Ben Line*,[179] memorably described by HWR Wade as the case in which *Strathcona* met its Waterloo – or rather its Trafalgar.[180] But *De Mattos* was called back from its watery grave by Browne-Wilkinson J in *Swiss Bank v Lloyds Bank*,[181] where he explained *De Mattos* as 'the counterpart in equity of the tort of knowing interference with contractual rights';[182] this was not considered on appeal. There are a number of reasons why the doctrine has received only chequered support outside its real property heartland. Wade, an eminent property lawyer, pointed out that whereas in land law the incidents of covenants are carefully defined by law, if the doctrine expanded to chattels there would appear to be no limits on the restrictions that could be attached to the property – save for the imagination of the parties! The problem with this, of course, is the violation of the rule that contracts do not bind third parties, and the virtual destruction of the line between contract and property. Simon Gardner concurs with this, pointing out the oddity that the *De Mattos v Gibson* cases do not define the content of the restrictions that may bind later purchasers: 'This is quite abnormal for a proprietary obligation'.[183] The law generally favours the transfer of unencumbered title to property. Indeed, this had led to some reluctance to accept the principle even in the real property cases. A decade before *Tulk v Moxhay* Lord Brougham LC had rejected a similar doctrine, holding that it would be 'clearly inconvenient both to the science of the law and to the public weal' if 'incidents of a novel kind [could] be devised and attached to the property at the fancy or caprice of the owner'.[184] Gardner argues that if the *De Mattos* principle is to apply to all kinds of property, the permissible categories of restrictions should be laid down by legislation. The leisurely and experimental common law method used to work out the limits of *Tulk v Moxhay* in land cases would be unacceptable in modern conditions.

A further reason for caution about allowing contracts to bind later owners of property is concern about the doctrine of notice into commercial law. As Lindley LJ classically explained, 'notice' is quite acceptable in conveyancing, which takes place at a leisurely pace precisely to allow the investigation of title. However, 'if we were to extend the doctrine of constructive notice to commercial transactions we should be doing infinite mischief and paralysing the trade of the country'.[185] As so often in law, the context matters.

---

[177] *Barker v Stickney* [1919] 1 KB 121.

[178] *Lord Strathcona Steamship Co Ltd v Dominion Coal Co Ltd* [1926] AC 108.

[179] [1958] 2 QB 146.

[180] HWR Wade, 'Contract – Ship – Purchase with Notice of Contract of Charter' [1958] *CLJ* 169.

[181] [1979] Ch 548.

[182] Ibid, p. 575.

[183] S Gardner, 'The Proprietary Effect of Contractual Obligations Under *Tulk v. Moxhay* and *De Mattos v. Gibson*' (1982) 98 *LQR* 279, 317.

[184] *Keppel v. Bailey* (1834) 2 Myl & K 517.

[185] *Manchester Trust v Furness* [1895] 2 QB 539, 545.

Even in the real property context, holding later owners bound by contracts relating to the land has proved controversial. Roger Smith criticizes the tort in *Lumley v Gye*[186] for subverting basic principles of land law.[187] He cites *Esso Petroleum v Kingswood Motors*, in which the purchaser of a petrol station was liable for inducing breach of contract (undertaking to buy petrol only from Esso) by its previous owner.[188] But as Smith points out, the undertaking was neither a registered nor an overriding interest and so according to the basic principles of land registration the defendant should have taken the land free of the restriction. It is not sensible for tort to hold a party bound by obligations when land law holds him free of them. If there is conflict between the two, land law should prevail: property lawyers have been grappling with such issues for centuries whereas the tort is in its comparative infancy. Its parallel application creates great uncertainty. One possible solution suggested by Smith is to allow unencumbered property rights to be raised as a justification defence to an action based on *Lumley v Gye*, although he admits that there are no English precedents for this. Even property lawyers do not enthusiastically accept that promises should bind third parties in all situations.

CONCLUSIONS

It is generally accepted that contract law does not, and should not, impose positive obligations on unwilling third parties. However, if we widen our attention to tort and property law, it will be seen that promises may indeed generate liabilities for third parties. These are in effect negative duties, not to induce breach of another's contract (*Lumley v Gye*)[189] or not to break a restrictive covenant made by another (*Tulk v Moxhay*).[190] Both areas are controversial. *Lumley v Gye* has been fiercely attacked on grounds of economic inefficiency, and even class bias (given its primary use as a weapon against trade unions). The courts have been wary about extending *Tulk v Moxhay* from the real property context, fearing a proliferation of obligations attaching to property, restricting alienability. Two conclusions may be drawn. First, it is important not to take a blinkered view of the limits of contract law. There are no watertight compartments separating it from aspects of tort, property, estoppel and unjust enrichment (for example). Secondly, we should question the syllogism in which contracts are promises, breaking promises is wrong, and therefore people must always perform their contracts. This is beguiling in its simplicity and possesses undoubted moral appeal. However, it is *too* simple. There are other matters of social and legal policy that should, quite legitimately, be taken into account. The stark clarity of moralistic reasoning may lead the law into error, by requiring that all other considerations must be ignored. Arguably, *Lumley v Gye* is a prime example of such a mistake, however much that conclusion

---

[186] (1853) 2 E & B 216.
[187] R.J. Smith, 'The Economic Torts – Their Impact on Real Property' [1977] *Conv* 318.
[188] [1974] QB 142.
[189] (1853) 2 E & B 216.
[190] 2 Phillips 774.

'stinks in the nostrils of those who think it advantageous to get as much ethics into the law as they can'.[191]

Further Reading

Third-party rights

P. Kincaid, 'Third Parties: Rationalising a Right to Sue' [1989] *CLJ* 243.

S.A. Smith, 'Contracts for the Benefit of Third Parties: In Defence of the Third-Party Rule' (1997) 17 *OJLS* 643.

A. Burrows, 'The Contracts (Rights of Third Parties Act) 1999 and Its Implications for Commercial Contracts' [2000] *LMCLQ* 540.

R. Stevens, 'The Contracts (Rights of Third Parties) Act 1999' (2004) 120 *LQR* 292.

H. Beale, 'A Review of the Contracts (Rights of Third Parties) Act 1999' In A. Burrows and E. Peel (eds), *Contract Formation and Parties* (Oxford University Press, 2010).

Promisee's remedies

B. Coote, 'The Performance Interest, *Panatown*, and the Problem of Loss' (2001) 117 *LQR* 81.

A. Burrows, 'No Damages for a Third Party's Loss' (2001) 1 *OUCLJ* 107.

E. McKendrick, 'The Common Law at Work: The Saga of *Alfred Mc Alpine Construction Ltd v. Panatown Ltd*' (2003) 3 *OUCLJ* 145.

Effects on third parties

D. Howarth, 'Against *Lumley v Gye*' (2005) 68 *MLR* 195.

M.R. Macnair, 'Free Association versus Juridification' (2011) 39 *Critique* 53.

---

[191] O.W. Holmes, 'The Path of the Law' (1897) 10 *Harvard LR* 457.

INDEX

agreed remedies, *see* remedies, party-agreed

battle of the forms, 14–27
  gap-filling approach to, 17–20
  restitutionary solutions to, 21–4
  traditional approach to, 14–17, 72
  see also offer and acceptance, formation
    of contract, implied terms

certainty, 25, 163–4
consideration, 29–41, 44–53
  Atiyah-Treitel debate, 31–2
  history of, 30–1
  see also modification of contracts
construction, *see* interpretation
consumer protection, 76–7, 83, 85–7,
  205–9, 228

damages, *see* remedies, judicial
De Mattos v Gibson, rule in, *see* property
  ownership, effect of contract upon
disclosure of information, 8, 153–62

economic duress, 185–96
  illegitimate pressure, 190–3
  threat to breach contract, whether
    illegitimate, 49–50, 193–6
  vitiated consent, theory of, 185–7
  see also modification of contracts
efficient breach, *see* remedies, judicial
  (breach, efficient, toleration of)
entire agreement clause, 70, 74, 80–4, 96
  effect on misrepresentation, 81–3
estoppel, 53–66
  cause of action, as, 55, 62–3

remedies for, 58–61, 65–6
unconscionability as basis of, 57–8
see also reliance theory of obligation
exclusion clauses, 81–3, 272–4

fairness, procedural and substantive, 203–5
formalism, 71–4, 83–4
  see also entire agreement clause,
    interpretation (textual), offer and
    acceptance, signature rule
formalities, 36, 38–41
  facilitative role of, 40
  peppercorn, 39
  relationship with promissory estoppel,
    59, 63
  Scythians, 39, 40
  seal 36, 39
  stipulatio, 13, 38–9, 40
formation of contract
  Civilian tradition, 4–5, 6
  flexibility in finding, 24–7, 273
  mistakes, effect of, 7–9
  objective approach, 1–7, 75
  see also offer and acceptance, battle of
    the forms, signature rule
frustration, 120–52
  force majeure clauses, 137–9
  illegality, supervening, 121–2
  impracticability, 122–4
  justice, 124–6, 145–50
  remedies for, allocating loss, 145–8
  remedies for, reversing unjust
    enrichment, 142–5
  risk-allocation, upholding, 52, 126–31,
    133–7, 139–40

good faith, absence from English contract
    law of, 114–15, 147, 154–5, 156–7,
    212, 216–19

implied terms, 106–19
    default rules ('implication by law'),
        18–19, 86–7, 111–19
    economic analysis of, 115–19
    filling gaps ('implication in fact'), 18,
        107–11
inducing breach of contract, tort of,
    287–92, 294
intention to create legal relations, 39, 41–4
interpretation, 89–106
    artificially restrictive approach, 101–5
    contextual 70–1, 72–4, 91–2
    prior negotiations, admissibility, 97–9
    purposive, 92, 95
    rectification, relationship with, 99–101
    termination clauses, use in controlling,
        219–21
    textual, 93–5

liquidated damages, see remedies, party-
    agreed (penalty clause)
Lumley v Gye, tort in, see inducing breach
    of contract, tort of

mistake, 163–84
    common mistake, 174–9
    equity, mistake in, 164–5, 180–3
    historical development, 165–7
    identity, mistakes of, 167–73
    remedies for, 179–84
    see also formation of contract (mistakes,
        effect of), non est factum
modification of contracts, 44–54, 62–3
    change of circumstances, 50–2
    consideration 44–8
    contractual allocation of risk,
        upholding, 51–3
    economic duress, 49–50
    opportunism, 49–53
    practical benefit, 45–7, 48
    see also economic duress, frustration

non est factum, 173–4
non-disclosure, see disclosure of
    information

offer and acceptance, 9–14
    formalism, 9, 12–13, 72
    pragmatism, 11–12, 144
Owl and the Pussycat, The
    perfect example of stipulatio, includes, 13

parol evidence rule, 78–80
    see also entire agreement clause
penalty clause, see remedies, party-agreed
performance interest, see remedies, judicial
privity of contract, see third party rights
property ownership, effect of contract
    upon, 292–4
    see also mistake (identity, mistakes of)

relational contract, 69–70, 74
reliance theory of obligation, 25–6, 53–4,
    55, 56–7, 63–6, 179–80, 231, 235
    see also estoppel, remedies for
remedies, judicial, 230–64
    breach, efficient, toleration of, 46, 53,
        225–6, 232, 235–43, 255–6
    damages, market price rule, 247–8
    damages, substitutionary, 246–52
    damages, Wrotham Park, basis of, 257–63
    labels, proliferation of, 246
    performance, right to, vindication of,
        46, 233–6, 243–8, 256–7, 262–3, 277,
        285–6
    profits, disgorgement of, 224–5, 252–7,
        258, 260–2
    punitive, 225, 252–7
    specific performance, 243–6
    taxonomy of, 230–2
    see also remedies, promisee's in three
        party situation; restitution
remedies, party-agreed, 211–29
    termination, control of, 216–21
    termination, when granted by law,
        213–16
    penalty clause, 221–8

penalty clause, economic analysis of, 225–7

remedies, promisee's in three party situations, 276–86

performance interest, 280–5

surrogate claim, 277–80

see also remedies, judicial (performance, right to, vindication of), third party rights

remoteness of damage

efficient default rule, as, 116–18

restitution

quantum meruit, 21–4, 64

'skimping' performance, damages as response to, 251–2

total failure of condition (or 'consideration'), 251, 270

see also frustration (remedies for, reversing unjust enrichment), remedies, judicial (damages, *Wrotham Park*, basis of), (profits, disgorgement of)

signature rule, 15–16, 21, 26, 75–8, 87

specific performance, *see* remedies, judicial

standard forms, 15, 16, 68, 84–7

see also battle of the forms, signature rule

termination, *see* remedies, party-agreed

third party rights, 266–76

see also remedies, promisee's in three party situations

Tulk v Moxhay, rule in, *see* property ownership, effect of contract upon

unconscionability, 200–3

see also fairness, procedural and substantive

undue influence

'claimant' or 'defendant' sided doctrine, whether, 196–200

written contracts, *see* entire agreement clause, parol evidence rule, signature rule, standard forms

This book is due for return on or before the last date shown below.

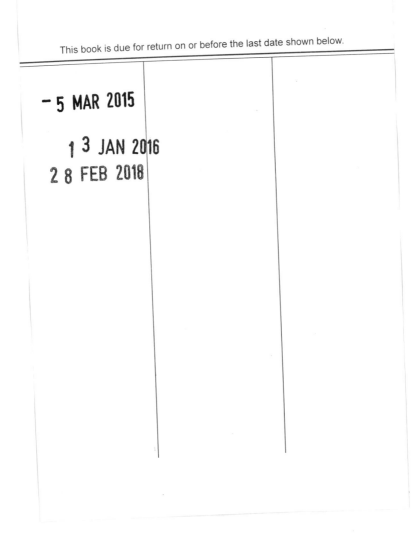

- 5 MAR 2015

1 3 JAN 2016

2 8 FEB 2018